OCCUPATIONAL STRESS INJURIES

This book explores the stress faced by public safety professionals across an array of occupational fields, such as police, correctional officers, paramedics, and firefighters.

Bringing together leading scholars from around the world, it showcases cutting-edge quantitative and qualitative research from across three continents and multiple regions within six countries, introduces key concepts related to occupational and organizational stressors, and provides an overview of the state of current research in key topic areas. Those who have yet to be exposed to the concepts associated with occupational stress injuries, or to the range of theories and methodologies, will be provided with an informative introduction to this topic. It explores the state of current literature on this topic, identifies gaps in our knowledge and approaches to understanding the relationship between occupational stressors and different outcomes, and provides potential responses for reducing or ameliorating occupational stressors experienced by public safety personnel.

Aimed at students, academic researchers, public safety practitioners, law enforcement analysts, and public policy-makers, this book will appeal to readers who have some knowledge in this area and are interested in learning more about new and emerging research, as well as those who are well-versed on this topic.

Rosemary Ricciardelli is Professor in the School of Maritime Studies, and Research Chair in Safety, Security, and Wellness, at Memorial University's Fisheries and Marine Institute, Canada. Elected to the Royal Society of Canada, and a Fellow of the Canadian Academy of Health Sciences, her research centres on evolving understandings of gender, vulnerabilities, risk, and experiences and issues within different facets of the criminal justice system.

Joy C. MacDermid is Professor in the School of Physical Therapy at Western University, Canada, and the Scientific Director of FIREWELL, an independent knowledge translation platform and research collaborative with firefighters. Her research includes public safety personnel and Veteran health, work injury, and implementation science.

Lorna Ferguson is a Banting Postdoctoral Researcher at Memorial University of Newfoundland and is the Founder of the Missing Persons Research Hub. Lorna has a broad interest in policing research and developing evidence-based approaches to policing and crime prevention, including issues related to search and rescue, incident command, crime concentration, cybercrime, and persons with mental illness. Currently, she focuses on police responses to missing person cases.

Routledge Frontiers of Criminal Justice

Holistic Responses to Reduce Reoffending
Ian Mahoney and Rahmanara Chowdhury

Policing Rape
The Way Forward
Katrin Hohl and Elizabeth A. Stanko

Human Rights in Probation
Theory, Practice and Balance
Kyros Hadjisergis

Corporate Criminal Liability and Sanctions
Current Trends and Policy Changes
Edited by Michala Meiselles, Nicholas Ryder and Arianna Visconti

Crime Prevention by Exclusion
Ethical Considerations
Edited by Sebastian Jon Holmen, Thomas Søbirk Petersen & Jesper Ryberg

Occupational Stress Injuries
Operational and Organizational Stressors Among Public Safety Personnel
Edited by Rosemary Ricciardelli, Joy C. MacDermid, and Lorna Ferguson

For more information about this series, please visit: www.routledge.com/Routledge-Frontiers-of-Criminal-Justice/book-series/RFCJ

OCCUPATIONAL STRESS INJURIES

Operational and Organizational Stressors Among Public Safety Personnel

Edited by Rosemary Ricciardelli, Joy C. MacDermid, and Lorna Ferguson

Routledge
Taylor & Francis Group
LONDON AND NEW YORK

Designed cover image: Getty Images

First published 2025
by Routledge
4 Park Square, Milton Park, Abingdon, Oxon OX14 4RN

and by Routledge
605 Third Avenue, New York, NY 10158

Routledge is an imprint of the Taylor & Francis Group, an informa business

British Library Cataloguing-in-Publication Data
A catalogue record for this book is available from the British Library

Library of Congress Cataloging-in-Publication Data
Names: Ricciardelli, Rose, 1979– editor. | MacDermid, Joy, editor. |
Ferguson, Lorna (Criminologist), editor.
Title: Occupational stress injuries : operational and organizational stressors
among public safety personnel / edited by Rosemary Ricciardelli, Joy C. MacDermid
and Lorna Ferguson.
Description: Abingdon, Oxon ; New York, NY : Routledge, 2025. |
Series: Routledge frontiers of criminal justice |
Includes bibliographical references and index.
Identifiers: LCCN 2024032887 (print) | LCCN 2024032888 (ebook) |
ISBN 9781032543086 (hardback) | ISBN 9781032542966 (paperback) |
ISBN 9781003424253 (ebook)
Subjects: LCSH: Job stress. | Police–Job stress. | First responders–Job stress. |
Correctional personnel–Job stress.
Classification: LCC HF5548.85 .O265 2025 (print) |
LCC HF5548.85 (ebook) | DDC 158.7/2–dc23/eng/20240905
LC record available at https://lccn.loc.gov/2024032887
LC ebook record available at https://lccn.loc.gov/2024032888

ISBN: 9781032543086 (hbk)
ISBN: 9781032542966 (pbk)
ISBN: 9781003424253 (ebk)

DOI: 10.4324/9781003424253

Typeset in Galliard
by Newgen Publishing UK

CONTENTS

FIGURES

TABLES

CONTRIBUTORS

Sam Ainslie is Senior Lecturer in Criminology and Criminal Justice at Sheffield Hallam University and previously worked as a probation officer and manager. She has undertaken research focusing on desistance-supportive probation practice, emotional labour, and burnout in probation work and development of critically reflective practice in probation practitioners.

Alan M. Batt is an internationally educated and experienced paramedic, researcher, and educator at Monash University, Australia. He uses mixed-methods approaches to explore health professions education, the care of vulnerable and under-served populations, social and structural determinants of health, the evolving role of paramedicine, and paramedic well-being. He is based in Ontario, Canada.

Sarah Britto is Associate Professor of Criminal Justice Administration. She received her PhD from the College of Criminology and Criminal Justice at Florida State University. Much of her research focuses on media portrayals of the criminal justice system, and on the relationship between media consumption and crime-related public perceptions.

Robin Campbell Bromhead completed her PhD at Dalhousie University and works as a Research Project Coordinator at Western University, Canada. Her research explores the occupational experiences of volunteer firefighters and other public safety personnel that impact mental health and well-being. She is a former volunteer firefighter and currently serves as a reservist in the Canadian Armed Forces.

Mary Ann Campbell is Professor of Psychology and Director of the Centre for Criminal Justice Studies & Policing Research at the University of New Brunswick, Canada. She consults with first responder organizations on psychological health and wellness and conducts research on criminal behaviour, crime reduction intervention, and police psychology.

Marina Carbonell is a PhD student in Maritime Studies (Public Safety) at Memorial University's Fisheries and Marine Institute, Canada. Her research focuses on public safety personnel, exploring risk, occupational stress, mental health, and workplace wellness.

R. Nicholas Carleton is Professor of Psychology at the University of Regina, Canada. He is also a registered clinician, scientific director for the Canadian Institute for Public Safety Research and Treatment, a Canadian Academy of Health Sciences Fellow, and a Royal Society of Canada College member. He has completed 240+ peer-reviewed articles and 500+ conference presentations and received $72M+ in research funding.

Heidi Cramm is Professor in the School of Rehabilitation Therapy, Queen's University, Canada. In her role as research lead for the Families Matter Research Group, she focuses on the mental health and well-being of defence and public safety families.

Stephen Czarnuch is Associate Professor of Biomedical Engineering, joint-appointed to the Faculties of Medicine and Engineering and Applied Science at Memorial University of Newfoundland, Canada. His research focuses on developing health-related technological interventions, commonly based on autonomously tracking human motion. His technical focus is on machine learning, deep learning, and computer vision.

Crystal Dieleman is Occupational Therapist and Associate Professor at Dalhousie University, Canada, focusing on the social, political, and occupational factors experienced by criminalized populations. She examines the intersection of health and criminal justice, including ideologies, approaches, processes, and mechanisms of criminal justice systems that shape opportunities for rehabilitation and recovery.

Jacqueline M. Drew is a police scholar with the School of Criminology and Criminal Justice and Griffith Criminology Institute, Griffith University, Australia, and has a PhD in psychology. She has 25 years of experience, focusing on the impacts of organizational contexts on police personnel. Jacqueline is passionate about improving the mental health and well-being of police, working across Australia and the USA.

Kerry Ellis Devitt has 25 years' experience as a researcher in the public, private, academic and charity sectors. Formally a Criminal Justice Senior Lecturer, Kerry now heads up the Practice Research Unit at Interventions Alliance in the UK. Kerry's research interests include domestic abuse, community justice interventions, and women's probation services delivery.

Walter Eppich is Professor of Work Integrated Research at the University of Melbourne, Australia. He builds on a clinical background as paediatric emergency doctor and a PhD in Health Professions Education to study intersections between simulation and workplace learning. His research seeks to delineate the contribution of workplace talk and team interactions to collaborative learning and team performance and the impacts on health delivery.

Lorna Ferguson is a PhD(c) at Western University, Canada, and the Founder of the Missing Persons Research Hub. She has a broad interest in criminal justice research and developing evidence-based approaches to policing and crime prevention, including issues related to crime concentration, cybercrime, drug crises, and police reform. Her specialization is police responses to missing persons.

Andrew Fowler is Senior Lecturer in Criminology and Community Justice at Sheffield Hallam University, UK. He has undertaken research across the criminal justice system, focusing on the intersection between policy and practice in the field of probation. He has carried out research on emotional labour, staff well-being, sexual offending, and pracademia.

Lena Gryshchuk is a PhD student in Clinical Psychology at the University of New Brunswick, Canada, working under the supervision of Dr. Mary Ann Campbell. Lena's research interests include risk assessment, intimate partner violence, as well as mental health and wellness of first responders and their families.

Sara A. Jahnke has over a decade of research experience on firefighter health and has led FEMA and NIH-funded studies focusing on the health of women firefighters, behavioural health, risk of injury, cancer, cardiovascular risk factors, and substance use. She has more than 100 publications in peer-reviewed medical literature.

Mark Jones is a research assistant at Memorial University of Newfoundland, Canada. His research focuses on policing, corrections, and occupational stressors. He holds an Honours Specialization (BA) Degree in Criminology and has published numerous papers in reputable journals. Mark is dedicated to advancing knowledge with the criminology field and solving complex problems through innovative research.

Marije Keulen-de Vos is the Head of the Research Department at Forensic Psychiatric Center de Rooyse Wissel in Venray, the Netherlands. Her research interests are sexual health, sexual violence, forensic treatment, and rehabilitation. She is also affiliated to Maastricht University's Faculty of Psychology and Neuroscience.

Maria D. H. Koeppel is Associate Research Scientist and Postdoctoral Fellow at NDRI-USA, Inc., USA. Her work has focused on women firefighters, mental health, and cancer. She has received funding from FEMA and NIH to examine DEI in the fire service as well as alcohol use among EMS providers. She is also active in the field as a firefighter/EMT.

Nadine Leduc is a researcher with the Atlantic Canada Public Safety Research and Innovation Lab at Memorial University of Newfoundland, Canada. Her research relates to organizational culture and its impact on the well-being of emergency communicators. As a former public safety communicator, she is passionate about researching the mental well-being of communicators.

Joy C. MacDermid is Professor in the School of Physical Therapy at Western University, Canada, and the Scientific Director of FIREWELL, an independent knowledge translation platform and research collaborative with firefighters. Her research includes public safety personnel and Veteran health, work injury, and implementation science.

Sherri A. Martin is National Director of Wellness Services for the Fraternal Order of Police, USA, the largest organization of law enforcement officers in the world. She is a retired law enforcement officer, holds a Master's degree in Clinical Counseling Psychology, and is licenced as a Professional Counselor Associate.

Mark Norman is a postdoctoral fellow in the Fisheries and Marine Institute at Memorial University of Newfoundland, Canada. His research interests include occupational experiences and mental health in correctional work and sport, physical activity, and incarceration.

Laurett Nwaonumah is the Wellness and Crisis Intervention Coordinator with the Saint John Police Force, Canada. She works to support victims of crime and tragic loss in the Saint John area. In addition, she leads the development, delivery, and evaluation of wellness programming within the organization.

Temitope Osifeso is a PhD candidate in Health and Rehabilitation Science at Western University, Canada, where she is researching chronic pain, workplace disability, and musculoskeletal and mental health disorders of public safety personnel (PSP).

Michelle O'Toole is a teacher practitioner in the School of Medicine and Researcher in RCSI SIM, Centre for Simulation Education and Research in the Royal College of Surgeons (RCSI), Dublin, Ireland. She is a former firefighter/advanced paramedic, and family member to serving personnel. She is an experienced health professions educator/researcher, and peer supporter in critical incident stress and psychotraumatology. As a PhD student in Monash University, she researches optimal training and support pathways for families and friends of first responders internationally.

Jake Phillips is Reader in Criminology at Sheffield Hallam University, UK. He has undertaken research across the criminal justice system, focusing on the intersection between policy and practice in the field of probation. He has carried out research on emotional labour, staff well-being, people who die whilst under supervision, inspection, and privatization in criminal justice.

Rosemary Ricciardelli is Professor in the School of Maritime Studies, and Research Chair in Safety, Security, and Wellness, at Memorial University's Fisheries and Marine Institute, Canada. Elected to the Royal Society of Canada, her research centres on evolving understandings of gender, vulnerabilities, risk, and experiences and issues within different facets of the criminal justice system.

Funda Sanci is a forensic psychologist at the Psychotrauma Expertise Centre in the Netherlands. During her career she developed a particular interest in personality disorders, trauma, sexual transgressive behaviour, risk assessment, and management in outpatient services.

Kathryn E. Sinden is Assistant Professor in the School of Kinesiology at Lakehead University, Canada. Her research aims to prevent and reduce the human and financial impact of workplace injuries through applied ergonomics and identifying determinants of occupational task performance.

Sara M. Stretton is a PhD candidate at Western University, Canada, in the Department of Health and Rehabilitation Sciences, under the supervision of Dr. Joy MacDermid. Her research areas include chronic stress, occupational stressors, and mental wellness strategies. Sara's current research undertaking focuses on the link between stress and heart disease among firefighters.

Linna Tam-Seto is Assistant Professor in the Department of Occupational Science and Occupational Therapy, Temerty Faculty of Medicine at the University of Toronto, Canada. Linna holds a PhD in Rehabilitation Science with a research focus on the health and well-being of Canada's military members, Veterans, public safety personnel, and families.

Chalen Westaby is Senior Lecturer in Law Sheffield Hallam University, UK. Her research focuses on emotions and emotional labour in probation and legal practice. Chalen has engaged in research relating to emotional labour in probation, researchers, legal professionals, and judges as well as work–life spillover and burnout in probation practice.

Brett Williams is Professor of Paramedicine at Monash University, Australia, and holds an Adjunct Professorial position at the Jordan University of Science and Technology in Jordan. Brett has been an academic leader in paramedicine educational research, scholarship, and mentorship for over 25 years. He is committed to professionalizing paramedicine, and building capacity for paramedics personnel internationally.

R. Michael Young is responsible for Criminal Investigation Divisions with the Saint John Police Force, Canada, and has also served as Inspector for Patrol Services and Commander for Emergency Tactical Services. He has an interest in evidence-based policing and best practices for management and employee psychological health.

INTRODUCTION TO OCCUPATIONAL STRESS INJURIES

Operational and Organizational Stressors Among Public Safety Personnel

Rosemary Ricciardelli, Joy C. MacDermid, and Lorna Ferguson

Introduction

Public safety personnel (PSP) have long been argued to experience rates of potentially psychologically traumatic event exposures and other occupational stressors much more frequently than the general public (Liberman et al., 2002; Rivard et al., 2002). In the House of Commons Report of October 4, 2016, entitled *Healthy Minds, Safe Communities: Supporting Our Public Safety Officers Through a National Strategy for Operational Stress Injuries*, PSP were recognized as being at risk for operational stress injuries (OSIs) (i.e., injuries resultant from exposure to events that are potentially psychologically trauma which occurs directly because of their requirement to fulfill their occupational responsibilities) relative to the general public (Oliphant, 2016). In the House Report, exposure to potentially psychologically traumatic events was acknowledged as the "rule" for these professionals who support and protect public safety rather than the "exception." The exposures were identified as correlates of several OSIs, including but not limited to diagnosable mental health disorders.

PSP include police, correctional workers, firefighters, paramedics, public safety communicators, intelligence officers, search and rescue, coast guard, border services, and other groups whose work strives to ensure public safety. The psychological strain inherent to the profession and the effect of psychological strain on police officers are increasingly recognized in public safety research (Carleton, et al., 2017, Carleton, Afifi, Turner, Taillieu, LeBouthillier et al., 2018, Carleton et al., 2019; Carleton et al., 2020; Duxbury, Higgins, & Halinski, 2015; Ricciardelli, Carleton, Groll, et al., 2018; Ricciardelli, Carleton, Mooney et al., 2018; 2020; Sommer et al., 2020), alongside the

DOI: 10.4324/9781003424253-1

implications of physical strain and the impact on compromised health more generally. Regarding the former, for instance, police researchers have been studying police stress since at least the 1970s, with many influential studies about police stress being published in the early 1980s (Grier, 1983; Jackson & Maslach, 1982; Lester, 1982; Lester & Gallagher, 1980; Stratton, 1984). The impact of stressors on police can be, and often are, wide-ranging, from negatively impacting their attitudes toward the public to mounting frustration with systems of justice (Ellison & Genz, 1978). This is no different from the experiences of other PSP, where the experiences of stressors and psychological strain can also result in a diversity of mental health challenges.

Lieutenant Colonel (Retired) Stéphane Grenier coined the phrase "operational stress injury" (OSI) to legitimize and destigmatize the mental health sequelae of serving in vocations involving extreme stress and to describe the broad array of associated potential symptoms following exposure to one or more potentially psychologically traumatic events while serving (Oliphant, 2016). An occupational stress injury includes both **organizational stressors** (those tied to job context, e.g., shift work, administrative processes) and **operational stressors** (those connected to inherent job content, e.g., responding to calls for service). Specifically, occupational stress injuries can refer broadly to symptoms associated with mental health disorder symptoms that approach or meet specific diagnostic criteria (e.g., posttraumatic stress disorder [PTSD], major depressive disorder, and generalized anxiety disorder [Canadian Institute for Public Safety Research and Treatment, 2022]). However, if we turn to the latter, physical implications and recognition required by occupational stress injuries are not just psychological. For instance, the association between stress and cardiovascular disease or chronic musculoskeletal (MSK) pain too constitutes an occupational stress injury. Moreover, there is a complex and longstanding tension in the relationship between physical, mental, and social health, where each intensifies the other, and one cannot be resolved in isolation from the other. Taking this standpoint, in the current book, we bring to the fore the connection between physical, psychological, and social health to understand the impacts, presentation, and trajectory of occupational stress injuries among PSP internationally and try to elucidate some responses to the seemingly impossible problem. Indeed, potentially psychologically traumatic event exposures are inherent to public safety professions yet are also a precursor to some occupational stress injuries; thus, such adverse events cannot be eliminated, but efforts are necessary to reduce the health impacts of such exposures.

As noted, among PSP, OSIs are tied in part to experiences of increased risk of exposure to potentially psychologically traumatic events commonly associated with many different clinically significant symptoms (e.g., chronic pain) (Carleton et al., 2018b). Tomblin, in her 2002 study of Royal Canadian Mounted Police (RCMP) officers, did not find any changes in response to members being asked about their emotional health between 1994 and 1998. However, Tomblin (2002) did find that members' mental health was associated with exposure to occupational stressors and argued that "police work may have a negative effect on the psychological health of the members" (p. 91). Stearns and Moore (1993), nearly three decades ago, sampled 290 officers to learn about elements that contributed to police stress, writing: "Psychological well-being was consistently found to be one of the strongest correlates of three of the four MBI [Maslach Burnout Inventory] burnout scales (i.e., Emotional Exhaustion, Depersonalization, and Total Burnout Score)" (p. 127). The Stearns and Moore (1993) study occurred before the OSI construct was operationalized (i.e., obtained a structured definition), and their investigation did not study mental health disorder prevalence. Nevertheless, Stearns and Moore (1993) argued that police officers experiencing burnout would perceive all elements in their lives more negatively than officers without burnout – that their psychological well-being would be lacking.

Lee and Stoneham (1993) surveyed the RCMP to identify specific occupational stressors, finding evidence that excessive paperwork (among all ranks), understaffing, and risks tied to working alone among constables were considered critically problematic stressors. Violanti and Aron (1994) also found evidence that occupational stressors for police included inadequate support from the employer and an incompatible patrol partner. Mearns and Mauch (1998) studied a small group of 56 police officers from urban centers, finding evidence that high levels of occupational-related stress were tied to experiences of physical and emotional distress.

Duxbury and Higgins (2012), in their survey of 25 police services, found evidence that key stressors for police include multiple competing work demands, the performance of work that falls outside their mandate, understaffing and lack of backfill when officers are on leave, the court system, and managing public expectations. Further, their data continues to support how organizational stressors, in essence, could be alleviated, while operational stressors are inherent to the nature of the occupational work as first responders. Moreover, when investigating stress at work, workload, and work–life issues among police officers, Duxbury and Higgins (2012) found that 50 percent of their sample of police reported high stress levels, while 46 percent reported moderate levels of stress, with only 4 percent of the sample reporting low stress levels. In addition, 30 percent of police in the sample from Duxbury and Higgins (2012) reported high levels of depressed mood, 40 percent of respondents reported moderate levels of depressed mood, and the remaining 30 percent reported low levels of depressed mood. Among correctional workers, Norman and Ricciardelli (2021), as well as Ricciardelli (2019), have found that occupational stress injuries resulting from operational and organizational stress are the norm rather than the exception.

Within the field of correctional services, providers do and will continue to be impacted by the experience of diverse operational and organizational stresses, including exposure to potentially psychologically traumatic events despite if they work in institutions, the community, or in an administrative role (Galatzer-Levy et al., 2011; Komarovskaya et al., 2011; Ricciardelli, 2019; Ricciardelli et al., 2020; Ricciardelli & Power, 2020). Correctional service providers are exposed to, mainly when working in prisons, substances that are toxic or lethal, physical, sexual, or verbal assault, and unwanted or uncomfortable sexual experiences; they may engage in combat, be held in captivity, and or threatened with life-changing illness or injury – even death (Carleton et al., 2019). Correctional officers, for example, fear becoming infected with sexually transmitted infection blood born infections (STBBI) due to contact, accidental or threatened, with bodily fluids through fecal bombing or being accidentally or intentionally pricked by sharps (Hartley et al., 2013). They may be harmed when, as occupational mandated, made to intervene in an altercation or escalating situation or when responding to an attempted murder or death by suicide (Ricciardelli, 2019; Ricciardelli & Power, 2020; Ricciardelli et al., 2018). These service providers may develop mental health disorders or have to manage thoughts of attempts tied to suicide (Berger et al., 2012; Carleton et al., 2018b, 2020; Faust et al., 2014; Haugen et al., 2012; Neria et al., 2011; Oliphant, 2016; Ricciardelli et al., 2019). Yet, each of these experiences constitutes an occupational stress injury with dire implications for providers' social, physical, and psychological health.

These findings are not unique to policing or correctional service providers; organizational and operational stressors are relevant to the prevalence of OSIs, including PTSD, among PSP more broadly (Carleton et al., 2020). Yet, the depth of research we see in policing has yet to be replicated among other PSP, albeit this is a burgeoning line of scholarship. Broadly examining OSIs for public safety professionals has uncovered several notable findings that span across multiple roles. In one study by Carleton and colleagues (2020) investigating OSIs, nearly 30 percent of PSP reported thoughts of suicide, and almost 5 percent had actually attempted suicide. Another study found a significantly higher presence (approximately 45 percent) of one or more mental health disorders, like panic disorder, generalized anxiety disorder, and social anxiety disorders, among public safety professionals (Carleton et al., 2020). Elevated rates of PTSD have been well-documented across multiple public safety professional roles, including around 20 percent of paramedics and just up to 40 percent of firefighters, compared to up to 9 percent of the general public experiencing PTSD (Carleton et al., 2020; Sareen, 2022; Wagner et al., 2020; Bryant, 1995; Ellis & Korman, 2022). Research on firefighters has revealed that around 59 percent suffered from sleep deprivation, and 58 percent exhibited binge-drinking behaviors due to work stress (Carey et al., 2011; Ellis & Korman, 2022).

Turning to occupational and operational stress, there are two general approaches to understanding these matters in relation to public safety professionals more broadly in the literature: first, there is a focus on worker characteristics, such as PSP's abilities to cope or their personality characteristics. The second research theme highlights the work conditions in these areas, such as job demands, shift work, and job insecurity. Regarding the latter organizational stressors, PSP self-reported as being most impacted by staff shortages, a lack of resources, unequal sharing of work responsibilities, inconsistent leadership styles, bureaucratic red tape, dealing with co-workers, favoritism, feeling they must prove themselves to the organization, excessive administrative duties, and constant changes in policy or legislation. For operational stressors, PSP self-reported being most impacted by paperwork, fatigue, and the aforementioned finding time for physical fitness. As an example, research on firefighters highlights that occupational stress spans forces beyond those within the organization, like job insecurity, feelings of self-esteem in the workplace, mental health, frustration with work, and inadequate support systems to include customs, traditions, and cultures that affect firefighting, such as work ethics, government standards and regulations, and poor attitudes toward chronic illnesses (see, e.g., Beaton et al., 1995; Murphy, 1999; Jahnke et al., 2016). As a reminder, operational and organizational stress can and often do underpin experiences of OSIs. Indeed, organizational and operational stressors are correlated with positive screens for PTSD and other mental health disorders (i.e., OSIs) across occupational groups (Carleton et al., 2020).

The above are just a few examples of the many operational and organizational stressors affecting PSP. Though, R Nicholas Carleton et al. (2020), in a large sample of PSP, found that of all organizational stressors, police and correctional employees self-reported the highest levels of stress in comparison to other public safety populations sampled (e.g., municipal/provincial police, paramedics, firefighters, public safety communicators). Moreover, the police subsample, as well as the paramedic subsample, also reported higher levels of stress in response to operational stressors in comparison to other public safety subpopulations sampled – although Carleton and colleagues (2020) used different survey items and definitions of organizational and operational stressors than Duxbury and Higgins (2012). Still, what we can see is that across all groups of public safety professionals, there are repeated patterns of OSIs and occupational and operational stressors that are specific to their work and have ripple effects beyond the organization.

In this edited collection, we present a comprehensive volume of papers from some of the leading scholars from around the world. Researchers conducting cutting-edge quantitative and qualitative research from across three continents and multiple regions within six countries provide rich discussions of the stress faced by public safety professionals across an array of occupational fields, such as police, paramedics, public safety communicators, and firefighters. This book explores the state of current literature on this topic. It identifies gaps in our knowledge and approaches to understanding the relationship between occupational stressors and different outcomes, as well as provides potential responses for reducing or ameliorating occupational stressors experienced by PSP and their impacts.

Aimed at a diverse audience – including students, academic researchers, public safety practitioners, law enforcement analysts, and public policy-makers – our goal in this edited collection is to provide vital and contemporary information on occupational stress among public safety professions in an accessible and interesting way, fulfilling an empirical gap in the knowledge base while theoretically developing the scholarship across interdisciplinary fields. Our specific objectives in the collection are to first, as we have done in this introduction, introduce fundamental concepts related to occupational and organizational stressors faced by PSP. Second, we incorporate the variety of research methodologies and theories that can be employed in understanding this phenomenon – neither prioritizing nor privileging a certain method over another nor using multidisciplinary approaches to understanding the phenomenon under study. Indeed, we take issue that the study of different groups is often restricted to a particular field (e.g., the restriction of prison research to the discipline of punishment and prison studies) and instead work to draw attention to how PSP work in areas of diversity such as public health and justice and thus call on researchers to engage across the discipline in study of the realms. Our third objective is to provide an overview of the state of current research in key topic areas; and, finally, we hope to advance and enhance academic research and public safety practice by presenting different ways of thinking about, and responding to, occupational stress injuries.

The Collection Roadmap

We have structured this edited collection into four parts, with each concentrated on the different public safety roles that give rise to occupational stressors (e.g., firefighters, paramedics, police, and public safety communicators). Throughout this book, four main themes are examined: (1) the environmental factors faced by public safety professionals in their work, including political and social climates and how these impact these personnel; (2) the comparison and contrast between different roles, environmental stressors, resources, and beyond, within and across occupational groups, jurisdictions, and countries; (3) the individual and social impacts of stress for PSP, their families, their organizations, and implications for society; and (4) the responses, referring to explorations of the strengths and limitations of different resources for addressing operational and organizational stress (e.g., wellness programs, peer-counseling).

Police

Part I brings together four chapters on police. In Chapter 1, Mark Norman, Rosemary Ricciardelli, and Mark Jones examine the occupational experiences of Detachment Service Assistants (DSAs), non-sworn public servants within detachments or specialized units of the RCMP. They discuss the various operational and organizational stressors related to DSA work and that contribute to OSIs. Investigating the occupational experiences of DSAs allows for suggestions on minimizing OSIs in this area of police work and how the RCMP can better support DSAs when experiencing OSIs. Chapter 2 by Sarah Britto describes how media representations of police, even if fictional, can have implications for the mental well-being of officers. Drawing on a content analysis of popular Canadian police procedurals (e.g., "Rookie Blue"), Britto contributes vital insights into the attention paid to certain OSIs, the inattention to others, and the implications of these issues. Chapter 3, written by Jacqueline Drew and Sherri Martin, discusses the results of a United States-wide survey of police on community relations, workplace stress, and well-being in the context of contemporary critical issues in policing (e.g., mass demonstrations, defunding, and anti-police sentiment). Crucial information is offered on the workplace and community factors causing harm to police, as well as practical, actionable strategies for healthier workplaces for police agencies and leaders. In Chapter 4, Marije Keulen-de Vos and Funda Sanci describe the traumatic nature of work conducted by police investigating cases involving child sexual exploitation material, resulting in secondary trauma. After examining existing knowledge on the impacts, risks, and protective factors for secondary trauma in police officers investigating child sexual exploitation cases, implications for practice and recommendations to advance the scholarship are explored in this chapter.

Corrections

Part II includes three chapters on corrections. In Chapter 5, Kerry Ellis Devitt discusses the need for tailored, gender-responsive support and services for women on probation, given the complex and multiple needs of this group and being involved in a system primarily designed for men. Drawing on qualitative research in an English Community Rehabilitation Company, the experiences of female probation staff with practical and emotional stressors and the concept of emotional labor in probation are unpacked through a gendered lens. This chapter offers meaningful learning for better supporting women practitioners working with women on probation. In Chapter 6, Jake Phillips, Sam Ainslie, Andrew Fowler, and Chalen Westaby investigate the extent and key correlates of burnout among a sample of probation workers and managers in England and Wales. In light of the findings, an intervention in the fields of community correctional services and occupational stress in criminal justice is presented. In Chapter 7, Marina Carbonell, Joy C. MacDermid, and Rosemary Ricciardelli propose a simplified job stress analysis checklist (JSAC) for employers to unpack job stress and inform job support change in corrections. The authors suggest this checklist as it addresses the gaps in current stress assessment measures, barriers to self-reporting, and limitations to studying workplace stress. This chapter thus provides an accessible stress assessment tool to aid in responding to existing challenges when measuring stress in complex workplaces such as prisons.

Firefighters

Part III includes four chapters on firefighters. In Chapter 8, Sara Stretton and Joy C. MacDermid explore the link between stress and cardiac outcomes in firefighters. Specifically, they consider the quality of evidence on this topic and the extent to which evidence supports the causation of firefighting as an independent risk factor for heart disease. A future research agenda is then set, given the state of the evidence. In Chapter 9, Sara A. Jahnke and Maria D.H. Koeppel present a comprehensive account of how the work-related stressors firefighters experience relate to mental health outcomes (e.g., anxiety, depression, PTSD), substance use, and sleep. They also offer an account of the gender differences in the experiences and impacts of stressors. This chapter concludes with guidelines regarding support, resources, and program development to improve the well-being of firefighters. Written by Joy C. MacDermid, Temitope Osifeso, and Kathryn Sinden, Chapter 10 proposes a Unified Neuromatrix Allostatic Load and Resiliency Model (UNALARM) that integrates different theories/models on stress or leading exposures that consider the cumulative impacts of mental and physical health exposures experienced by firefighters within a biopsychosocial framework. Further, these authors conducted a meta-analysis of the relationship between psychological stress and MSK pain and firefighters and other PSP to assess whether there is evidence to support UNALARM. In Chapter 11, Robin Campbell Bromhead and Crystal Dieleman discuss how social media is an occupational stressor for volunteer firefighters and other first responders, considering how social media impacts both occupational performance and mental health. Bromhead and Dieleman conclude this chapter with a clear discussion on managing stress related to social media for volunteer firefighters.

Public Safety Personnel

Part IV comprises four chapters focusing broadly on PSP and occupational groups not included in the previous collection sections. In Chapter 12, Mary Ann Campbell, R. Michael Young, Laurett Nwaonumah, and Lena

Gryshchuk draw upon their experiences working with Atlantic Canadian public safety organizations to present a research-informed psychological health survey process framework to guide organizations. They specifically discuss the following for organizations: what knowledge to seek, how to implement a survey on the psychological health needs of their employees, and how to identify strengths and gaps in existing support services and operational processes affecting employee wellness. Written by Nadine Leduc, Stephen Czarnuch, and Rosemary Ricciardelli, Chapter 13 investigates the impact of organizational culture on the mental well-being of public safety communicators. Results from this pan-Canadian qualitative survey study highlighted that organizational culture is a crucial factor in employee well-being, but it varies considerably across agencies. Chapter 13 concludes with considerations of the role of organizational culture in helping to reduce the severity and frequency of communicator OSIs. In Chapter 14, Michelle O'Toole, Alan Batt, Walter Eppich, and Brett Williams focus on the protective role of social support, including family and friends, as an early intervention strategy for attenuating vicarious trauma experienced by PSP. They announce a call for practical education interventions to prepare families for critical conversations with first responders, including how to encourage self-care, break down barriers to support, bolster existing support, and reduce help-seeking stigma. Lastly, Chapter 15, written by Linna Tam-Seto, Heidi Cramm, Rosemary Ricciardelli, and R. Nicholas Carleton, highlights how occupational stressors among PSP affect the health and well-being of family members. They take on the systems theory approach to understand the experiences and consequences of PSP careers on their health, well-being, and families.

In the book's concluding chapter, Rosemary Ricciardelli and Joy C. MacDermid synthesize the information from 15 commissioned chapters and offer suggestions for moving forward. Specifically, this book concludes with a comprehensive but succinct summary of each chapter's key findings, documenting the various ways in which they contribute to the scholarship and the similarities and differences across jurisdictions and sectors. This chapter ends with a brief note focusing on guiding researchers in their approach to collaborating with diverse sectors and supporting efforts to mitigate occupational stress injuries.

We hope readers worldwide can look to the chapters and their lessons as a roadmap for improving operational and organizational stressors among PSP and the related OSIs.

References

Beaton, R., Murphy, S., Pike, K., & Jarrett, M. (1995). Stress-symptom factors in firefighters and paramedics. In S. L. Sauter & L. R. Murphy (Eds.), *Organizational risk factors for job stress* (pp. 227–245). American Psychological Association. https://doi.org/10.1037/10173-014

Berger, W., Coutinho, E. S. F., Figueira, I., Marques-Portella, C., Luz, M. P., Neylan, T. C., Marmar, C. R., & Mendlowicz, M. V. (2012). Rescuers at risk: A systematic review and meta-regression analysis of the worldwide current prevalence and correlates of PTSD in rescue workers. *Social Psychiatry and Psychiatric Epidemiology*, *47*(6), 1001–1011.

Bryant, R.A., & Harvey, A.G. (1995) Posttraumatic stress in volunteer firefighters. *The Journal of Nervous and Mental Disease*, *183*, 267–271.

Canadian Institute for Public Safety Research and Treatment. (2022). Glossary of terms: A shared understanding of the common terms used to describe psychological trauma (version 2.0).

Carey, M. G., Dean, G. E., Sessanna, L., Finnell, D. S., & Al-Zaiti, S. S. (2011) Sleep problems, depression, substance use, social bonding, and quality of life in professional firefighters. *Journal of Occupational and Environmental Medicine*, *53*, 928–933.

Carleton, R. N., Afifi, T. O., Taillieu, T., Turner, S., El-Gabalawy, R., Sareen, J., & Asmundson, G. (2018). Anxiety-related psychopathology and chronic pain comorbidity among public safety personnel. *Journal of Anxiety Disorders*, *55*, 48–55.

Carleton, R. N., Afifi, T. O., Taillieu, T., Turner, S., Krakauer, R., Anderson, G. S., . . . Groll, D. (2019). Exposures to potentially traumatic events among public safety personnel in Canada. *Canadian Journal of Behavioural Science/Revue canadienne des Sciences du comportement*, *51*(1), 37.

Carleton, R. N., Afifi, T. O., Taillieu, T., Turner, S., Mason, J. E., Ricciardelli, R., . . . Krakauer, R. L. (2020). Assessing the relative impact of diverse stressors among public safety personnel. *International Journal of Environmental Research and Public Health*, *17*(4), 1234.

Carleton, R. N., Afifi, T. O., Turner, S., Taillieu, T., Duranceau, S., LeBouthillier, D. M., . . . Asmundson, G. J. G. (2018). Mental disorder symptoms among public safety personnel in Canada. *The Canadian Journal of Psychiatry*, *63*(1), 54–64. https://doi.org/10.1177/0706743717723825

Carleton, R. N., Afifi, T., Turner, S., Taillieu, T., El-Gabalawy, R., Sareen, J., & Asmundson, G. (2017). Chronic pain among public safety personnel in Canada. *Canadian Journal of Pain*, *1*(1), 237–246.

Carleton, R. N., Afifi, T. O., Turner, S., Taillieu, T., LeBouthillier, D. M., Duranceau, S., . . . Groll, D. (2018). Suicidal ideation, plans, and attempts among public safety personnel in Canada. *Canadian Psychology/Psychologie canadienne*, *59*(3), 220–231. https://doi.org/10.1037/cap0000136

Duxbury, L., & Higgins, C. A. (2012). *Caring for and about Those Who Serve: Work-life Conflict and Employee Well Being within Canada's Police.*

Duxbury, L., Higgins, C., & Halinski, M. (2015). Identifying the antecedents of work-role overload in police organizations. *Criminal Justice and Behavior*, *42*(4), 361–381.

Ellis, J., & Korman, M. B. (2022, September). Development of an evidence-informed solution to emotional distress in public safety personnel and healthcare workers: The Social Support, Tracking Distress, Education, and Discussion CommunitY (STEADY) Program. *Healthcare*, *10*(9), 1777. MDPI.

Ellison, K. W., & Genz, J. L. (1978). The police officer as burned-out Samaritan. *FBI Law Enforcement Bulletin*, *47*, 1.

Galatzer-Levy, I. R., Madan, A., Neylan, T. C., Henn-Haase, C., & Marmar, C. R. (2011). Peritraumatic and trait dissociation differentiate police officers with resilient versus symptomatic trajectories of posttraumatic stress symptoms. *Journal of Traumatic Stress*, *24*(5), 557–565.

Faust, K. L., & Ven, T. V. (2014). Policing disaster: An analytical review of the literature on policing, disaster, and post-traumatic stress disorder. *Sociology Compass*, *8*(6), 614–626.

Grier, K. S. (1983). A study of job stress in police officers and high school teachers.

Hartley, D. J., Davila, M. A., Marquart, J. W., & Mullings, J. L. (2013). Fear is a disease: The impact of fear and exposure to infectious disease on correctional officer job stress and satisfaction. *American Journal of Criminal Justice*, *38*, 323–340.

Haugen, P. T., Evces, M., & Weiss, D. S. (2012). Treating posttraumatic stress disorder in first responders: A systematic review. *Clinical Psychology Review*, *32*(5), 370–380.

Jackson, S. E., & Maslach, C. (1982). After-effects of job-related stress: Families as victims. *Journal of Organizational Behavior*, *3*(1), 63–77.

Jahnke, S. A., Poston, W. S. C., Haddock, C. K., & Murphy, B. (2016). Firefighting and mental health: Experiences of repeated exposure to trauma. *Work*, *53*(4), 737–744.

Komarovskaya, I., Maguen, S., McCaslin, S. E., Metzler, T. J., Madan, A., Brown, A. D., ... & Marmar, C. R. (2011). The impact of killing and injuring others on mental health symptoms among police officers. *Journal of Psychiatric Research*, *45*(10), 1332–1336.

Lee, D., & Stoneham, B. (1993). Survey of work stress. *Health Services Directorate, Royal Canadian Mounted Police.*

Lester, D. (1982). Perceived stress in police officers and belief in locus of control. *Journal of General Psychology*, *107*, 157.

Lester, D., & Gallagher, J. (1980). Stress in police officers and department store managers. *Psychological Reports*, *46*(3, Pt 1), 882. https://doi.org/10.2466/pr0.1980.46.3.882

Liberman, A. M., Best, S. R., Metzler, T. J., Fagan, J. A., Weiss, D. S., & Marmar, C. R. (2002). Routine occupational stress and psychological distress in police. *Policing: An International Journal of Police Strategies & Management*, *25*(2), 421–439. https://doi.org/10.1108/13639510210429446

Mearns, J., & Mauch, T. G. (1998). Negative mood regulation expectancies predict anger among police officers and buffer the effects of job stress. *The Journal of Nervous and Mental Disease*, *186*(2), 120–125.

Murphy, S. A., Beaton, R. D., Pike, K. C., & Johnson, L. C. (1999). Occupational stressors, stress responses, and alcohol consumption among professional firefighters: A prospective, longitudinal analysis. *International Journal of Stress Management*, *6*(3), 179–196.

Neria, Y., DiGrande, L., & Adams, B. G. (2011). Posttraumatic stress disorder following the September 11, 2001, terrorist attacks: A review of the literature among highly exposed populations. *American Psychologist*, *66*(6), 429.

Norman, M., & Ricciardelli, R. (2021). Operational and organisational stressors in community correctional work: Insights from probation and parole officers in Ontario, Canada. *Probation Journal.* https://doi.org/10.1177/0264550520984253

Oliphant, R. (2016). Healthy Minds, Safe Communities, Supporting Our Public Safety Officers through a National Strategy for Operational Stress Injuries: Report of the

Standing Committee on Public Safety and National Security. Canada. Parliament. House of Commons. Standing Committee on Public Safety National Security.

Ricciardelli, R. (2019) *Also serving time: Canada's provincial and territorial correctional officers*. Toronto: University of Toronto Press.

Ricciardelli, R., Carleton, R. N., Groll, D., & Cramm, H. (2018). Qualitatively unpacking Canadian public safety personnel experiences of trauma and their well-being. *Canadian Journal of Criminology and Criminal Justice*, *60*(4), 1–12.

Ricciardelli, R., Carleton, R. N., Mooney, T., & Cramm, H. (2018). "Playing the system": Structural factors potentiating mental health stigma, challenging awareness, and creating barriers to care for Canadian public safety personnel. *Health*, *0*(0), 1363459318800167.https://doi.org/10.1177/1363459318800167

Ricciardelli, R., Czarnuch, S., Afifi, T., Taillieu, T., & Carleton, R. N. (2020). Public Safety Personnel's interpretations of potentially traumatic events. *Occupational Medicine*, *70*(3), 155–161.

Ricciardelli, R., & Power, N. (2020). How "conditions of confinement" impact "conditions of employment": The work-related wellbeing of provincial correctional officers in Atlantic Canada. *Victims and Violence*, *35*(1), 88–107. doi:10.1891/0886-6708.VV-D-18-00081

Rivard, J. M., Dietz, P., Martell, D., & Widawski, M. (2002). Acute dissociative responses in law enforcement officers involved in critical shooting incidents: The clinical and forensic implications. *Journal of Forensic Science*, *47*(5), 1–8.

Sareen, J. (2022). Posttraumatic Stress Disorder in Adults: Epidemiology, Pathophysiology, Clinical Manifestations, Course, Assessment, and Diagnosis [Internet].. Previously available at: www.uptodate.com/contents/posttraumatic-stressdisorder-in-adults-epidemiology-pathophysiology-clinical-manifestations-course-assessment-and-diagnosis/print#:~{}:text=PTSDprevalence-Thelifetimeprevale...1/32www.uptodate.com

Sommer, J. L., El-Gabalawy, R., Taillieu, T., Afifi, T. O., & Carleton, R. N. (2020). Associations between trauma exposure and physical conditions among public safety personnel. *The Canadian Journal of Psychiatry*, *65*(8), 548–558. doi: 10.1177/0706743720919278. Epub 2020 Apr 10. PMID: 32275461; PMCID: PMC7361655.

Stearns, G. M., & Moore, R. J. (1993). The physical and psychological correlates of job burnout in the Royal Canadian Mounted Police. *Canadian Journal of Criminology*, *35*(2), 127–147.

Stratton, J. G. (1984). *Police passages*. Glennon Publishing Company, Manhattan Beach, CA.

Tomblin, L. (2002). *Health trends in a Canadian police force: A cross-sectional and longitudinal study*. Memorial University of Newfoundland,

Violanti, J. M., & Aron, F. (1994). Ranking police stressors. *Psychological Reports*, *75*(2), 824–826.

Wagner, S.L., White, N., Fyfe, T., Matthews, L.R., Randall, C., Regehr, C., White, M., Alden, L.E., Buys, N., Carey, M., et al. (2020). Systematic review of posttraumatic stress disorder in police officers following routine work-related critical incident exposure. *American Journal of Industrial Medicine*, *63*, 600–615.

PART I

Police

1

"IT DOES SCREW WITH YOUR MENTAL STATE"

The Occupational Experiences of Detachment Services Assistants Working for the Royal Canadian Mounted Police

Mark Norman, Rosemary Ricciardelli, and Mark Jones

Introduction and Context

While the concept of operational stress injuries originated in research on armed forces personnel, such injuries are now recognized among many other public safety personnel (PSP), injuries that result from their work (Oliphant, 2016). Rather than operational stress injuries, in the current chapter, we speak to occupational stress injuries (OSIs), which are constituted by both operational (i.e., job content) and organizational (i.e., job context) stresses in the workplace. Long recognized is how PSP can experience various forms of detrimental mental health outcomes due to the risks and stresses inherent (i.e., operational) to their jobs (e.g., Carleton et al., 2018, 2019) as well as those derived from their organization of employment, such as structures and processes. In Canada, recent efforts have expanded the definition of PSP and, with it, the recognition of how workers in a diversity of public safety roles can experience OSIs (Oliphant, 2016). Yet, there remain groups of public safety workers whose experiences of operational stress go largely unacknowledged. In this chapter, we analyse the occupational experiences of one such group: Detachment Services Assistants (DSAs), who are non-sworn public servants who perform a variety of administrative and support roles within detachments or specialized units of the Royal Canadian Mounted Police (RCMP). DSAs work for the RCMP, the Canadian federal law enforcement service—which provides both federal policing and local police services in communities across the country. The occupational responsibilities of DSAs vary, depending on the size and needs of the detachment served; however, DSAs regularly are the first point of contact with the public by phone or in

DOI: 10.4324/9781003424253-3

person at the reception desk. Moreover, DSAs may perform criminal record checks, review and transcribe case-related materials, enter records and instances into electronic databases, and can be the lifeline to officers responding to calls for service.

Notably, despite working within police detachments or units, DSAs are employed as *public servants* of the Canadian government, in contrast to other non-sworn staff (e.g., laboratory specialists or information technology experts) who are classified as *civilian members* of the RCMP. Compounded with the fact that over 90% of public servants working in the RCMP are women, in contrast to the masculinized culture and workforce of the organization, DSAs have reported feeling they occupy a lower status than both RCMP members and civilian members (Norman & Ricciardelli, 2023). As the role of non-sworn staff continues to grow in Canada's police services, the RCMP now employs over 8,300 public servants and 3,000 civilian members, with public servants accounting for 27% of the organization's labour force (Royal Canadian Mounted Police [RCMP], 2021). Given their importance to the RCMP's operations, DSAs' occupational experiences and stresses are worthy of greater scholarly and public attention.

In the current chapter, we draw from semi-structured interviews with 54 DSAs to explore how DSAs understand their contributions to public safety, experience operational stress (namely, vicarious trauma), and perceive organizational stresses to contribute to damaging mental health outcomes. Following the work of other policing researchers (e.g., Duxbury & Higgins, 2015; Ricciardelli, 2018), we utilize the framework of operational stressors (i.e., related to the content of the job) and organizational stressors (i.e., arising from wider factors within the organization) to situate DSAs' experiences of occupational stress. We argue that DSAs, and other personnel who perform support roles for frontline PSP, should be considered within the definition of PSP and have their risks of experiencing OSIs acknowledged and supported. For DSAs, who often feel their experiences of vicarious trauma are unrecognized or underacknowledged within the RCMP culture, organizational stressors can compound the challenges of inherent secondary operational exposure to events and materials that are traumatic, including potentially psychologically traumatic events (PPTE). PPTE refer to "events that have the potential to cause PTSD and other trauma-related mental health conditions" (CIPSRT, 2020a, para. 3), and we differentiate between events and materials given that secondary trauma exposure among DSAs and other PSP often occurs through documents, images, or videos. As such, DSAs' experiences and contributions to public safety should be taken seriously, and their risk of OSI should be acknowledged. The remainder of the chapter is structured such that we first provide a brief overview of both OSIs and the

DSA role within the RCMP before presenting our findings. We conclude with recommendations for how the mental health of DSAs might be better supported.

Methods

Data analysed in the current chapter are derived from 54 semi-structured interviews with DSAs. Participants were asked to explain their occupational experiences, describe their workplaces, discuss the aspects of the job they interpreted as rewarding or challenging, and elaborate on how their work affected their health and well-being. Following a semi-structured approach meant that while we used an interview guide to loosely follow conversational paths within the interview, our use of open-ended questions and follow-up probes was intended to enable participants to direct the flow and focus of the discussion and share what they considered the most relevant information. The union representing DSAs (Union for Safety and Justice Employees) both funded the study and assisted with recruitment by distributing study information via an internal email listserv. The study received approval from Memorial University of Newfoundland (#20201029) and the RCMP's HR Research Review Board. Interviews were transcribed verbatim and collaboratively coded in an open-ended fashion. We followed a semi-grounded constructed approach to data analysis (Charmaz, 2014; Glaser & Strauss, 1967; Ricciardelli et al., 2010), attempting to allow our theoretical interpretations to emerge (but not be created) directly from participants' words because our own biographies and scholarly training inevitably inform the interpretive process.

Prior to interviews, participants submitted a short demographic survey, enabling us to report data on their demographics and occupational experiences. All 54 participants (100%) were female and between 25 and 74 years of age. Most participants (n = 49; 90.7%) identified their race as white, while the remainder (n = 5; 7.4%) identified as Indigenous, Latin American, or chose not to self-identify their race. Although most participants (n = 42; 77.8%) were employed as DSAs at the time of the interview, some (n = 12; 22.2%) had moved from DSA roles into supervisory or specialized administrative positions within the RCMP; the latter groups were asked only about their previous employment as a DSA. Participants' tenure in the RCMP ranged from 2 to 31 years, with the median being 13 years of employment with the organization. Many participants (n = 23; 42.6%) had worked as a DSA in multiple detachments or in other roles or RCMP units (n = 27; 50.0%), meaning that participants held a diverse range of RCMP work experiences. Participants were employed in nine of Canada's ten provinces.

Defining Operational Stress Injuries: Is There Room for DSAs?

Operational stress injury is a relatively new term in the occupational stress and injury literature. According to an interim report from the Senate of Canada (2015), the label is awarded to:

> any persistent psychological difficulty resulting from an operational duty performed while serving in the Canadian Armed Forces or as a member of the Royal Canadian Mounted Police [and describes the] broad range of emotional problems … that interfere with a person's life.
>
> *(p. 1)*

The term was first coined in 2001 by former Lieutenant Colonel Stéphane Grenier to study the negative mental health challenges military personnel and veterans experienced from their work and to destigmatize mental health and legitimize mental health injuries to the same level as physical injuries (Oliphant, 2016; Senate of Canada, 2015).

As Norris et al. (2018) point out, much of the early literature on operational stress injuries in the 20th century was centred on studying the prevalence of posttraumatic stress disorder, major depressive disorder, and general anxiety disorder among military personnel and the negative effects these injuries had on military members and their families. Research on operational stress injuries has since expanded to study PSP because they share some similarities with military personnel in their exposure to PPTE and propensity to develop negative mental health outcomes when compared to the general population (Carleton et al., 2018, 2019; Easterbrook et al., 2022; Rusu et al., 2016; Stelnicki et al., 2021; Thompson et al., 2016). Despite these parallels, armed forces and public safety personnel face different struggles, scenarios, and barriers unique to their job and work environment. Therefore, for this reason, PSP warrant careful consideration within current and future research to account for their occupational nuance (Oliphant, 2016).

Because the psychological injuries people experience persist across occupations outside of public safety and armed forces work, research has expanded to explore and investigate operational stress injuries in other areas like medical work, civilian PSP work, emergency-response jobs, and correctional jobs (Lentz et al., 2020; Moustaka & Constantinidis, 2010; Ricciardelli & Carleton, 2022; Varker et al., 2022). Likewise, research in the area has also broadened in scope to include the study of the effects of operational stress injuries on the families of PSP (Hawryluk et al., 2021; Ricciardelli et al., 2018), the barriers and stigma PSP endure from having such an injury (Krakauer et al., 2020; Martin et al., 2021; Ricciardelli, Carleton et al., 2020, Ricciardelli et al., 2021; Stuart, 2017), and other unique facets resultant or causal of operational stress injuries such as moral injury or distress and substance abuse

(Corthésy-Blondin et al., 2022; Lentz et al., 2021; Roth et al., 2022a, 2022b; Smith-MacDonald et al., 2021).

OSIs include, but are not limited to, operational stress injuries (those derived from the operational realities of the job) and organizational stresses (the realities of how their work is organized). Operational stress can be intensified by those within the organization, or managed, and the interconnecting relationship between job context and content guides our discussion to focus on OSIs, rather than isolate our studies to operational stress injuries. Central here is the recognition that, for various reasons, PSP are more vulnerable to developing compromised mental health when compared to the general population, with roughly 45% of Canadian PSP screening positive for at least one mental health disorder compared to approximately 10% of the general population (Carleton et al., 2018). One notable explanation for the disparity stems from the prolonged and routine exposure PSP have to different PPTE and high-pressure situations throughout the course of their career (Carleton et al., 2019; Ricciardelli, Carleton et al., 2020; Ricciardelli, Czarnuch, Afifi et al., 2020)—often alongside managerial challenges and organizational stress (Ricciardelli, 2018). Similarly, both organizational stressors (e.g., staff turnover and shortages, fatigue, shift work, limited training and resources, lack of social support, and role conflict) and operational stressors (e.g., PPTE exposures, critical incidents, responding to calls for service) are strongly correlated to the high rates of OSIs found in PSPs (Carleton et al., 2020; Chan & Andersen, 2020; Konyk et al., 2021; Ricciardelli, Czarnuch, Carleton et al., 2020).

Our focus in this chapter is the occupational experiences of DSAs, a group not typically considered in discussions of OSIs. DSAs have been found to experience operational stresses, primarily arising from vicarious exposure to PPTE and materials (Huey et al., 2023). Different from being directly exposed to PPTE, vicarious or secondary trauma results from "the emotional, cognitive, and physical consequences of providing professional services to victims or perpetrators of trauma" (Severson & Pettus-Davis, 2013, p. 7). Furthermore, DSAs experience a diversity of organizational stresses—tied to, for example, feeling unsupported, technological challenges, and inadequate resources—which can exacerbate the mental health toll of vicarious trauma (Norman et al., forthcoming). As such, we argue that the experiences of DSAs should be considered within the OSI framework.

"It's part of the job, but it's horrifying": Understanding DSAs as Public Safety Personnel

Before analysing DSAs' experiences of occupational stress, we first situate the DSA role within the framework of PSP to demonstrate why the occupational group should be included in discussions and policies about OSIs. PSP is a term used by Public Safety Canada (2019) "that broadly encompasses front-line personnel who ensure the safety and security of Canadians across all jurisdictions" (p. 3). Public Safety Canada (2019) specifically identifies several roles that fall under the definition of PSP, including police, firefighters, paramedics, dispatchers, and those working in correctional, border, and intelligence services, among others. Having been broadened from its initial formulation to include a wider array of public safety professions, PSP continues to be a flexible concept that recognizes these workers as sharing professional duties that maintain the safety of Canadians (Canadian Institute for Public Safety Research and Treatment [CIPSRT], 2020b). DSAs were adamant that their contributions were vital to the effective functioning of police operations and, more broadly, to public safety; yet, they often felt their contributions were devalued within their detachments and the broader organization:

Interviewer: Do you feel acknowledged for your role in public safety?

P50: I know that I do make a difference, but on a larger scale no. We hear all the time, "Bravo for the police officers and what they do," and of course, they deserve that, absolutely 100%... [And] "bravo to the 911 operators for what you do on a regular basis," obviously what they do is 100% crucial and critical to people's safety.... We hear the "bravo, good job" for them, but never for detachment services assistants. And there's a lot of us, and we do a lot of good work, and I don't feel that we get that recognition and support and respect.

P50 describes how, in the course of their regular duties, DSAs perform a vital, if unacknowledged, public safety role. In rarer cases, some DSAs completed tasks far outside their job description to support their colleagues and meet public safety needs, including handling evidence (e.g., one participant was required to package and ship human remains), providing emergency dispatch support to officers responding to service calls, comforting victims or providing childcare for their children at the detachment, or assuming some duties of sworn officers if all the members were occupied. For example, P36 described an instance where all on-duty officers were attending an emergency call in a rural area, and she received a call about a traffic accident in town. Because she had some medical training, she decided to assist on the scene until officers were able to arrive:

> I had my medic ticket from working at the mines here. And one of the other ladies said to me, "You gotta go, [the officers] are going to be 10 minutes at least before they get into town." And so I went out. There was another member in the office, he was off-duty, so him and I went over. And he smashed the window out of the truck, and him and another bystander got the guy out of the truck, and I did CPR on him until the ambulance arrived

and the other members arrived, which was probably about 20 minutes. And then I went back to work.... It's part of the job, but it's horrifying.

As P36 and P50 explain, DSAs perform important duties in support of frontline police officers and, in exceptional circumstances, may even perform frontline duties beyond their job description. While the latter experiences are rare, and often limited to DSAs in small and under-resourced detachments, they speak to the fact that some administrative staff do take on tasks beyond their job description because they perceive these to be, in the words of P36, "part of the job." Indeed, many DSAs, particularly those in small detachments, expressed a view that their role was to support the public safety work of sworn RCMP members in whatever way possible: P1 stated that "you wear a lot of hats [and] you just get handed everything and anything all the time," while P3 stated that, as a DSA, "you're part of the team.... [sworn members] need you." Clearly, whether performing regular or exceptional duties, many DSAs perceive their work to be contributing to public safety in a meaningful way. Yet, as participants like P50 indicate, many DSAs feel they are rarely acknowledged within their workplace or the broader RCMP for their PSP duties and contributions. Furthermore, as P50's statement indicates, DSAs may suffer "horrifying" experiences in the line of duty—that is, they may be exposed to PPTE or materials, either directly or vicariously. It is to such vicarious exposure that we next turn.

"It does screw with your mental state": Vicarious Exposure to PPTE and Materials

While DSAs occasionally experience direct exposure to PPTE, the most significant operational stress described by participants was vicarious exposure to PPTE and materials. While we detail these exposures and their mental health impacts elsewhere (see Huey et al., 2023), herein, we provide a brief summary to situate these impacts within the framework of OSIs affecting DSAs. Vicarious exposure to PPTE largely came in the form of interactions with the public—as DSAs are typically the first point of contact with the public, either at the front counter or on the telephone—or hearing, either in-person or over the police radio, about events that affected frontline officers. For example, DSAs described experiences such as assisting the families of recently deceased victims, receiving phone calls from people contemplating or planning suicide, and overhearing officers' explicit discussions about crime or accident scenes.

Vicarious exposure to potentially psychologically traumatic materials occurred through DSA's operational duties, such as transcribing statements by victims or offenders and preparing or organizing case files. These job tasks could expose DSAs to graphic details and, in the case of case files, images of crimes and accidents. Exposure to materials involving the death or sexual assault of children was described as particularly difficult. P21, whose duties included handling evidence for such crimes, summarized these impacts by stating, "Those things, you can't get out of your mind." Like P21, other DSAs discussed the mental health toll of vicarious exposure to PPTE and materials. For example, P41 stated:

> You hear things and you know things and you see things that most people don't on a day-to-day basis when they go to work.... It does screw with your mental state quite a bit at certain points.... Any person who says that working for a policing agency does not give you some sort of PTSD in some way shape or form is out of their mind.

Participants' statements highlight the potential of DSA work for acquiring OSIs. A first step to addressing this risk is to recognize the work of DSAs, and other support staff in public safety organizations, and include them in definitions of PSP. In a statement to Canada's Parliament in 2016, David Neufeld—then Vice-President of the Union of Solicitor General Employees—argued in favour of expanding the definition of PSP, stating that:

> several thousand other public servants including the federal sex offender registry analysts, who are exposed, on a daily basis, to details of the worst kinds of sexual abuse; transcription clerks, whose job it is to read and transcribe statements and files regarding offenders and their crimes on a daily basis.
>
> *(quoted in Oliphant, 2016, p. 6)*

Neufeld's statement speaks to the need to implement a wider definition of PSP, which includes support personnel, a fact recognized by the committee to which he spoke (Oliphant, 2016) and which we reiterate in our arguments. Neufeld's words also highlight the importance of recognizing the impacts of vicarious trauma among these PSPs. Researchers have shown the existence of a "trauma hierarchy" among PSP, in which "suffering is considered most legitimate if the exposure to trauma is direct, rather than indirect or cumulative" (Ricciardelli et al., 2020, p. 159). In organizations where such a "trauma hierarchy" is normative, the experiences of non-frontline staff may go unacknowledged. DSAs' experiences, however, speak to the need to recognize both their experiences of trauma and their contribution to the public safety goals of their organization.

Fuel to the Fire: The Impact of Organizational Stressors on OSIs

DSAs experience a wide range of organizational stresses, some of which affect the mental health impact of their vicarious exposure to PPTE and materials.

Many DSAs expressed feelings of being of lower status than the uniformed officers in their detachment, creating feelings that "higher-ups in the RCMP generally don't really care about support staff.... I feel separate" (P29). These findings align with broader research on civilian personnel in police services, an occupational group who can feel excluded from the organization and inferior to uniformed personnel (Boogaard & Roggeband, 2010; Loftus, 2008; McCarty & Skogan, 2013; Norman & Ricciardelli, 2023), as well as other PSP in support roles, such as emergency dispatchers (Beamer et al., 2023; Burke, 1995; Gurevich et al., 2006). The feeling of being unsupported was consequential for DSAs' experience of exposure to PPTE and materials, as some felt their experiences were devalued compared to those of frontline officers. For example, P30 states:

> One day, we were upstairs having coffee...and [the officers] were talking about PTSD, and I piped up and said something about some of the things that I've encountered. And they looked at me and they said, "what the hell do you know about post-traumatic stress?"

P30's experience points to how organizational culture can devalue DSAs' experiences of exposure to PPTE and materials and delegitimize their potential experience of OSI. Further, a widespread lack of consideration for DSAs' experiences was described by some participants, such as P42, as a barrier to pursuing mental health support. She described communication about mental health resources as "mumbo-jumbo...that's [not] going to prompt me to do anything," instead expressing a desire for her uniformed colleagues to personally acknowledge her experiences of occupational stress:

> If someone reached out to me and talked to me and said, "You know, the thing that happened, how did you deal with it?" Or if they involve you in a debriefing.... If I had someone physically and, and personally reach out and say to me "come into the detachment and see a psychologist" or someone just tapped on your door and took a minute to chat with you.... Then, I might be more tempted to actually think about [my mental health].

Of particular import for participants' sense of value within the organization, and feelings of validation for the occupational stress they endure, was inclusion or exclusion from Critical Incident Stress Management (CISM) meetings, events which gave staff an opportunity to collectively debrief PPTE. P50, who had worked for the RCMP for 15 years, stated, "In all of my career with the RCMP, I was invited to one debriefing." Others explained how only in the past few years did DSAs start to be included in CISM. Even where DSAs were routinely invited to debriefings, they did not always feel they could share as openly as the frontline officers. P25 stated:

> When they do the debriefings for critical incidents...personally I feel like the members who were on the scene, and actually hands-on, deserve that time more than I did. I would have rather had just a debriefing where the public service employees could just say how it makes them feel.

In these words, P25 highlights there may be times when, even if they are included in the debriefing, DSAs feel they should restrain themselves out of respect for the officers who had direct exposure to a PPTE. This may also be indicative of a trauma hierarchy within police institutions, as civilian staff might internalize certain sentiments around their exposure to vicarious trauma and, in the process, minimize those traumatic experiences when they are compared to the more direct trauma experienced by their police counterparts. As such, P25 suggests having separate debriefings for DSAs and other public servant staff. Clearly, for P25 and many other DSAs, organizational factors exacerbate the operational stresses experienced by DSA in the course of their duties—with significance for their mental health and well-being.

Conclusion

DSAs are public servants, vital to the functioning of RCMP services in Canada. DSAs feel underacknowledged in terms of their exposure to OSIs, which are organizational or operational in nature. Vicarious trauma is a central concern for DSAs, which is often compounded by organizational stresses as well as other operational realities; indeed, they are often the lifeline for officers who are dispatched to a call for service, and they provide essential support for public safety personnel as well as first responders. The variability in the DSA role also requires recognition, as the job is variable and in flux between detachments, a reality which also reduces the understanding of how best to support DSAs in fulfilling their occupational responsibilities. As police services like the RCMP increasingly rely on non-sworn civilian staff to perform key operational duties, it would be beneficial to develop robust job descriptions which not only encompass the wide-ranging roles and duties these staff may perform on a daily basis, but also account for the various stressors and injuries unique to their line of work.

Within the RCMP, the supports for OSIs available to sworn officers may not be appropriate for DSAs, suggesting careful consideration of the DSA role (as well as that of civilian RCMP members) is needed to best support these workers as they cope with the organizational and operational stresses they experience. Broader organizational shifts in how the organization both acknowledges and handles vicarious trauma may help legitimize the experiences of non-sworn staff, such as DSAs, and create more inclusive spaces in which all forms of trauma are recognized and appropriately handled. While all qualitative studies have limitations, and the experience of DSAs with OSIs demands future enquiry, our study provides rich insight into how DSAs understand the mental health impacts of their work and lays an important foundation for scholarship. Future research on the OSIs impacting DSAs is required, as well as greater acknowledgement of the roles of all persons supporting PSP and first responders to ensure a healthy labour force and safe society.

References

Beamer, A. T., Thomas, T. D., White, S. L., & Van Hasselt, V. B. (2023). Emergency communications operators. In M.L. Bourke, V.B. van Hasselt, & S.J. Buser (Eds.), *First responder mental health: A clinician's guide* (pp. 81–95). Springer.

Boogaard, B., & Roggeband, C. (2010). Paradoxes of intersectionality: Theorizing inequality in the Dutch police force through structure and agency. *Organization, 17*(1), 53–75.

Burke, T. W. (1995). Dispatcher stress. *FBI Law Enforcement Bulletin, 64*(10), 1–6.

Canadian Institute for Public Safety Research and Treatment. (2020a). Potentially psychologically traumatic event (PPTE)/Psychologically traumatic event/ Potentially psychologically traumatic stressor/Psychologically traumatic stressor (PTS)/Traumatic event/Traumatic stressor. *Glossary of Terms*. Available at: www.cipsrt-icrtsp.ca/en/glossary/psychologically-traumatic-event-psychologically-traumatic-stress-psychologically-traumatic-stressor

Canadian Institute for Public Safety Research and Treatment. (2020b). Public Safety Personnel (PSP). *Glossary of Terms*. Available at: www.cipsrt-icrtsp.ca/en/glossary/public-safety-personnel-psp/

Carleton, R. N., Afifi, T. O., Taillieu, T., Turner, S., Krakauer, R., Anderson, G. S., MacPhee, R. S., Ricciardelli, R., Cramm, H. A., & Groll, D. (2019). Exposures to potentially traumatic events among public safety personnel in Canada. *Canadian Journal of Behavioural Science/Revue Canadienne Des Sciences Du Comportement, 51*(1), 37–52.

Carleton, R. N., Afifi, T. O., Taillieu, T., Turner, S., Mason, J. E., Ricciardelli, R., McCreary, D. R., ... & Griffiths, C.T. (2020). Assessing the relative impact of diverse stressors among public safety personnel. *International Journal of Environmental Research and Public Health, 17*(4), 1234.

Carleton, R. N., Afifi, T. O., Turner, S., Taillieu, T., Duranceau, S., LeBouthillier, D. M., Sareen, J., Ricciardelli, R., MacPhee, R. S., & Groll, D. (2018). Mental disorder symptoms among public safety personnel in Canada. *The Canadian Journal of Psychiatry, 63*(1), 54–64.

Chan, J. F., & Andersen, J. P. (2020). *Influence of organizational stress on reported depressive symptoms among police. Occupational Medicine, 70*(7), 496–502. https://doi.org/10.1093/occmed/kqaa141

Charmaz, K. (2014). *Constructing grounded theory*. SAGE.

Corthésy-Blondin, L., Genest, C., Dargis, L., Bardon, C., & Mishara, B. L. (2022). Reducing the impacts of exposure to potentially traumatic events on the mental health of public safety personnel: A rapid systematic scoping review. *Psychological Services, 19*(S2), 80–94

Duxbury, L., Higgins, C., & Halinski, M. (2015). Identifying the antecedents of work-role overload in police organizations. *Criminal Justice and Behavior, 42*(4), 361–381.

Easterbrook, B., Brown, A., Millman, H., Blyderveen, S. V., Lanius, R., Heber, A., McKinnon, M., & O'Connor, C. (2022). The mental health experience of treatment-seeking military members and public safety personnel: A qualitative investigation of trauma and non-trauma-related concerns. *Health Promotion and Chronic Disease Prevention in Canada, 42*(6), 252–260.

Glaser, B. G., & Strauss, A. L. (1967). The *discovery of grounded theory: Strategies for qualitative research*. Aldine Publishing.

Gurevich, M., Halpern, J., Brazeau, P., Defina, P., Schwartz, B., & Bishop, S. (2006). Frontline stress behind the scenes: Emergency medical dispatchers [paper presentation]. *2006 Association of Public Safety Communications Officials Conference*, Toronto, Canada. Available at: www.researchgate.net/profile/Janice-Halpern/publication/228796157_Frontline_Stress_behind_the_Scenes_Emergency_Medical_Dispatchers/links/0fcfd5101759d4bcd3000000/Frontline-Stress-behind-the-Scenes-Emergency-Medical-Dispatchers.pdf

Hawryluk, H., Popik, J., & Tam-Seto, L. (2021). Reimagined connection: New possibilities for virtual mental health support for children and youth of public safety personnel affected by operational stress injuries. *Journal of Military, Veteran and Family Health, 7*(2), 110–115.

Huey, L., Norman, M., Ricciardelli, R., & Spencer, D. C. (2023). "I've seen more dead people than I thought I would": Vicarious trauma exposure among police support personnel. *Criminal Justice and Behavior, 50*(4), 541–558. https://doi.org/10.1177/0093854822114353

Konyk, K., Ricciardelli, R., Taillieu, T., Afifi, T. O., Groll, D., & Carleton, R. N. (2021). Assessing relative stressors and mental disorders among Canadian provincial correctional workers. *International Journal of Environmental Research and Public Health, 18*(19), 1–25. https://doi.org/10.3390/ijerph181910018

Krakauer, R. L., Stelnicki, A. M., & Carleton, R. N. (2020). Examining mental health knowledge, stigma, and service use intentions among public safety personnel. *Frontiers in Psychology, 11*, 949.

Lentz, L., Silverstone, P. H., & Krameddine, Y. I. (2020). High rates of mental health disorders in civilian employees working in police organizations. *Frontiers in Psychology 11*, 1031.

Lentz, L. M., Smith-MacDonald, L., Malloy, D., Carleton, R. N., & Brémault-Phillips, S. (2021). Compromised conscience: A scoping review of moral injury among firefighters, paramedics, and police officers. *Frontiers in Psychology, 12*, 681.

Loftus, B. (2008). Dominant culture interrupted: Recognition, resentment and the politics of change in an English police force. *The British Journal of Criminology, 48*(6), 756–777.

Martin, K., Siddiqui, A., Ricciardelli, R., Lentz, L., & Carleton, R. N. (2021). Differences in mental health, help-seeking and barriers to care between civilians and sworn members working in law enforcement: A research note. *Journal of Police and Criminal Psychology, 36*(3), 627–633.

McCarty, W. P., & Skogan, W. G. (2013). Job-related burnout among civilian and sworn police personnel. *Police Quarterly, 16*(1), 66–84.

Moustaka, E., & Constantinidis, T. C. (2010). Sources and effects of work-related stress in nursing. *Health Science Journal, 4*(4), 210.

Norman, M., & Ricciardelli, R. (2023). "I think it's still a male-dominated world": Detachment Services Assistants' perceptions and experiences of a gendered police organization." *Feminist Criminology 18*(3), 183–204. https://doi.org/10.1177/15570851231153713

Norman, M., Ricciardelli, R., & Huey, L. (forthcoming). "I feel separate": The impact of operational and organizational stressors on non-sworn police support personnel.

Norris, D., Eichler, M., Cramm, H., Tam-Seto, L., & Smith-Evans, K. (2018). Operational stress injuries and the mental health and well-being of veteran spouses: A scoping review. *Journal of Family Theory & Review, 10*(3), 657–671.

Oliphant, R. (2016). *Healthy minds, safe communities: Supporting our public safety officers through a national strategy for operational stress injuries.* Report of the Standing Committee on Public Safety and National Security. House of Commons, Standing Committee on Public Safety National Security.

Public Safety Canada. (2019). *Supporting Canada's Public Safety Personnel: An Action Plan on Post-Traumatic Stress Injuries.* Government of Canada. Available at: www.publicsafety.gc.ca/cnt/rsrcs/pblctns/2019-ctn-pln-ptsi/2019-ctn-pln-ptsi-en.pdf

Ricciardelli, R. (2018). "Risk it out, risk it out": Occupational and organizational stresses in rural policing. *Police Quarterly, 21*(4), 415–439.

Ricciardelli, R., & Carleton, N. (2022). A qualitative application of the Job Demand-Control-Support (JDCS) to contextualize the occupational stress correctional workers experience. *Journal of Crime and Justice, 45*(2), 135–151. https://doi.org/10.1080/0735648X.2021.1893790

Ricciardelli, R., Carleton, R. N., Groll, D., & Cramm, H. (2018). Qualitatively unpacking Canadian public safety personnel experiences of trauma and their well-being. *Canadian Journal of Criminology and Criminal Justice, 60*(4), 566–577.

Ricciardelli, R., Carleton, R. N., Mooney, T., & Cramm, H. (2020). "Playing the system": Structural factors potentiating mental health stigma, challenging awareness, and creating barriers to care for Canadian public safety personnel. *Health, 24*(3), 259–278.

Ricciardelli, R., Clow, K. A., & White, P. (2010). Investigating hegemonic masculinity: Portrayals of masculinity in men's lifestyle magazines. *Sex Roles, 63*(1), 64–78.

Ricciardelli, R., Czarnuch, S., Afifi, T. O., Taillieu, T., & Carleton, R. N. (2020). Public Safety Personnel's interpretations of potentially traumatic events. *Occupational Medicine, 70*(3), 155–161.

Ricciardelli, R., Czarnuch, S., Carleton, R. N., Gacek, J., & Shewmake, J. (2020). Canadian public safety personnel and occupational stressors: How PSP interpret stressors on duty. *International Journal of Environmental Research and Public Health, 17*(13), 4736.

Ricciardelli, R., Haynes, S. H., Burdette, A., Keena, L., McCreary, D. R., Carleton, R. N., Lambert, E. G., & Groll, D. (2021). Mental health stigma, gender and seeking treatment: Interpretations and experiences of prison employees. *Applied Psychology in Criminal Justice, 16*(1), 107–127.

Roth, S. L., Andrews, K., Protopopescu, A., Lloyd, C., O'Connor, C., Losier, B. J., Lanius, R. A., & McKinnon, M. C. (2022a). Development and preliminary evaluation of the moral injury assessment for public safety personnel. *Traumatology, 29*(2), 301–308.

Roth, S. L., Andrews, K., Protopopescu, A., Lloyd, C., O'Connor, C., Losier, B. J., Lanius, R. A., & McKinnon, M. C. (2022b). Mental health symptoms in public safety personnel: Examining the effects of adverse childhood experiences and moral injury. *Child Abuse & Neglect, 123*, 105394.

Royal Canadian Mounted Police. (2021). About the RCMP. www.rcmp-grc.gc.ca/en/about-rcmp

Rusu, C., Zamorski, M. A., Boulos, D., & Garber, B. G. (2016). Prevalence comparison of past-year mental disorders and suicidal behaviours in the Canadian Armed Forces and the Canadian general population. *The Canadian Journal of Psychiatry, 61*(1_suppl), 46S–55S.

Senate of Canada. (2015). Interim report on the operational stress injuries of Canada's veterans: Standing Senate Committee on national security and defence, subcommittee on veterans affairs. Ottawa, Canada.

Severson, M., & Pettus-Davis, C. (2013). Parole officers' experiences of the symptoms of secondary trauma in the supervision of sex offenders. *International Journal of Offender Therapy and Comparative Criminology, 57*(1), 5–24.

Smith-MacDonald, L., Lentz, L., Malloy, D., Brémault-Phillips, S., & Carleton, R. N. (2021). Meat in a seat: A grounded theory study exploring moral injury in Canadian public safety communicators, firefighters, and paramedics. *International Journal of Environmental Research and Public Health, 18*(22), 12145.

Stelnicki, A. M., Jamshidi, L., Fletcher, A. J., & Carleton, R. N. (2021). Evaluation of before operational stress: A program to support mental health and proactive psychological protection in public safety personnel. *Frontiers in Psychology, 12*, 511755.

Stuart, H. (2017). Mental illness stigma expressed by police to police. *The Israel Journal of Psychiatry and Related Sciences, 54*(1), 18–23.

Thompson, J. M., VanTil, L. D., Zamorski, M. A., Garber, B., Dursun, S., Fikretoglu, D., Ross, D., Richardson, J. D., Sareen, J., & Sudom, K. (2016). Mental health of Canadian Armed Forces veterans: Review of population studies. *Journal of Military, Veteran and Family Health, 2*(1), 70–86.

Varker, T., Dennison, M. J., Bancroft, H., Forbes, D., Nursey, J., Sadler, N., Creamer, M., Khoo, A., Metcalf, O., & Putica, A. (2022). Mental health, operational stress, and organizational stress among sworn and unsworn police personnel. *Traumatology, 29*(2), 330–337.

2

POLICE PROCEDURALS' CONSTRUCTION OF UNREALISTIC IMAGES OF POLICING

Implications for Officer Stress

Sarah Britto

Introduction

Media representations, even fictional representations, of police can be vital for shaping public perceptions of justice and may have implications for attitudes toward the police, public policy, and the mental well-being of police officers. With a few exceptions (Chatelain, 2020; Cummings & King, 2017; Donovan & Klahm, 2015), scant research in this area has focused on how critical incidents and the mental health of characters are portrayed in police procedurals. In this chapter, I present findings from a content analysis of three popular Canadian police procedurals, *Motive*, *19-2*, and *Rookie Blue*, and examine how these media representations have the potential to either counter or contribute to stereotypes about mental health and how officers manage stress and trauma experienced during their occupation.

Employment in law enforcement and other public safety professions brings an increased risk of exposure to potentially psychologically traumatic incidents, and there is psychological pressure associated with coping with these incidents (Richards et al., 2021). Exposure puts police officers at a higher risk of developing mental health disorders or "operational stress injuries" (Oliphant, 2016). In a survey of public safety personnel in Canada, Carleton et al. (2018) found that over one-third of municipal/provincial officers and over one-half of Royal Canadian Mounted Police (RCMP) officers screened positive for a recent mental health disorder. Treatment for mental health disorders is a key component of officers' well-being; however, there are many barriers to seeking help for mental health, including lack of knowledge about mental health services, difficulty accessing mental health services, concerns about job consequences, lack of social support at home and among law enforcement

DOI: 10.4324/9781003424253-4

leadership, and a police culture that has traditionally stigmatized mental health and seeking treatment (Ricciardelli et al., 2018; Richards et al., 2021).

The inclusion of storylines that emphasize potentially psychologically traumatizing experiences police officers face in the course of their work has the potential to defy or reify stigma related to help-seeking among police officers and their families. After a brief introduction to research on the pattern of portrayals on crime dramas and how they shape attitudes and beliefs, research on three recent Canadian police procedurals[1] will show the portrayal of basic demographic characteristics of police officers, their efficiency in solving crimes, and exposure and responses to potentially psychologically traumatic events. I conclude with a discussion of the implications of these findings on police stress and mental well-being.

Police Procedurals and the Social Construction of Policing

Police procedurals are a staple of many Canadians' media consumption, and while it is obvious to most viewers that these TV programs are fictional, crime drama programs help to shape public perceptions of police, the justice system and notions of what justice means in our society (Surette, 2015; Reiner, 2003). Gerbner's (1998) cultivation theory argued that mass-produced television (TV) content cultivates an image of society as a dangerous, scary place, or "mean world." In this "mean world," police are positioned as societal protectors who risk their lives to fight the crime problem (Gerbner & Gross, 1976). With a media-cultivated understanding of the world as a dangerous and scary place also come higher levels of fear of crime, positive attitudes toward the police as crime fighters, and support for punitive attitudes (Callanan & Rosenberger, 2017). The influence of fictional portrayals of police may be amplified because most of the public have little contact with police and only a superficial understanding of the policing occupation (Bielejewski, 2016; Cummins et al., 2014; Reiner, 2003; Surette, 2015). Two types of research methods dominate research in this area: content analyzes that examine how police and police organizations are portrayed in crime dramas and surveys of audience members and police officers to assess the impact of these portrayals.

Content Analysis Research on Crime Dramas

Content analyzes have found that policing on TV is dominated by a quite simple narrative where police use their detective skills to solve serious crimes, which leads to arrests and prosecutions of those who transgress the law (Eschholz et al., 2004; Reiner, 2003; Surette, 2015). Serious and violent crimes are often the focus of crime drama programs, with murder being the most frequently depicted crime (Britto et al., 2007; Donovan & Klahm, 2015; Rhineberger-Dunn et al., 2008; Soulliere, 2004). Policing on TV can be exciting, glamorous, and sexy (Garland et al., 2018; Huey & Broll, 2015) and effective, with most cases being solved (Britto et al., 2007; Donovan & Klahm, 2015; Eschholz et al., 2004; Rhineberger-Dunn et al., 2016). However, policing in practice is more complicated than what is depicted on TV and requires police officers to work patrol, manage bureaucracy and paperwork, adjust to shift work, and cope with the routine, mundane, and "dirty"[2] nature of much of their work (Cummins et al., 2014; Huey & Broll, 2015). Despite, or perhaps because of, this discordance, police procedurals can serve to legitimize traditional reactive policing in the public eye by portraying policing as an effective form of crime control and infrequently showing community and problem-oriented policing (Donovan & Klahm, 2015; Reiner, 2003). Ericson and Haggerty (2018) have long noted the tension between the "mass-mediated image of the police as crime fighters" (p. 20) and the reality of police as knowledge workers who dedicate a large portion of their time to report writing and other bureaucratic duties. This creates challenges for police when interacting with individuals whose expectations are based on TV crime fighters, and internally for officers, who may experience frustration at the lack of time they devote to crime-fighting (Ericson & Haggerty, 2018).

Content analyzes frequently measure and compare how racial and gender diversity is depicted in crime dramas compared to the police agencies these programs portray. A lack of diversity and inclusion in police professions is frequently criticized and pointed out as a reason why women and racialized individuals in policing face role strain, harassment, and other job-related stressors at higher rates than their male and non-racialized counterparts (Rabe-Hemp, 2018). Depictions of women and racialized people in the media may help women and racialized people to imagine themselves entering criminal justice professions and to diversify police agencies (Stringer & Murphy, 2020). In recent years, gains have been made in the diversity of police officers in Canada and on TV. Statistics Canada (2023) reports that the number of women in Canadian police services has increased from 4% in 1986 to 23% in 2022. Since the 2000s, studies have routinely found crime dramas slightly over-represent women as police officers compared to their real-life counterparts, but these fictional portrayals still fall short of being representative of the populations where these programs are set (Eschholz et al., 2004; Garland et al., 2018; Soulliere, 2004). DeTardo-Bora (2009) notes another area where female characters have made gains in recent years how, "compared to their male counterparts, female characters were equally assertive, self-confident, and competitive" (p. 153). Despite these gains and regular depictions of women as crime fighters in crime dramas, studies continue to report that the way many female officers are portrayed suggests they often must choose to "become 'one of the boys' or engage in sexualized behavior to fit in and be accepted" and were frequently shown as the victims of crime (DeTardo-Bora, 2009; Garland et al., 2018, p. 613).

Similarly, minority representation in crime dramas is improving, with studies in the 2000s finding greater minority representation than in the past (Eschholz et al., 2004; Soulliere, 2004), and as Tukachinsky et al. (2015) note, crime dramas do better than other genres in presenting Black people as part of ensemble casts. Unfortunately, the development of storylines around these characters has often been categorized as superficial compared to their white counterparts (Chatelain, 2020; Eschholz et al., 2004; Soulliere, 2004; Tukachinsky et al., 2015). A recent study conducted by the USC Annenberg Norman Lear Center found that although the representation of racialized characters in the United States (U.S.) crime dramas has increased in recent years, there were few storylines that included the presence of racial tensions between police and communities, and this lagged behind conversations about policing found in society (Robinson, 2020). This report also noted that crime drama programs rarely discussed criminal justice reform designed to reduce police brutality or improve relationships between police agencies and their communities. Rhineberger-Dunn and Rader (2017) researched the portrayal of intellectual authority on popular crime dramas in the U.S. and found that "White characters present nearly eight times more crime-related facts than Black characters or those of other races" (p. 217). Ongoing research on racialized identities and gender is needed as police agencies and crime drama programming continue to evolve.

Consistent with research on actual police culture (Porter & Lee, 2023), crime dramas emphasize an "us" versus "them" view of the world that can lead to social isolation and the belief that officers are tough enough to handle the stress of the job on their own (Reiner, 2003). In a recent study of retired police officers' perceptions of their experience as police, Porter and Lee (2023) report that police officers identified machismo, unwillingness to accept weakness, in-group identity, feeling underappreciated, and exposure to trauma as key elements of police culture. Cummins and King (2017) argue that media representations of police officers reflect these traditional notions of police culture and normalize the depiction of police officers as "stressed-out, dysfunctional officer[s]" (p. 838) obsessed with fighting crime. Media representations often show police officers drowning their worries at the pub, withdrawing from their spouses and other social supports, and operating in "burnout" mode (Cummings & King, 2017). These dysfunctional portrayals show police officers using excessive force, self-medicating with drugs and alcohol, and breaking the law to manage occupational stress injuries (Chatelain, 2020; Cummings & King, 2017; Donovan & Klahm, 2015). While entertaining and dramatic, these representations rarely show efforts by police agencies and individual officers to promote officers' mental health.

Survey Research on Crime Dramas

Survey research has connected watching crime dramas with increased fear of crime (Eschholz et al., 2003), positive attitudes toward the police, including the belief that police officers only use force when necessary (Donovan & Klahm, 2015), and punitive attitudes (Kort-Butler & Sittner-Hartshorn, 2011). In combination, these attitudes suggest a general understanding of the crime problem as primarily caused by "bad offenders" who deserve severe punishment after being caught by benevolent police officers who bravely man the dividing line between "good" and "evil" in crime drama viewers' communities. The complexity of the crime problem and the role of multiple government agencies and non-profit organizations in addressing crime may be minimized when viewing crime from this perspective. The amplification of positive sentiment toward police officers may also raise expectations of police officers to be as efficient and effective as their TV counterparts (Cummins et al., 2014; Huey, 2010). These high expectations may create stress for actual police officers, who may not always look and act like the police officers depicted in crime dramas.

Interviews with police officers suggest crime dramas may influence expectations of police behavior in real life, placing unrealistic expectations on police officers to solve every crime, and to easily manage the stress that comes with working in a public safety profession (Huey, 2010; Huey & Broll, 2015; Perlmutter, 2000). Additionally, by depicting detective work inaccurately this may also lead to interruptions in their work because they must spend time educating the public on how investigative and other police work is carried out in real life (Cummins et al., 2014; Ericson & Haggerty, 2018; Huey & Broll, 2012). Finally, interviews with police officers (Huey & Broll, 2015) and criminal justice majors (Stringer & Murphy, 2020) suggest that crime dramas may act as a recruiting mechanism for law enforcement. In qualitative interviews of police officers, Cummins et al. (2014) found that a small number of officers felt that some recruits come into policing with problematic stereotypes garnered from watching crime dramas. As survey research suggests that crime dramas may impact public perceptions in several areas, research is needed to examine how critical incident exposure is depicted on police procedurals.

Methods

In this study, I conducted a content analysis to examine three, roughly overlapping, seasons of three of the most popular police procedurals set in Canada. *Rookie Blue*, *19-2*, and *Motive* were selected because they were highly rated, long-running programs that were still in production in 2015 when the study was initiated.[3] Conveniently, these programs also purport to represent the municipal police departments of the three largest metropolitan areas in Canada, Toronto, Montreal, and Vancouver, each with a population of over 2 million. *Rookie Blue* and *19-2*, set in Toronto and Montreal, respectively, are patrol-based programs that show officers policing a district, while *Motive* is set in the homicide unit of the Vancouver Police Department.

A coding instrument including quantitative and qualitative measures of how police are portrayed in crime dramas was developed based on previous content analyzes of crime dramas (Britto et al., 2007; Eschholz et al., 2004). These instruments included items like the race, sex/gender, age, and rank of officers, as well as their efficiency at solving crimes. Items identifying critical incidents experienced by TV officers and elements of TV officers' mental health were developed, including exposure to critical incidents, posttraumatic stress disorder symptoms (PTSD), and qualitative descriptions of specific responses to critical incidents. Data was collected on all police characters with a speaking role. To begin, two research assistant coders (one who had a summer position and helped with refining the initial coding instrument, and another who coded throughout the entire project) completed a collaborative training session with the author that concluded with coding an initial episode and discussing the coding instrument. After the training session, three episodes were coded by all three coders and reviewed for consistency. Minor changes were then made to the coding instrument to include if an officer participated in mental health treatment and to make the data easier to input on the data forms. An entire season of *19-2* was then coded by the author and a research assistant to assess interrater reliability. For nominal and ordinal measures utilized in this chapter, measures of Cohen's Kappa ranged from .75 to 1.00, and for age, which was measured as a continuous variable, the Interclass Correlation Coefficient (ICC) was .80. The remaining episodes were coded by either the author or a research assistant. Three entire seasons of each of the programs were coded for a total of 107 episodes, including 37 from *Rookie Blue*, 30 from *19-2*, and 40 from *Motive*. The analysis focuses on portrayals of police officers' responses to traumatic events in Canadian police procedurals.

For each police officer with a speaking role in an episode, the demographic characteristics of race, age, and sex/gender were recorded. This coding was based on visual (physical characteristics that would indicate an individuals' race, gender, or age) and verbal cues (such as specific references to a character's age, race, or gender/sex) provided within the program. The coders did not rely on information outside the actual program that described the actors because, in the entertainment industry, actors may play characters that do not reflect the actual age, race, or sex or gender identity of the actor and the instrument is designed to capture how an audience member would perceive a character. The measures of PTSD symptoms were adapted from *DSM-5* (2013) diagnostic criteria and only captured symptoms that could be reflected onscreen. Finally, thematic analysis (Braun & Clarke, 2006) was utilized to code the qualitative descriptions of TV officers' responses to experiencing a critical incident. The data were reviewed and coded through an iterative process where patterns of responses to critical incidents were organized into themes.

Results

The construction of police on Canadian police procedurals included physical, occupational, and emotional components. Physically, police characters, especially women, represent what De Tardo-Bora (2009) calls "Hollywood-style" attractiveness, which includes being young, single, stylish, and physically fit. This combination of portrayals, coupled with TV police officers' ability to solve almost every crime, can lead to an image of police work as glamorous and sexy (Huey & Broll, 2015). TV female police officers were depicted as significantly younger (M = 33) than male police officers (M = 37) (p = .000). In terms of race/ethnicity and sex/gender, Canadian police procedurals over-represent racialized people (30% of all officers) and women (34% of all officers) in the police service compared to police services in Canada, where in 2017, 13% of all officers were racialized, and 21% of all officers were women (Conor, 2018). Most of the racialized officers shown were Black, Asian, or Latin American Canadian, with few portrayals of other racialized groups. Over-representation of women and racialized groups relative to police agencies is a positive and potentially empowering trend; however, Indigenous police characters were largely absent from police procedurals, and none of these three programs featured a recognized Indigenous police character in their ensemble casts. It should be noted, as mentioned above, that the coding of race/ethnicity was based on physical and verbal cues provided in the programs.[4] The lack of storylines about Indigenous police characters continues a history of representational erasure in the entertainment industry and is consistent with findings on U.S. programs (Tukachinsky et al., 2015). "Actively writing Indigenous people out of the domain of contemporary representation is tantamount to an erasure of entire ethnic groups and has devastating psychological consequences for young Indigenous people" (Elliot-Groves & Fryberg, 2018, p. 2). While the representation of women, Black, Asian, and Latin American Canadians show progress in representing diversity, the lack of Indigenous characters suggests this progress is not finished.

Occupationally, TV police are efficient and effective at their jobs. Contrary to the research suggesting that a major source of police stress is boredom, and much of their time is spent on routine patrol and doing paperwork (Richard et al., 2021), TV police officers spend almost all their time fighting crime and responding to emergencies. Disdain for the more mundane aspects of policing is evidenced by characters like Officer McNally on *Rookie Blue*, who states, "This shift is going to be full of the stupidest calls ... noise complaints and stealing garden gnomes." Another example of the negative characterization of routine calls is Officer Epstein, who responds to a call about a car idling in a driveway – "better step on it, the planet needs our help." In contrast, the officers are always ready to respond to violent crimes. The focus on the crime-fighting portion of their job may reinforce unrealistic images of the police profession (Donovan & Klahm, 2015; Reiner, 2003). Furthermore, TV officers in this study cleared 90% of their cases, and often did so in a single program that only represents a day or, at most, a couple of weeks. Scholars have long noted that the condensation of time that occurs in crime dramas is necessitated by the one-hour time frame (with commercials) that encapsulates an episode, while also finding that the focus on violent crimes, extremely fast and accurate forensic methods, and high clearance rates may create confusion among members of the general public about the scope and efficacy of actual police services (Britto et al., 2007; Donovan & Klahm, 2015; Eschholz et al., 2004; Rhineberger-Dunn et al., 2016; Surette, 2015).

Emotionally, TV police characters live in a dangerous world where their work leads them to be hypervigilant, suspicious, and cynical. Crime in police procedurals is violent, and its portrayal reflects what Surette (2015) calls the law of opposites, where TV portrays the crime problem in a manner that directly conflicts with reality. Approximately 80% of the crimes shown on Canadian police procedurals were violent, with assault, and murder being the most frequently portrayed offenses. Almost all episodes of *Motive* focused on a murder, which is not surprising given that the show portrays a homicide unit. *Rookie Blue* and *19-2* also showed murders but balanced them with aggravated assaults. Kidnapping, hostage-taking, and human trafficking were also common elements of the plot lines in the three programs. For comparison, the Uniform Crime Reports show that property crimes are almost three times more likely than violent crimes, and murder is the least frequently occurring violent crime in Canada (Statistics Canada, 2022). The focus on murder and other serious crimes is consistent with other studies of crime dramas (Cavender & Deutsch, 2007; Eschholz et al., 2004; Rhineberger-Dunn et al., 2008; Soulliere, 2004). These crimes are likely chosen for their dramatic value and ability to get the audience invested in storylines.

To capture the portrayal of officers' exposure and reaction to potentially psychologically traumatic events, exposure to critical incidents was recorded for each police character. Coders used the following Correctional Service Canada (2007) definition to identify critical incidents:

> A traumatic event, outside the usual range of human experience, which could happen in an institution or in the community, which can cause a strong emotional reaction with the potential to affect one's ability to cope with the after-effects. [Including events such as]: death of a colleague in the line of duty; hostage taking; death or injury of any person during use of force in the conduct of duties; witnessing of another person being mutilated

> or dying; being the victim of physical violence; suicide of a colleague; suicide of an offender; any incident where there is intensive or negative media coverage.
>
> (*p. 1*)

Rookie Blue, *19-2*, and *Motive* all portrayed policing as extremely dangerous and stressful. Officers routinely drew their weapons and faced a lethal threat on an almost episodic basis. It was not uncommon for officers to be shot, stabbed, or blown up, only to survive and keep doing their jobs. There were 176 portrayals of an officer experiencing a critical incident shown on the three programs over three years, for an average of 1.6 critical incident exposures per episode. This provides an example of Gerbner and Gross's (1976) characterization of TV as presenting a "mean world" to audience members.

In total, 62% of all the police officers shown were involved in a critical incident, many of which involved drawing a firearm. As a rough real-world comparison, in a study of police use of force in Canadian Cities, Hall et al. (2013) found that less than 1% of police calls result in the use of force, of which only 10% of those calls involve the use of a firearm. Similarly, Baldwin et al. (2018) estimated that only 0.08% of police–public interactions resulted in the use of force for a large Canadian law enforcement agency. For police in the real world, critical incidents such as seeing a badly beaten adult, seeing the body of someone recently deceased, seeing an animal that has been severely neglected or tortured, interacting with a sexually assaulted adult, and participating in a life-threatening high-speed chase all happen more frequently than incidents were an officer is directly threatened with a weapon or draws their firearm (Chopko et al., 2015). Canadian police procedurals also depicted these more common critical incidents described by Chopko et al. (2015).

Table 2.1 shows that critical incidents were much more common for characters on *19-2* and *Rookie Blue*, averaging 2.1 and 2.3 per episode, respectively, compared to 0.7 per episode for *Motive*. This difference is likely based on the patrol emphasis of *19-2* and *Rookie Blue* compared to the detective focus of *Motive*. Critical incidents were not isolated events in these programs; rather, they were normalized as an everyday part of policing. As an example, Officer Andy McNally on *Rookie Blue* experienced 23 critical

TABLE 2.1 Police officers who experienced critical incidents on Canadian police procedurals

	All Programs	*19-2*	*Motive*	*Rookie Blue*
Number of critical incidents	176	62	28	86
Average officers exposed per episode	1.6	2.1	.7	2.3

incidents over the course of three seasons yet walked away relatively unscathed. She once joked with her police officer boyfriend, Sam Swarek, "I'm invincible, apparently. How many girlfriends have you had that could walk away from a bomb unscathed." To which, he deadpanned – "three." Most major characters that were part of the programs' ensemble casts experienced from five to ten critical incidents in the three-year period. While officers in real life do face critical incidents as a part of their job (Chopko et al., 2015), it is rarely a weekly occurrence, especially in the case of having to draw one's weapon (Hall et al., 2013). There is some experimental evidence that exposure to fictional police use-of-force videos is related to elevated audience perceptions of police use of force and the perception that officers use force too often (Boivin et al., 2017). Research that is specific to watching police procedurals is needed in this area.

TV officers' responses to critical incidents were measured in two ways, (1) through a checklist of PTSD symptoms from the literature that could be observed on a TV program, including items that attempted to capture the categories of intrusive memories (such as flashbacks to a traumatic event, or obsessive thinking about an event), avoidance (such as avoiding places or people tied to a traumatic event), negative changes in thinking and mood (such as emotional numbness, negative beliefs, and disinterest in significant events), and changes in physical and emotional reactions (such as insomnia, hypervigilance, reckless or self-destructive behavior) and (2) qualitative descriptions of officers behaviors after experiencing a critical incident that was analyzed using thematic analysis. Four thematic responses emerged from the qualitative data on responses to critical incidents: business as usual, emotional reaction, an immediate violent response, and positive coping strategies. The typical response to a critical incident on Canadian police procedurals was business as usual, often followed by a drink at a local bar. Most officers continued to do their jobs in a professional manner and displayed few signs, other than a slow smoldering angst, about the incidents impacting them. For example, Detective Angie Flynn from *Motive*, who experienced 12 critical incidents during three years of programming, was known for keeping her cool. Her critical incident scenes were often followed by her drinking a glass of wine at home. In many ways, these portrayals represent the archetypical crime fighter who is impervious to emotional pain and handles any emotional discomfort they may feel on their own.

The next most common response, depicted by approximately one-quarter of the officers after a critical incident, fits the theme of an emotional reaction of expressed fear, anger, sadness, guilt, panic, relief, or shock. The third theme was an immediate violent response that could, in most cases, be characterized as excessive force in the situation. This included officers threatening cuffed suspects with a gun, slamming cuffed suspects into the hood of police vehicles, and beating suspects. A theme of positive coping strategies was also identified, and these included responses such as exercise, focused breathing, and talking with a loved one. In addition, 10% of the officers' experiences with critical incidents resulted in an injury so severe they were hospitalized, and there was no measurable, immediate response.

Although there were several storylines that included flashbacks after a psychologically traumatic incident, prolonged self-destructive behavior such as abusing alcohol and drugs, responding violently when triggered, and avoiding people and places associated with the traumatic incident, the possibility of most police officers needing psychological services following critical incidents was largely unacknowledged. Of the 176 officers who witnessed or participated in a critical incident, only 12, or 7%, were shown receiving any type of treatment or counseling. Critical incidents are clearly integral to police procedurals; yet, meeting with a mental health professional following a traumatic experience was not often highlighted.

There was a frequent underlying message, consistent with research on traditional police culture (Reiner, 2003), that emotions should be kept to oneself or between officers and that the best treatment was a drink at the bar with other officers after work. For example, Sergeant Oliver Shaw on *Rookie Blue* responded to the obvious emotional distress of an officer by stating, "This case got to you … everything is going to hurt a bit more and that's okay, that is how it is supposed to be, except the hurting part bites," rather than encouraging the officer to seek help. There were also a couple of public service-type announcements, such as when Sgt. Julien Houle from *19-2* states, "Just as a reminder, counseling is available, I know some of you are mandated to go, but it is for everybody, and it is a good thing" during a shift briefing. Announcements like this were made in passing with very little follow-up.

A small number of transformative character arcs focused on the mental health of a character. These character arcs have the potential to bring much-needed attention to some of the mental health challenges faced by officers, yet, these portrayals were gendered in ways that reinforced stereotypes.

For example, Marlo Cruz in *Rookie Blue* effectively but secretly managed her bipolar disorder for some time. She kept her diagnosis and need for medication a secret because she did not want to be stigmatized or lose her career in policing. She stopped taking her medication when she started to fall in love and wanted to "feel it," which led to the reemergence of her bipolar symptoms. These symptoms included insomnia, increased activity, racing thoughts, an obsession with a case, and stalking an individual off duty. When this is discovered, her colleagues rally around her to cover her misconduct by faking log entries and supporting her efforts to resume medication and treatment. This example demonstrates the real fear faced by many officers that disclosing mental health treatment or conditions will hurt their career and go against a police subculture that stresses "autonomy, emotional control, and self-sufficiency" (Arter & Ménard, 2018, p. 31), while also depicting the potential for officers, albeit in an illegal manner (consistent with traditional police culture that places a priority on loyalty to other officers) to support each other in treatment.

The most prominent mental health character arc for females involved PTSD following life-threatening violence and sexual assault. There were two officers with similar character arcs, Audrey Pouliot on *19-2* and Gail Peck on *Rookie Blue*. They were portrayed as strong, independent, and competent police officers who were violently sexually assaulted on duty. Both characters were hospitalized and had PTSD symptoms (although the term PTSD was never actually used), and both characters engaged in treatment. Gail Peck was portrayed with symptoms that were primarily intrusive and avoidance. Audrey Pouliot responded with increased arousal and frequent aggressiveness. On one call, she shot a dog, and on another, she attacked a man and erratically screamed at a crowd, leading to protests against the police. Treatment helped both characters develop coping strategies for the fear and anger associated with their mental health disorders. Their storylines were complex and showed trauma significantly impacting everything from their personal lives to their work. They also both epitomized a slow recovery, which focused on building resilience and personal growth. Despite the gendered portrayal of female officers as victims that has been found in other studies of crime dramas (DeTardo-Bora, 2009; Garland et al., 2018), the inclusion of storylines where individuals received effective mental health treatment and then continued their successful police careers show progress in terms of humanizing depictions of police officers and destigmatizing mental health treatment in policing.

For men with a clear PTSD character arc, the message was that treatment was largely ineffective, and although it was not something to be embarrassed about, it was something that you were forced to do and go through the motions, but it did not work. For example, Dov Epstein in *Rookie Blue* states, "I tried therapy after my brother died – talking doesn't really help, I went once, it was stupid…," he later gives advice to a colleague for dealing with her PTSD symptoms, "teen fiction novels and wildlife documentaries will help you get through the night." Nick Barron, on *19-2*, self-medicated with alcohol and contemplated suicide with a gun to his head. What kept him alive was thinking about how his suicide would hurt his son and his colleague intervening at the scene. The next day, he returned to work as a damaged but functioning police officer. Also, on *19-2*, Ben Chartier, whose father had a substance use disorder, is required to go to mandatory counseling sessions following his shooting of a school shooter. Although Ben's behavior, including using a dangerous chokehold on a suspect, struggling with his relationships, withdrawal, and irritability, shows that he is struggling with trauma, the mandatory counseling sessions he attends are portrayed as ineffective. Thus, the messaging is that men need to deal with trauma on their own as treatment is ineffective for recovery from a mental health disorder – but treatment does work for women, who are backhandedly portrayed as lacking the inner strength of their male colleagues.

Conclusion

The image of Canadian police organizations presented on Canadian police procedurals distorts the reality of the day-to-day work performed by most police officers and greatly overstates the frequency of the need to use force during patrol and detective work. Violent crimes, particularly murders, are frequently shown, while property crimes predominate in society (Statistics Canada, 2022). As a result, the operational stress injuries portrayed largely relate to trauma in response to critical incidents, while organizational stressors caused by repetitive routine tasks and operating within a hierarchical bureaucracy receive little attention – whereas both types of injuries constitute occupational stress injuries.

A CSI effect is the phenomenon where portrayals of crime dramas shape viewers' perceptions and evaluations of the criminal justice system and could influence interactions with the police, jury decision-making, and public policy (Desmarais et al., 2008; Deutsch & Cavendar, 2008). The efficacy of police organizations shown on police procedurals has the potential to set unrealistic expectations for police officers in their community. "Public scrutiny adds to the routine stress and high demands of policing" (Anderson et al., 2015, p. 2). In interviews with police officers about their perceptions of how the expectations of the public, shaped by crime dramas, impact their interactions with civilians, Huey (2010) found some evidence of role strain among officers who were challenged by members of the public expecting crime drama technology and had to spend valuable investigative time debunking media myths. Cummins et al. (2014) note that many individuals are drawn to policing based on the dramatic representations of the job they see on TV. Managing this discordance is a challenge faced by new law enforcement officers.

Critical incidents are a staple of Canadian police procedurals, and their regular inclusion in these programs ensures intense drama and characterizes police as heroes who navigate an extremely stressful and dangerous profession, often at the expense of their health and relationships. Implied in this coverage is how police officers should be able to handle traumatic events stoically. Many of the officers portrayed in Canadian police portrayals align with Cummins and King's (2017) characterization of a "stressed-out, dysfunctional officer" (p. 838). These images allow viewers the "dystopian pleasure of seeing police officers' lives disintegrate before the[ir] eyes" (p. 843). The examination of police responses to potentially psychologically traumatic events evidenced a reproduction of a police culture that stigmatizes help-seeking (Reiner, 2003; Richards et al., 2021), along with a continued normalization of self-medicating through alcohol, drugs, one-night stands, and other risky behavior (Cohen et al., 2019; Menard & Arter, 2013). The exception is storylines of female police officers who, after experiencing sexual assaults, participate in mental health treatment that is transformative and essential for their careers.

These findings are noteworthy as avoidant coping, as modeled on these programs, is the least effective coping method (Carver et al., 1989) and yet is the method most consistent with a police subculture that stigmatizes showing weakness (Blau, 1994; Fox et al., 2012). These depictions align with Menard and Arter's (2013) research on real police officers' responses to exposure to critical incidents, which found that abusing alcohol and other negative coping strategies, such as avoidance, disengaging, and dissociation, were more common than help-seeking. The consequences of police officers not developing positive coping skills for managing the stress of policing include higher rates of substance abuse and suicide, reduced efficiency on the job, and being more prone to violence (International Public Safety Association, 2019).

A potentially positive aspect of these programs is the portrayal of police departments as more diverse than the agencies in the cities they depict. Images of female and visible minority officers send an inclusive message about policing and could potentially attract more diverse applicants to this profession (O'Sullivan, 2005). As with U.S. crime dramas (Tukachinsky et al., 2015), the inclusion of Indigenous police characters on Canadian police procedurals still falls behind their representation in Canadian police agencies and the population. Future research should include more recent crime dramas, such as Cardinal (produced in Canada) and, Alaska Daily (produced in the U.S. with some location work done in Canada), and Dark Winds (produced in the U.S.), all of which feature Indigenous characters. More diverse police organizations, as portrayed on police procedurals, represent an aspirational goal, and perhaps also an aspirational society where common stressors faced by women and minorities pursuing a career in policing are rarely present.

Understanding that media portrayals, especially fictitious ones, do not accurately reflect the reality of law enforcement work can go a long way toward better understanding the mental health concerns faced by officers. Education and information literacy are critical to reducing the ability of law enforcement portrayals on police procedurals to impact interactions between the police and the public, juror decision-making, and policy decisions about police organizations. Similarly, promoting a realistic understanding of the range of normal responses to critical incidents and how building resilience and coping skills, fostering strong social supports, and destigmatizing seeking treatment for mental health can reduce the lasting negative impacts of occupational stress injuries can counter inaccurate portrayals in police procedurals.

There were several limitations to this study. First, this study analyzed three years of three of the most popular police procedurals that were in production in 2015 in Canada and may no longer represent the state of police procedurals, and the interpretation of 2015 productions in the 2023 context can be problematic. This study only utilized a content analysis to examine how police officers and the justice system are shown on police procedurals and did not examine whether these specific portrayals affect public perceptions. Finally, all media research is complicated by the issue of causality and determining whether people with certain attitudes are drawn to particular types of programs or whether media content shapes audience perceptions. It is also possible that the relationship between watching crime dramas and crime-related public perceptions is reciprocal. Future research is needed to explore how role depictions of police officers in police procedurals may affect public perceptions, and the direct or indirect impacts of these portrayals may have on police and their families.

Acknowledgments

The author would like to thank Vanessa Jerkovits (Sprentz) for her coding work on this project while a research assistant at the University of Regina.

Notes

1 Police procedural is used throughout to refer to fictional crime drama programs that portray law enforcement investigating and solving crimes, usually within a single episode.
2 The occupation of policing includes performing activities that involve getting physically dirty, exposure to substances such as dirt, saliva, blood, and urine, and responding to calls where individuals are upset or in crisis (Cummins et al., 2014; Huey & Broll, 2015).
3 This timeframe of the data collection should be taken into consideration when reflecting on the findings as it may not be representative of more recent seasons of Canadian police procedurals.
4 It is possible that an Indigenous actor played a police officer in one or more of these programs, who was not an identifiable Indigenous character in the police procedural.

References

Andersen, J. P., Papazoglou, K., Nyman, M., Koskelainen, M., & Gustafsberg, H. (2015). Fostering resilience among the police. *Journal of Law Enforcement*, *5*(1), 1–13.

Arter, M. L. & Ménard, K. S. (2018). An examination of the reasons police officers fail to seek treatment for occupational stress. *Law Enforcement Executive Forum*, *18*(1), 30–42.

Baldwin, S., Hall, C., Blaskovits, B., Bennell, C., Lawrence, C., & Semple, T. (2018, Sept–Oct). Excited delirium syndrome (ExDS): Situational factors and risks to officer safety in non-fatal use of force encounters. *International Journal of Law and Psychiatry*, *60*, 26–34.

Bielejewski, A. (2016). Gangbusters, mavericks, and the cop next door. *Kriminologisches Journal*, *48*(2), 106–127.
Blau, T. H. (1994). *Psychological services for law enforcement.* John Wiley & Sons.
Boivin, R., Gendron, A., Faubert, C., & Poulin, B. (2017). The malleability of attitudes toward the police: Immediate effects of the viewing of police use of force videos. *Police Practice and Research*, *18*(4), 366–375.
Braun, V., & Clark, V. (2006). Using thematic analysis in psychology. *Qualitative Research in Psychology*, *3*(2), 77–101. https://doi.org/10.1191/1478088706qp063oa
Britto, S., Hughes, T., Saltzman, K., & Stroh, C. (2007). Does "special" mean young, white and female? Deconstructing the meaning of "special" in Law & Order: Special victims unit. *Journal of Criminal Justice & Popular Culture*, *14*(1), 39–57.
Callanan, V. J., & Rosenberger, J. S. (2017). Cultivation theory: Gerbner, fear, crime, and cops. In C. P. Campbell (Ed.), *The Routledge companion to media and race* (pp. 31–42). Routledge.
Carleton, R. N., Afifi, T. O., Turner, S., Taillieu, T., Duranceau, S., LeBouthillier, D. M., Sareen, J., Ricciardelli, R., MacPhee, R. S., Groll, D., Hozempa, K., Brunet, A., Weekes, J. R., Griffiths, C. T., Abrams, K. J., Jones, N. A., Beshai, S., Cramm, H. A., Dobson, K. S., Hatcher, S., Keane, T.M., Stewart, S. H. & Asmundson, G. J. G. (2018). Mental disorder symptoms among public safety personnel in Canada. *Canadian Journal of Psychiatry*, *63*(1), 54–64. https://doi.org/10.1177/0706743717723825
Carver, C. S., Scheier, M. F., & Weintraub, J. K. (1989). Assessing coping strategies: A theoretically based approach. *Journal of Personality and Social Psychology*, *56*(2), 267–283. https://doi.org/10.1037/0022-3514.56.2.267
Cavender, G., & Deutsch, S. (2007). CSI and moral authority: The police and science. *Crime, Media, Culture*, *3*, 67–81.
Chatelain, M. E. (2020). Minority representations in crime drama: An examination of roles, identity, and power. University of the Pacific Scholarly Commons. Master's Thesis. https://scholarlycommons.pacific.edu/cgi/viewcontent.cgi?article=4708&context=uop_etds
Chopko, B. A., Palmieri, P. A., & Adams, R. E. (2015). Critical incident history questionnaire replication: Frequency and severity of trauma exposure among officers from small and midsize police agencies. *Journal of Traumatic Stress*, *28*(2), 157–161.
Cohen, I. M., McCormick, A. V., & Rich, B. (2019). Creating a culture of police officer wellness. *Policing: A Journal of Policy & Practice*, *13*(2), 213–229. https://doi.org/10.1093/police/paz001
Conor, P. (2018). Police resources in Canada, 2017. Ottawa, ON: Canadian Centre for Justice Statistics. www150.statcan.gc.ca/n1/pub/85-002-x/2018001/article/54912-eng.htm
Correctional Service Canada (2007). Critical incident stress management. Government of Canada. www.csc-scc.gc.ca/lois-et-reglements/253-2-gl-eng.shtml
Cummins, I., Foley, M., & King, M. (2014). '... And after the break': Police officers' views of TV crime drama. *Policing: A Journal of Policy & Practice*, *8*(2), 205–211. https://doi-org.libproxy.csudh.edu/10.1093/police/pau014
Cummins, I., & King, M. (2017). "Drowning in here in his bloody sea": exploring TV cop drama's representations of the impact of stress in modern policing. *Policing*

& Society, 27(8), 832–846. https://doi-org.libproxy.csudh.edu/10.1080/10439463.2015.1112387

Desmarais, S., Price, H., & Read, J. D. (2008). "Objection, your Honor! Television is not the relevant authority." Crime drama portrayals of eyewitness issues. *Psychology, Crime & Law, 14*(3), 225–243. https://doi-org.libproxy.csudh.edu/10.1080/10683160701652583

DeTardo-Bora, K.A. (2009). Criminal justice "Hollywood Style": How women in criminal justice professions are depicted in prime-time crime dramas. *Women in Criminal Justice, 19*(2), 153–168. https://doi.org/10.1080/08974450902791336

Deutsch, S. K. (2008). CSI and forensic realism. *Journal of Criminal Justice and Popular Culture, 15*(3), 34–53.

Diagnostic and statistical manual of mental disorders: DSM-5 (5th ed.). (2013). American Psychiatric Association.

Donovan, K. M., & Klahm, C. F. (2015). The role of entertainment media in perceptions of police use of force. *Criminal Justice and Behavior, 42*(12), 1261–1281. https://doi-org.libproxy.csudh.edu/10.1177/0093854815604180

Elliott-Groves, E., & Fryberg, S. A. (2018). "A future denied" for young Indigenous people: From social disruption to possible futures. *Handbook of Indigenous education*, 631–649. Springer Nature.

Ericson, R. V., & Haggerty, K. D. (2018). *Policing the risk society*. University of Toronto Press. https://doi.org/10.3138/9781442678590

Eschholz, S., Chiricos, T., & Gertz, M. (2003). Television and fear of crime: Program types, audience traits, and the mediating effect of perceived neighborhood composition. *Social Problems, 50*, 395–415. https://doi.org/10.1525/sp.2003.50.3.395

Eschholz, S., Mallard, M., & Flynn, S. (2004). Images of prime time justice: A content analysis of "NYPD Blue" and "Law & Order." *Journal of Criminal Justice & Popular Culture, 10*(3), 161–180.

Fox, J., Desai, M. M., Britten, K., Lucas, G., Luneau, R., & Rosenthal, M. S. (2012). Mental-health conditions, barriers to care, and productivity loss among officers in an urban police department. *Connecticut Medicine, 76*(9): 525–531.

Garland, T. S., Blackburn, A. G., Browne, J. A., & Blanfort, C. D. (2018). Prime-time representations of female federal agents in television dramas. *Feminist Criminology, 13*(5), 609–631. https://doi-org.libproxy.csudh.edu/10.1177/1557085117693089

Gerbner, G. (1998). Cultivation analysis. *Mass Communication & Society, 1*(3/4), 175–194. https://doi.org/10.1080/15205436.1998.9677855

Gerbner, G., & Gross, L. (1976). Living with television: The violence profile. *Journal of Communication, 26*, 173–199.

Hall, C., Votova, K., & Wood, D. (2013). *Prospective analysis of police use of force in four Canadian cities*. Defence Research and Development Canada. https://publications.gc.ca/collections/collection_2016/rddc-drdc/D68-3-011-2013-eng.pdf

Huey, L. (2010). "I've seen this on CSI": Criminal investigators' perceptions about the management of public expectations in the field. *Crime, Media, Culture, 6*(1), 49–68. https://doi.org/10.1177/1741659010363045

Huey, L., & Broll, R. (2012). 'All it takes is one TV show to ruin it': A police perspective on police-media relations in the era of expanding prime time crime markets. *Policing & Society, 22*(4), 384–396. https://doi.org/10.1080/10439463.2011.641556

Huey, L., & Broll, R. (2015). 'I don't find it sexy at all': Criminal investigators' views of media glamorization of police 'dirty work.' *Policing & Society, 25*(2), 236–247. https://doi.org/10.1080/10439463.2013.864654

International Public Safety Association (2019, October). Policing through the pain: How trauma impacts police officers. www.joinipsa.org/resources/Publications/Policing%20through%20the%20Pain%20-%20How%20Trauma%20Impacts%20Police%20Officers%20-%20International%20Public%20Safety%20Association%20-%20October%202019.pdf

Kort-Butler, L., & Sittner-Hartshorn, K. (2011). Watching the detectives. Crime programming, fear of crime, and attitudes about the criminal justice system. *The Sociological Quarterly, 52*, 36–55. https://doi.org/10.1111/j.1533-8525.2010.01191.x

Menard, K. S., & Arter, M. L. (2013). Police officer alcohol use and trauma symptoms: Associations with critical incidents, coping, and social stressors. *International Journal of Stress Management, 20*(1), 37–56. https://psycnet.apa.org/doi/10.1037/a0031434

Oliphant, R. (2016). Healthy minds, safe communities: Supporting our public safety officers through a national strategy for operational stress injuries. *Report of the Standing Committee on Public Safety and National Security.* Published under the authority of the Speaker of the House of Commons. Retrieved from https://publications.gc.ca/collections/collection_2016/parl/xc76-1/XC76-1-1-421-5-eng.pdf

O'Sullivan, S. (2005). UK Policing and its television portrayal: 'Law and order' Ideology or modernising agenda? *Howard Journal of Criminal Justice, 44*(5), 504–526. https://doi-org.libproxy.csudh.edu/10.1111/j.1468-2311.2005.00394.x

Perlmutter, D. (2000). *Policing the media: Street cops and public perceptions of law enforcement.* Sage Publications. https://dx.doi.org/10.4135/9781452233314

Porter, C. N., Lee, R. (2023). The policing culture: An exploration into the mental health of former British police officers. *Current Psychology*, 1–15. https://doi.org/10.1007/s12144-023-04365-y

Rabe-Hemp, C. E. (2018). *Thriving in an all-boys club: Female police and their fight for equality.* The Rowman & Littlefield Publishing Group.

Reiner, R. (2003). *The politics of the police.* Oxford University Press.

Rhineberger-Dunn, G., Briggs, S., & Rader, N. (2016). Clearing crime in prime-time: The disjuncture between fiction and reality. *American Journal of Criminal Justice, 41*(2), 255–278. https://doi-org.libproxy.csudh.edu/10.1007/s12103-015-9300-z

Rhineberger-Dunn, G., & Rader, N. E. (2017). Race, criminal justice professionals, and intellectual authority in fictional crime dramas. *Journal of Ethnicity in Criminal Justice, 15*(2), 205–225. https://doi.org/10.1080/15377938.2017.1310684

Rhineberger-Dunn, G. M., Rader, N.E., & Williams, K. D. (2008). Constructing juvenile delinquency through crime drama: An analysis of Law & Order. *Journal of Criminal Justice and Popular Culture, 15*(1), 94–116.

Ricciardelli, R., Carleton, R. N., Mooney, T., & Cramm, H. (2018). Playing the system: Structural factors potentiating mental health stigma, challenging awareness, and creating barriers to care for Canadian public safety personnel. *Health, 24*(3), 259–278. https://doi.org/10/1177/1363459318800167

Richards, N. K., Suarez, E. B., & Arocha, J. F. (2021). Law enforcement officers' barriers to seeking mental health services: A scoping review. *Journal of Police & Criminal Psychology*, *36*(3), 351–359. https://doi.org/10.1007/s11896-021-09454-x

Robinson, R. (2020). Normalizing injustice: The dangerous misrepresentation that define television's scripted crime genre. *Color of Change Hollywood*. https://hollywood.colorofchange.org/crime-tv-report/#key

Soulliere, D. M. (2004). Policing on prime-time: A comparison of television and real-world policing. *American Journal of Criminal Justice*, *28*(2), 215–234. https://doi-org.libproxy.csudh.edu/10.1007/BF02885873

Statistics Canada (2022). Canada at a Glance 2022. www150.statcan.gc.ca/n1/pub/12-581-x/2022001/sec10-eng.htm

Statistics Canada (2023). Decrease in the rate of police strength in Canada 2022. www150.statcan.gc.ca/n1/daily-quotidien/230327/dq230327a-eng.htm

Stringer, E. C. & Murphy, J. (2020). Major decisions and career attractiveness among criminal justice students. *Journal of Criminal Justice Education*, *31*(4), 523–541. https://doi.org/10.1080/10511253.2020.1814829

Surette, R. (2015). *Media, crime, and criminal justice: Images, realities, and policies.* Cengage Learning.

Tukachinsky, R., Mastro, D., & Yarchi, M. (2015). Documenting portrayals of race/ethnicity on primetime television over a 20-year span and their association with national-level racial/ethnic attitudes. *Journal of Social Issues*, *71*(1), 17–38.

3

COMMUNITY RELATIONS, WORKPLACE STRESS, AND WELL-BEING IN THE CONTEXT OF MASS DEMONSTRATIONS, DEFUNDING, AND ANTI-POLICE SENTIMENT

A National Study of the Experiences of United States Law Enforcement

Jacqueline M. Drew and Sherri Martin

Introduction

Those working in policing are at increased risk of experiencing psychological harms from their work (Kyron et al., 2022; Syed et al., 2020), with high prevalence of depression and posttraumatic stress (posttraumatic stress disorder [PTSD]) often reported. A recent systematic review found that one in seven police meets the criteria for PTSD and major depressive disorder (MDD) diagnoses (Syed et al., 2020). The prevalence of psychological ill-health in police cohorts and the causes of those outcomes demand attention.

It is with this focus that in 2021, the US National Fraternal Order of Police (NFOP), the largest organization of law enforcement officers in the world, distributed a national survey to their US law enforcement members. The survey was designed by NFOP in collaboration with an academic partner (Griffith University, Australia).[1] The 'NFOP Biennial Critical Issues in Policing' survey (referred to, from here on, as the 'Critical Issues in Policing' survey) had several aims: to understand what officers believe are the most serious issues facing policing right now; to capture the prevalence of burnout, psychological distress, mental health diagnoses, and suicidality among officers; to measure and compare various sources of stress experienced by law enforcement personnel; and to measure the effects of current social and cultural events on officer well-being and policing practice.

The purpose of this chapter is to present a summative and broad overview of the range of findings that have been produced from the Critical Issues in Policing survey (see Drew and Martin [2023] for a specific topic paper

DOI: 10.4324/9781003424253-5

drawn from the survey data on the availability, access, and effectiveness of police wellness initiatives). For this chapter, based on an analysis of the Critical Issues in Policing survey data, we draw several conclusions that are relevant for police services and their leaders as they seek to navigate the current challenges impacting policing practice and the health and well-being of their officers.

Critical Issues in Policing Survey

The NFOP is guided by an overarching mission of improving the lives and working conditions of police officers. Under this mandate, the NFOP recognizes the importance of officer well-being. In 2018, the NFOP began a practice of surveying its membership of law enforcement officers across the United States to gather information about officer health (NFOP, 2023). The organization's initial survey was a short pulse check undertaken in collaboration with NBC News Channel 4 in New York City. The purpose of the survey was for a media segment on officer mental health. It highlighted the concerns and challenges being faced by members of law enforcement with respect to mental health and well-being in the profession. Given the high response rate to the survey, it was clear that officers wanted to talk more about mental health. In particular, the impacts of the police workplace and the profession on their overall well-being. Anecdotally, the viewpoint of officers has long been a missing part of this conversation. It seemed that they wanted to talk more about their working conditions and their experiences working in a law enforcement career. As such, the NFOP began directing additional resources towards the development of wellness initiatives for its members. It also committed to the practice of surveying members biennially to track and identify changes in officer experiences. The NFOP sought to recognize new and emerging trends that impact officer wellness.

Buoyed by the success and impact of the first national survey conducted in collaboration with NBC News, the NFOP has committed to surveying its members every two years about critical issues in policing and wellness. The first and more simplistic iteration of the survey conducted with NBC News in 2018 has now grown into a comprehensive survey instrument. The current Critical Issues in Policing survey measures over 35 separate variables.

The Critical Issues in Policing survey, first deployed in 2021, is the focus of this chapter. As already highlighted, it has been co-produced with an academic partner (Griffith University, Australia). Leveraging academic experts has allowed an evidence-informed approach to both survey development and analysis to be undertaken. More attention has been given to the methodological rigour of the survey instrument, using validated scales and clearly defined theoretical constructs. Further, survey development involved extensive input from leaders and scholars working in the law enforcement profession. This included committee members of the NFOP Wellness Committee, who are all current or retired law enforcement officers. Both the academic and practitioner expertise sought during survey development ensured the robustness of the survey design.

The Critical Issues in Policing survey had several aims, including:

- to understand what officers believe are the most serious issues facing policing right now;
- to investigate the prevalence of burnout, psychological distress, and suicidality among officers;
- to examine the availability, access, and perceived effectiveness of wellness services;
- to measure and compare various sources of stress experienced by officers; and
- to measure the impact of current social and cultural events on officer well-being.

Method

Sample

The Critical Issues in Policing survey deployed in 2021 included responses from 5,854 active (n=3,994) and retired (n=1,860) police officers across the United States.[2] The binary gender breakdown was broadly reflective of the current gender composition of US police agencies, 84% males and 15% females. On average, across the United States, female officers comprise around 13% of agencies (National Institute of Justice, 2019). Most respondents identified as White (84%), with the remainder of respondents representing various other ethnic groups (7% Hispanic/Latino, 4% African American/Black, 1% American Indian/Alaskan, 1% Asian/Asian American, 1% Native Hawaiian/Pacific Islander, and 2% Other). Considering active officers only, most respondents had 21+ years of service (39%), followed by 16–20 years (20%) and 11–15 years of service (17.0%). Most respondents were officers, patrols, or deputies (37%), with the next largest category being corporals or sergeants (25%). The largest group of respondents were general patrol or were undertaking operational duties (47%), followed by detectives or plain clothes (20%). Respondents were drawn from all 50 states, the District of Columbia, and the US territory of Guam.

Survey Instrument and Procedure

An online, quantitative survey, delivered via the Survey Monkey platform, was marketed to all NFOP members. Participation in the survey was voluntary and those accessing the survey link were provided with a comprehensive information sheet and consent form, detailing information such as confidentiality and anonymity of survey responses. Ethics approval for the research was obtained from the Griffith University Human Research Ethics Committee.

At the time of survey deployment, the NFOP had a membership of approximately 350,000 active and retired police officers with lodges in all 50 states and the District of Columbia. Given the composition of the NFOP, the survey was able to include a group who are often underrepresented in police research, those who had retired from the police profession. The survey was deployed to NFOP members via email and other internal communication channels (e.g., promotion through internal newsletters). The survey was not promoted through open channels, such as social media, to minimize the likelihood that non-law enforcement personnel would access the survey. Survey deployment occurred between September and November 2021.

It is important to note the context in which the survey was deployed; what was happening before and during the survey period. At the time, there was increased public attention on the law enforcement profession, including calls for defunding, reimagining policing, and greater police accountability. The profession had just experienced over a year of uncertainty, increased danger for officers, and other changes to police work resulting from the global health pandemic (COVID-19). Further, instability ensued in the wake of various high-profile deaths of Black US citizens (Eric Garner, Breonna Taylor, Michael Brown, Jr., and others) at the hands of US law enforcement. This climaxed following the death of George Floyd in Minneapolis, Minnesota. Many communities across the nation experienced mass demonstrations railing against law enforcement and calling for defunding of police departments.

Despite extensive coverage by mainstream media and the reporting of significant public outcry, law enforcement and the general public seldom heard from members of law enforcement who were experiencing these events on the ground. Officers were coping with significant shifts happening in the profession and extreme negativity. The Critical Issues in Policing survey provided a mechanism through which to capture the viewpoints and experiences of law enforcement practitioners – from rank-and-file through to police leadership. Through the survey a more complete picture, which focused on the collation of the views of officers about the policing landscape, can be provided.

The full survey measured over 35 different variables of interest. The current chapter provides summative data related to a sub-set of variables. These include critical issues in policing, psychological health prevalence, police stressors, and the impact of the current context on motivation, community relations, and police practices.

Critical Issues Measure

To measure critical issues in policing, officers were asked to rate a list of 19 issues (including 'other' response option) which were likely of concern for officers. The list of critical issues was generated through consultation with the NFOP Wellness Committee, a committee which includes both active and retired law enforcement officers. The issues related to three categories: crime problems, community relations, and the police profession. Officers completing the survey rated the seriousness of each issue using a 10-point Likert scale, ranging from 'not an issue at all' to 'extremely serious'. Means for each item were calculated and the 'top five' critical issues were identified for each of the three categories listed above.

Prevalence Data Measures

The survey incorporated several measures related to psychological health, including burnout, psychological distress, mental health diagnoses, and suicidal behaviours. Burnout was measured using the eight-item exhaustion sub-scale of the Oldenburg Burnout Inventory (Demerouti et al., 2003). Officers rated each item using a 7-point Likert scale and mean scores were calculated. Low, medium, and high categories were generated following the methodology provided by Delgadillo et al. (2018). Psychological distress was measured using the ten-item Kessler Psychological Distress (K10) scale (Kessler et al., 2002). Each statement was rated on a 5-point Likert response scale, ranging from 1 (none of the time) to 5 (all of the time). Based on sum scale scores, four categories were generated (well [scores under 20], mild distress [scores between 20 and 24], moderate distress [scores between 25 and 29], and severe distress [scores of 30 and above]). Officers indicated whether they had received a formal diagnosis of PTSD, depression, and/or anxiety during their employment as a police officer. Three questions were asked regarding suicidal behaviours. Information was collected from officers about suicidal ideation, suicide attempts, and suicide plans. Officers were asked whether they had experienced each type of suicidal behaviour within the previous 12 months or at any time during their police career.

Stress Measures

Three sets of stressors were measured in the survey: stress stemming from the experience of trauma and critical incidents, and stress resulting from both operational and organizational factors. The trauma measure captured stress caused by the experience of various critical incidents relevant to policing. An adapted version of Weiss et al.'s (2010) Critical Incident History Questionnaire for police was used. The measure included 18 items. Officers were asked whether they had experienced the event and if they had, to indicate the level of stress that each incident had caused them using a 3-point Likert scale. Responses ranged from no stress at all (1) to a great deal of stress (3). Mean scale scores for each item were calculated.

Operational stress and organizational stress were measured using the Police Stress Questionnaire-Operational (PSQ-Op) and Police Stress Questionnaire-Organizational (PSQ-Org) scales, respectively (McCreary & Thompson, 2006; McCreary et al., 2017). Active officers rated each item using a 1–3 scale, with responses ranging from no stress at all (1) to a great deal of stress (3). While the scales were designed to produce an overall mean score, the data in this chapter is presented at the item level to identify which specific operational and organizational factors caused the highest level of stress for police. Mean scores for items were calculated.

Motivation, Community Relations, and Police Practices Measures

For all scales used to measure motivation, community relations, and police practices, officers rated each scale item using a 5-point Likert scale. Responses ranged from strongly disagree (1) to strongly agree (5). Three categories, including low, medium, and high, were created for each scale. The percentage of officers who fell into each category was calculated.

For motivation, three single items were constructed to measure the impact of anti-police rhetoric, mass demonstrations, and negative publicity on the motivation to 'do the job' of policing. Scores of 1 and 2 were grouped as low agreement, a score of 3 was medium agreement, and scores of 4 and 5 were grouped as strong agreement.

With respect to community relations, four variables were measured: war on cops; likelihood of being criminally prosecuted, civilly sued, or fired; audience legitimacy; and dangers of policing. War on cops was measured based on a scale developed by Nix et al. (2018). Active officers were asked to indicate their level of agreement with three statements, each measuring officer perceptions of citizen behaviour towards police. Based on the total mean score for the scale, low agreement represented scores between 3 and 6, medium agreement were scores between 7 and 10, and strong agreement were scores between 11 and 15.

Three single items were used to collect information from active officers on their concerns regarding being criminally prosecuted, civilly sued, or fired for doing their job. Concerns were grouped into three categories: low (scores of 1 and 2), moderate (score of 3), and high (scores of 4 and 5).

Audience legitimacy was measured using Nix and Wolfe's (2017a) five-item measure. Audience legitimacy refers to 'how the police believe they are viewed by the public' (Nix, Pickett & Wolfe, 2020, p. 218). Using the total mean score for the scale, low agreement included officers who scored between 5 and 11, medium agreement included scores between 12 and 18, and strong agreement included scores between 19 and 25.

Dangers of policing were measured using two items derived from a measure developed by Nix and Wolfe (2017b). The items focused on whether officers felt that negative publicity had made it more dangerous to be a police officer. Based on the total mean scale score, low agreement included scores between 2 and 4, medium agreement were scores between 5 and 7, and strong agreement included scores between 8 and 10.

With respect to police practices, the survey included a measure of de-policing. A three-item scale developed by Nix and Wolfe (2017b) was used. Using the total mean score, low agreement was represented by scores between 3 and 6, medium agreement scores were between 7 and 10, and strong agreement included scores between 11 and 15.

Survey Findings

Critical Issues

Often, there are discussions amongst politicians, policymakers, lobby groups, criminologists, think tanks, police strategic forums, and senior police leaders about the critical issues facing contemporary policing. A group that is perhaps less well represented in such discussions includes those on the frontline; law enforcement personnel who are most directly involved in delivering policing services to the public. It is vital to understand from their perspective what they view as critical issues facing them. Their understanding, knowledge, and job motivation can offer insights into how policing services are delivered on the ground and how officers are engaging with communities. Further, understanding perceptions and concerns about enacting their police role provides insights into their choice to remain or leave the police profession. Three factors were examined: crime problems, community relations, and concerns related to the police profession.

Crime Problems

Beginning with crime problems (see Figure 3.1), the crime problem rated as the most serious issue was violent crime. This was followed by illegal narcotics and policing emotionally disturbed and mentally ill citizens within the

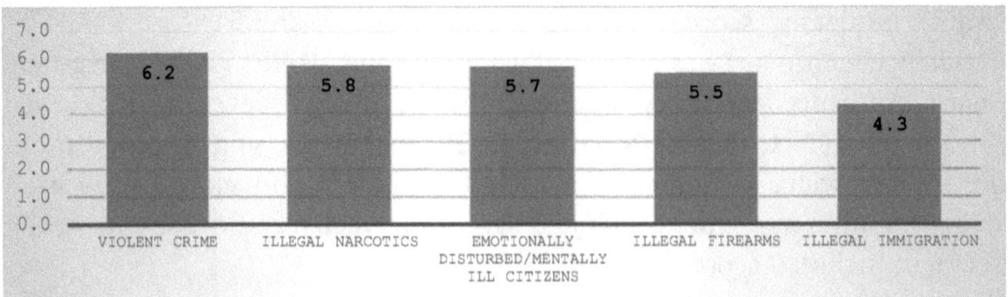

FIGURE 3.1 Critical issues: Crime problems.

community. The finding that serious crime was the top issue rated by officers is unsurprising. Increases in violent crime across the United States have attracted attention in the last few years. While the rates do not reach those seen in the 1990s, some do report that violent crimes, particularly homicide rates, have shown an uptick, beginning as early as 2014 (Berk, 2023; Gramlich, 2022). Violent crime is certainly on the agenda, not just for law enforcement but also for the broader community (Gramlich, 2022).

Current perceptions by police regarding the seriousness of violent crime may have been fuelled, in part, by the environment in which officers were operating at the time of survey deployment. As discussed earlier, the survey was distributed in 2021 after the mass demonstrations and protests which were ignited by the death of George Floyd. Many officers had experienced firsthand, unprecedented levels of negative and violent interactions with their communities.

Community Relations

Turning to community relations (see Figure 3.2), our research indicates that negative news media about law enforcement and other anti-police rhetoric was the most serious community relations issue identified by officers. This was followed by calls to defund police, racial tensions between police and their communities, and mass public demonstrations and protests. The top two issues are reflective of the tensions that were omnipresent during the time of the survey. The impact of these issues was further explored in the survey through the measurement of concepts, such as 'war on cops', audience legitimacy, and the impact of negative publicity on the dangers and motivation 'to do the job of policing'. Data on these are presented in a later discussion of the survey findings.

Police Profession

Within the police profession category, the greatest concern identified by officers was the removal of qualified immunity.

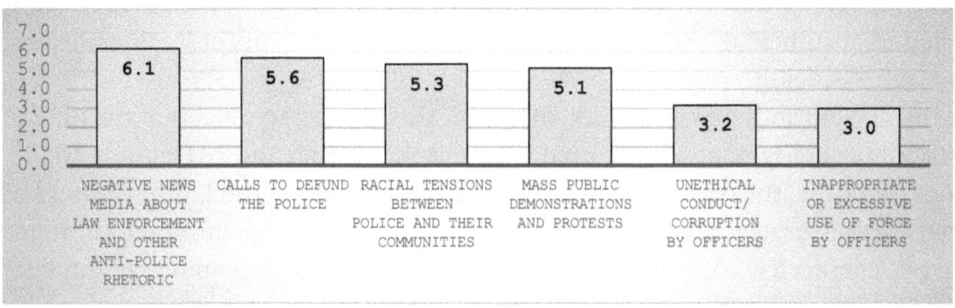

FIGURE 3.2 Critical issues: Community relations.

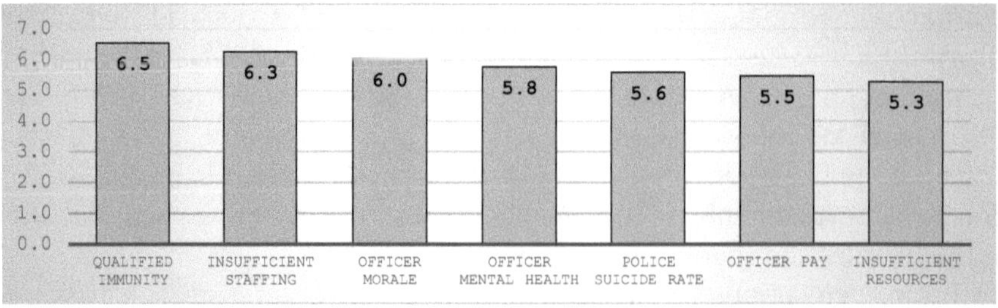

FIGURE 3.3 Critical issues: Police profession.

TABLE 3.1 Qualified immunity (active officers)

	Low (%)	*Moderate (%)*	*High (%)*
Criminally Prosecuted	15.9	17.4	66.7
Civilly Sued	15.1	16.2	68.7
Fired	29.2	17.6	53.2

In several states across the United States, there had been discussion surrounding the removal of qualified immunity for law enforcement. Qualified immunity 'protects a government official from lawsuits alleging that the official violated a plaintiff's rights, only allowing suits where officials violated a "clearly established" statutory or constitutional right' (Legal Information Institute, 2022). If qualified immunity were removed, it would make officers more vulnerable to being criminally prosecuted and/or civilly sued. For many officers, this may make the job simply untenable due to such risks. Our research provides evidence to suggest that officers were highly concerned with this type of outcome. Over half the sample (see Table 3.1) (53.2%) of active officers were concerned about being fired 'just for doing their job'. More than six in ten officers held serious concerns about being criminally prosecuted and civilly sued.

Returning to the overall data focused on the police profession, the next most highly endorsed issues, following the removal of qualified immunity, included insufficient staffing, levels of officer morale, officer mental health, and police suicide.

Insufficient staffing was already of significant concern to officers at the time of the survey deployment (distributed between September and November 2021). Since that time, the recruitment and retention crisis across the United States has been further exacerbated. Police agencies have seen rising numbers of police leave their services, and they are facing genuine difficulties in attracting new officers into their ranks (Young & Sayers, 2022). Despite increased attention and effort by US law enforcement agencies and policymakers, as well as the development of additional incentives offered to prospective police recruits, the numbers of interested and qualified candidates remain at unprecedented low levels (PERF, 2019). Research conducted following the death of George Floyd found that voluntary resignations in the Western US agencies under study increased by 279% (compared to synthetic control expectations) and were likely to continue to increase (Mourtgos et al., 2021). Many agencies may simply not have enough human resources to fulfill frontline duties. The result of this strain on officers who work in understaffed agencies is likely to be even poorer psychological health, increased rates of burnout, and less efficiently functioning police organizations.

Officers rated mental health and officer suicide as the fourth and fifth most serious issues in the US police profession, respectively. The basis of these concerns is likely two-fold. One, of course, is the personal experience of officers themselves and the impacts they are experiencing because of working in policing. The other relates to the increasing spotlight that has been placed on officer mental health and suicide (Carleton et al., 2019; Drew & Martin, 2023; Law Enforcement and Mental Health Wellness Act, 2017). It is likely that officers are becoming more aware that psychological health is a significant concern for all those who work within the police profession.

Prevalence Data

A key aim of the survey was to provide insight into burnout, psychological distress, mental health diagnoses, and suicidal behaviours of law enforcement officers across the United States. Given the plan to conduct the current survey every two years, the resultant information will allow for national tracking of the overall rates of each of these mental health indicators. The inclusion of both active and retired officers in this survey provides insight into the rates of psychological distress of both cohorts. With the inclusion of retired officers, the findings of the survey provide important information about the need for ongoing mental health support following the end of a police career.

Burnout (Exhaustion)

For the active officer sample, we found that around eight in every ten officers reported medium to high burnout, with over 50% indicating high levels of burnout. To put this in context, we can compare police burnout data with data collected from other employed population groups from a similar time period. Comparative research has found that five in ten employees, across a range of industries in the United States, are similarly experiencing medium to high workplace burnout (Aflac, 2022). The rate of burnout in policing, approximately 30% higher in policing compared to other industries, is concerning and requires immediate attention.

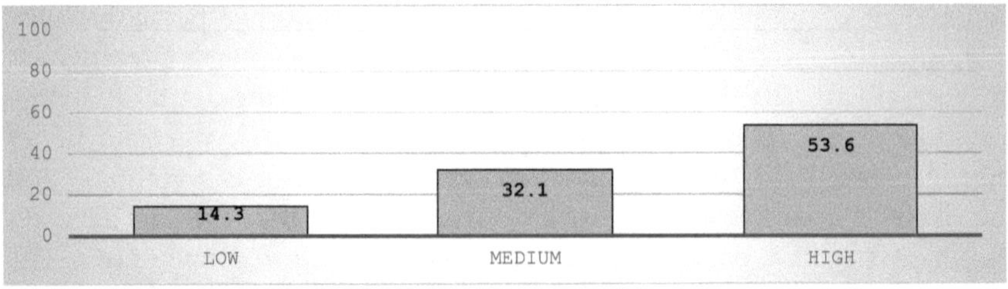

FIGURE 3.4 Burnout categories for police (active officers).

Psychological Distress

The survey findings indicated that 44% of active and almost 31% of retired officers are experiencing some level of psychological distress. For comparison, in a US national study of employed adults, 22.6% reported psychological distress (National Health Interview Study data; Daly, 2022).

Of concern, 11% of active officers and 7% of retired officers reported symptoms that constitute severe distress. Comparisons to the National Health Interview Study data reveal that only 4% of respondents in that sample indicated this level of distress (Daly, 2022). Our data reinforces the work of others (e.g., Kyron et al., 2022; Syed et al., 2020) who have undertaken prevalence research in police populations. Police cohorts represent a group that experiences higher than average levels of psychological distress resulting from their work. In particular, the percentages of police reporting psychological distress at the higher end of the distress continuum must be recognized and action must be taken.

Our research provides data on the retired police cohort. This research revealed that psychological distress remains relatively high following retirement from the profession. Ongoing support for psychological health needs to be considered. Given that retired officers can no longer access psychological services provided by police agencies, the provision of psychological support and services for retired officers, many of whom may have given an entire career to law enforcement, remains largely unaddressed.

Mental Health Diagnoses

The three types of mental health conditions that are most often identified within police populations were included in the survey. Active and retired officers were asked whether they had a formal diagnosis of PTSD, depression,[3] and/or anxiety[4] during their employment as a police officer. Respondents were able to indicate if they had more than one diagnosis given the high occurrence of comorbidity of depression, anxiety, and PTSD in police (Bowler et al., 2016).

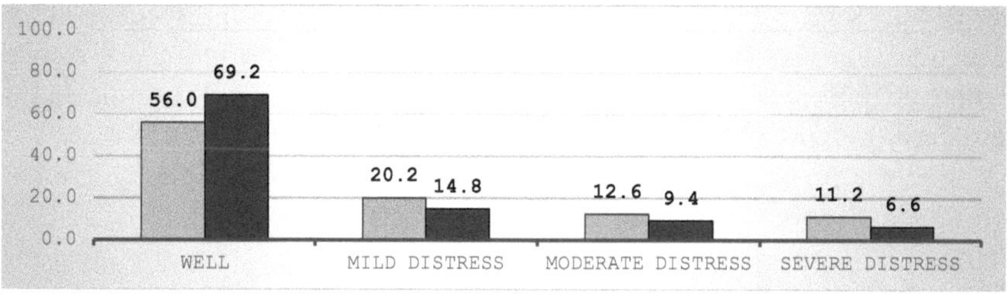

FIGURE 3.5 Psychological distress categories for police (active and former officers).

The current research demonstrates similar numbers of officers across the active and retired cohorts who reported PTSD (active: 12.4%; retired: 13.9%), depression (active: 14.1%; retired: 15.3%), and anxiety (active: 17.0%; retired: 15.8%). Anxiety was the most reported condition, followed by depression and PTSD, respectively.

While acknowledging variability in specific rates reported in previous research findings, often driven by different methodological designs and cohorts studied (e.g., nationality of sample, type of police role, and exposure or not to extreme traumatic incidents) (Regehr et al., 2021), the current data is largely consistent with other police prevalence research. Research with police cohorts often finds that depression and anxiety occur at higher rates than PTSD diagnoses (Beyond Blue, 2018; Stevelink et al., 2020). A recent study of over 40,000 active police officers in the United Kingdom found rates of 4.0% for PTSD, 9.0% for depression, and 7.5% for anxiety (Stevelink et al., 2020). In a large Australian study, diagnosed mental health disorders in the police cohort totalled 13.8% for PTSD, 26.2% for depression, and 23.8% for anxiety (Beyond Blue, 2018).

The rates of diagnoses found in the current study are also analogous with others who compared police and general population data. Numerous studies have reported that police officers experience higher rates of PTSD, anxiety, and depression, compared to the general population (National Center for Health Statistics, 2021; National Center of PTSD, 2023; National Institute of Mental Health, 2023).

Suicidal Behaviours

Three questions were asked regarding suicidal behaviours. The survey measured suicidal ideation, suicide attempts, and suicide plans. The data indicated that 6.2% of officers (both active and retired) had suicidal ideation during the previous 12 months and a career prevalence of 18.5%. Some research from US police cohorts has reported a lifetime prevalence of suicide of around 20% (Violanti et al., 2009). For the Royal Canadian Mounted Police (RCMP), rates of 25.7% have been found (Carleton et al., 2018). With respect to more recent ideation (i.e., within two weeks), a US study reported a prevalence of 8.8% (Chopko et al., 2014) and a Canadian study of police indicated a prevalence (i.e., over one year period) of 9.9% (Carleton et al., 2018).

Within the previous 12 months, 2.2% of officers had made a suicide plan, and 6.8% had done so at some time during their career. In terms of suicide attempts, 0.3% of officers had made a suicide attempt within the previous 12 months, and 0.7% had made a suicide attempt during their police career. Recent research with Canadian police reported similar, but generally slightly higher, prevalences of suicide attempts and suicide planning (Carleton et al., 2018).

In 2021, based on the US National Survey on Drug Use and Health, 4.8% of adults (during the preceding year) had serious thoughts about suicide, 1.4% made a suicide plan, and 0.7% had attempted suicide (Substance Abuse and Mental Health Services Administration, 2022). As such, the prevalence of suicidal ideation and suicide plans are comparatively higher in the policing cohort surveyed for this research. This interpretation is made with an acknowledgement that comparisons with general population rates must be considered with regard to specific population effects. Specifically, police populations are numerically male-dominated and suicide deaths are generally higher in male cohorts.

Multi-faceted Nature of Police Stressors

An aim of the survey was to capture the various types of stressors experienced by US police. By understanding sources of stress, we can begin to better understand which specific stressors are connected to well-being outcomes. In turn, we are then better informed on how best to direct resources and efforts to decrease the prevalence of burnout, psychological distress, and mental health concerns within police cohorts. Drawing on the work of Carleton et al. (2020) and others (Drew & Carroll, 2022; Drew et al., 2023), police stress was conceptualized in this study as falling within three groups: trauma or critical incident stress, other operational stress, and organizational stress.

It should be noted that operational stress is sometimes narrowly conceptualized and focuses on stress resulting from traumatic events or critical incidents. However, the concept of operational stress has been expanded by some to be more inclusive. For instance, measurement of police operational stress, based on the work of McCreary et al. (2017), includes a range of factors that relate to the broader context in which the job of policing is enacted. This includes stressors such as fatigue, work-related activities on days off, managing work-life balance, and physical health impacts (McCreary et al., 2017). The approach taken in this research to study operational stressors and trauma and critical incident stressors as separate groups is supported by recent research.

Research has found that a broad range of operational stressors, beyond critical incident traumas, cause as much, if not more, harm (Carleton et al., 2020; Drew & Carroll, 2022; Sherwood et al., 2019).

Trauma and Critical Incident Stress

The experience of traumatic events and critical incidents forms an inevitable part of policing and officers will experience a high frequency of exposure to such events (Rose et al., 2002; Wagner et al., 2020). There are two ways to consider critical incident stress felt by officers as a result of potentially psychologically traumatic events (PPTEs). The first is to ensure that when we study stress, we divide the sample into those who have and have not experienced the specific stressor, rather than considering responses from officers who may not have been exposed to the critical incident being examined. In cases where an officer has not experienced the event, officers are simply 'guessing' about the stress they would feel in such a circumstance, or they report no stress because they have not experienced it. For example, fewer officers would experience killing someone in the line of duty given it is a relatively rare event, compared to attending a domestic violence call which is experienced by almost all officers.

Examining the dataset, which included only stress ratings of those officers who had experienced the event, the top three most stressful events were: colleague being killed, killing someone in the line of duty, and responding to a call where a child was badly beaten, sexually assaulted, or severely neglected. Officers were highly concerned with the physical dangers posed by policing, whether to themselves, their colleagues, or others in the community. Only one type of traumatic event in the top five related to the content of police work (i.e., responding to a call where a child was badly beaten, sexually assaulted, or severely neglected).

This research indicates that the danger of policing is generally perceived as more stressful in comparison to the traumatic content of police work. This is consistent with other research that has found police are surprisingly resilient to the potentially psychologically traumatic nature of police work itself (Hartley et al., 2013; McCaslin et al., 2006). Research finds that the dangers associated with police work are often the most impactful (Hartley et al., 2013; McCaslin et al., 2006).

Operational Stress

As discussed earlier, operational stress can be extended beyond simply measuring trauma and critical incidents. More broadly, operational stress, as defined by McCreary et al. (2017), refers to a broader range of stressors that are related to the context of the police role. The current research revealed that the top five operational stress factors reported by officers are: fatigue, negative

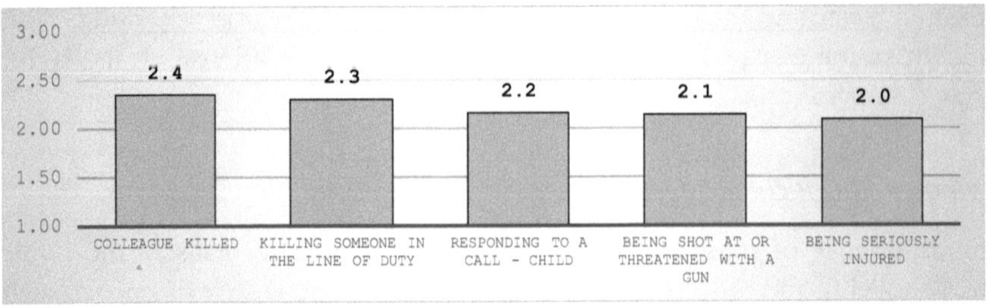

FIGURE 3.6 Trauma/critical incident stressors – Top five (active officers).

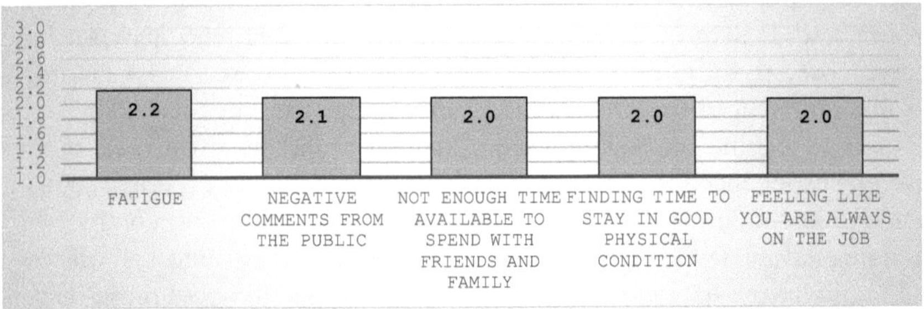

FIGURE 3.7 Operational stressors – Top five (active officers).
Operational stressors were listed in order, using the second decimal place; not included in figure.

comments from the public, not having enough time available to spend with friends and family, finding time to stay in good physical condition, and feeling like you are always on the job.

The experience of fatigue as the top stressor is not surprising. Not having enough time to spend with family and friends, difficulty in finding time to stay in good physical condition, and feeling like they are always on the job were also identified as significant sources of stress for officers. Likely, all three factors are connected to and/or are exacerbating fatigue. These findings, particularly with respect to fatigue, are consistent with previous research. Oscar Kilo (2023), a national police well-being service in the United Kingdom, has made significant investments in interventions designed to combat officer fatigue. These initiatives were based on the findings of their 2019 national (UK) well-being survey. That survey revealed fatigue was the biggest area of well-being concern reported by police.

The finding that officers are experiencing stress resulting from negative comments from the public is consistent with the critical issues findings, presented earlier. Negativity of the media towards law enforcement was the top community relations concern, and based on this finding, it causes significant stress for officers.

Organizational Stress

Organizational stress refers to those stressors that are associated with the organizational culture of policing and/or the police agency (McCreary et al., 2017). Examples of organizational stressors include: leadership and supervision issues, constant changes in policy or legislation, favouritism, and always having to prove oneself in the agency (McCreary et al., 2017). The current research indicates that the top five organizational stress factors reported by officers are: staff shortages, bureaucratic red tape, feeling that different rules apply to different people, inconsistent leadership style, and constant changes in policy and legislation.

At the time of survey deployment, stress experienced due to the staff shortages likely stemmed from a sustained period of policing mass demonstrations and protests. In addition, there was the impact on police agencies resulting from the COVID-19 pandemic. During COVID-19, police agencies struggled to cope with understaffing. For example, at one point, 19.8% of the New York Police Department (NYPD) staff were out sick (NYPD, 2020). Other research, such as the study undertaken by Drew and Martin (2021), highlighted the negative impacts of COVID-19 on stress and mental health of US police. Due to current and ongoing recruitment and retention challenges in the United States, police services are likely to continue to experience the stress of staff shortages.

The stress created by bureaucratic red tape or overwhelming administrative burdens is not a new phenomenon in policing. Of some concern, but consistent with other research (Carleton et al., 2020; Drew et al., 2023; Drew & Carroll, 2022), were the findings around favouritism and leadership within police agencies. Police often report concerns with promotion systems and the fairness of these processes (Drew & Saunders, 2019). The central role leaders play in the experience of policing is unquestionable. Leaders shape the experience of subordinate officers, both in their direct impact on policing practices and the experience of the organizational context (Drew et al., 2023). Policing is characterized by constant changes in policy and legislation. Organizational change is a commonly reported stressor in policing and was perhaps exacerbated during a global health pandemic that required changing police priorities and functions during that time (Maskaly et al., 2021).

Comparing Stressors

As introduced earlier, recent research has examined stress by focusing on the three categories of trauma and critical incidents, other operational, and organizational factors. Of interest is the proportionality of harms caused by each type (Carleton et al., 2020; Drew & Carroll, 2022; Sherwood et al., 2019). Similar to other studies (Carleton et al., 2020; Drew & Carroll, 2022; Sherwood et al., 2019), the survey data highlighted, when comparing all three groups of stressors, that

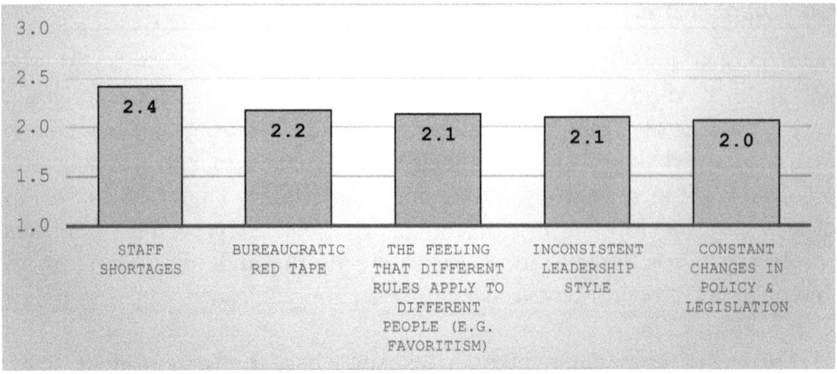

FIGURE 3.8 Organizational stressors – Top five (active officers).

Stressors were listed in order, using the second decimal place; not included in figure.

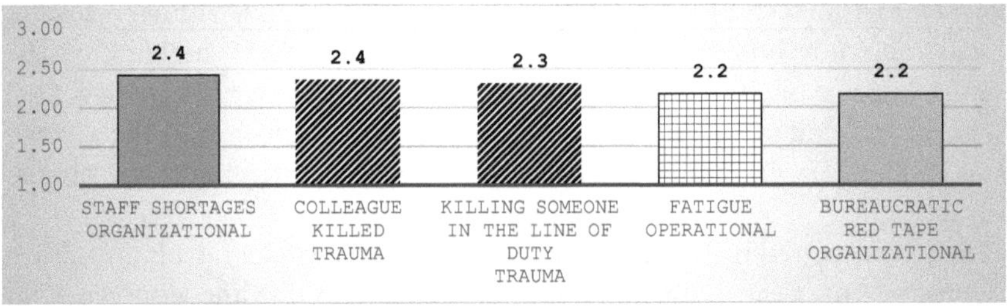

FIGURE 3.9 Comparison of stressors – Top five (active officers).

organizational and operational stress play a prominent role. In the top five most highly-rated stressors, the current research revealed two organizational stress factors and two trauma/critical incident factors (see Figure 3.11). One operational stressor, fatigue, fell in the top five most stressful experiences.

It is extraordinary that staff shortages were rated as more stressful than a colleague being killed or killing someone in the line of duty. Further analysis using data from the Critical Issues in Policing survey is currently underway to explore the interconnections between those factors and their direct relationship with well-being outcomes. A critical avenue of enquiry is to explore not only what officers rate as most stressful *but* also which factors are connected to the most harm.

The Impact of Current Context on Motivation, Community Relations, and Police Practice

Arguably, the impact of negativity of the news media, calls to defund police, threats of removal of qualified immunity, and the tensions between many communities and police resulting in mass demonstrations and protests, will continue to have a sustained impact. The following data collected via the Critical Issues in Policing survey provides insight into how these factors influence motivation, community relationships, and police practices.

Motivation to 'Do the Job'

A central aim of the survey was to understand how anti-police rhetoric, mass demonstrations, and negative publicity impact on the motivation to 'do the job' of policing. Negative publicity was the most highly endorsed factor impacting motivation; over 77% of officers indicated that they 'somewhat', 'quite a bit', or 'very much agreed'. Using similar metrics, over 70% of officers indicated that mass demonstrations and anti-police rhetoric negatively impacted their motivation.

Dangers in Policing

Exploring officer perceptions of the impact of negative publicity, over 90% of officers 'agreed' or 'strongly agreed' that negative publicity increased the danger of policing. This finding is reflective of data presented earlier with respect to the stress caused by different types of traumatic and critical incidents. The dangers associated with doing the job of policing were reported by officers as comparatively more stressful than the content of police work itself.

Community Relations and Legitimacy

The perceptions of officers regarding how they are viewed by the community can be examined through the concepts of 'war on cops' and audience legitimacy. 'War on cops' is a term used to capture an environment where the media and community are focused on scrutiny of police behaviours (MacDonald, 2016; Nix et al., 2018).

Data from the Critical Issues in Policing survey indicated around eight in ten police strongly endorsed the perception that there is a current 'war on cops'. This research found police strongly endorsed statements that citizens have become less compliant, are more willing to resist arrest, and are more likely to assault police. These views are likely reinforced by the increasing numbers of reports in the United States of violent and felonious attacks on police, inclusive of the rise, since 2020, of ambush-style killings (COPS Office, 2022).

Relevant to understanding 'war on cops' is perceived audience legitimacy. While the 'war on cops' captures action-oriented responses by citizens, audience legitimacy focuses more on police perceptions of how they are viewed by the community. Audience legitimacy captures what police believe are the views of citizens with respect to the rightful authority of law enforcement to enact

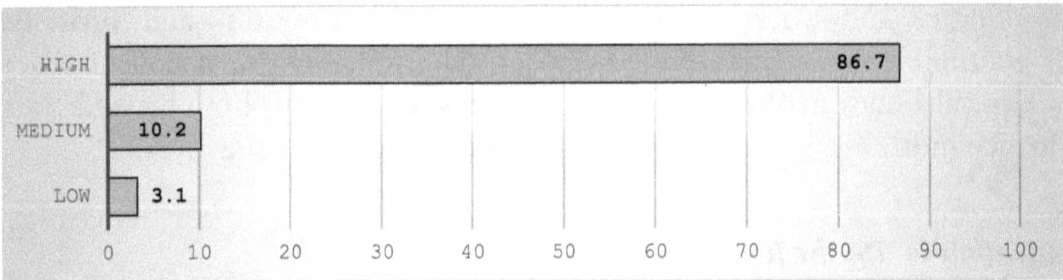

FIGURE 3.10 War on cops (active officers).

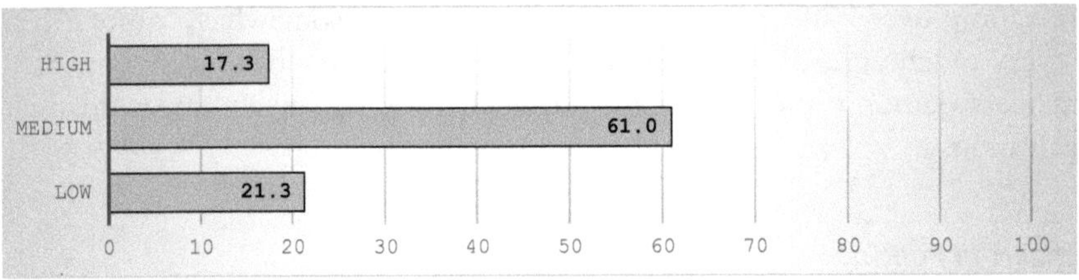

FIGURE 3.11 Audience legitimacy (active officers).

their police function (Nix et al., 2020, p. 218; Bottoms & Tankebe, 2012). The data revealed almost four in five officers 'moderately' or 'highly' endorsed the perception that police are viewed by the community as lacking legitimacy. We conclude that officers who were surveyed in this study are experiencing a crisis of legitimacy. This is of significant concern. Perceptions of low audience legitimacy can affect the likelihood that officers will exercise procedural justice when policing the community and may result in greater use of more coercive forms of control (Jonathan-Zamir & Harpaz, 2018; Nix et al., 2020; Tankebe & Mesko, 2015). The influence of perceptions of a war on cops and low audience legitimacy has implications for the willingness of officers to engage in more proactive policing activities (i.e., de-policing). The following section addresses these de-policing outcomes.

Impact on Police Practice

Several researchers have examined the inter-relationships between the war on cops, audience legitimacy, and de-policing outcomes. De-policing, a concept originally developed in the 1980s by Black and Baumgartner (1987), has attracted contemporary interest following the death of Michael Brown Jr and the 2014 riots in Ferguson, Missouri. Discussions began about disengagement by police from more active police work due to the intense scrutiny (often perceived as unfair or overly intense) that police came under (Oliver, 2017). When designing the current research, in the aftermath of riots across the United

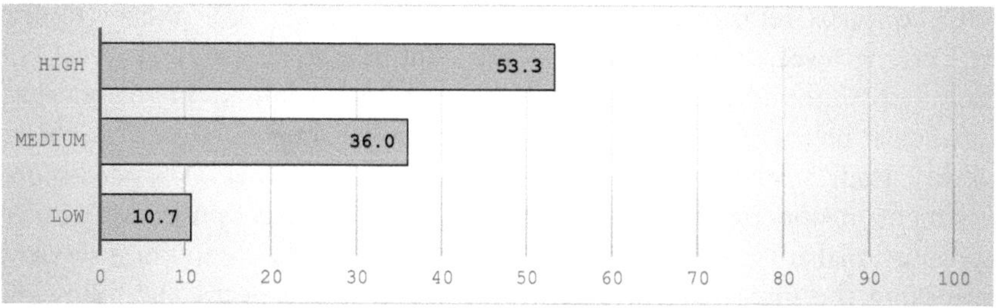

FIGURE 3.12 De-policing (active officers).

States following the death of George Floyd, de-policing was determined to be again a key variable of interest that needed to be explored.

The current data indicates that over half of the officers surveyed strongly endorsed statements that are reflective of de-policing. Statements, such as being less proactive on the job and less likely to work with community members, were strongly endorsed by officers. De-policing that occurred in the aftermath of the riots sparked in Ferguson, Missouri, was often referred to as the Ferguson effect (Capellan et al., 2020). Perhaps what we are now experiencing, following George Floyd's death and the wave of mass demonstrations and protests that ensued, is the Minneapolis effect. The effect refers to a perception held by police of a war on cops, which when coupled with excessive negative media scrutiny, encourages the threat of increasing crime rates. This results from a combination of factors, including police working less proactively, retreating from communities, and lower engagement in police activities that keep communities safe (Nix et al., 2018; Shjarback et al., 2017).

Practical Considerations for Police Services

The preceding discussion has provided an overview of a large proportion of data that was collected as part of the 2021 Critical Issues in Policing survey. The data collected provides insight into the views of police, what they are experiencing, and how the environment in which police operate impacts them personally, and their policing practice. As such, the research provides an opportunity to draw several summative conclusions relevant to police agencies and their leaders. The research provides information for leaders who seek to navigate contemporary challenges related to policing practice and the health and well-being of their officers.

Prevalence of Mental Health Concerns in Policing

The data collected provides further evidence that despite investment in wellness interventions by police services and relevant stakeholders, mental health concerns remain at concerning levels within the US police cohort. The current research reveals that police continue to report high levels of burnout, psychological distress, diagnoses of compromised mental health, and suicidal behaviours. There is more work to be done. US police services and their leaders cannot be complacent about police wellness. We need more investment in understanding *how and why* police cohorts continue to suffer disproportional adverse outcomes due to their work. Why are wellness services not making the impact on prevalence that we would expect? The following discussion, which addresses the need to consider the multi-faceted nature of police stressors and the proportionality of harms caused by each, may be one promising way forward.

The data on retired members of law enforcement is important. Further analysis of the retired cohort is still to be undertaken, but the preliminary analysis presented here indicates consideration must be given to how to better support the transition out of a police career and how to better support a healthy retirement following exit. It would be naïve to suggest that health and wellness simply 'bounces back to normal levels' after a career in law enforcement.

Sources of Police Stress and Their Impact

The current research adds to other recent evidence (e.g., Carleton et al., 2020), highlighting the importance of the impact of operational and organizational stressors, beyond trauma and critical incidents, on police cohorts. This research has two clear implications for US police agencies. The first relates to the need to consider all three groups of stressors, trauma and critical incidents, a more expansive definition of operational stress, and organizational stress. Disentangling the proportional harms being caused by the multidimensional stressors of police work is important; we need to better understand stress caused by the content of police work, the inherent dangers, the unique factors associated with doing the job, and factors associated with the organizational culture of policing and/or the police agency.

The second implication extends the first. The work of many agencies, agencies which have embraced the need to prepare officers for the inevitability of trauma and its consequences, must be continued. However, our research and that of others (e.g., Carleton et al., 2020; Drew & Carroll, 2022; Drew et al., 2023) point to the need to consider how we reform police workplaces. Other operational factors (beyond critical incidents and trauma) and organizational factors are causing significant impacts. By focusing on these causes of stress a true primary prevention approach can be pursued. This approach provides focus on those modifiable factors that are within the control and mandate of police agencies and will lead to the better identification and removal of causes of harm before they have a chance to negatively impact on officer health.

Acknowledging the multidimensional causes of stress experienced by police is a first step. From here, wellness prevention and response interventions that focus on the organization of police work and how it is enacted within organizational structures must be developed. Police leaders at all levels of the agency have a role to play in not only recognizing and addressing the risks and harms that stem from the organizational and operational contexts that characterize policing but also taking action. Trauma is somewhat of an uncontrollable risk; other types of operational stressors and organizational factors are perhaps more pliable and amenable to modification by police agencies and their leadership (Drew et al., 2023). Addressing organizational and operational factors is our best chance at reducing alarming prevalence rates of psychological ill-health because they are amendable. Given that they are in many cases the most significant cause of harms, addressing these factors is also likely to have the largest impact.

Continuous Monitoring of Factors in Contemporary Environment

The landscape of policing is always changing. While some factors will be enduring simply due to the role and function of police in our communities, even these 'always present' factors may rise and fall in importance. For example, the dangers of policing are likely to be of even more concern in an environment such as the one that has recently been experienced by police across many parts of the United States. It has been an environment where there has been increased and at times, sustained negative and often violent interactions, between the police and communities.

Some factors in the policing landscape will be unique to a particular time and/or place. These are factors that may be relevant right now but may not be as important in the future. The Critical Issues in Policing survey measured several factors that were specifically relevant to the US policing landscape at the time of survey deployment. Police were significantly affected by negative news media that were driving calls to defund police and threats of removal of qualified immunity. These are the types of factors that are likely to be most reflective of current circumstances and may not represent issues that persist over long time periods. While they may only have short-term relevancy, their impact on police health and practice needs to be captured and addressed. This research has revealed the critical need for real-time data about the contemporary environmental or societal factors influencing police wellness and police practice. Research may quickly become out-of-date when there is a significant delay in communicating findings and, as such, over time become less useful for police agencies and leaders.

A collaboration between an academic institution and a practitioner organization was established to conduct this research, resulting in a robust approach, informed by academic expertise and lived experience. Addressing the issue of timeliness of research as identified above, the benefit of this collaboration was the ability to report the findings of such a robust and rigorous research project quickly. Academic research, even when conducted with practitioner partners, often takes months, if not years, to be available via academic publications. In the case of the Critical Issues of Policing survey, the collaboration we formed prioritized the efficient delivery of the survey findings back to agencies and leaders. Within weeks of the first analyses of data being undertaken, law enforcement agencies and leaders were able to reference findings of the survey to lobby for and make changes to legislation, policy, and practice. We deployed the survey in September and November 2021, and the first presentation of findings was given at the NFOP Leadership Matters conference in early February 2022. The efficient delivery of the research findings better supports police leaders in their efforts to continually monitor how factors at a broader societal level are impacting on the causes and prevalence of stress and well-being outcomes for their officers. Initiatives such as the Critical Issues in Policing survey are one mechanism through which timely information can be collected about contemporary issues impacting the police profession and have the capacity to be fed back to agencies and leaders expeditiously for use in practice. Greater engagement between academics and practitioner organizations such as that achieved here is likely to improve the usability and effectiveness of research conducted with police agencies and should be encouraged.

Study Limitations

Despite its strengths, limitations of the current study should be noted. The study included officers from across the United States; however, the officers participating in the research were largely drawn from the NFOP membership. Replication of the research with officers not associated with NFOP would test the generalizability of findings. Also, the impact of findings of the specific events which had occurred and societal context in which police were operating at the time of survey deployment is acknowledged. Whether the findings simply capture the impact of experiences of officers at a specific period, or whether the impacts are persistent over time, needs further study.

Conclusions

In conclusion, the current chapter sought to collate and discuss many of the findings derived from the 2021 NFOP Biennial Critical Issues in Policing survey. Through this research, we explored the contemporary and critical issues faced by law enforcement officers (both active and retired officers). Stress and well-being within the police profession formed a specific focus of the research.

Our research has reinforced the need for police services and their leaders to consider, beyond traditional critical incident and trauma events, organizational and other operational factors that are causing significant stress. Stress in policing is multidimensional and must be understood from multiple perspectives. We have demonstrated the need for research to be timely, focusing on understanding the impacts of contemporary environmental, contextual, and societal factors impacting police.

There is a clear need to ensure information, such as that collected through the collaborative project between NFOP and Griffith University, is quickly and efficiently fed back to police services and leaders. Most research will contribute to our knowledge and understanding, but an important aim, from our perspective, is the delivery of research to agencies and their leaders as close to 'real time' as possible. Through an evidence-informed approach, agencies and leaders will be resourced to better respond to factors that are negatively impacting officers in the contemporary context. Through these adaptive responses, we hope the deterioration of the health and well-being of officers, who already represent a group at high risk of psychological ill-health, will be more effectively addressed.

Notes

1 No financial funding was secured via external grants or allocated by FOP for the design and analysis of the survey. The FOP provided access to the sample through distribution of the survey to their members. Personnel at FOP and Griffith University contributed to the project via in-kind support.

2 An accurate response rate is not able to be calculated. The survey was promoted to all FOP members via emails and other FOP communication channels. It is unable to be determined how many of the 350,000 (approx.) active and retired police officers were successfully contacted and, as such, chose or not to participate in the survey.

3 A clinical term for major depressive disorder (MDD) was not stated, only referenced depression.

4 A clinical term for generalized anxiety disorder (GAD) was not stated, only referenced anxiety.

References

Aflac (2022). *Aflac workforces report.* Accessed 21 March 2023 from www.aflac.com/docs/awr/pdf/2022-overview/2022-aflac-awr-executive-summary.pdf

Berk, R. (2023). *Is violent crime increasing?* Department of Criminology, University of Pennsylvania. Accessed from https://crim.sas.upenn.edu/fact-check/violent-crime-increasing

Beyond Blue Ltd. (2018). *Answering the call national survey, National Mental Health and Wellbeing Study of Police and Emergency Services – Final report.* Accessed from www.beyondblue.org.au/docs/default-source/resources/bl1898-pes-full-report_final.pdf

Black, D. & Baumgartner, M.P. (1987). On self-help in modern society. *Dialectical Anthropology, 12*, 33–44.

Bottoms, A. & Tankebe, J. (2012). Beyond procedural justice: A dialogic approach to legitimacy in criminal justice. *Journal of Criminal Law and Criminology, 102*, 119–170.

Bowler, R.M., Kornblith, E.S., Li, J., Adams, S.W., Gocheva, V.V., Schwarzer, R. & Cone, J.E. (2016). Police officers who responded to 9/11: Comorbidity of PTSD, depression, and anxiety 10-11 years later. *American Journal of Industrial Medicine, 59*, 425–436.

Capellan, J.A., Lautenschlager, R. & Silva, J.R. (2020). Deconstructing the Ferguson effect: A multilevel mediation analysis of public scrutiny, de-policing, and crime. *Journal of Crime and Justice, 43*(2), 125–144.

Carleton, R.N., Afifi, T.O., Taillieu, T., Turner, S., Krakauer, R., Anderson, G.S., McCreary, D., Ricciardelli, R., Cramm, H.A., Groll, D. & McCreary, D.R. (2019). Exposures to potentially traumatic events among public safety personnel in Canada. *Canadian Journal of Behavioural Science, 51*(1), 37–52.

Carleton, R.N., Afifi, T.O., Taillieu, T., Turner, S., Mason, J.E., Ricciardelli, R. et al. (2020). Assessing the relative impact of diverse stressors among public safety personnel. *International Journal of Environmental Research and Public Health, 17*, 1234–1259.

Carleton, R.N., Afifi, T.O., Turner, S., Taillieu, T., LeBouthillier, D.M., Duranceau, S., Sareen, J., Ricciardelli, R., MacPhee, R.S., Groll, D., Hozempa, K., Brunet, A., Weekes, J.R., Griffiths, C.T., Abrams, K.J., Jones, N.A., Beshai, S., Cramm, H.A., Dobson, K.S. et al. (2018). Suicidal ideation, plans, and attempts among public safety personnel in Canada. *Canadian Psychology / Psychologie canadienne, 59*(3), 220–231.

Chopko, B.A., Palmieri, P.A. & Facemire, V.S. (2014). Prevalence and predictors of suicidal ideation among U.S. law enforcement officers. *Journal of Police and Criminal Psychology, 29*(1), 1–9.

Daly, M. (2022). Prevalence of psychological distress among working-age adults in the United States, 1999–2018. *American Journal of Public Health, 112*(17), 1045–1049.

Delgadillo, J., Saxon, D. & Barkham M. (2018). Associations between therapists' occupational burnout and their patients' depression and anxiety treatment outcomes. *Depression and Anxiety, 35*(9),844–850.

Demerouti, E., Bakker, A.B., Vardakou, I. & Kantas, A. (2003). The convergent validity of two burnout instruments. *European Journal of Psychological Assessment, 19*(1), 12–23.

Drew, J.M., Bartels, S. & Herrington, V.L. (2023). *Leadership for wellness: A strategy for developing police and public safety leaders*. Leadership Development White Paper. A Collaboration between Griffith Criminology Institute, Griffith University and AIPM. AIPM: Sydney.

Drew, J.M. & Carroll, K. (October, 2022). Early identification of police workplace health and performance. Presentation to International Association of Chiefs of Police, Dallas, Texas.

Drew, J.M. & Martin, S. (2021). Policing during a global health pandemic: Exploring stress and wellbeing of police and their families. *Journal of Community Safety and Well-Being, 6*(3), 104–111.

Drew, J.M. & Martin, S. (2023). Mental health and wellness initiatives supporting United States law enforcement personnel: The current state-of-play. *Journal of Community Safety and Well-Being, 8*(Suppl 1), S12–S22.

Drew, J.M. & Saunders, J. (2019). Navigating the police promotion system: A comparison by gender of moving up the ranks. *Police Practice and Research: An International Journal, 21*(5), 476–490.

Gramlich, J. (2022). *Violent crime is a key midterm voting issue, but what does the data say?* Pew Research Center. Accessed from www.pewresearch.org/fact-tank/2022/10/31/violent-crime-is-a-key-midterm-voting-issue-but-what-does-the-data-say/

Hartley, T.A., Sarkisian, K., Violanti, J.M., Andrew, M.E. & Burchfiel, C.M. (2013). PTSD symptoms among police officers: Associations with frequency, recency, and types of traumatic events. *International Journal of Emergency Mental Health, 15*(4), 241–253.

Jonathan-Zamir, T. & Harpaz, A. (2018). Predicting support for procedurally just treatment: The case of the Israel National Police. *Criminal Justice and Behavior, 45*, 840–62.

Kessler, R., Andrews, G., Colpe, L., Hiripi, E., Mroczek, D., Normand, S., Walters, E.E. & Zaslavsky, A. (2002). Short screening scales to monitor population prevalences and trends in non-specific psychological distress. *Psychological Medicine, 32*(6), 959–976.

Kyron, M.J., Rikkers, W., LaMontagne, A., Bartlett, J. & Lawrence, D. (2022). Work-related and nonwork stressors, PTSD, and psychological distress: Prevalence and attributable burden among Australian police and emergency services employees. *Psychological Trauma: Theory, Research, Practice, and Policy, 14*(7), 1124–1133.

Law Enforcement and Mental Health and Wellness Act. (2017). United States.

Legal Information Institute. (2022). *Qualified immunity.* Accessed from www.law.cornell.edu/wex/qualified_immunity

MacDonald, H. (2016). *The war on cops.* New York, NY: Encounter Books.

Maskaly, J., Ivkovic, S.K. & Neyroud, P. (2021). Policing the COVID-19 pandemic: Exploratory study of the types of organizational changes and police activities across the globe. *International Criminal Justice Review, 31*(3), 266–285.

McCaslin, S.E., Rogers, C.E., Metzler, T.J., Best, S.R., Weiss, D.S. et al. (2006). The impact of personal threat on police officers' responses to critical incident stressors. *Journal of Nervous and Mental Disease, 194*(8), 591–597.

McCreary, D.R., Fong, I. & Groll, D.L. (2017). Measuring policing stress meaningfully: Establishing norms and cut-off values for the operational and organizational police stress questionnaires. *Police Practice and Research, 18*(6), 612–623.

McCreary, D.R. & Thompson, M.M. (2006). Development of two reliable and valid measures of stressors in policing: The operational and organizational police stress questionnaires. *International Journal of Stress Management, 13*(4), 494–518.

Mourtgos, S.M., Adams, I.T. & Nix, J. (2021). Elevated police turnover following the summer of George Floyd protests: A synthetic control study. *Criminology and Public Policy, 21*(1), 9–33.

National Center for Health Statistics. (2021). *Estimates of Mental Health Symptomatology, by Month of Interview: United States, 2019.* Accessed from www.cdc.gov/nchs/data/nhis/mental-health-monthly-508.pdf

National Center for PTSD. (2023). *PTSD: National Center for PTSD.* Accessed from www.ptsd.va.gov/understand/common/common_adults.asp

National Fraternal Order of Police. (2023). *Wellness surveys*. Accessed from https://NFOP.net/officer-wellness/survey/

National Institute of Justice. (2019). *Women in policing: Breaking barrier and blazing a path*. Accessed from www.ojp.gov/pdffiles1/nij/252963.pdf

National Institute of Mental Health. (2023). *Major depression*. Accessed from www.nimh.nih.gov/health/statistics/major-depression

New York Police Department (NYPD). (May 29, 2020). *Tweets (NYPDNews)*. Retrieved October 28, 2020.

Nix, J., Pickett, J.T. & Wolfe, S.E. (2020). Testing a theoretical model of perceived audience legitimacy: The neglected linkage in the dialogic model of police–community relations. *Journal of Research in Crime and Delinquency, 57*(2), 217–259.

Nix, J. & Wolfe, S.E. (2017a). Management-level officers' experiences with the Ferguson effect. *Policing: An International Journal, 41*(2), 262–275.

Nix, J. & Wolfe, S.E. (2017b). The impact of negative publicity on police self-legitimacy. *Justice Quarterly, 34*(1), 84–108.

Nix, J., Wolfe, S.E. & Campbell, B.A. (2018). Command-level police officers' perceptions of the "War on Cops" and de-policing. *Justice Quarterly, 35*(1), 33–54.

Office of Community Oriented Policing Services (COPS Office). (2022). *Law Enforcement Officers Shot in the Line of Duty: 2021 Year-End Summary*. Washington, DC: Office of Community Oriented Policing Services.

Oliver, W.M. (2017). De-policing: Rhetoric or reality? *Criminal Justice Policy Review, 28*(5), 437–461.

Oscar Kilo. (2023). *Sleep and fatigue interventions*. Accessed from www.oscarkilo.org.uk/services/healthy-living/sleep-and-fatigue-interventions

Police Executive Research Forum (PERF). (2019). *The workforce crises and what police agencies are doing about it*. Accessed from www.policeforum.org/assets/WorkforceCrisis.pdf

Regehr, C., Carey, M.G., Wagner, S., Alden, L.E., Buys, N., Corneil, W., Fyfe, T., Matthews, L., Randall, C., White, M., Fraess-Phillips, A., Krutop, E., White, N. & Fleischmann, M. (2021). A systematic review of mental health symptoms in police officers following extreme traumatic exposures, *Police Practice and Research, 22*(1), 225–239.

Rose, S.C., Bisson, J., Churchill, R. & Wessely, S. (2002). *Psychological debriefing for preventing post traumatic stress disorder (PTSD)*. Cochrane Database of Systematic Reviews, Issue 2. Art. No.: CD000560.

Sherwood, L., Hegarty, S., Vallieres, F., Hyland, P. et al. (2019). Identifying the key risk factors for adverse psychological outcomes among police officers: A systematic literature review. *Journal of Traumatic Stress, 32*, 688–700.

Shjarback, J.A., Pyrooz, D.C., Wolfe, S.E. & Decker, S.H. (2017). De-policing and crime in the wake of Ferguson: Racialized changes in the quantity and quality of policing among Missouri police departments. *Journal of Criminal Justice, 50*, 42–52.

Stevelink, S.A.M., Opie, E., Pernet, D., Gao, H., Elliott, P., Wessely, S., et al. (2020) Probable PTSD, depression and anxiety in 40,299 UK police officers and staff: Prevalence, risk factors and associations with blood pressure. *PLoS ONE, 15*(11), e0240902.

Substance Abuse and Mental Health Services Administration. (2022). *Key substance use and mental health indicators in the United States: Results from the 2021 National*

Survey on Drug Use and Health (HHS Publication No. PEP22-07-01-005, NSDUH Series H-57). Center for Behavioral Health Statistics and Quality, Substance Abuse and Mental Health Services Administration. www.samhsa.gov/data/report/2021-nsduh-annual-national-report

Syed, S., Ashwick, R., Schlosser, M., et al. (2020). Global prevalence and risk factors for mental health problems in police personnel: A systematic review and meta-analysis. *Occupational and Environmental Medicine, 77*, 737–747.

Tankebe, J. & Mesko, G. (2015). Police self-legitimacy, use of force, and pro-organizational behavior in Slovenia. In Mesko, G. & Tankebe, J. (eds). *Trust and legitimacy in criminal justice*. New York, NY: Springer.

Violanti, J.M., Fekedulegn, D., Charles, L.E., Andrew, M.E., Hartley, T.A., Mnatsakanova, A. & Burchfiel, C.M. (2009). Suicide in police work: Exploring potential contributing influences. *American Journal of Criminal Justice, 34*(1–2), 41–53,

Wagner, S.L., White, N., Fyfe, T., Matthews, L.R., Randall, C., Regehr, C., White, M., Alden, L.E., Buys, N., Carey, M.G., Corneil, W., Fraess-Phillips, A., Krutop, E. & Fleischmann, M. (2020). Systematic review of posttraumatic stress disorder in police officers following routine work-related critical incident exposure. *American Journal of Industrial Medicine, 63*, 600–615.

Weiss, D.S., Brunet, A., Best, S.R., Metzler, T.J., Liberman, A., Pole, N., Fagan, J.A. & Marmar, C.R. (2010). Frequency and severity approaches to indexing exposure to trauma: The critical incident history questionnaire for police officers. *Journal of Traumatic Stress, 23*(6), 734–743.

Young, R. & Sayers, D.M. (2022, February 3). *Why police forces are struggling to recruit and keep officers*. Cable News Network. www.cnn.com/2022/02/02/us/police-departments-struggle-recruit-retain-officers/index.html

4

SECONDARY TRAUMA IN POLICE OFFICERS INVESTIGATING CHILD SEXUAL EXPLOITATION MATERIALS

Marije Keulen-de Vos and Funda Sanci

Introduction

Starting from an early age, grades, rankings, and achievements are considered fundamental for defining personal identity. More and more companies, professions, and services are held to so-called key performance indicators, or quantifiable indicators of progress towards an intended result. Work also plays a central role in how we perceive our physical, psychological, and social functioning. However, work can be a source of both satisfaction and stress. Work-related stress can lead to symptoms such as fatigue, tension, irritability, lability, loss of concentration, insomnia, and ultimately burnout, a severe and long-term form of being overworked. Besides a reduced quality of life for the affected person, considerable costs are associated with work tied to sick leave and turnover intent, among other factors that compromise wellness. Therefore, taking care of employee well-being is of social importance.

Different stresses arise in different occupational settings, where exposure to different traumas can be direct, secondary, vicarious, etc. Focusing on secondary trauma, Bride and Kintzle (2011) use secondary trauma in reference to occurrences of posttraumatic stress symptoms following indirect exposure to psychologically traumatic events—being exposed through a close personal or professional relationship(s). Individuals working in certain occupational realms appear at greater risk for secondary trauma because of their consistent exposure to troubling social problems and affected people. Studies reveal how individuals working in (mental) health care, child protection service, and public safety (e.g., firefighters and police officers) are among the occupational groups at a higher risk of experiencing secondary trauma (Baum, 2016; Carleton et al., 2020; Foley et al., 2022). In the current chapter, we focus on

DOI: 10.4324/9781003424253-6

secondary trauma among police officers investigating offences involving child sexual exploitation materials (CSEM).

Legal Definitions and CESM Prevalence

"Child sexual exploitation materials" (CSEM), sometimes also referred to as child sexual abuse materials, have different legal definitions in different countries. Generally, CSEM are defined as imagery or videos depicting a minor who may be engaged in explicit sexual activity. People who commit sex crimes online are most likely to use CSEM, and in Canada, in 2015, 95% of the reports of online sex crimes had youth victims (Canadian Centre for Child Protection, 2016). Offences involving CSEM have proliferated over the past two decades. For example, the *National Center for Missing & Exploited Children* (NCMEC) in the United States received over 40 million reports of suspected CSEM over the past 20 years (NCMEC, 2019). The *Australian Centre to Counter Exploitation* (ACCE) received over 21,000 reports of CSEM in 2019–2020, which was a considerable increase (+50%) compared to previous years (Australian Centre to Counter Child Exploitation, 2019). The volume of CSEM being produced and the number of people accessing CSEM have increased enormously, which presents challenges and pressure for police services internationally to identify victims and perpetrators.

In most countries, specialist units of the police service are dedicated to the investigation of (potential) CSEM cases. These police officers perform regular tasks such as investigation, interrogation, and collecting evidence for prosecution. But they are also set apart from other police units by their requirement to perform a number of investigative tasks such as checking (dark web) websites for illegal content, viewing thousands of graphic images, classifying material according to content depicted, and viewing and hearing videos of young children of various age ranges (i.e., infant to adolescent) being sexually assaulted as they strive to identify and protect victims and to locate perpetrators. These specific tasks may leave CSEM officers vulnerable to experiencing secondary trauma. In this chapter, we examine existing knowledge relating to secondary trauma among police officers and potential protective factors specific to CSEM investigators. Next, implications for practice and recommendations to take this area of research forward are considered.

Impact on Police Officers

The prevalence of secondary trauma across public service providers, such as paramedics and firefighters, is well-recognized, but for specialist sexual offending police work prevalence remains largely unclear (Foley et al., 2022). Studies suggest that a majority of specialist police staff, including CSEM investigators, generally cope well with the demands of their jobs (Powell et al.,

2014). However, also recognized is how they can experience a wide variety of psychological trauma-related symptoms resulting from their job. Police officers investigating CSEM may experience signs and symptoms of secondary trauma at some point in their career as they are exposed to difficult material and may face internal and external pressure to cover the overwhelming number of leads they receive to substantiate cases and save lives (O'Brien et al., 2024; Parkes et al., 2019). CSEM investigators may experience physical, cognitive, emotional, behavioural, and social consequences on themselves from performing their occupational responsibilities (Powell et al., 2015).

First, regarding physical consequences, physical complaints often include headaches, intestinal upsets, severe tiredness, sleep deprivation or difficulty sleeping, depressed immunity, elevated heart rate, and general ill health (Krause, 2009). For example, Burns et al. (2008) interviewed 14 members of a Canadian police team dedicated to investigating (potential) CSEM cases. Many participants described experiencing physical reactions to work, including headaches and extreme fatigue, which often prevent them from engaging in normal activities during and outside work (Burns et al., 2008).

Second, in reference to cognitive outcomes, some investigators describe experiencing emotional and cognitive consequences due to viewing CSEM, such as anger or moodiness, nightmares, intrusive imagery, hypervigilance with regard to child safety, and a distortion of an individual's outlook on the world (Burns et al., 2008; Hernandez-Wolfe et al., 2015; Perez et al., 2010). For example, Powell et al. (2015) examined reactions to viewing child exploitation materials in a sample of 32 investigators across several Australian jurisdictions. Their findings show how investigators experienced CSEM-related intrusive thoughts and flashbacks outside of work and in their dreams, and these occurrences affected their mood. This is unsurprising as unpleasant images tend to lead to stronger sensory reactivation over time (Bowen & Kensinger, 2017; Bowen et al., 2018). Another emotional consequence of watching CSEM videos and images is the sense that someone is "at the end of one's rope." In fact, emotional exhaustion or burnout is one of the most common consequences of secondary trauma. Those suffering can experience emotional symptoms such as irritability, low morale, and reduced self-esteem and attitudinal symptoms such as pessimism and cynicism (Foley & Massey, 2021). For example, Perez et al. (2010) examined the impact of viewing CSEM among 28 police officers. Their results reveal that 54% suffered from high levels of emotional exhaustion and secondary traumatic stress.

Third, tied to emotional consequences, secondary trauma may underpin poor work performance, avoidance of work tasks (absenteeism), impatience, a reluctance to take on new casework or to view material, and sloppy paperwork (MacEachern et al., 2011; Powell et al., 2014).

Finally, referring to the interconnection between behavioural and social consequences is how exposure to disturbing photographs and videos and intense contact with perpetrators and victims can affect an officer's social and personal life. For example, many officers experience sexual problems within their own intimate relationships, struggle with the enjoyment of physical contact with their own children or become reluctant to interact with children, and withdraw from social activities with family, partner, and friends (Perez et al., 2010; Powell et al., 2015). Similarly, the tasks that police officers regularly do are sometimes associated with doing "dirty work" because they are involved in dealing with people who are (allegedly) involved in socially, morally, and physically undesirable sexual activities (Tracy & Scott, 2006). These police activities may be socially tainted, which may ultimately lead to social repugnance and withdrawal by family, partners, and friends (Ashforth & Kreiner, 1999; Marier & Moule, 2019).

Risk Factors

Certain factors increase the likelihood of developing secondary trauma in CSEM investigators. For example, life experiences, especially in early childhood (e.g., adverse childhood events), have been shown to increase vulnerability to psychologically traumatic stress and may determine the response to distressing activities (Tehrani, 2018; Tortella-Feliu et al., 2019). Adverse childhood experiences (e.g., child sexual abuse) are known to have a cascading effect by influencing cognition (e.g., interpretations) and emotional and behavioural self-regulation and subsequently influencing adult mental and physical health (Jones et al., 2020; Masten & Cicchetti, 2010). There seems to be a relationship between adverse childhood experiences and adult psychological distress across genders (Cloitre et al., 2019; Rudenstine et al., 2019). Some surveys have shown how child abuse investigators are often more likely to have experienced early life abuse than other occupational groups and that there is a relationship between these experiences and experiences of secondary trauma. For example, Tehrani (2018) examined the effects of personal experiences of childhood abuse on symptoms of secondary trauma in 2798 child abuse investigators (both male and female) and reported a significant relationship between these two factors. Perhaps, an investigator who has experienced childhood sexual abuse has an intrinsic motivation to protect others from abuse but may have lower resilience to the impacts of their work compared to those without a history of abuse (Krause, 2009; Wortley et al., 2014). Also suggested is how an officer's personality may influence one's risk of developing secondary trauma (Krause, 2009). In a study by Tehrani (2016), 126 internet child abuse investigators from 2 police services in the United Kingdom completed a personality test and a secondary traumatic stress questionnaire. Among these participants (both male and female), there was a higher incidence of secondary trauma in investigators who were introverted or neurotic. Moreover, personality traits like introversion and neuroticism

(Gray & Rydon-Grange, 2019), where introversion is associated with lower social engagement, whereas neuroticism is a personality trait characterized by sadness, moodiness, and emotional instability, may make an officer susceptible to secondary trauma.

The potential impact of CSEM investigative activities is also determined by the duration and intensity of CSEM exposure and the nature of the materials (Krause et al., 2009). For example, Perez et al. (2010) examined the impact of exposure to CSEM on 28 police officers (both male and female). Greater exposure to CSEM was related to higher levels of stress and exhaustion (Perez et al., 2010). Similarly, studies show that the cumulative effects of exposure to psychologically traumatic images may increase the risk of secondary stress-related emotional exhaustion among police officers (Kohan & Mazmanian, 2003). The study conducted by Powell et al. (2015) showed child exploitation materials of victims under the age of six years old, and materials showing a large age difference between the victim and perpetrators are generally considered as most disturbing and thus have the strongest effect on police officers. The degree to which the sexual act violates conventional societal norms also has a strong effect. For example, displays of mothers offending against their own children are against the stereotypical view against women (e.g., caring, nurturing role). Also, sadistic behaviour typically has a strong effect on those viewing the materials, as such behaviour amplifies one's perceptions of the victim's helplessness (Powell et al., 2015). Finally, organizational stressors such as high workloads, cumbersome administrative processes, perceived unfairness, lack of adequate rewards and recognition, and lack of autonomy may influence secondary psychological trauma in CSEM investigators (Maslach et al., 2001; Paton et al., 2009; Perez et al., 2010; van der Velden et al., 2013). Nevertheless, not all police officers investigating CSEM will develop secondary psychological trauma symptoms. The interplay between risk and protective factors increases the likelihood of developing work-related trauma symptoms.

Protective Factors

Several factors can reduce or counteract the risk of secondary psychological trauma among police officers who investigate (potential) CSEM cases. First, resilience is a protective factor in navigating the emotional impact of CSEM investigations. According to Sollie et al. (2017), resilience in the context of criminal investigations can be defined as

> the outcome of a coping process in which internal and external resources enable a criminal investigator to continue to function throughout stressful situations and to recover from such situations in a sustainable manner while retaining their motivation to carry on with their investigative work.
>
> *(p. 1594)*

The ability to cope with work-related stressors may depend on one's appraisal of the situation, one's coping strategy, and one's ability to use this strategy (Sollie et al., 2017). Coping ability aligns with Lazarus' transactional model of stress, which states that stress results from the appraisal where particular demands exceed one's individual resources (i.e., coping; Lazarus, 1999). Coping strategies can have different purposes. For example, problem-focused coping is aimed at changing the problem (i.e., the stressful situation), whereas emotion-focused coping is aimed at dealing with the strong emotions triggered. CSEM officers can also use dissociation strategies, for example, not looking at the eyes of the victim, searching for meaning in adversity (i.e., meaning-focused coping), or using instrumental coping strategies (e.g., gaining social support; Powell et al., 2014; Sollie et al., 2017).

Criminal investigators may employ a range of different coping strategies. Active and instrumental coping strategies have been associated with good adaptation to secondary stress, while more passive or avoidant strategies (e.g., excessive alcohol intake) are often considered maladaptive, negative coping strategies (Acquadro Maran et al., 2015; Bourke et al., 2014; Hennig-Fast et al., 2009; Sherwood et al., 2019). Whether one can use positive coping strategies may depend on individual characteristics, such as the ability to form social relationships, being generally comfortable with sexual matters, having a sense of (gallows) humour, having a stable personal life, and being emotionally stable (Bogaerts, 2013; Krause, 2009; Powell et al., 2014; Sollie et al., 2017).

Second, having peer and social support is a protective factor (Burns et al., 2008; Jones et al., 2022; Perez et al., 2010). For example, Davidson and Moss (2008) reported how law enforcement officers (both male and female) who used the social support of their romantic partners were less likely to experience secondary trauma symptoms. Schwarzer et al. (2014) also state that high levels of social support can help improve resilience and protect against psychological distress in police officers, whereas low levels of support have been associated with the onset of symptoms of depression. However, officers often attempt to shield their spouses and families from the negative aspects of their jobs. CSEM investigators may avoid sharing much information about their day-to-day work experiences because of the (perceived) burden their experiences might place on others (Craun et al., 2015). Evans et al. (2013) highlight how, although officers may not always want to talk about the psychologically traumatic events which have occurred, the use of humour and banter is a way of both giving and receiving social support.

Third, physical exercise can be an effective factor in combatting physical symptoms relating to secondary trauma (Singo & Shilubane, 2022). When a person experiences stress, the body prepares to respond to the challenge by producing the hormones epinephrine, norepinephrine, and cortisol (Jackson, 2013). The result of the production is a cascade of physiological reactions that make up the stress response. These responses may include increases in heart and respiration rates, blood pressure, and hypervigilance. Physical exercise improves how the body handles stress because of changes in hormone responses that affect mood and behaviours (Eriksen et al., 2022; Romas & Sharma, 2022). A systematic review by McKeon et al. (2022) shows how physical exercise reduces post-traumatic stress disorder (PTSD)-like symptoms in medical and public service personnel, including police officers. For example, Burns et al. (2008) examined coping strategies employed by a Canadian police team investigating internet child sexual exploitation. Results indicated that physical fitness and lifestyle education were helpful to the police officer's well-being.

Practical Implications

Implications on the Individual Level

There are always CSEM cases waiting to be carried out. The work, specifically locating perpetrators and victims, is never done. Thus, realistic expectations about what one can personally achieve within the time available to complete the work are necessary. Having realistic expectations helps maintain a healthy level of stress intensity. For example, Petrou et al. (2015) reported how reducing demands had a positive reciprocal link with exhaustion, and exhaustion negatively predicted performance in a sample of 950 police officers in the Netherlands. Another way for officers to navigate the stress of the job is to find a symbolic way to switch off at the end of the day. For example, in a study by Powell et al. (2014), some police officers examining CSEM cases reported that they took a shower after a shift to symbolize that their work was over and to disengage their minds from the workplace. Others spend quite some time cleaning their work desk to de-stress or seek psychological support (Burns et al., 2008; Powell et al., 2014). Investigators may also try to avoid identifying with the human suffering they encounter in house searches, reviewing footage, and conducting interviews. To protect or detach themselves, officers may adopt an analytic attitude and avoid emotional connections. For example, when classifying materials, they analytically trace any leads in the videos and pictures but avoid looking at the eyes and facial expressions of the victims as much as possible (Sollie, 2017).

Implications on the Team Level

As peer support can help protect against developing secondary trauma, socializing with colleagues can provide short opportunities for respite during the workday (Bakker et al., 2010; Burns et al., 2008; Powell et al., 2014). Regular (in)formal debriefing with team members can also assist in the process of cognitive reappraisal, in seeing the material as evidence. For example, a meta-analysis by Webb et al. (2012) showed that perspective-changing reappraisal is more effective for regulating strong emotions than strategies that focus on the suppression of thoughts and emotions. Similarly, Aldao et al. (2010) reported that strategies such as rumination, avoidance, and suppression were associated with more psychological symptoms (i.e., anxiety and depression), whereas acceptance and reappraisal strategies were associated with fewer symptoms. Talking with colleagues about CSEM case material can help shift the appraisal of the material. Therefore, allowing for informal socializing opportunities during the workday is important.

Implications for the Organizational Level

Cumulative exposure to disturbing images and videos of child sexual abuse may increase the risk of secondary trauma. An organizational implication is to limit the time one is exposed to CSEM in terms of both the number of consecutive hours an investigator can view CSEM without substantial breaks and the number of years an investigator can work in a CSEM unit. Training about how and when to view, classify and analyse photographs may also reduce exposure reactions. For example, remaining analytical and focusing on the evidence in the images or following a mental template and working systematically to gather the information required from the images for the investigation may allow individuals to remain more objective. Also, Burns et al. (2008) reported that the ability of a police officer to determine when, where, and how to view child sexual exploitation material during work hours may increase an officer's sense of control, which helps them cope with the demands of the job. For example, some officers only want to view CSEM in the morning in hopes of returning home at the end of the day with fewer reminders of the materials, which simplifies the transition from one world to another (Sollie, 2017). Having supervisors who understand the effect of CSEM work is also considered necessary because these managers are able to support their team members in their coping behaviours (Burns et al., 2008).

In addition, psychological interventions designed to educate CSEM officers about the work, common reactions, and how to cope may also offer a sense of support and may diminish the sense of isolation officers might experience. Stress management techniques, such as biofeedback, are a powerful tool for learning how to manage stress responses (Yu et al., 2018). Similarly, the use of wearable sensors might offer police officers a direct way to monitor their physiological responses over time. Relatedly, organizations could offer individual consultations with a qualified and trained clinician to their CSEM team members. These clinicians should have a strong theoretical grounding in psychological trauma therapy, pay attention to both conscious and unconscious aspects of psychological trauma, and create a mutually respectful interpersonal climate in their sessions (Hayden et al., 2015; Hunter & Schofield, 2006).

Finally, supervisors and colleagues play a central supporting role in how the team members deal with the demands of the job in a realistic way (Breevaart et al., 2015). Determining in consensus what is achievable in terms of work output makes the stress resulting from examining CSEM more manageable.

Fundamental here is an organizational culture that takes such workload regulation into account. Furthermore, secondary psychological trauma symptoms require normalization—symptoms are nothing to be ashamed of and can be discussed without judgement. An open and inviting climate can lower the threshold for help-seeking.

Future Research

In the current chapter, we discussed the potential impact of investigating CSEM cases and factors which may increase or decrease the likelihood of developing secondary trauma in police officers who examine these materials. We propose four topics that might be useful to examine in the future and may help this crucial topic of research further.

Prevention and innovative strategies. Classifying CSEM can be labour intensive, and the volume of CSEM is likely to increase in the next decennium. Future studies should examine how technological advances, such as artificial intelligence and data science, can help in aiding CSEM investigations and, by proxy, aid in preventing secondary trauma among police officers examining these cases. Furthermore, we should examine how physical, psychological, social, and environmental factors are interrelated with the prevention of secondary trauma.

Long-term impact, treatment strategies, and change mechanisms. Longitudinal studies would help assess how stable secondary psychological trauma is throughout one's career and whether symptoms persist after a transition to a new job outside the CSEM field (e.g., jobs in different police units or jobs outside the police force). Next, several studies indicate there is a general link between exposure to images of violence and subsequent aggression (Engelhardt et al., 2011; Krahé et al., 2011). Whether, for instance, officers turn to criminalized actions due to viewing CSEM is unknown and should be explored. Another area to be addressed in future research is potential sexual health concerns in CSEM officers. Researchers show secondary trauma can lead to short-term reduced sexual desires and lack of physical intimacy within marital relationships; however, less is known about the long-term impact on the sexual health of CSEM police officers. Finally, research should focus on factors either mediating or moderating the relationship between job-related characteristics and secondary stress, such as personality traits, knowledge about sexual violence, attachment style, and empathy.

Generalizability across gender and culture. People from different cultures and backgrounds have different demeanours and ways of carrying themselves.

In the last decade, there has been a growing recognition of the role that cultural diversity plays in our daily lives as well as in (online) offending behaviour. Less is known about the impact of culture on the impact of CSEM investigative activities carried out by police officers. For example, there is a need to examine whether cultural beliefs influence the development and symptoms of secondary stress in CSEM investigators. Also, research should explore whether secondary psychological trauma is more common in police officers with specific cultural backgrounds and whether gender-specific risk and protective factors exist. Furthermore, it is unknown whether interventions targeting (prevention of) secondary stress are equally beneficial for CSEM police officers with different gender identities and cultural backgrounds. For example, there are some studies reporting resilience training is effective in female officers in general (Chitra & Karunanidhi, 2021), but we do not know whether these findings also generalize to female CSEM officers and across other gender identities.

Conceptual issues. There are several theories or perspectives on the development of psychological stress (at work), such as the transactional model of stress (Lazarus, 1999), the person–environment fit perspective (Cummings & Cooper, 1979), the Conservation of Resources theory (Hobfoll, 1989), the Job–Demands–Control model (Karesek, 1979), the stress response theory (Horowitz, 1986), and the two-factor learning model (Mowrer, 1960). Future research should examine whether these conceptual models and theories apply to secondary psychological trauma in general and in police officers examining CSEM and whether the field can move towards an integrative theory on secondary psychological trauma in the public service.

Concluding Remarks

The work involved in investigating cases of child sexual exploitation material places police officers at risk of developing work-related stress and psychological health difficulties, which all constitute occupational stress injuries. We have some understanding of the factors likely to increase or decrease the likelihood of developing secondary psychological trauma. In the years to come, we need to learn more about how secondary stress involving CSEM investigations generalizes across gender and culture, how secondary stress progresses over time, and which treatment strategies are most effective for whom and under which circumstances. To reduce the risk of psychological problems and promote long-term sustainability, we advise the police service, managers, and academics to (continue to) invest in and examine the various personal, team, and organization-related resources that promote the resilience of CSEM investigators. In doing so, we must learn from adjacent workforces (e.g., fire and paramedic services, child protection services) and studies in (organizational) psychology, criminology, health, and sociology.

References

Acquadro Maran, D., Varetto, A., Zedda, M., & Ieraci, V. (2015). Occupational stress, anxiety and coping strategies in police officers. *Occupational Medicine, 65*(6), 466–473. https://doi.org/10.1093/occmed/kqv060

Aldao, A., Nolen-Hoeksema, S., & Schweizer, S. (2010). Emotion regulation strategies across psychopathology: a meta-analytic review. *Clinical Psychology Review, 30*, 217–237. https://doi.org/10.1016/j.cpr.2009.11.004

Ashforth, B.E., & Kreiner, G. (1999). How can you do it? Dirty work and the challenge of constructing a positive identity. *Academy of Management Review, 24*(3), 413–434. http://dx.doi.org/10.5465/amr.1999.2202129

Australian Centre to Counter Child Exploitation. (2019). Blueprint 2019–2021. Australian Federal Police. www.accce.gov.au/sites/default/files/2020 12/ACCCE%20Blueprint%202019-2021_online.pdf. Retrieved on November 29, 2022.

Bakker, A.B., van Veldhoven, M., & Xanthopolou, D. (2010). Beyond the demand-control model: thriving on high job demands and resources. *Journal of Personnel Psychology, 9*, 3–16. https://doi.org/10.1027/1866-5888/a000006

Baum, N. (2016). Secondary traumatization in mental health professionals: a systematic review of gender findings. *Trauma, Violence & Abuse, 17*(2), 221–235. https://doi.org/10.1177/1524838015584357

Bogaerts, S. (2013). *Professional resilience of police personnel: a review.* Research and Documentation Centre (WODC).

Bourke, M.L., & Craun, S.W. (2014). Secondary traumatic stress among internet crimes against children task force personnel: impact, risk factors, and coping strategies. *Sexual Abuse, 26*(6), 586–609. https://doi.org/10.1177/1079063213509411

Bowen, H.J., Kark, S.M. & Kensinger, E.A. (2018). NEVER forget: negative emotional valence enhances recapitulation. *Psychonomic Bulletin & Review, 25*, 870–891. https://doi.org/10.3758/s13423-017-1313-9

Bowen, H.J., & Kensinger, E.A. (2017). Recapitulation of emotional source context during memory retrieval. *Cortex, 91*, 142–156. https://doi.org/10.1016/j.cortex.2016.11.004

Breevaart, K., Bakker, A.B., Demerouti, E., & van den Heuvel, M. (2015). Leader-member exchange, work engagement, and job performance. *Journal of Managerial Psychology, 30*(7), 754–770. https://doi.org/10.1108/JMP-03-2013-0088

Bride, B., & Kintzle, S. (2011). Secondary traumatic stress, job satisfaction, and occupational commitment in substance abuse counselors. *Traumatology 17*(1), 22–28. https://doi.org/10.1177/1534765610395617

Burns, C.M., Morley, J., Bradshaw, R., & Domene, J. (2008). The emotional impact on and coping strategies employed by police teams investigating internet child exploitation. *Traumatology, 14*, 20. https://doi.org/10.1177/1534765608319082

Canadian Centre for Child Protection. (2016). *Child sexual abuse images on the internet: a cybertip.ca analysis.* Canadian Centre for Child Protection.

Carleton, R.N., Afifi, T.O., Taillieu, T., Turner, S., Mason, J.E., Ricciardelli, R., McCreary, D.R., Vaughan, A.D., Anderson, G.S., Krakauer, R.L., Donnelly, E.A., Camp, R.D., Groll, D., Cramm, H.A., MacPhee, R.S., & Griffiths, C.R. (2020). Assessing the relative impact of diverse stressors among public safety personnel.

International Journal of Environmental Research and Public Health, *17*, 1234. https://doi.org/10.3390/ijerph17041234

Chitra, T., & Karunanidhi, S. (2021). The impact of resilience training on occupational stress, resilience, job satisfaction, and psychological well-being of female police officers. *Journal of Police and Crime Psychology*, *36*, 8–23. https://doi.org/10.1007/s11896-018-9294-9

Cloitre, M., Khan, C., Mackintosh, M.-A., Garvert, D.W., Henn-Haase, C.M., Falvey, E.C., & Saito, J. (2019). Emotion regulation mediates the relationship between ACES and physical and mental health. *Psychological Trauma: Theory, Research, Practice, and Policy*, *11*(1), 82–89. https://doi.org/10.1037/tra0000374

Craun, S.W., Bourke, M.L., & Coulson, F.N. (2015). The impact of internet crimes against children work on relationships with families and friends: an exploratory study. *Journal of Family Violence*, *30*, 393–402. https://doi.org/10.1007/s10896-015-9680-3

Cummings, T.G., & Cooper, C.L. (1979). *Cybernetic framework for studying occupational stress.* Minnesota Press.

Davidson A.C., & Moss S.A. (2008). Examining the trauma disclosure of police officers to their partners and officers' subsequent adjustment. *Journal of Language and Social Psychology*, *27*(1), 51–70. https://doi.org/10.1177/0261927x07309511

Engelhardt, C.R., Bartholow, B.D., Kerr, G.T., & Bushman, B.J. (2011). This is your brain on violent video games: neural desensitization to violence predicts increased aggression following violent video game exposure. *Journal of Experimental Social Psychology*, *47*(5), 1033–1036. https://doi.org/10.1016/j.jesp.2011.03.027

Eriksen, H.R. Ihlebaek, C., Mikkelsen, A., Gronningsaeter, H., Sandal, G.M., & Ursin, H. (2022). Improving subjective health at the worksite: a randomized clinical trial of stress management training, physical exercise and an integrated health programme. *Occupational Medicine*, *25*(7), 383–391. https://doi.org/10.1093/occmed/52.7.383

Evans, R., Pistrang, N., & Billings, J. (2013). Police officers' experiences of supportive and unsupportive social interactions following traumatic incidents. *European Journal of Psychotraumatology*, *4*(1), 19696. https://doi.org/10.3402/ejpt.v4i0.19696

Foley, J., Hassett, A., & Williams, E. (2022). "Getting on with the job": a systematised literature review of secondary trauma and post-traumatic stress disorder (PTSD) in policing within the United Kingdom (UK). *The Police Journal: Theory, Practice and Principles*, *95*(1), 224–252. https://doi.org/10.1177/0032258x21990412

Foley, J., & Massey, K.L.D. (2021). The "cost" of caring in policing: from burnout to PTSAD in police officers in England and Wales. *The Police Journal: Theory, Practice and Principles*, *94*(3), 298–315. https://doi.org/10.1177/0032258x20917442

Gray, C., & Rydon-Grange, M. (2020). Individual characteristics, secondary trauma and burnout in police sexual and violent offending teams. *The Police Journal*, *93*(2), 146–161. https://doi.org/10.1177/0032258X19847499

Hayden, S.C.W., Williams, D.J., Canto, A.I., & Finklea, T. (2015). Shelter from the storm: addressing vicarious traumatization through wellness-based clinical supervision. *The Professional Counselor*, *5*(4), 529–542. https://doi.org/10.15241/scwh.5.4.529

Hennig-Fast, K., Werner, N.S., Lermer, R., Latscha, K., Meister, F., Reiser, M., Engel, R.R., & Meindl, T. (2009). After facing traumatic stress: brain activation, cognition and stress coping in policemen. *Journal of Psychiatry Research*, *43*, 1146–1155. https://doi.org/10.1016/j.jpsychires.2009.03.001

Hernandez-Wolfe, P., Killian, K., Engstrom, D., et al. (2015). Vicarious resilience, vicarious trauma, and awareness of equity in trauma work. *Journal of Humanistic Psychology, 55*(2), 153–172. https://doi.org/10.1177/0022167814534322

Hobfoll, S. (1989). Conservation of resources: a new attempt at conceptualizing stress. *The American Psychologist, 44*(3), 513–524.

Horowitz, M.J. (1986). *Stress response syndromes* (2nd ed.). Jason Aronson.

Hunter, S.V., & Schofield, M.J. (2006). How counsellors cope with traumatized clients: personal, professional, and organizational strategies. *International Journal for the Advancement of Counselling, 28*, 121–138. https://doi.org/10.1007/s10447-005-9003-0

Jackson, E.M. (2013). The role of exercise in stress management. *ACSM's Health & Fitness Journal, 17*(3), 14–19.

Jones, C.M., Merrick, M.T., & Houry, D.E. (2020). Identifying and preventing adverse childhood experiences: implications for clinical practice. *JAMA, 323*(1), 25–26. https://doi.org/10.1001/jama.2019.18499

Jones, C.M., Salter, M., & Woodlock, D. (2022). "Someone who has been in my shoes": the effectiveness of a peer support model for providing support to partners, family and friends of child sexual abuse material offenders, victims & offenders. *Victims & Offenders: An International Journal of Evidence-Based Research, Policy and Practice.* https://doi.org/10.1080/15564886.2022.2051108

Karasek, R.A. (1979). Job demands, job decision latitude and mental strain: implications for job redesign. *Administrative Science Quarterly, 24*, 285–308. https://doi.org/10.2307/2392498

Kohan, A., & Mazmanian, D. (2003). Police work, burnout, and pro-organizational behavior: a consideration of daily work experiences. *Criminal Justice and Behavior, 30*(5), 559–583. https://doi.org/10.1177/0093854803254432

Krahé, B., Möller, I., Huesmann, L.R., Kirwil, L., Felber, J., & Berger, A. (2011). Desensitization to media violence: links with habitual media violence exposure, aggressive cognitions, and aggressive behavior. *Journal of Personality and Social Psychology, 100*(4), 630–646. https://doi.org/10.1037/a0021711

Krause, M. (2009). Identifying and managing stress in child pornography and child exploitation investigators. *Journal of Police, Crime and Psychology, 24*, 22–29. https://doi.org/10.1007/s11896-008-9033-8

Lazarus, R.S. (1999). *Stress and emotion: A new synthesis.* Free Association.

MacEachern, A.D., Jindal-Snape, D., & Jackson, S. (2011). Child abuse investigation: police officers and secondary traumatic stress. *International Journal of Occupational Safety and Ergonomics, 17*(4), 329–339. https://doi.org/10.1080/10803548.2011.11076898

Marier, C.J., & Moule, R.K. (2019). Feeling blue: officer perceptions of public antipathy predict police occupational norms. *American Journal of Criminal Justice, 44*, 836–857. https://doi.org/10.1007/s12103-018-9459-1

Maslach, C., Schaufeli, W.B., & Leiter, M.P. (2001) Job burnout. *Annual Review of Psychology, 52*, 397–422. https://doi.org/10.1146/annurev.psych.52.1.397

Masten, A.S., & Cicchetti, D. (2010). Developmental cascades. *Development and Psychopathology, 22*(3), 491–495. https://doi.org/10.1017/S0954579410000222

McKeon, G., Steel, Z., Wells, R., Fitzpatrick, A., Vancampfort, D., & Rosenbaum, S. (2022). Exercise and PTSD symptoms in emergency service and frontline medical workers: a systematic review. *Translational Journal of the ACSM*, *7*(1), e000189. https://doi.org/10.1249/tjx.0000000000000189

Mowrer, O.H. (1960). *Learning theory and behavior.* Wiley.

National Center for Missing & Exploited Children. (2019). *Child sexual exploitation reports explode.* www.missingkids.org/blog/2019/pre-update/cse-reports-explode. Retrieved on November 29, 2022.

O'Brien, J.E., Gewirtz-Meydan, A., & Mitchell, K.J. (2024). Emotional wellbeing and cognitive appraisals among law enforcement exposed to child sexually explicit materials. *Criminal Justice and Behavior*, *51*(3), 420–439. https://doi.org/10.1177/00938548231224815

Parkes, R., Graham-Kevan, N., & Bryce, J. (2019). 'I put my "police head" on': coping strategies for working with sexual offending material. *The Police Journal*, *92*(3), 237–263. https://doi.org/10.1177/0032258X18808294

Paton, D., Violanti, J.M., Burke, K., & Gehrke, A. (2009). *Traumatic stress in police officers: a career-length assessment from recruitment to retirement.* Charles Thomas Pub Ltd.

Perez, L.M., Jones, J., Englert, D.R., & Sachau, D. (2010). Secondary traumatic stress and burnout among law enforcement investigators exposed to disturbing media images. *Journal of Police, Crime and Psychology*, *25*, 113–124. https://doi.org/10.1007/s11896-010-9066-7

Petrou, P., Demerouti, E., & Schaufeli, W.B. (2015). Job crafting in changing organizations: antecedents and implications for exhaustion and performance. *Journal of Occupational Health Psychology*, *20*(4), 470–480. https://doi.org/10.1037/a0039003

Powell, M.B., Cassematis, P., Benson, M., Smallbone, S., & Wortley, R. (2014). Police officers' strategies for coping with the stress of investigating internet child exploitation. *Traumatology: An International Journal*, *20*(1), 32–42. https://doi.org/10.1037/h0099378

Powell, M.B., Cassematis, P., Benson, M., Smallbone, S., & Wortley, R. (2015). Police officers' perspectives of their reactions of viewing internet child exploitation material. *Journal of Police, Crime and Psychology*, *30*, 103–111. https://doi.org/10.1007/s11896-014-9148-z

Romas, J.A., & Sharma, M. (2022). *Practical stress management: a comprehensive workbook.* Academic Press.

Rudenstine, S., Espinosa, A., McGee, A. B., & Routhier, E. (2019). Adverse childhood events, adult distress, and the role of emotion regulation. *Traumatology*, *25*(2), 124–132. https://doi.org/10.1037/trm0000176

Schwarzer, R., Bowler, R.M., & Cone, J.E. (2014). Social integration buffers stress in New York police after the 9/11 terrorist attack. *Anxiety, Stress & Coping*, *27*(1), 18–26. https://doi.org/10.1080/10615806.2013.806652

Sherwood, L., Hegarty, S., Vallières, F., Hyland, P., Murphy, J., Fitzgerald, G., & Reid, T. (2019). Identifying the key risk factors for adverse psychological outcomes among police officers: a systematic literature review. *Journal of Traumatic Stress*, *32*, 688–700. https://doi.org/10.1002/jts.22431

Singo, C., & Shilubane, H.N. (2022). How do police officers cope with stress? A qualitative study. *Journal of Police and Criminal Psychology*, *37*, 984–992. https://doi.org/10.1007/s11896-022-09556-0

Sollie, H. (2017). *Alledaagse magie: mentale weerbaarheid van kinderporno- en forensische rechercheurs* [Everyday magic: mental resilience of CSEM and forensic investigators]. Boom Criminologie. https://doi.org/10.5553/tvc/0165182x2014056004005

Sollie, H., Kop, N., & Euwema, M.C. (2017). Mental resilience of crime scene investigators: how police officers perceive and cope with the impact of demanding work situations. *Criminal Justice and Behavior*, *44*(12), 1580–1603. https://doi.org/10.1177/0093854817716959

Tehrani, N. (2016). Extraversion, neuroticism and secondary trauma in Internet child abuse investigators. *Occupational Medicine*, 66(5), 403–407. https://doi.org/10.1093/occmed/kqw004

Tehrani, N. (2018). Psychological well-being and workability in child abuse investigators. *Occupational Medicine*, 68(3), 165–170. https://doi.org/10.1093/occmed/kqy016

Tortella-Feliu, M., Fullana, M.A., Pérez-Vigil, A., Torres, X., Chamorro, J., Littarelli, S.A., Solanes, A., Ramella-Cravaro, V., Vilar, A., González-Parra, J.A., Andero, R., Reichenberg, A., Mataix-Cols, D., Vieta, E., Fusar-Poli, P., Ioannidis, J.P.A., Stein, M.B., Radua, J., & Fernández de la Cruz, L. (2019). Risk factors for posttraumatic stress disorder: an umbrella review of systematic reviews and meta-analyses. *Neuroscience & Biobehavioral Reviews*, *107*, 154–165. https://doi.org/10.1016/j.neubiorev.2019.09.013

Tracy, S.J., & Scott, C. (2006). Sexuality, masculinity, and taint management among firefighters and correctional officers: getting down and dirty with 'America's heroes' and the 'scum of law enforcement'. *Management Communication Quarterly*, *20*(6), 6–38. http://dx.doi.org/10.1177/0893318906287898

van der Velden, P.G., Rademaker, A.R., Vermetten, E., Portengen, M., Yzermans, J.C., & Grievink, L. (2013). Police officers: a high-risk group for the development of mental health disturbances? A cohort study. *BMJ Open*, *3*, e001720. https://doi.org/10.1136/bmjopen-2012-001720

Webb, T. L., Miles, E., & Sheeran, P. (2012). Dealing with feeling: a meta-analysis of the effectiveness of strategies derived from the process model of emotion regulation. *Psychological Bulletin*, *138*, 775–808. https://doi.org/10.1037/a0027600

Wortley, R., Smallbone, S., Powell, M., & Cassematis, P. (2014). *Understanding and managing the occupational health impacts on investigators of internet child exploitation*. Griffith University & Deakin University.

Yu, B., Funk, M., Hu, J., Wang, Q., & Feijs, L. (2018). Biofeedback for everyday stress management: a systematic review. *Frontiers*, *5*. www.frontiersin.org/articles/10.3389/fict.2018.00023

PART II
Corrections

5

THE PRACTICAL AND EMOTIONAL DEMANDS OF WORKING WITH WOMEN ON PROBATION

Kerry Ellis Devitt

Introduction

In the Probation Service for England and Wales, occupational stress and burnout are common amongst those in front-facing probation roles. Reasons for this include target expectations and managerialism (Tidmarsh, 2020a), high caseloads, a lack of time for reflective supervision (Burrell, 2022; Coley, 2020; Petrillo, 2022), and the challenges and responsibilities of working directly with vulnerable, disengaged, and sometimes potentially dangerous individuals (Gladfelter & Haggis, 2022; Morran, 2008; Phillips, Waters et al., 2020). In addition, the Probation Service has seen more disruption than any other part of the Criminal Justice System (CJS). For example, in the last decade, there have been two major structural reforms; the most recent has seen the Probation Service move from a bifurcated model – with privately owned Community Rehabilitation Companies (CRCs) responsible for the supervision of individuals classified as low-to-medium risk and the former National Probation Service responsible for high-risk individuals – to a now unified probation service. The last change, taking place during the first two years of the COVID-19 pandemic, required all probation staff in England and Wales to adjust quickly to the Exceptional Delivery Model (where unpaid work and accredited programmes were paused, and probation supervision was predominantly through telephone calls).

However, though much scholarship tied to probation work considers these common occupational stressors and, more recently, how they have intensified amidst the additional challenges of delivering services while adhering to public health measures during COVID-19 (e.g., Dominey et al., 2021; Ellis Devitt et al., 2022; Herzog-Evans & Sturgeon, 2022; Phillips et al., 2021) and

DOI: 10.4324/9781003424253-8

through the latest structural reform (e.g., Burrell, 2022; HM Inspectorate of Probation, 2022), investigation of the occupational stress of working in probation through a gendered lens has had notably less attention – specifically, the nuances of supervising women on probation.

Working with Women on Probation

Women in the CJS often have complex needs and may struggle with being unhoused, compromised mental health, substance misuse problems, and relationship difficulties (Ministry of Justice [MoJ], 2018). In addition, they are likely to have experienced victimization, abuse, or trauma (Burman et al., 2018; Dominey & Gelsthorpe, 2020), as well as revictimization in adulthood (Petrillo, 2022). Women on probation are also found to face different variations of hurdles in comparison to men when working towards desistance (Gelsthorpe & Sharpe, 2015, p.118). To exemplify, in 2007, Baroness Corston released a ground-breaking investigation into women in the CJS in England and Wales. The Corston Report (2007) revealed the failures of the system in meeting the specific and unique needs of vulnerable women, calling for a more holistic, woman-centred approach to service delivery. The report underscored the need for a system to help women develop the resilience, life skills, and emotional literacy required to successfully move forward.

Though the challenges facing women in the CJS continue to be discussed, often highlighting how much more progress is necessary (e.g., Women in Prison, 2017), what has had substantially less attention is the experiences of those who *work* with women in criminal justice professions – like in probation. Though pockets of dedicated research do exist in the area (e.g., Burman et al., 2018; Goldhill, 2019; Petrillo, 2022; Shepherd, 2022), the scholarship remains limited, but given that the strength, value, and sustainability of public services rely heavily on the individuals upholding them, these perspectives are essential.

In response, I ask, what are the challenges for staff tasked with supervising women on probation? Though one of the main responsibilities of the probation officer is to ensure the individuals on their caseload adhere to the parameters of their Court Order (their conditions of release), working with women probationers means the probation officer must also be sensitive to their complex needs. As such, there are certain practices required; each is considered essential for working effectively with women on probation. Many practices, however, simultaneously come at a cost to the individual practitioner.

Emotional Labour and Trauma-Informed Practice

Emotional labour, a term characterized by Hochschild (1983), explains the process of managing one's emotions as required by certain professions, drawing a distinction between deep acting, referring to where the worker makes an effort to align inner feelings with the emotion they are displaying, and surface acting, where the worker's inner feelings differ from the emotions they are displaying. Emotional labour exists where emotional work, which involves regulating or suppressing emotions, is exchanged for something else, e.g., wages or some other type of valued compensation (Jeung et al., 2018).

Simply said, workers perform emotional labour to manage their emotions, the presentation of their emotions, and the emotions of others. Emotion management may be used to hide emotions considered inappropriate in the circumstances, or to "invoke an emotional response in the person with whom someone is interacting" (Phillips, Westaby et al., 2020, p.5). Phillips, Westaby et al. (2020) explain how emotional labour involves "display rules" and draws on experiences of a "trained imagination"; and "genuine emotional responses". With the latter, genuine emotions, there is a natural alignment between the worker's feelings and the emotional expectations of the organization; however, emotional labour is still required as emotions must be regulated to be displayed "appropriately" (Phillips, Westaby et al., 2020, p.5).

Though emotional labour is not exclusive to women practitioners, nor exclusive to working with women on probation, emotional labour requires skills often culturally associated with women. As Goldhill (2019) observes, "gendered characteristics of emotional labour, such as gaining compliance through being pleasant and caring, suggest that certain 'femininities', are seen as normal for women workers (p.55)". Burman et al. (2018) too, drawing on their own research around vicarious trauma, add how effective practice with women and girls typically means "a personal and empathic engagement between the service provider and individual woman or girl, demanding emotional labour as a key component of the work (p.8)". For the authors, when working with women, emotional labour was an absolute necessity.

Working with women on probation also requires practitioners to be trauma-informed when completing their occupational duties (MoJ, 2018; National Offender Management Servic [NOMS], 2015). Trauma-informed practice refers to approaches grounded in the understanding that exposure to trauma can impact an individual's neurological, biological, psychological, and social development (Office for Health Improvement & Disparities, 2022). Trauma-informed practice generally operates around six basic principles – safety, trustworthiness, choice, collaboration, empowerment, and cultural consideration (or inclusivity; Petrillo, 2022) – and recognizes the necessity of appropriate approaches and support through "a knowledge of the impact of trauma on behaviour" (Petrillo, 2022, p.14). As McCartan (2020) explains, a trauma-informed approach marks a change in perspective from "What's wrong with you?" to "What happened to you?" (p.8). Being trauma-informed means engaging in emotional work, particularly "deep acting". Moran and Asquith (2020) usefully observe how the priorities of trauma-informed practice mean "belief cannot be performed (surface acting); it must be authentic and embodied (deep acting)" (p.3). Staff tasked with working in trauma-informed ways must engage with the expected emotions required by their profession and equally work to ensure those emotions are genuine.

However, working in trauma-informed ways can leave the individual practitioner unprotected from their own exposure to psychological trauma. Subsequently, trauma-informed practice opens up the possibility of psychological harm – a significant occupational stress. Arguably, "vicarious trauma" – occurring when people who are indirectly exposed to trauma (e.g., through reading or hearing of it) experience psychological distress *because* of that exposure – can negatively affect the individual, creating feelings of mistrust, low self-esteem, pessimism, alienation, and withdrawal (Lee, 2017, p.375). Reflecting a common understanding of most women on probation having some level of psychological trauma in their past, the risks of trauma being absorbed to some extent by the professionals who work with them are very real. Though emotional labour and trauma-informed practice are requirements for *all* front-facing probation staff, and the risks of burnout and vicarious trauma a possibility for anyone working within the sector, these considerations are particularly acute for probation officers supervising women.

Importantly, when talking about exploring occupational stress in front-facing probation roles through a gendered lens, I refer not only to the unique challenges of supervising women on probation but also to the gender of the staff themselves. Though male practitioners *can* and *do* supervise women on probation, the task largely falls to female practitioners. When discussing the experiences of supervising women on probation, as I now proceed to do, this doubly gendered phenomenon requires attention. Thus, to do so, I explore the practical and emotional demands of supervising women on probation from women's perspectives.

A word on gender – in addressing this topic, I consider how, as a social construct, gender is not restricted to a dichotomous understanding. As Cox et al. (2024) and others (Barr et al., 2016; Valcore et al., 2021) argue, describing gender as a dichotomy or binary has the capacity to exclude and pathologize those who do not identify or fit neatly into traditional gender categories, as per their social construction. Treating sex as immutable denies the existence of trans individuals (Cox et al., 2024, p.149). Although I refer to "women on probation" and "female practitioners" (amongst other terms), I use these as broad indicators to provide distinction to "men on probation" and "male practitioners" and not as reductive terms suggesting there to be only two gendered perspectives available.

Background to This Research

In recent years, His Majesty's Prison and Probation Service (HMPPS) has become increasingly concerned with its awareness and responsiveness to the gender-specific needs of women in the CJS. Women-centred probation service delivery has become a priority area, with various probation regions creating a dedicated role for supporting women on probation. Based on research undertaken in 2020 (Ellis Devitt, 2020), in the current chapter, I explore the experiences of women probation staff who supervised women probationers at the former Kent, Surrey and Sussex CRC – a role known commonly as "Women's Leads".[1] My original purpose in the research was to closely examine the realities and complexities of the Women's Lead (WL) role in hopes to improve the experiences of women on probation. Here, I offer a broader and deeper understanding of how staff managing women on probation experience gender-specific, job-related stress.

Methodology

The research involved a qualitative study to explore the holistic experiences of WLs in delivering women-led probation services at KSS CRC. My research questions included:

- What are the "realities" of delivering women-led probation services?
- How do staff conceptualize their own resilience and well-being when working as a WL?
- What needs to happen to ensure the sustainability of the WL role?

Data was collected via 12 semi-structured interviews, comprising 8 WLs and 4 managers of WLs, and an online survey involving an additional 13 WLs. WLs were recruited through two introductory emails explaining the research and inviting people to take part in individual interviews or, due to the COVID-19 pandemic's onset during data collection, which inhibited participation in the interview, an online survey. Managers were contacted by email using an "opt-in" approach, as all participation was voluntary.

For confidentiality, personal information was anonymized, and unique stories were summarized or generalized. I also refrain from disclosing participant geographical location to further support confidentiality.

Data collection occurred between December 2019 and July 2020 (December to February for the interviews; June and July for the survey). Interview participants agreed on times and dates by email, and interviews were conducted individually, although two participants were interviewed as a pair. During COVID-19, interviews were conducted over the telephone; prior to the pandemic, they were conducted in person in private spaces on KSS

CRC property. There were no discernible differences between telephone and face-to-face respondents – interviews lasted approximately 60 minutes, and participants spoke candidly in both contexts. The paired interview was longer, given the two participants, lasting approximately 100 minutes.

All the interviews were digitally recorded and later transcribed, with the exception of one, where the decision was not to record the interview. Here, with the permission of the two participants, a second researcher took detailed notes instead.

To explore the data – from both the interviews and the survey – I used an inductive thematic analysis, similar to Braun and Clarke (2006). After familiarizing myself with the data, I generated initial codes, entailing research assistant support, and then manually coded the transcripts. Codes were then sorted into main themes (e.g., practicalities of the job; well-being and mental health; organizational culture; creating a sustainable workforce) and sub-themes (e.g., factors around working with women probationers; support networks; examples of emotional labour; ways to improve the WL role), which I visualized in Excel. Finally, I "define(d) and refine(d)" the themes (Braun & Clarke, 2006, p.87), named each to establish what they "meant" and clarified how they would enable making sense of the data.

Results

Working with Women on Probation: Practicalities and Routes In

Widely understood as a demanding role, and one seeing a considerably higher turnover of staff than other front-facing probation jobs, the WL role expected much from the women occupying it. Beyond the general duties of a probation officer, being a WL meant specialist training in trauma-informed practice, attending women's only reporting sessions, working closely with specialist local women's services, and assisting in delivering the "Believe and Succeed" programme – an in-house women-only programme designed to meet the specialized needs of women in the CJS. Participants also indicated that the role was accompanied by several gender-specific challenges. For instance, women on probation were said to require a greater need for empathy, listening, and compassion (compared with their male counterparts). There was more required in finding and accessing appropriate services to support gender-specific needs, and staff spoke of generally spending more time worrying about the safety and well-being of the women outside of the supervisory context. There was also the ever-present difficulty for staff in balancing women's offending and the recognition and response to their psychological trauma. For example:

> [Men] are quite open to doing like structured work, you can kind of go in and have an interview session say, "right today we're gonna talk about this

> thing" and "we're going to do some offence focused work". I find that with women, there's a whole different kind of work that's needed.
>
> *(Women's Lead)*

Where offence-focused work was required, the professional relationship would sometimes feel the strain – an effect consistent across research (e.g., Goldhill, 2019, p.60). One manager spoke of the specific risks of *not* including trauma-informed approaches in their practice in terms of the potential to cause further harm:

> I have seen people do more damage because they are very much pushing the, I don't want to go super feminist, but I will, like patriarchal, toxic masculine ideas around violence and victim blaming, and not understanding women as survivors first and foremost, and a perpetrator of a crime as the secondary item of what we're dealing with. So, trust is given, but then it has also to be earnt [sic] and kept, and that's down to how we work.
>
> *(Women's Lead Manager)*

Speaking to their occupational entry, participants had mixed responses. Some were motivated by a passion for working with vulnerable women – "wanting to make a difference". Others were drawn to the job through a natural evolution from what they were already doing or had done before (e.g., other front-facing roles working with women) – " 'occupational drift" – a phenomenon noted elsewhere (e.g., Ricciardelli & Martin, 2017). And for a minority, they talked of being propelled into the role. For these participants, the WL role was one that most probation staff sought to avoid. As a manager suggested, "Many staff are just *put* into those roles, told to do it". She continues, "No-one wants to do it because they have seen the impact this role has had on other staff members". Of note, several were drawn to the role because of their personal history of trauma – they felt they could understand the women they worked with and, further, saw the role adding to their own recovery:

> Women who get drawn to women's work generally have a reason behind that, whether it's trauma in their own lives or understanding [the] trauma [of] people close to them, because there's something healing and supportive in being someone that then supports others.
>
> *(Women's Lead Manager)*

A similar effect is reported in Petrillo's (2022) research into trauma-informed practice in probation settings. Reflecting on the predominantly female staff base and how most front-facing work with women on probation is undertaken by female practitioners, Petrillo (2022) notes how participants' own experiences of gendered victimization influenced their commitment to being trauma-informed in their approach to practice (p.16). The findings from both these studies appear to reinforce the notion that experiencing psychological trauma can be a precursor to wanting to help alleviate similar trauma in others.

Despite different pathways into the WL role, participants shared similar views regarding their training for it. Participants universally felt that staff entering the role were not adequately prepared for the numerous and often far-reaching mental, emotional, and practical challenges. Participants spoke of feeling "chucked in the deep end" and having to "wing it" in the job. Others said the mandatory trauma-informed training often came quite late on, for some up to a year after being on the job, which often left (particularly less experienced) staff isolated, alienated, and overwhelmed. Relatedly, participants spoke of the shortage of qualified probation officers and the subsequent requirement of probation services officers (staff without a probation qualification) to take on more complex cases – something Burrell (2022) suggests as reflective of CRC organizational policies and the attrition of probation practitioner posts (p.437). As this participant shares:

> I was a Women's Lead pretty much from the get-go. I don't think that was helpful for me, starting off in a job, especially holding those kinds of cases. I was split between female cases and under 25-year-olds – two very hectic groups. [I] basically ended up going off sick, from an accumulation of stress.
>
> *(Women's Lead)*

Ultimately, though most participants felt capable of doing the job, the training was often said to be a "crash course", requiring them to learn very quickly what was expected of them. Job-related stress subsequently occurred when staff were placed in a role for which they did not feel qualified to do or lacked experience and training in.

The Emotional Demands of Supervising Women

Working with women on probation requires emotional labour – particularly around the enactment of empathy. Empathy is a necessary skill for probation officers, with research consistently highlighting empathy's value in building trusted professional relationships (e.g., Bonta et al., 2008; Lewis, 2014; HM Inspectorate of Probation, 2020; Westaby et al., 2020). However, empathy can also bring harm. For some participants, the emotional toll was expressed in their holding of stories of pain and psychological trauma as experienced by the women probationers. For example, in experiencing repeated disclosures of self-harm and suicide ideation in group work, one participant commented, "to provide someone support when they've got emotional issues like that require[s] empathy, and for me, empathy takes from me". For others, empathy was in seeing consistent examples of "deep and painful grief". As one participant explained, "it just wears you down emotionally". Empathy was also in the difficult task of seeing the person beyond the offence. Reflecting on her previous role as a WL, a manager described the emotional impact of conducting a home visit whilst a woman probationer nursed her new baby – "[she was breastfeeding] as we are talking about theft and other crimes, and it really gets me, whilst their child is touching them, whilst they are holding them". As Phillips, Westaby et al. (2020) observe, to convey empathy, the practitioner needs to suppress or emphasize emotions to achieve the aims of the job (pp.5–6). Moreover, it was this constant requirement to suppress and emphasize emotions, which unfortunately left many staff members feeling emotionally depleted.

Participants also explained how empathy simultaneously needed to be regulated – again echoing findings from Phillips, Westaby et al. (2020) and Westaby et al. (2020). Beyond *having* and *displaying* empathy, the worker must also *monitor* and *regulate* empathy by paying close attention to the borders of empathy – ever mindful of appearing appropriate, controlled, and ultimately professional. Phillips, Westaby et al. (2020) speak of the "display rules" in emotional labour, specifically, that of "genuine emotional response" – e.g., the alignment between the practitioner's feelings and the emotional expectations of an organization (p.5). Here, this prevailed when participants spoke of having to temper authentic feelings of compassion to ensure they did not overstep. An example is a participant's comments concerning a distressed woman under her supervision – "[I] just wan[ted] give her a hug, but you can't because you've got to maintain that professional boundary". The challenges of observing professional boundaries, as fundamental to the ethical principles of probation practice (Probation Institute, 2020), were particularly hard when the call for physical reassurance and comfort felt profoundly necessary.

Adhering to "display rules" was also evidenced in how WLs managed challenging and sometimes aggressive behaviour amongst their supervised women – in these instances, requiring the WLs to engage in "surface acting". Participants described situations where fears and frustrations sometimes resulted in displays of anger amongst the women probationers, leaving staff feeling unsettled and intimidated yet needing to appear calm and be able to diffuse the situation. Reminiscing on Westaby et al.'s (2020) research into how probation staff must manage "negative" emotions, staff had to neutralize their own feelings to be able to carry on doing the work.

> I've had another case that, she was on the phone telling me that she's going to jump off a bridge and kill herself. So I obviously did everything that I needed to do, I rung the police, did a welfare check, got the police to go out and see her, and then the next day she's ringing me saying I've ruined her life and that I shouldn't have told the police and that she

> doesn't want the police involved and you can't, there's a no-win situation. And I think they take it out on you because you're there, and they haven't got anybody else.
>
> *(Women's Lead)*

Emotional labour often appeared gendered, for instance, when WLs engaged women probationers in offence-focused work, a participant stated, "[women] bring all these issues and it's really difficult to be like 'ok that's fine, put that aside, I need you to do this' ". Thus, in striving for their compliance, WLs had to compromise their own intention and work.

Emotional work was additionally evident in how participants managed their stress and anxiety, particularly regarding worries about the well-being of the women they supervised. Intrusive thoughts and questions of whether they had ever "done enough" were commonplace, as was the struggle of trying to leave worries (often related to the women probationers' personal safety) at work. As one participant shared, "there's no way you can't bring that home". Exploring similar concerns of the "spillover" of probation work into homelife, Westaby et al. (2016) noted how despite probation officers' best intentions, "the temporal boundary between work and family life is not always so easy to maintain" (p.118). As they observe, unlike the prison officer, who may be able to physically leave their work behind, the probation officer has no such option. Participants knew that when leaving their work in the office, the women they worked with may be without formal supports for extended periods. Concerns for the women's well-being rested with fears tied to professional liability. Continual reflection on the robustness of their own professional judgment peppered participants' accounts. For example, this participant questioned their own decisions:

> Have I just opened a conversation with a woman that you know is suicidal? Have I just opened-up a conversation about their abuse that's going to lead them to go and kill themselves? And if they do, is that my fault? It just eats you up.
>
> *(Women's Lead)*

Participants experienced a constant background of worry regarding whether they had adequately protected the vulnerable women they worked with but also suffered through fears of what may happen to them if they were found to be professionally negligent.

The Perils of Vicarious Trauma

Working with women on probation saw practitioners also navigate the risky terrain of vicarious trauma. Victimization, abuse, and psychological trauma are common experiences among women on probation (Burman et al., 2018; Dominey & Gelsthorpe, 2020; Petrillo, 2022), and hearing these repeated stories weighed heavily on staff. Burnett (2017), speaking to compassion fatigue, references Figley's (1995) coining of the phenomenon as the "cost of caring" due to the trauma worker's use of empathy with survivors (Burnett, 2017, p.1). The potential for vicarious trauma was compounded for those who had histories of abuse themselves and who additionally felt the risks of "over empathizing" due to their own experiences.

> Working with women, realizing that the trauma work that you have done yourself to recover from your own trauma, often you then are encountered with other people's trauma a lot of the time you've find yourself absorbing little bits of their trauma. When you're sitting with somebody, sitting with their trauma, it's difficult to deal with. It can be very re-traumatizing for yourself.
>
> *(Women's Lead)*

Managers, too, had concerns about vicarious trauma, intensified by known psychological trauma in a staff member's past. Reflecting on such risks and the related concerns of suitability for the role, a manager commented, "it's so much harder if they have experienced [trauma] themselves. We have one staff member, she had something awful happen to her and I thought, you can't go into that role". For managers, the fear of adding to a staff member's psychological trauma, due to their position working with traumatized others, was a significant risk factor in increasing their own stress.

High Caseloads but Minimal Time

A perennial issue within the Probation Service is how to balance high caseloads, and this issue was elevated for staff supervising women on probation. Women were said to require considerably more time than men during supervisory meetings. They were perceived as more reliant on staff, more likely to "overshare", and generally took longer to arrive at change because of all they were (mentally and emotionally) carrying. As one participant said, "With difficult men, they don't speak. You are struggling to get 15 minutes out of them. With difficult women, they will be there an hour". The outcome created additional anxieties for WLs trying to maintain or create boundaries between themselves and the women probationers – evidenced by efforts to ensure appointments stayed within their allocated time. One WL commented, "It makes you feel like you're putting an end to a really important conversation". Viewed as an unfortunate outcome of a system more suited to men, gender was considered a factor impacting the supervision requirement, leaving WLs unsure if they could fully meet the needs of women under their supervision.

> The model we work to is not set up to accommodate women. See our diaries; they are in 30-minute slots. With a woman, you use double that time and then don't have any time to write up your notes, or plan for anything. It is a caseload issue. There are some reductions, but not enough. Women's cases take significantly longer. You can't expect staff to supervise similar amounts of women's cases.
>
> *(Women's Lead Manager)*

Though it may be argued that appointment times may benefit from being longer for both men and women; those for women probationers were seen as clearly not long enough. Both managers and WLs alike stated that women's cases demanded more time, and further, not having that time subsequently created more occupational stress.

Participants also experienced stress through the time needed to find and access gender-specific services for their women probationers (e.g., women's centres, child social services, women-only substance misuse services, and various multi-agency risk management forums). The experiences were problematized because of the sparsity of such services and the "uphill struggle" to ensure non-gender specific agencies would work with the women. The additional demands translated into case-allocation debates. Arguing why WLs' caseloads should be reduced, a WL commented, "[you] do all the other work alongside trying to coordinate all of these agencies for all your women, and you just end up with no time. And to me, that's a big, big thing".

Participants frequently spoke of feeling overwhelmed. One described the situation as "soul-destroying" as she sought to do her best but had neither the time nor resources to do so. Another described the isolation of the role – (typically, there were only one or two WLs operating in each geographic area, meaning those undertaking the role had little opportunity to share their experiences with others). Reflecting research elsewhere (e.g., Petrillo, 2022; Tidmarsh, 2020a), such concerns were described as systemic, where processes rather than people were perceived to be the metric of value.

> Unfortunately, it's the sort of system that tells you that if you can't do the job, they'll find someone else who will. And that's how it feels a lot of the time, and unfortunately, that person then comes into the role, and you watch the exact same thing that has just happened to you happen to them, and it's like, why the hell did I bother kicking up any sort of fuss, say anything at all, because they haven't learnt from it, and this poor sod over here is just going through exactly what I went through.
>
> *(Women's Lead)*

As the participant's words reveal, many WLs feel undervalued, or reduced to their experience – i.e., not expecting any supportive changes. As several also suggested, being overwhelmed with work contributed to sick leave use.

Sources of Support

Probation officers work in emotionally demanding occupations, thus requiring significant support – for participants, this predominantly came from turning to their colleagues. With these colleagues, they "check-in", "offload" about difficult or complex cases, or seek reassurance for prior decisions and actions. Lee (2017, p.383) considers such practices to be particularly helpful strategies for managing vicarious trauma exposure. Participants also found support in line-managers. Here, value was felt when managers took the time to listen to concerns, offer opportunities for reflective supervision, and provide practical solutions to high caseload challenges. However, echoing the findings of Westaby et al. (2021), a few participants also suggested that managers themselves were time-constrained, especially regarding supervision. Participants additionally cited family and friends as part of their support structure, most commonly by their role in providing an impartial ear to talk through difficulties, but with limitations. Though loved ones might be able to listen and sympathize, by not being in the role themselves, they were less able to understand and empathize.

> If they don't do the job, they're not part of the service, they don't understand, [they don't] know what it's like to have a woman come in and be like, "I'm suicidal because I was raped", like that's not in [their] day to day, and unless it is in your day to day, no one really knows how they're going to deal with that, and they hypothesize about how they might cope with that and how they might deal with it, but they don't know.
>
> *(Women's Lead)*

Finally, some participants discussed formal support, including group-based clinical supervision. This form of clinical supervision gave WLs the chance to meet with a clinical practitioner and other WL colleagues, in a group setting, a few times a year to discuss challenges and concerns in their supervision of women probationers. Participants spoke of the benefits of group-based clinical supervision as: a space to air worries and grievances, comfort and not being alone in their experiences, and the space to process difficult feelings. The drawbacks of the practice were multiple, however. First, some participants found accessing the supervision impractical; for example, clinical supervision sessions were only offered in certain geographic locations, and the sessions did not account for busy work schedules – specifically, staff were not allocated time to attend (similar findings are also observable in Petrillo's [2022] study).

Second, participants were not always comfortable voicing concerns to a group, suggesting that discussions became "diluted" because people did not want to disclose. For example:

> You're in a room with people from other offices that you don't know very well, who don't know your caseload and you often can end up in a position where you feel very uncomfortable. I don't think people want to talk about it, other professionals don't feel comfortable talking about it, and it leads to an environment where you feel like you are the only person who cannot manage [your] caseload.
>
> *(Women's Lead)*

Though staff highly valued having such a resource at their disposal, restructuring the supervision to be more responsive to practitioner needs was thought to result in more service use.

Keeping Staff in the Women's Lead Role: A Sustainable Model

Participants offered considerations for how to make their work more sustainable, including those tied to gender-conscious caseload allocations. Calls for giving WLs more time and fewer cases were common, as well as for the additional flexibility for women's cases to be divided among more staff. The reliance on just one or two people to do the role was felt to carry too many risks (e.g., burnout and sick leave).

> It's like getting whiplash. It's emotional whiplash, and it's exhausting. And the only way to deal with that is having a limited number of [women on your caseload], and it being spread out throughout a team; otherwise, it's just, I strongly believe that people are just gonna continue to go off sick, and continue to get ill, and continue to leave the role.
>
> *(Women's Lead)*

As Petrillo (2022) observes, unmanageable workloads are "a cause and consequence" of staff shortages (p.28).

Sustainability was also suggested to include maintaining professional relationships with other women-focused agencies or organizations. WLs highly valued the support from such agencies, considering it to be a significant benefit to their practice and wellness. Speaking of a woman's support worker from another agency, a participant said:

> I'm absolutely mortified she's got another job, and I'm worrying already. I co-work with her a lot [and] it's taken a lot of the stress when I don't have time to take stuff on. I do depend on her heavily. I've got a big caseload

> and she's a pillar of support towards that. I think that's essential because otherwise, you feel on your own again.
>
> *(Women's Lead)*

Other considerations included investing in supporting officer experience through better supervision and more attention to staff well-being. Participants desired a more reflective model of supervision, rather than a solely managerial model, where, as one participant commented, "business needs eclipse staff well-being needs". For one manager, using reflective supervision was deemed essential: "it's more time consuming but without it, my staff wouldn't be ok, and our women wouldn't be as looked after". Participants noted that probation workplace culture centred "the service user experience" while often overlooking the well-being of staff. With staff being expected to be trauma-informed in their practice, feeling unsupported indicated a challenge warranting future attention.

> It feels like we are being told constantly that we need to be hyper-vigilant and hyper aware of our service users' trauma, and yet the second it comes to a member of staff struggling in that way, all of that trauma-informed behaviour that [is] instilled in us [is] launched out of the window. Because you're a member of staff, you don't have trauma. You don't count.
>
> *(Women's Lead)*

Problems within probation workplace culture when it comes to staff well-being are also discussed by Kirton and Guillaume (2015). Echoing my findings, the authors highlight recurring themes of stress and anxiety around lack of inclusion, lack of consultation, and low morale, leaving staff feeling devalued within the organization.

Finally, participants requested practical support (i.e., a company laptop and mobile phone) and instrumental changes (e.g., having a day out of the office to finish administrative activities); the latter was particularly desirable:

> I think for our own well-being and our own sanity, to have a day out of the office where we can do all the practical bits but without the distraction of anyone coming to you and talking to you about other cases. Because it can get so overwhelming, and you know when you're busy, like yesterday I was on duty, and I was trying to, I was dealing with all of this stuff, and I had reception ringing me with this and that, and trying to pass on stuff that really, it could have just been an email.
>
> *(Women's Lead)*

The overall sentiment was that changes to support sustainability were possible and necessary, particularly given the emotional labour engaged in by WLs. As one participant said, "It's a hard role, and I think if you're gonna do it, you've gotta be like fully committed and you've got to have a passion for it, because otherwise it just won't work".

Conclusion

My findings provide insight into the experiences of women probation officers who supervise women on probation. Given the practical demands of the job (e.g., tasks required in supervising women; finding and accessing gender-specific services; balancing offence-focused work with trauma-informed practice), organizational obstacles (e.g., inexperienced/unqualified staff being thrust into the role; the lateness of training; varying levels of support), and the requirement of constant and complex emotional labour (e.g., the expectation that staff must manage and regulate their own emotions and those of their probationers; the risks of vicarious trauma), participants described the WL role as one asking a lot of practitioners. Participants also spoke of feeling impacted by their own historical, psychological trauma. As found by Petrillo (2022), psychological trauma is a strong precursor to wanting to help alleviate psychological trauma in others. Finally, participants desired to increase the sustainability of the WL role through more frequent and reflective supervision, gender-conscious caseload allocations, better connections with other agencies and women's services, and offering staff more time and flexibility in their work day.

There is an opportunity to improve WLs and women probationer's experiences through, for example, gender-specific training and recognition of emotional labour (i.e., emotional costs tied to, for example, repeated exposure to psychological trauma without adequate protections in place). Stress and burnout, common in probation contexts (Gladfelter & Haggis, 2022; Phillips, Waters et al., 2020; Morran, 2008), are acute risks for WLs. As Phillips et al. (2016), reflecting on their own research with probation practitioners, concisely note, "A workforce that suffers from high levels of stress, and that is not supported sufficiently, is unlikely to be able to deliver the high-quality work that is required of them" (p.189). Incumbent upon the Probation Service is to strive to better understand and respond to the needs of their WLs to ensure they can provide optimal supervision to those under their care. Future research is required to understand how intersectionality impacts WL as they supervise women.

The core of effective service delivery for women on probation is ensuring staff can perform their occupational responsibilities as desired and with emotional safety. By paying closer attention to the emotional well-being of those tasked with the Probation Service's upkeep, one might be in a substantially better place to offer a women-centric probation service that is robust, specialized, and, crucially, sustainable.

Note

1 The specific Women's Lead role to which this chapter refers no longer exists due to the closure of all the CRCs in June 2021; however, the role is still in operation in very similar ways across the Probation Service, with many regional probation areas still referring to these roles using them same terminology.

References

Barr, S. M., Budge, S. L. & Adelson, J. L. (2016). Transgender community belongingness as a mediator between strength of transgender identity and wellbeing. *Journal of Counseling Psychology*, *63*(1), 87. https://doi.org/10.1037/cou0000127

Bonta, J., Rugge, T., Scott, T., Bourgon, G. & Yessine, A. (2008). Exploring the black box of community supervision. *Journal of Offender Rehabilitation*, *47*(3), 248–270. https://doi.org/10.1080/10509670802134085

Braun, V. & Clarke, V. (2006). Using thematic analysis in psychology. *Qualitative Research in Psychology*, *3*(2), 77–101. https://doi.org/10.1191/1478088706qp063oa

Burman, M., Robinson, R. & Crowley, A. (2018). Working with women and girls: Researching experiences of vicarious traumatisation. The Scottish Centre for Crime and Justice Research. www.sccjr.ac.uk/wp-content/uploads/2020/04/Vicarious-Traumatisation-Research-Report-02.-2018_.pdf

Burnett, H. (2017). Revisiting the compassion fatigue, burnout, compassion satisfaction, and resilience connection among CISM responders. *Journal of Police Emergency Response*, *7*(3), 1–10. https://doi.org/10.1177/2158244017730857

Burrell, A. (2022). The reflective practitioner in transition. Probation work during reintegration of probation services in England and Wales. *Probation Journal*, *69*(4), 434–451. https://doi.org/10.1177/02645505221117537

Coley, D. (2020). Probation staff supervision: Valuing 'me time' within congested spaces. *Probation Journal*, *67*(3), 228–245. http://doi.org/10.1177/0264550520926581

Corston, J. (2007) The Corston Report: A review of women with particular vulnerabilities in the criminal justice system. London: Home Office.

Cox, C. Ellis Devitt, K. & Sugiura. L. (2024). Female researcher identities in male spaces and places. In K. J. Stockdale and M. Addison (Eds.), *Marginalised Voices in Criminology* (pp. 148–165). Routledge. https://doi.org/10.4324/9781003260967

Dominey, J., Coley, D., Ellis Devitt, K. & Lawrence, J. (2021). Putting a face to a name: Telephone contact as part of a blended approach to probation supervision. *Probation Journal*, *68*(4), 394–410. https://doi.org/10.1177/02645505211050870

Dominey, J. & Gelsthorpe, L. (2020). Resettlement and the case for women. *Probation Journal*, *67*(4), 393–409. https://doi.org/10.1177/0264550520939154

Ellis Devitt, K. (2020). *Resilience, wellbeing and sustainability in women-led probation service delivery: Exploring the 'Women's Lead' role*. KSS CRC. https://interventionsalliance.com/exploring-the-womens-lead-role/

Ellis Devitt, K., Coley, D., Lawrence, J. & Musimbe-Rix, S. (2022). A view of probation and mental health after the pandemic. In C. Brooker and C. Sirdifield (Eds.), *Probation, Mental Health and Criminal Justice* (pp. 155–164). Routledge. https://doi.org/10.4324/9781003193456

Figley, C. R. (1995). Compassion fatigue as secondary traumatic stress disorder: An overview. In C. Figley (Ed.), *Compassion Fatigue: Coping with Secondary Traumatic Stress Disorder in Those Who Treat the Traumatized* (pp. 1–20). Routledge. https://doi.org/10.1192/S0007125000026179

Gelsthorpe, L. & Sharpe, G. (2015). Women and sentencing: Challenges and choices. In J. Roberts (Ed.), *Exploring Sentencing Practice in England and Wales* (pp. 118–136). Palgrave Macmillan. https://link.springer.com/chapter/10.1057/9781137390400_7

Gladfelter, A.S. & Haggis, W. (2022). Burnout among probation officers: The importance of resilience. *International Journal of Offender Therapy and Comparative Criminology*, 1–7 (June 2022, online ahead of print). https://doi.org/10.1177/0306624X221102835

Goldhill, R. (2019). The complexities of managing gendered violence in an English probation setting. *European Journal of Probation*, *11*(2), 53–71. https://doi.org/10.1177/2066220319862773

Herzog-Evans, M. & Sturgeon, J. (2022). Remote probation by phone in France and Scotland during the 2020 lockdown. *European Journal of Probation*, *14*(1), 60–78. https://doi.org/10.1177/20662203211056545

HM Inspectorate of Probation. (2020). *Supervision Skills*. www.justiceinspectorates.gov.uk/hmiprobation/research/the-evidence-base-probation/models-and-principles/supervision-skills

Hochschild, A.R. (1983). *The Managed Heart: Commercialization of Human Feeling*. University of California Press. www.jstor.org/stable/10.1525/j.ctt1pp0cf

Jeung, D.-Y., Kim, C. and Chang, S.-J. (2018). Emotional labour and burnout: A review of the literature. *Yonsei Medical Journal*, *59*(2), pp. 187–193. https://doi.org/10.3349/ymj.2018.59.2.187

Kirton, G. and Guillaume, C. (2015). *Employment Relations and Working Conditions in Probation after Transforming Rehabilitation: With a Special Focus on Gender and Union Effects*. Queen Mary University of London. www.napo.org.uk/employment-relations-and-working-conditions-probation-after-tr

Lee, R. (2017). The impact of engaging with clients' trauma stories: Personal and organizational strategies to manage probation practitioners' risk of developing vicarious traumatization. *Probation Journal*, *64*(4), 372–387. https://doi.org/10.1177/0264550517728783

Lewis, S. (2014). Learning from success and failure: Deconstructing the working relationship within probation practice and exploring its impact on probationers, using a collaborative approach. *Probation Journal*, *61*(2), 161–175. https://doi.org/10.1177/0264550514523816

McCartan, K. (2020). *Trauma-Informed Practice*. HM Inspectorate of Probation. www.justiceinspectorates.gov.uk/hmiprobation/wp-content/uploads/sites/5/2020/07/Academic-Insights-McCartan.pdf

Ministry of Justice (MoJ). (2018). *Female Offender Strategy*. https://assets.publishing.service.gov.uk/government/uploads/system/uploads/attachment_data/file/719819/female-offender-strategy.pdf

Moran, R.J. & Asquith, N.L. (2020). Understanding the vicarious trauma and emotional labour of criminological research. *Methodological Innovations*, *13*(2), 1–11. https://doi.org/10.1177/2059799120926085

Morran, D. (2008). Firing up and burning out: The personal and professional impact of working in domestic violence offender programmes. *Probation Journal, 55*(2), 139–152. https://doi.org/10.1177/0264550508090272

National Offender Management Service (NOMS). (2015). *Better outcomes for women offenders.* https://assets.publishing.service.gov.uk/government/uploads/system/uploads/attachment_data/file/457922/Better_Outcomes_for_Women_Offenders_September_2015.pdf

Office for Health Improvement & Disparities. (2022). *Working definition of trauma-informed practice.* www.gov.uk/government/publications/working-definition-of-trauma-informed-practice/working-definition-of-trauma-informed-practice

Petrillo, M. (2022). *Working with trauma in adult populations.* HM Inspectorate of Probation. www.justiceinspectorates.gov.uk/hmiprobation/wp-content/uploads/sites/5/2022/03/Working-with-trauma-in-adult-probation.pdf

Phillips, J., Waters, J., Westaby, C. & Fowler, A. (Eds.). (2020). *Emotional Labour in Criminal Justice and Criminology.* Routledge. https://doi.org/10.4324/9780429055669

Phillips, J., Westaby, C. & Fowler, A. (2016). 'It's relentless': The impact of working primarily with high-risk offenders. *Probation Journal, 63*(2), 182–192. https://doi.org/10.1177/0264550516648399

Phillips, J., Westaby, C. & Fowler, A. (2020). *Emotional Labour in Probation.* HM Inspectorate of Probation. www.justiceinspectorates.gov.uk/hmiprobation/wp-content/uploads/sites/5/2020/04/Emotional-Labour-in-Probation.pdf

Phillips, J., Westaby, C. & Fowler, A. (2021). 'I don't like this job in my front room': Practising probation in the COVID-19 pandemic. *Probation Journal, 68*(4), 426–443. https://doi.org/10.1177/02645505211050867

Probation Institute. (2020). Code of Ethics. https://static1.squarespace.com/static/5ec3ce97a1716758c54691b7/t/6077fcc51b514306fac41ebb/1618476230561/Code+of+Ethics.pdf

Ricciardelli, R. & Martin, K. (2017). Why corrections? Motivations for becoming a Canadian provincial or territorial correctional officer. *Journal of Criminological Research Policy and Practice, 3*(2), 274–286. https://doi.org/10.1108/JCRPP-01-2017-0001

Shepherd, B. (2022). Women working with women – vicarious trauma in the probation service. *Probation Quarterly, 24*, 24–28. https://doi.org/10.54006/XWXW8220

Tidmarsh, M. (2020a). The probation service in England and Wales: A decade of radical change or more of the same? *European Journal of Probation, 12*(2), 129–146. https://doi.org/10.1177/2066220320947243

Valcore, J., Fradella, H.F., Guadalupe-Diaz, X., Ball, M.J., Dwyer, A., DeJong, C. & Worthen, M.G. (2021). Building an intersectional and trans-inclusive criminology: Responding to the emergence of "gender critical" perspectives in feminist criminology. *Critical Criminology, 29*(4), 687–706. https://doi.org/10.1007/s10612-021-09590-0

Westaby, C., Fowler, A. & Phillips, J. (2020). Managing emotion in probation practice: Display rules, values and the performance of emotional labour. *International Journal of Law, Crime and Justice, 61*, 1–11. https://doi.org/10.1016/j.ijlcj.2019.100362

Westaby, C., Phillips, J. & Fowler, A. (2016). Spillover and work–family conflict in probation practice: Managing the boundary between work and home life. *European Journal of Probation*, *8*(3), 113–127. https://journals.sagepub.com/doi/epub/10.1177/2066220316680370

Westaby, C., Phillips, J., Fowler, A. & Ainslie, S. (2021). *An Evaluation of the Implementation of Reflective Practice Supervision Standards in the National Probation Service*. Sheffield Hallam University. http://shura.shu.ac.uk/28842/1/SEEDS2%20RPSS%20Report%20Final.pdf

Women in Prison. (2017). *Corston+10: The Corston Report 10 Years On*. https://womeninprison.org.uk/media/downloads/corston-report-10-years-on.pdf

6

BURNING OUT IN PROBATION

An Exploration of Organizational, Operational, and Personal Stressors Amongst Probation Workers in England and Wales

Jake Phillips, Sam Ainslie, Andrew Fowler, and Chalen Westaby

Introduction

Probation work can be incredibly demanding and stressful, and as a result, probation officers are at a high risk of experiencing burnout. Burnout is a state of physical, emotional, and mental exhaustion caused by prolonged and excessive stress (Leiter et al., 2015). Burnout can lead to feelings of cynicism, detachment, and a reduced sense of accomplishment, which can negatively impact the quality of the work being done by probation officers. The demanding nature of probation work can stem from a variety of internal and external factors. For example, probation officers are often responsible for managing a large caseload of clients who may have complex needs and challenging behaviours. This can involve conducting frequent meetings with clients, attending court hearings, and completing extensive paperwork (Canton and Dominey, 2017). In addition, probation officers may be exposed to situations that are potentially dangerous, such as working with individuals who have a history of violence or substance abuse.

The combination of these stressors can lead to burnout and have consequences for the probation officer and those under their supervision (i.e., their clients or probationers). Burnout refers to the emotional depletion and loss of motivation resulting from prolonged exposure to chronic emotional and interpersonal stress on the job (Leiter et al., 2015) and can lead to increased absenteeism, decreased job satisfaction, and higher staff turnover. Burnout can also negatively affect the quality of services provided by probation officers, which can compromise public safety and the well-being of their clients. To prevent burnout, probation officers must prioritize self-care and stress management techniques. However, just as crucial is for organizations

DOI: 10.4324/9781003424253-9

to recognize the risks of burnout and provide adequate resources and support for their probation officers, such as training, supervision, and opportunities for professional development. In this chapter, we explore the extant evidence on burnout in the field of probation work and present an original analysis of data collected from probation practitioners in England and Wales.

Burnout in Probation Work

A growing body of literature suggests that staff working in criminal justice are at risk of burnout and compromised well-being. Burnout is defined by three dimensions: emotional exhaustion (feeling 'burned out' from your work); depersonalization (becoming more cynical and detached); and having a sense of ineffectiveness and lack of accomplishment (Maslach et al., 2001). Burnout, then, is a chronic condition linked to low job satisfaction and high levels of stress, which leads to lower levels of efficacy and people choosing to leave their jobs. That said, there is still debate about the direction of causation here, and the relationship with mental health is complex. Some have argued that burnout causes compromised mental health (Toppinen-Tanner et al., 2005), while others have argued that people with poor mental health are more predisposed to burnout and people who are psychologically healthier are less likely to experience burnout (Maslach et al., 2001).

Burnout results from a range of factors, from the organizational through operational to the individual (Maslach et al., 2001; and see Table 6.3). Organizational factors include high and unmanageable workloads, role conflict, lack of support, limited autonomy, and a lack of organizational feedback. All of these are correlated with higher levels of burnout. Operationally, burnout is correlated with work involving a high level of caring, with emotion-work variables correlated with higher levels of burnout. Thus, jobs demanding a high degree of emotional labour (Hochschild, 1983) can account for higher levels of burnout. In the context of criminal justice work, evidence suggests that perceived or actual threats to personal safety from those under their supervision can also result in burnout (Ricciardelli & Carleton, 2021).

Much of the existing literature points to the primacy of organizational stressors in explaining burnout amongst probation officers around the world. A significant implication of this – as Brown (1987) states – is that if burnout is caused by the organization, individual stress-reducing techniques are likely to have little effect. For organizations, knowing what causes burnout is critical when trying to reduce it. Brown (1987) goes so far as to call burnout an 'organizational disease,' arguing – although without a great deal of empirical evidence – that the most significant influence on burnout is the work environment. Dir et al. (2019) explored levels of burnout amongst juvenile probation officers, again, in the United States (US) and found that a participatory atmosphere (i.e., where mental health stigma was low) was correlated with lower levels of burnout. Meanwhile, Uncel (2018) found a significant relationship between high caseloads and burnout in the US and Australia; it was found that 'role ambiguity, role conflict, and lack of participation in decision making' – mainly organizational factors – were significant contributors to burnout although the authors also point to the role of different personality types amongst younger practitioners (Holgate & Clegg, 1991, p. 325). Undoubtedly then, organizational stressors can contribute to stress and burnout, with one systematic review suggesting that 'role in the organization, rewards at work, supervisory relationships at work and the organizational structure and climate' are all central organizational stressors in criminal justice (Finney et al., 2013, p. 10). Finney and colleagues' (2013, p. 3) analysis suggests that 'organizational structure and climate' have the strongest link with stress and burnout in correctional work, again pointing to the argument that solutions to burnout cannot reside solely in individuals' actions.

Taking a more occupational-oriented perspective, Rhineberger-Dunn et al. (2017) found probation officers in the US were more likely to experience emotional exhaustion than less qualified residential workers suggesting the differences in the job role (most notably the extent to which offending behaviour is discussed) are invaluable. Similarly, Lewis et al. (2013) found occupational stressors appeared to be most strongly correlated with burnout, reporting in their sample of 309 US probation officers,

> officers who reported violent and sexual recidivism on their caseloads, offender suicide, and threats and/or assaults in the line of duty scored significantly higher on measures of traumatic stress and burnout than officers who did not experience these caseload event.
>
> *(p. 78)*

In relation to individual factors, Whitehead (1985, 1989) found that US probation staff with greater seniority (i.e., more experienced) were more likely to report higher levels of burnout. Although, overall, he reported that burnout did not appear to be as big a problem as one might expect. Through analysis of a sample of 115 Turkish probation officers, Ersayan et al. (2021) suggest attitudes towards clients are a significant predictor of burnout. Staff with negative attitudes towards prisoners are more likely to experience depersonalization, but there was no correlation between attitudes and emotional exhaustion. Also supporting the idea of how individual factors can explain burnout, Wirkus et al. (2021) tested levels of burnout against probation practitioners' preferred method of coping. In their sample of Polish probation officers, they found that staff who adopted an emotion-focused coping style were more likely to experience emotional exhaustion and, in response, recommended that practitioners adopt a more problem-focused approach to dealing with stressful situations.

There is, however, a significant emotional dimension to probation work and concomitant occupation stressors. Emotional labour – the management of emotions for a wage – has been found to be an inherent part of probation practice. Put simply, emotional labour asks practitioners to use their emotions to achieve the goals of the organization. Although emotions have been neglected in policy in probation in England and Wales (Fowler et al., 2020), research has found that practitioners perform emotional labour to develop relationships with service users, convey empathy, and assess risk (Westaby et al., 2019). Knight (2014) found that probation practitioners need a high degree of emotional literacy to practice effectively, as they must understand both their own emotions as well as those of people under supervision. Emotional labour – as a potential occupational stressor – is critical to consider because certain forms of emotional labour have been shown to correlate with a risk of burnout. In particular, occupations requiring high levels of surface acting – the suppression of one emotion and the display of another, more appropriate emotion – can result in higher levels of burnout (Guy et al., 2008; Hülsheger & Schewe, 2011). Considering probation practice involves high levels of emotional labour, one might assume these features of probation work may lead to more burnout amongst probation practitioners.

In all likelihood, burnout is the culmination of a complex combination of factors that individual staff members and groups of staff will experience in different ways. Norman and Ricciardelli's study of Canadian probation and parole officers in which interview data pointed to the importance of organizational and operational stressors: 'exposure to potentially psychologically traumatic events and secondary trauma, as well as three predominant organizational stressors: paperwork and administrative tasks, insufficient human resources, and workplace relationships and tensions' were all highlighted (2021, p. 2). These factors affect 'the mental health and well-being of community correctional workers, which in turn compromises their ability to effectively supervise and support individuals on their caseload' (Norman and Ricciardelli, 2021, p. 2).

Although burnout is defined using the three concepts of emotional exhaustion, depersonalization, and low perception of attainment, it manifests differently in different settings. Thus, Salyers et al. (2015) sought to explore how probation officers in the US experience burnout. They found that staff experience burnout as a sense of dread about going to work, apathy, and going through the motions, although the majority described burnout in terms of 'feeling overwhelmed and less caring about their job.' Confirming Norman and Ricciardelli's (2021) argument, Salyers et al. (2015) found that staff experiencing burnout reported being less tolerant and more directive with clients and doing the 'bare minimum.' In turn, their findings suggest burnout can lead to a lower standard of care and less effective practitioners and organizations. Evidence from other settings suggests that criminal justice workers are at a relatively raised risk of burnout, and probation practice entails many of the stressors correlated to burnout. Moreover, due to the lack of research conducted on the topic, this study was designed to explore the key factors behind variations in levels of burnout amongst probation staff working for the National Probation Service (NPS) in England and Wales.

Study Context

Before proceeding, it is necessary to outline the context in which probation is delivered in England and Wales. In 2014, the Government partially privatized the service and created the NPS and 20 privately run Community Rehabilitation Companies (CRC). The NPS was responsible for supervising people who had been assessed as posing a high risk of harm as well as writing reports for the courts. CRCs meanwhile supervised those deemed to pose a low- and medium risk of harm and delivered Unpaid Work (community service). In June 2021, CRCs ceased to exist, and all staff and service users were moved to a newly formed state-run Probation Service, which now supervises all people in England and Wales serving a community sanction or period of supervision following release from prison. The research in this chapter was undertaken in the NPS one year prior to the abolition of CRCs. Alongside these changes in the structure and governance of probation, the overarching aims of the service – and thus the nature of the job itself – have changed. Over recent decades governments have shifted the focus of the service to be more punitive in the context of what Garland (2001) has called the 'culture of control.' Probation in England and Wales is now a critical part of a punitive, enforcement-focused criminal justice landscape.

Methods

The data presented in this chapter were generated as part of a wider study which sought to evaluate the implementation of a new model of staff supervision in the NPS in England and Wales called the Reflective Practice Supervision Standards. The new model was intended to improve the quality of supervision provided to probation workers by recognizing the emotional impact of probation work and providing a framework of supervision which encouraged workers to make their own defensible decisions through reflective supervision sessions and observations of practice (Ainslie et al., 2022; Westaby et al., 2021). As part of the wider study, we generated data through a survey with probation workers and senior probation officers around burnout (by measuring levels of emotional exhaustion and depersonalization) and some potential stressors which may or may not be correlated with higher levels of burnout. In our analysis, we explore these connections by answering the research question: what correlations exist between organizational, operational, and individual stressors and variations in emotional exhaustion and depersonalization across participants in our sample?

The survey was administered using the online survey software Qualtrics. The survey link was sent to a total of 6,780 probation officers, probation services officers,[1] trainee probation officers, and senior probation officers across England and Wales in February 2020. A follow-up email was sent after two weeks. Then, the UK entered a period of lockdown due to the COVID-19 coronavirus pandemic, and so no further reminder emails were sent. The survey was left open for a further two weeks. A total of 1,727 probation workers responded to the survey from all regions of the NPS, representing a response rate of 25.5%. A breakdown of our sample can be found in Tables 6.1 and 6.2.

Burnout was measured using questions from the Maslach Burnout Inventory, in line with the process undertaken by Adams and Mastracci (2020). A latent variable and the Cronbach alpha were calculated for emotional exhaustion

TABLE 6.1 Breakdown of sample according to gender, ethnicity, and role

		N	*Percentage of sample*
Gender	Man	323	18.7
	Woman	919	53.2
	Prefer not to say/other	38	2.2
	Missing	447	25.9
Ethnicity	White	1119	64.8
	Mixed	39	2.3
	Asian	35	2.0
	Black	71	4.1
	Any other ethnic background	3	0.5
	Missing	454	26.3
Role	PQIP student (trainee probation officer)	246	14.2
	Probation service officer	360	20.8
	Probation officer	557	34.7
	Senior probation officer	218	12.6
	Other	224	13
	Missing	122	7.1

TABLE 6.2 Breakdown of sample according to age and length of service

	Range	*Mean*	*SD*
Age (years)	18–73	43.1	12.1
Length of service (years)	0–45	11.9	9.4

TABLE 6.3 Organizational, occupational, and individual stressors in probation

Organizational stressors	*Occupational stressors*	*Individual stressors*
Caseloads	Role	Gender
Perceived lack of organizational support	Extent of surface acting performed	Age
Division in which they work	Extent of deep acting performed	Ethnicity
Overtime worked		Amount of sleep
		Emotional awareness of others
		Emotional self-awareness

TABLE 6.4 Emotional exhaustion and depersonalization amongst probation practitioners in England and Wales

	N	*Mean*	*Std. deviation*	*Std. error mean*
Emotional exhaustion	1347	4.1	1.5	.04
Depersonalization	1361	3.7	1.4	.04

(0.874) and depersonalization (0.629). Both variables passed the test for reliability and are therefore included in the analysis below.

To assess the effect of different types of stressors on our two dependent variables, we undertook an analysis of the effect of the following variables as we considered these to be potentially significant in light of the findings from previous literature, we previously outlined (see Table 6.3).

Independent samples t-tests and one-way ANOVAs were carried out to calculate the difference in means across the different groups for gender, role, and ethnicity. All other independent variables were measured on a 7-point Likert scale, and, in response, we undertook Pearson coefficient correlations to assess the strength and direction of correlations between these variables.

Results

Table 6.4 shows the mean scores for emotional exhaustion and depersonalization amongst our sample. Both emotional exhaustion and depersonalization were measured on a seven-point Likert scale. For comparison, police officers in Adams and Mastracci's (2020) US-based study reported mean scores of 4.49 for emotional exhaustion (n = 175) and 5.30 for depersonalization (n = 172).

The two variables are correlated, as shown in Table 6.3, where Pearson's correlation coefficient shows a medium-strength correlation. Thus, participants who were more likely to report higher levels of emotional exhaustion were also more likely to report higher levels of depersonalization.

TABLE 6.5 Correlation between emotional exhaustion and depersonalization amongst probation practitioners in England and Wales

		Emotional exhaustion	*Depersonalization*
Emotional exhaustion	Pearson correlation	1	.394**
	Sig. (2-tailed)		.000
	N	1347	1341
Depersonalization	Pearson correlation	.394**	1
	Sig. (2-tailed)	.000	
	N	1341	1361

**. Correlation is significant at the 0.01 level (2-tailed).

TABLE 6.6 Emotional exhaustion and depersonalization amongst probation practitioners, by gender

	What is your gender?	*N*	*Mean*	*Std. deviation*	*Std. error mean*
Emotional exhaustion	Man	320	3.8	1.5	.08
	Woman**	901	4.2	1.5	.04
Depersonalization	Man	322	3.8	1.4	.08
	Woman	913	3.7	1.4	.05

** = p<0.001

Individual and Demographic Level Stressors

Gender and Ethnicity

Burnout manifests differently between women and men, with men more likely to show signs of burnout as depersonalization, whilst women are more likely to experience burnout as emotional exhaustion (Artz et al., 2022). Independent samples t-tests of emotional exhaustion and depersonalization across men and women in our sample (Table 6.6) reveal how women reported statistically significant ($t = -3.23$, $p = 0.001$) higher levels of emotional exhaustion. Although men reported higher levels of depersonalization, the finding was nonsignificant ($t = 1.419$, $p = .155$).

Burnout has been shown to be the product of organizational stressors, including a lack of organizational support and the fact that recent work undertaken in probation in England and Wales has found a high degree of racial inequality exists within the service (HMI Probation, 2021b), one might also expect one's ethnicity to be correlated with emotional exhaustion or burnout. Therefore, ANOVA tests were used to identify differences in

TABLE 6.7 Emotional exhaustion and depersonalization amongst probation practitioners, by ethnicity

Ethnicity	*Emotional exhaustion Mean (n=)*	*Depersonalization mean (N=)*
Black	3.8 (69)	3.3 (70)
Mixed	3.8 (38)	3.5 (39)
White	4.1 (1100)	3.7 (1113)
Asian	4.3 (35)	4.0 (35)
Any other ethnic group	4.9 (9)	3.9 (9)

emotional exhaustion and depersonalization between different ethnic groups in our sample. Table 6.7 shows that while there was some variance in the means, Tukey's post-hoc test showed none of these differences was statistically significant; thus, what may be attributed to ethnic differences may actually be inherent to their occupational work.

We were interested in the connection between age, length of service, and time spent supervising clients with burnout. One might expect people who have been in the service longer to be more likely to be experiencing burnout because burnout is a condition that builds up over time in situations of high stress. On the other hand, people develop coping strategies for burnout over time, and so – conversely – those with more life and work experience may report lower levels of burnout. The case could be, however, that those who experienced such high levels of burnout have left the service altogether or were too burnt out to participate.

Age is statistically significantly negatively correlated with emotional exhaustion (Table 6.8): older practitioners report lower levels of burnout. Depersonalization is statistically significantly and negatively correlated with all three variables here, meaning people who have been working on probation and supervising clients for longer and/or are older are more likely to report lower levels of depersonalization.

Sleep

Insufficient sleep has been shown to predict burnout (Söderström et al., 2012) because sleep 'is an essential biological purpose and has a major responsibility in recovery, energy conservation, and survival' (Mukherjee et al., 2015). However, there is a lack of knowledge about the direction of the association between sleep and burnout – does less sleep cause burnout, or does burnout create more sleep problems? Nonetheless, we explored the correlation between how much sleep our participants got on a nightly basis and reported levels of emotional exhaustion and depersonalization (Table 6.9). The amount of sleep people receive is statistically significantly correlated

TABLE 6.8 Emotional exhaustion and depersonalization amongst probation practitioners, by age and length of service

		Emotional exhaustion	*Depersonalization*
How many years have you been working in probation?	Pearson correlation	−.02	−.16**
	Sig. (2-tailed)	.290	.000
	N	1312	1323
How long have you supervised people on probation?	Pearson correlation	.06	−.09**
	Sig. (2-tailed)	.054	.004
	N	1009	1022
How old are you?	Pearson correlation	−.14**	−.23**
	Sig. (2-tailed)	.000	.000
	N	1201	1217

TABLE 6.9 Emotional exhaustion and depersonalization amongst probation practitioners, by hours of sleep

		Emotional exhaustion	*Depersonalization*
How many hours of sleep do you average in a 24-hour period?	Pearson correlation	−.154**	−.064*
	Sig. (2-tailed)	.000	.022
	N	1271	1284

**. Correlation is significant at the 0.01 level (2-tailed).
*. Correlation is significant at the 0.05 level (2-tailed).

with lower levels of both emotional exhaustion and depersonalization, albeit weakly (i.e., the more people sleep, the less emotional exhaustion and depersonalization they experience). It is not possible to test the direction of this association.

Emotional Intelligence

A Pearson's correlation found a weak but statistically significant correlation between emotional awareness of others (EOA) and emotional exhaustion $r = 0.054$, $p = .048$. This suggests probation practitioners who are more emotionally aware of others are more likely to report higher levels of emotional exhaustion. There was a nonsignificant correlation between EOA and emotional exhaustion.

Emotional Self-Awareness was found to be weakly negatively correlated with both emotional exhaustion ($r = -.116$, $p = .000$.) and depersonalization ($r = 0.054$, $p = .048$. Thus, the more emotionally self-aware probation practitioners are less likely to report higher levels of burnout.

TABLE 6.10 Emotional and depersonalization amongst probation practitioners, by emotional intelligence

		Emotional exhaustion	*Depersonalization*
Emotional awareness of others	Pearson correlation	.054*	-.018
	Sig. (2-tailed)	.048	.506
	N	1335	1350
Emotional self-awareness	Pearson correlation	-.116**	-.054*
	Sig. (2-tailed)	.000	.048
	N	1343	1357

** Correlation is significant at the 0.01 level (2-tailed).
* Correlation is significant at the 0.05 level (2-tailed).

Organizational Stressors

Caseload

Previous studies have found workload to be a strong predictor of burnout in several professions, and, in response, we sought to understand the link between workload and burnout in our participants. To do this, we used caseload as an imperfect proxy of workload. Caseload is an imperfect proxy because some clients demand much more time than others, and a simple measure of caseload does not account for this variation. Moreover, caseload does not reflect the other jobs which practitioners must do over and above supervising people on probation. For example, many practitioners hold specialist roles such as the women's champion, contact for youth offending team transfers, or link officers for trainees. None of these are equated in the workload management tool. Equally, they all perform 'duty officer' roles for colleagues on leave/sickness absence. We also have in our sample several practitioners who do not carry a caseload, such as programme facilitators or people who work solely in courts writing reports. These people are, therefore, excluded from the analysis below.

Nonetheless, we found a statistically significant correlation between caseload and emotional exhaustion ($r = .10$ $p=0.04$). No statistically significant correlation between caseload size and depersonalization was found.

Overtime

The number of hours worked as overtime is a useful alternative to caseload as a measure of workload. In total, 66.8% (N = 153) of our sample reported working more than their contracted hours, and 38.2% (N = 660) reported doing so weekly or daily. A chi-squared test and Cramer's V correlation

TABLE 6.11 Emotional exhaustion and depersonalization amongst probation practitioners, by caseload

		Emotional exhaustion	*Depersonalization*
How many clients are you currently supervising?	Pearson correlation	.102**	–.026
	Sig. (2-tailed)	.004	.459
	N	807	820

** Correlation is significant at the 0.01 level (2-tailed).

TABLE 6.12 Emotional exhaustion and depersonalization by probation practitioners, by overtime

	Do you ever work more than your contracted hours per week?	*N*	*Mean*	*Std. deviation*	*Std. error mean*
Emotional exhaustion	Yes	1134	4.1	1.5	.04
	No	145	3.5	1.5	.12
Depersonalization	Yes	1147	3.7	1.4	.04
	No	146	3.4	1.3	.10

were performed to find that probation officers (91.1%, N = 448) and senior probation officers (95.1%, N = 135) were statistically significantly more likely to work overtime, X^2 (4, N = 1295) = 16.192, p = .003, V = .112. To identify a difference between overtime and burnout, an independent samples t-test was carried out using emotional exhaustion and depersonalization as dependent variables and responses to the question 'Do you ever work more than your contracted hours per week?' as the independent variable.

The t-test revealed a statistically significantly higher mean for both emotional exhaustion and depersonalization amongst people who said they work more than their contracted hours. For emotional exhaustion, those who worked overtime (M = 4.1, SD = 1.5) were statistically significantly higher than those who did not (M = 3.569, SD = 1.497), t(1277) = 4.471, *p* = 0.001. Those who worked overtime (M = 3.7446, SD = 1.398) reported higher levels of depersonalization than those who did not (M = 3.493, SD = 1.306), t(1291) = 2.062, p = 0.001.

Perceived Organizational Support

Perceived organizational support has been found to be correlated with burnout amongst criminal justice practitioners and other professionals (Yaghoubi et al., 2014; Zeng et al., 2020). Perceived organizational support is seen to reduce

TABLE 6.13 Emotional exhaustion and depersonalization amongst probation officers, by perceived organizational support

		Emotional exhaustion	*Depersonalization*
Perceived organizational support	Pearson correlation	−.36**	−.24**
	Sig. (2-tailed)	.000	.000
	N	1286	1286

**. Correlation is significant at the 0.01 level (2-tailed).

burnout because support helps practitioners deal with the specific demands that the job makes of them. We thus sought to understand whether this stands up for probation practitioners in England and Wales.

A statistically significant moderate inverse correlation between perceived organizational support and emotional exhaustion (r = −.36, p = 0.001) and depersonalization (r = −.24, p = 0.001) was found. This mirrors research in other settings where probation practitioners in England and Wales with low levels of perceived organizational support are likely to report higher levels of both emotional exhaustion and depersonalization.

Division

In England and Wales, there is a significant difference across geographical divisions, with each local region having a degree of autonomy over how local services are run. Moreover, divisions experience different workloads and pressures in terms of who is on the caseload. Divisions covering the large cities (London, Greater Manchester, and Birmingham) are more likely to be working with people who pose a higher risk of harm because of the higher levels of organized crime, violence, and gang-related offending. HMI Probation – the body which has the responsibility for inspecting probation providers – has found significant differences in the quality of the work delivered by divisions. This has been put down – to some extent[2] – to high workloads. We thus explored whether there were differences in burnout between the different divisions through a Multivariate Analysis of Variance (MANOVA) calculation and Tukey's post-hoc test to discern differences in means across the divisions.

No statistically significant differences in the means for depersonalization were found. For emotional exhaustion, an F test found a statistically significant difference in means between the divisions ($F_{6,1332} = 3.204$, $p = 0.004$). Tukey's HSD Test for multiple comparisons found the mean value for emotional exhaustion amongst participants in London was significantly higher than in the Midlands and North West (p = <0.05, 95% C.I. = [4.2155, 4.6980], but there were no other statistically different means between divisions.

TABLE 6.14 Emotional exhaustion and depersonalization amongst probation providers, by division

	N	*Mean*	*Std. deviation*	*Std. error*
North West	239	3.9	1.4	.09
North East	110	4.3	1.5	.14
Wales	114	3.9	1.4	.13
South East	242	4.1	1.4	.09
Midlands	255	3.9	1.5	.10
London	133	4.5	1.4	.12
South West and South Central	246	3.9	1.5	.10

Occupational Stressors

The nature of one's work has also been found to be correlated with stress and burnout (Gladfelter & Haggis, 2022; McCarty et al., 2007; Oddie & Ousley, 2007) and we sought to understand the extent to which each plays out in probation in England and Wales.

Role

When this survey was carried out, the NPS held statutory responsibility for the assessment and management of people considered to pose a high risk of harm or who presented with complex needs requiring significant intervention and oversight. Working in such an organization is relentless and poses a risk to all staff's well-being (Phillips et al., 2016). However, the grade of staff determined the nature of work undertaken within the NPS, with POs shouldering the responsibility for supervising the highest risk individuals whilst PSOs and trainee probation officers (PQiP students) were responsible for oversight and intervention with those convicted of less serious offences or who were further through their period of supervision and deemed to have reduced the level of risk posed to others. As such, we explored the differences in burnout between different roles.

A Tukey's HSD test found that POs reported statistically significantly higher levels of emotional exhaustion than all other role types. POs also reported higher levels of depersonalization than all other roles except for PQIP students. SPOs reported statistically significantly lower levels of depersonalization than all other roles except for 'Other.'

Emotional Labour

As noted above, probation practitioners perform high levels of emotional labour as part of their jobs. This emotional labour is most likely to take place

TABLE 6.15 Emotional exhaustion and depersonalization amongst probation practitioners, by role

What is your role?		*Emotional exhaustion*	*Depersonalization*
Probation officer	Mean	4.5*	4.0*
	N	505	508
	Std. deviation	1.4	1.4
Probation service officer	Mean	3.8	3.6
	N	311	318
	Std. deviation	1.4	1.4
PQIP student	Mean	3.8	3.7
	N	197	200
	Std. deviation	1.4	1.3
Other (please specify)	Mean	3.5	3.5
	N	180	182
	Std. deviation	1.6	1.5
SPO	Mean	4.0	3.2*
	N	149	148
	Std. deviation	1.5	1.2
Total	Mean	4.1	3.7
	N	1342	1356
	Std. deviation	1.5	1.4

* Correlation is significant at the 0.001 level (2-tailed).

in the context of one-on-one work with people on probation. Moreover, the literature suggests a correlation between the performance of emotional labour and burnout (Jeung et al., 2018). We thus carried out a series of Pearson's coefficients to identify the extent certain ways of performing emotional labour are linked to emotional exhaustion and depersonalization within our sample.

All forms of emotional labour are statistically significantly correlated with higher levels of burnout. The strongest correlations were found between the performance of emotional labour, which involves the suppression of emotion, such as surface acting. The weakest correlation was found between deep acting and emotional exhaustion and depersonalization. The analysis shows how the more emotional labour probation practitioners do, the more likely they are to report high levels of both emotional exhaustion and depersonalization.

Discussion

Our analysis suggests that some personal, organizational, and operational stressors are correlated with higher levels of burnout among practitioners. The strongest connections were found between organizational and operational stressors, with perceived organizational support and overtime both being found to be moderately correlated with burnout.

TABLE 6.16 Emotional exhaustion and depersonalization amongst probation practitioners, by emotional labour variable

		Emotional exhaustion	*Depersonalization*
Pretend display rules	Pearson correlation	0.3**	0.3**
	Sig. (2-tailed)	.000	.000
	N	1326	1341
Suppression of emotion	Pearson correlation	0.3**	0.2**
	Sig. (2-tailed)	.000	.000
	N	1292	1306
Surface acting	Pearson correlation	0.4**	0.4**
	Sig. (2-tailed)	.000	.000
	N	1310	1323
Deep acting	Pearson correlation	0.1**	0.1**
	Sig. (2-tailed)	.000	.000
	N	1305	1318

**. Correlation is significant at the 0.01 level (2-tailed).

Emotionally exhausted practitioners are more likely to become risk averse as a coping mechanism against what might happen if something were to go wrong. Moreover, depersonalization – which can manifest as negative and excessively detached responses to colleagues and so has significant dysfunctional ramifications for both organizations and their members – can lead to absenteeism (Maslach & Jackson, 1981), reduced job satisfaction (Lee et al., 2011), reduced commitment, and turnover intentions (Halbesleben & Buckley, 2004). Our data show men are more likely to report higher levels of depersonalization, whilst women are more likely to report higher levels of emotional exhaustion. In terms of staff being able to identify when they might be experiencing burnout, they need to know whether and where to look for signs of these two key components of burnout. Similarly, as our data point to a higher prevalence of burnout amongst probation officers, it is this group which should be alert to signs of burnout. Knowing who is most at risk of emotional exhaustion and depersonalization within an organization represents a necessary step in terms of understanding how an organization functions but – more fundamentally – how an organization can protect its staff and continue being effective, thus supporting staff wellness.

We have reported elsewhere how staff supervision in the Probation Service is patchy (Westaby et al., 2021), and senior probation officers find themselves stuck between practitioners and the organization (Westaby et al., 2022), which has a deleterious impact on their ability to supervise practitioners effectively. Staff have also told us the employee support service provided is not fit for purpose whilst those who have received clinical supervision as part of their role have been very positive about the impact this has on their wider well-being (Phillips et al., 2016). Improving the extent to which people feel supported would – we hypothesize – reduce the levels of burnout amongst probation practitioners.

Our analysis would suggest one mechanism underpinning a connection between high caseloads and lower quality work (HMI Probation, 2021a) could be the increased amount of burnout amongst those people with high caseloads. These issues appear to have become more acute since the process of unification (i.e., after this research was conducted), and so it is reasonable to assume that the stressors which were contributing to higher levels of burnout amongst our participants in 2020 are even more pertinent post-unification.

How people in an organization feel is a strong indicator of how an organization is operating, and so our data raise potential implications for the oversight and governance of probation services. We would suggest that organizations which are responsible for quality-assuring probation (such as the Ministry of Justice and HMI Probation) should consider using measures of burnout within the inspection and other quality assurance processes. Probation work is underpinned by relational practice, and so organizations need people to be emotionally healthy to meet organizational roles and objectives.

Limitations

Although we have explored a range of variables and how they correlate with burnout, we have not been able to undertake an analysis which sheds light on which of these stressors has a lesser or greater effect on burnout using, for example, a linear regression model. Moreover, we did not test for variables which might have been happening outside of work (except for sleep), which may have an impact on burnout experienced at work. Considering probation practitioners have reported the presence of work–family conflict, this represents an important area for future research. Finally, we were unable to test for exposure to psychological or physical trauma (Norman & Ricciardelli, 2021) as we did not collect data on this variable. In future work, we would suggest using a more accurate measure of workload than caseload or overtime, as these fail to capture the breadth of what being overworked in probation might entail.

Conclusion

Probation work and probation organizations appear to create a risk of burnout for staff. A workforce that is emotionally exhausted and/or showing signs of depersonalization is likely to be less effective. In the context of probation, this means protecting the public becomes more difficult because it becomes more difficult for practitioners to develop constructive professional relationships which underpin good quality probation supervision because they have less emotional resilience to use when creating and nurturing professional relationships with those they supervise (Maslach & Jackson, 1981). Moreover, our analysis suggests burnout is an occupational and organizational problem: solutions which reside at the individual level are unlikely to be effective. Low levels of perceived organizational support, caseload, overtime, and operational stressors are the strongest predictors of burnout in our data, and this raises substantial implications for the Probation Service.

Criminal justice professionals have been found to be at risk of burnout, yet little research has explored the prevalence of burnout amongst probation practitioners in England and Wales. Although the causes of burnout are complex, research has suggested that personal, operational, and organizational stressors can all contribute. Our data suggest organizational and operational stressors appear more strongly correlated with burnout than individual stressors. Our findings raise ramifications for probation organizations more broadly in terms of supporting people with the risks that probation work poses. They may also explain why the Probation Service in England and Wales currently has high levels of stress-related absence, policy failures, and high staff turnover. Fundamentally, our data point to the importance of recognizing the risk of burnout amongst public safety personnel and taking action such that organizations continue to protect the public and support people in the criminal justice system.

Notes

1 Probation services officers undertake similar roles to probation officers but supervise low- and medium-risk cases. Probation Officers can supervise people who are assessed as high-risk.
2 Other explanations include the impact of organizational restructures, poor training, and supervision.

References

Adams, I. T., & Mastracci, S. H. (2020). Hidden in plain sight: Contrasting emotional labor and burnout in civilian and sworn law enforcement employees. In *Emotional Labour in Criminal Justice and Criminology*. Routledge.

Ainslie, S., Fowler, A., Phillips, J., & Westaby, C. (2022). 'A nice idea but....': Implementing a reflective supervision model in the National Probation Service in England and Wales. *Reflective Practice*, *0*(0), 1–14. https://doi.org/10.1080/14623943.2022.2066075

Artz, B., Kaya, I., & Kaya, O. (2022). Gender role perspectives and job burnout. *Review of Economics of the Household*, *20*(2), 447–470. https://doi.org/10.1007/s11150-021-09579-2

Brown, P. W. (1987). Probation officer burnout. *Federal Probation*, *51*(3), 17–21.

Canton, R., & Dominey, J. (2017) *Probation* (2nd edition). Routledge.

Dir, A. L., Saldana, L., Chapman, J. E., & Aalsma, M. C. (2019). Burnout and mental health stigma among juvenile probation officers: The moderating effect of participatory atmosphere. *Administration and Policy in Mental Health*, *46*(2), 167–174. https://doi.org/10.1007/s10488-018-0902-x

Ersayan, A. E., Çankaya, B., Erdem, G., Broers, N. J., & de Ruiter, C. (2021). The link between attitudes toward probationers and job burnout in Turkish probation officers. *Journal of Community Psychology*, *n/a*(n/a). https://doi.org/10.1002/jcop.22673

Finney, C., Stergiopoulos, E., Hensel, J., Bonato, S., & Dewa, C. S. (2013). Organizational stressors associated with job stress and burnout in correctional officers: A systematic review. *BMC Public Health*, *13*(1), 82. https://doi.org/10.1186/1471-2458-13-82

Fowler, A., Phillips, J., & Westaby, C. (2020). Emotions in context: The marginalisation and persistence of emotional labour in probation. In J. Phillips, J. Waters, C. Westaby, & A. Fowler (Eds.), *Emotional Labour in Criminal Justice and Criminology* (1st edition, pp. 54–68). Routledge.

Garland, D. (2001). *The Culture of Control: Crime and Social Order in Contemporary Society*. Clarendon.

Gladfelter, A. S., & Haggis, W. A. (2022). Burnout among probation officers: The importance of resilience. *International Journal of Offender Therapy and Comparative Criminology*, 0306624X221102835. https://doi.org/10.1177/0306624X221102835

Guy, M. E., Newman, M. A., & Mastracci, S. H. (2008). *Emotional Labor: Putting the Service in Public Service* (1 edition). Routledge.

Halbesleben, J. R., & Buckley, M. R. (2004). Burnout in organizational life. *Journal of management*, *30*(6), 859–879.

HMI Probation. (2021a). *Caseloads, workloads and staffing levels in probation services* (No. 2021/02; Research & Analysis Bulletin). HMI Probation.

HMI Probation. (2021b). *Race equality in probation: The experiences of black, Asian and minority ethnic probation service users and staff*. HMI Probation.

Hochschild, A. R. (1983). *The Managed Heart: Commercialization of Human Feeling*. University of California Press.

Holgate, A. M., & Clegg, I. J. (1991). The path to probation officer burnout: New dogs, old tricks. *Journal of Criminal Justice*, *19*(4), 325–337. https://doi.org/10.1016/0047-2352(91)90030-Y

Hülsheger, U. R., & Schewe, A. F. (2011). On the costs and benefits of emotional labor: A meta-analysis of three decades of research. *Journal of Occupational Health Psychology*, *16*(3), 361–389. https://doi.org/10.1037/a0022876

Jeung, D.-Y., Kim, C., & Chang, S.-J. (2018). Emotional labor and burnout: A review of the literature. *Yonsei Medical Journal*, *59*(2), 187–193. https://doi.org/10.3349/ymj.2018.59.2.187

Knight, C. (2014). *Emotional Literacy in Criminal Justice*. Palgrave Macmillan. www.dawsonera.com/abstract/9781137273215

Lee, J., Lim, N., Yang, E., & Lee, S. M. (2011). Antecedents and consequences of three dimensions of burnout in psychotherapists: A meta-analysis. *Professional Psychology: Research and Practice*, *42*(3), 252.

Leiter, M. P., Maslach, C., & Frame, K. (2015). Burnout. In R. L. Cautin & S. O. Lilienfeld (Eds.), *The Encyclopedia of Clinical Psychology* (pp. 1–7). John Wiley & Sons, Ltd. https://doi.org/10.1002/9781118625392.wbecp142

Lewis, K. R., Lewis, L. S., & Garby, T. M. (2013). Surviving the trenches: The personal impact of the job on probation officers. *American Journal of Criminal Justice*, *38*(1), 67–84. https://doi.org/10.1007/s12103-012-9165-3

Maslach, C., & Jackson, S. E. (1981). The measurement of experienced burnout. *Journal of Organizational Behavior, 2*(2), 99–113. https://doi.org/10.1002/job.4030020205

Maslach, C., Schaufeli, W. B., & Leiter, M. P. (2001). Job burnout. *Annual Review of Psychology, 52*(1), 397–422. https://doi.org/10.1146/annurev.psych.52.1.397

McCarty, W. P., "Solomon" Zhao, J., & Garland, B. E. (2007). Occupational stress and burnout between male and female police officers: Are there any gender differences? *Policing: An International Journal of Police Strategies & Management, 30*(4), 672–691. https://doi.org/10.1108/13639510710833938

Mukherjee, S., Patel, S. R., Kales, S. N., Ayas, N. T., Strohl, K. P., Gozal, D., & Malhotra, A. (2015). An official American Thoracic Society statement: The importance of healthy sleep. Recommendations and future priorities. *American Journal of Respiratory and Critical Care Medicine, 191*(12), 1450–1458. https://doi.org/10.1164/rccm.201504-0767ST

Norman, M., & Ricciardelli, R. (2021). Operational and organizational stressors in community correctional work: Insights from probation and parole officers in Ontario, Canada. *Probation Journal*, 0264550520984253. https://doi.org/10.1177/0264550520984253

Oddie, S., & Ousley, L. (2007). Assessing burn-out and occupational stressors in a medium secure service. *The British Journal of Forensic Practice, 9*(2), 32–48. https://doi.org/10.1108/14636646200700011

Phillips, J., Westaby, C., & Fowler, A. (2016). 'It's relentless' the impact of working primarily with high-risk offenders. *Probation Journal, 63*(2), 182–192. https://doi.org/10.1177/0264550516648399

Rhineberger-Dunn, G., Mack, K. Y., & Baker, K. M. (2017). Comparing demographic factors, background characteristics, and workplace perceptions as predictors of burnout among community corrections officers. *Criminal Justice and Behavior, 44*(2), 205–225. https://doi.org/10.1177/0093854816666583

Ricciardelli, R., & Carleton, R. N. (2021). A qualitative application of the Job Demand-Control-Support (JDCS) to contextualize the occupational stress correctional workers experience. *Journal of Crime and Justice, 0*(0), 1–17. https://doi.org/10.1080/0735648X.2021.1893790

Salyers, M. P., Hood, B. J., Schwartz, K., Alexander, A. O., & Aalsma, M. C. (2015). The experience, impact, and management of professional burnout among probation officers in juvenile justice settings. *Journal of Offender Rehabilitation, 54*(3), 175–193. https://doi.org/10.1080/10509674.2015.1009967

Söderström, M., Jeding, K., Ekstedt, M., Perski, A., & Akerstedt, T. (2012). Insufficient sleep predicts clinical burnout. *Journal of Occupational Health Psychology, 17*(2), 175–183. https://doi.org/10.1037/a0027518

Toppinen-Tanner, S., Ojajärvi, A., Väänänen, A., Kalimo, R., & Jäppinen, P. (2005). Burnout as a predictor of medically certified sick-leave absences and their diagnosed causes. *Behavioral Medicine, 31*(1), 18–32. https://doi.org/10.3200/BMED.31.1.18-32

Uncel, T. D. (2018). *Predictors of Burnout in Community Corrections.* Texas A&M University-Commerce.

Westaby, C., Fowler, A., & Phillips, J. (2019). Managing emotion in probation practice: Display rules, values and the performance of emotional labour. *International Journal of Law, Crime and Justice, 61*(June 2020), 100362. https://doi.org/10.1016/j.ijlcj.2019.100362

Westaby, C., Phillips, J., Fowler, A., & Ainslie, S. (2021). *An evaluation of the implementation of reflective practice supervision standards in the national probation service*. Sheffield Hallam University. https://doi.org/10.7190/shu.HKCIJ.07.21

Westaby, C., Phillips, J., Fowler, A., & Ainslie, S. (2022). 'Pushed from above and pushed from below': Emotional labour and dual identities amongst senior probation officers in England and Wales. *European Journal of Probation*, *15*(1), 40–59.

Whitehead, J. T. (1985). Job Burnout in Probation and Parole: Its Extent and Intervention Implications. *Criminal Justice and Behavior*, *12*(1), 91–110. https://doi.org/10.1177/0093854885012001007

Whitehead, J. T. (1989). *Burnout in Probation and Corrections* (pp. xii, 159). Praeger Publishers.

Wirkus, Ł., Babicka-Wirkus, A., Opora, R., & Stasiak, K. (2021). Burnout among probation officers in Poland and the role of preferred styles of coping with stress. *International Journal of Environmental Research and Public Health*, *18*(1), Article 1. https://doi.org/10.3390/ijerph18010355

Yaghoubi, N. M., Pourghaz, A., & Toomaj, H. G. (2014). Study of perceived organizational support's relationship with job burnout. *International Journal of Academic Research in Business and Social Sciences*, *4*(6), 315–324. https://doi.org/10.6007/IJARBSS/v4-i6/961

Zeng, X., Zhang, X., Chen, M., Liu, J., & Wu, C. (2020). The influence of perceived organizational support on police job burnout: A moderated mediation model. *Frontiers in Psychology*, *11*. www.frontiersin.org/articles/10.3389/fpsyg.2020.00948

7

EVALUATING WORKPLACE STRESS IN CORRECTIONAL SERVICES

Marina Carbonell, Joy C. MacDermid, and Rosemary Ricciardelli

Introduction

Prison, living or working, is a society in itself. The correctional environment and services cross with the courts and police services but are unique in the duration of service provision to service users (Flaherty & Carceral, 2022). For example, a criminalized adult may interact with police when charged and the courts through conviction(s) but will interact with correctional services for the duration of their sentence – which can be life (i.e., their warrant expires at death). Thus, encounters with correctional environments are not as temporary as encounters with police or courts. In addition, correctional work exists in unique, distinctive, and complex work/living environments shaped by local processes and social norms (Carbonell & Ricciardelli, 2023; Ricciardelli & McKendy, 2020), as well as formalized rules and governance structures (Ricciardelli & McKendy, 2020; Sygit-Kowalkowska et al., 2023). Each prison workspace can have its own work culture, and workplaces change over time (Crawley & Crawley, 2007). This environment of prolonged carceral care involves intimate exposure to the lives of prisoners and peers; working long hours in a confined space obstructs privacy (Crawley & Crawley, 2007). In addition, Correctional Officers (COs) are responsible for the "custody, control and care of prisoners" (Ricciardelli & McKendy, 2020, p. 618), where prisoners are involuntarily incarcerated, and experiencing a loss of control, privacy, and opportunity while waiting for release (Flaherty & Carceral, 2022). The nature of correctional work within this purpose and mandate of correctional workers means staff will be exposed to unavoidable operational stressors inherent to the

DOI: 10.4324/9781003424253-10

occupation (Coulling et al., 2024), and the correctional workspace ostensibly includes occupational stresses, both organizational and operational stresses (Duxbury & Higgins, 2001; Johnson et al., 2024).

While researchers have explored the types of occupational stressors, both operational and organizational, for correctional officers and correctional workers and their impact on well-being, these identified factors may appear segmented and difficult to evaluate and understand for non-academics within the published literature. Developed stress evaluation measures can be complicated to use and, thus, inaccessible for employers, employees, and their advocates; they are often behind paywalls,[1] they can require skills in quantitative methods for a full analysis of a workplace, and they may focus on physical elements of stress while ignoring the social, cultural, and psychological elements of workplace stress.

In the current chapter, we explore occupational stress broadly, with a focus on the correctional workplace. Through discussion of the gaps in current stress assessment measures, barriers to self-reporting, and limitations to studying workplace stress, we present a broader, straightforward stress assessment tool that starts to respond to existing challenges when measuring stress in complex workplaces, such as prisons. Through valid monitoring and a clear, evidence-informed approach building on correctional stress literature, we seek to evaluate overall workplace stress to allow for a more comprehensive examination of employee experience, workplace safety, and wellness to facilitate a greater understanding of workplace stress within prisons and, more broadly, public safety workspaces.

Occupational Stress

Most public safety employees, like correctional workers, experience some level of stress when performing their occupational responsibilities (Ricciardelli et al., 2020). Sources of stress include physical, psychological, and social stresses, which constitute organizational and operational stresses (Rengamani & Murugan, 2012). Importantly, while operational stress is inherent to the content of the job and thus unavoidable, organizational stress is systemic and structural, influenced by interpersonal dynamics and rooted in interactions and workplace demands (Duxbury & Higgins, 2001). Organizational stressors are not inherent – they are created by organization processes and structures – and thus can be changed (Finney et al., 2013). In contrast, operational stress can extend beyond incidents to include physical hazards in the workplace, such as ladders, inaccessible workspaces, and environmental conditions, which can lead to injury or cognitive disengagement (Bridger et al., 2010). Nevertheless, because organizational stresses are situational within a workspace, they can be changed with organizational modifications and remedies for the context in which one works. However, major sources of stress may be rooted in organizational and psychological factors rather than the physical risks of the job (Leung et al., 2022; Suresh et al., 2013).

Organizational stresses include workload, job future ambiguity, underutilization of skills, inequity in pay, perception of in-job supports, and exclusion from decision-making (Bannerman, 1997; Finney et al., 2013). Administrative burdens such as paperwork, ineffective record keeping, and lack of job support can lead to organizational stress, resulting in overall job frustration (Ricciardelli et al., 2023). These stresses also include bureaucracy, lack of time for healthy eating, inadequate staffing, fatigue (Allen et al., 2008; Andrews et al., 2022), internal norms (Johnston et al., 2024) and policies, and amount of sick time available (Coulling et al., 2024), which all play a role in mental health. Shift work, circadian rhythm disruptions, environmental factors, noise, and motion can also contribute to workplace stress (Allen et al., 2008), as can the use of some types of personal protective equipment (PPE) (Leung et al., 2022). The internal culture around mental health and the stigma surrounding mental health needs and treatment have been shown to be a large contributor to stress for correctional workers correctional worker (Coulling et al., 2024; Johnston et al., 2022a, 2022b, 2023, 2024). Collectively, job stress from whichever origin predicts (and correlates with) occupational burnout (Ogungbamila & Fajemirokun, 2016; Sygit-Kowalkowska et al., 2023), with high costs, including cynicism and suspiciousness, emotional detachment from family, reduced efficiency, absenteeism, early retirement, excessive aggressiveness, alcoholism, marital or family problems, posttraumatic stress disorder (PTSD), health problems, and even suicide behaviours (Dowler & Arai, 2008, p. 124; Johnston et al, 2022a, 2022b, 2023, 2024; McKendy & Ricciardelli, 2023). Workplace stress can have physical health repercussions, such as chronic stress-related conditions (Grant, 2006).

Occupational stress affects the families of public safety personnel (PSP), as does family stress, have an impact on the PSP work environment – the relationship is cyclical (Casus & Benuto, 2022; Regehr et al., 2005). Families play a crucial support role, providing PSP loved ones with several types of support, including supporting practical and emotional needs, providing safe spaces, assisting with coping, monitoring PSP mental health, and providing reassurance and reframing (Tjin et al., 2022). In response, families can experience crossover stress – the effect on the spouse perceiving stress in their partner – which can affect the spouse at home and their own personal workplace stress (Cox, 2022; Tjin,2022; Young, 2014). The influence of occupational stress stretches beyond the workplace, extending into the support system (Young, 2014). Families of PSP need their own supports, including formal organizational supports and informal social supports and resources as they experience the negative repercussions of caring for a PSP family member (Tjin, 2022). For example, the uncertainty of the safety of a PSP family member can create family stress, and the unpredictability in scheduling and negative responses, attitudes, or mental and physical health symptoms because of the work of PSPs impact the family at home (Cox, 2022; Tjin, 2022). Families can experience role overload and logistical challenges due to their PSP family member's work responsibilities, reduced family time or absences during important family events, and challenges dealing with residual PSP behaviours from work when PSP family members have difficulty turning off work mode, during off-duty hours (Cox et al., 2022; Ricciardelli, 2020).

Attempts at evidence-informed stress reduction are necessary to improve the quality of life for employees (Suresh et al., 2013). Stress reduction can occur, for example, through employer-led programmes and initiatives or the increase of job-specific supports and solutions. Although studies have examined the prevalence of workplace stress in public safety sectors, including the correctional workplace, through an academic lens, few scholars have yielded study results or information that is easily accessible to employers. Identified stressors can appear siloed in academic works or located behind inaccessible paywalls, and evaluation measures can require quantitative analysis or access to specific resources beyond the capabilities of employers. Academic products must be translated for industry to ensure they can be unpacked to inform policies and practices, operationally.

The Correctional Workplace

Correctional services workspaces have a unique work culture. Culture varies by space (Farkas & Manning, 1997) but remains distinct from correctional services, where correctional officers gain acceptance in the workplace through performance (Carbonell & Ricciardelli, 2023). Correctional workers must personify meticulous action and perfection, as failure to meet expectations of behaviour can have lasting consequences of exclusion (Carbonell & Ricciardelli, 2023). Building trust, showing a strong work ethic, spending an adequate amount of time doing the right kind of correctional work, and showing respect, as well as a willingness to support the team, are vital to acceptance in the correctional workplace (Carbonell & Ricciardelli, 2023). Exclusion can lead to targeted gossip and interpersonal conflict, which can be primary sources of workplace stress for officers (Siqueira Cassiano & Ricciardelli, 2023). Underpinning the correctional worker workspace and culture is a risk (Siqueira Cassiano & Ricciardelli, 2023; Carbonell & Ricciardelli, 2023; Ricciardelli et al., 2020), how employees interpret their occupation (Cullen et al., 1985), and the uncertainty of the work (Siqueira Cassiano & Ricciardelli, 2023; Ricciardelli et al., 2020). The nature of correctional services creates an environment where staff are exposed to the real or perceived threat of harm as a regular part of their job duties (Adorjan, 2023; Cullen et al., 1985; Finney et al., 2013; Konyk et al., 2021; Ricciardelli et al., 2020). Correctional staff can experience violence through witnessing others harming themselves or being involved in physical altercations with prisoners (Coulling et al., 2024). The interpretation of an unsafe work environment necessitates correctional officers' prioritization of safety, individually and collectively (Siqueira Cassiano & Ricciardelli, 2023; Carbonell & Ricciardelli, 2023).

Stress can stem from the organization itself, its structure, and its climate (Finney et al., 2013). The lack of supports for staff, perceived internal justice, and administration dynamics can be sources of stress within correctional service work (Siqueira Cassiano & Ricciardelli, 2023; Finney et al., 2013; Ricciardelli et al., 2020). For example, how matters are handled internally, and the involvement of management in daily matters impacts perceptions in the workplace (Coulling et al., 2024). Stress can stem from a lack of resources (Konyk et al., 2021; Summerlin et al., 2010), the quality of supervision (Armstrong & Griffin, 2004; Griffin, 2006), and the level of supervisory support (Castle & Martin, 2006; Moon & Maxwell, 2004; Siqueira Cassiano & Ricciardelli, 2023; Sygit-Kowalkowska et al., 2023). The organizational structure of correctional workplaces and the hierarchical nature of organizations can also be a source of stress (Finney et al., 2013). Prison workspaces are structurally organized in a "military-style" hierarchy, which involves a specific chain of command laced with low independence (Sygit-Kowalkowska et al., 2023, p. 745), but hierarchies also exist between groups of workers (Carbonell & Ricciardelli, 2023; Siqueira Cassiano & Ricciardelli, 2023). Thus, stress in prisons can stem from interpersonal relationships (Carbonell & Ricciardelli, 2023; Konyk et al., 2021). Interpersonal relationships between correctional workers, specifically, can influence acceptance into social work groups within prisons (Carbonell & Ricciardelli, 2023; Crawley, 2004; Crawley & Crawley, 2007). The pressure for correctional workers to adhere to social norms in the workplace is high, and exclusion from peer groups can lead to bullying or a lack of support in performing job duties (Crawley, 2004; Crawley & Crawley, 2007).

In a systematic review, Finney and colleagues (2013) identified several factors specific to correctional officer stress that are intrinsic to the job, such as work overload, overtime, training, prison overcrowding, professional worth, limited resources, and understaffing. The type of work schedule, specifically shiftwork involving long hours, also affects correctional staff stress, and the requirement to work on-call, shift work, irregular work hours, and long hours negatively impact employee well-being (Johnston et al., 2022a; Lavender & Todak, 2021), as can overtime requirements and working alone at night (Konyk et al., 2021). Fatigue has been reported as the highest stressor when doing shift work and working overtime (Paleksić, 2020), and researchers agree that overtime incites stress (Lambert, 2004; Roy & Avdija, 2012; Rutter & Fielding, 1988).

Correctional staff experience obstacles to mental health, including "exposure to potentially psychologically traumatic events" (Johnston et al.,

2022a, p. 962), and the correctional work environment is laden with stigma towards mental health and mental health care (Johnston et al., 2022a; Ricciardelli et al., 2020). The social norms of the correctional workspace are intolerant of mental health needs (Johnston et al., 2024), and correctional workers cannot discuss mental health matters openly in the workplace for fear of reprisal, reduced support, judgement, and stigma (Johnston & Ricciardelli, 2023). The workplace culture focuses on strength, conformity, and stoicism – with no space for mental health discussions (Coulling et al., 2024). In a study related to the mental health needs of correctional workers in Canada, Johnston and colleagues (2022a) found access to mental health care as a barrier to staff coping (2022). Correctional services employees may have limits to the number of funded counselling sessions per year, lack early detection methods for mental health concerns, and lack of control in scheduling to facilitate access to care (Johnston et al., 2022a). Recent work illustrates the prevalence of mental health disorders among correctional staff in Canada, noting a prevalence of 58% of staff screening positive for at least one disorder (Ricciardelli, Carleton et al., 2024). While correctional officers report a clear desire for increased, comprehensive, and accessible mental health supports, the stigma surrounding mental health care and mental health leave remains (Johnston et al., 2022a).

Additional stressors are present in the correctional workplace that comes to the fore when considering the effects of gender and stress. While there are similarities in how stress is experienced by men and women correctional workers (Ricciardelli, 2019), women officers report experiencing harassment and discrimination (Griffin, 2006; Pogrebin & Poole, 1997; Ricciardelli & McKendy, 2020; Savicki et al., 2003; Stohr et al., 1998). They have reported safety as a higher concern than their male counterparts, while men in officer roles reported a higher influence of work–family conflict (Griffin, 2006). Griffin (2006) found higher stress levels in younger women officers as well as tenured women officers, compared with men who are officers. However, burnout can impact men and women correctional workers equally, with no significant difference in terms of organizational commitment by gender (Savicki et al., 2003). Some women correctional workers can view feminine skills as an advantage in the workplace, with soft skills enabling them in their job duties, despite corrections being a masculine-trait-centred workspace (Ricciardelli & McKendy, 2020). This emotional labour can be an added work stress, eroding well-being (Ricciardelli & McKendy, 2020). Women may garner more respect from prison residents, given their gender (Ricciardelli & McKendy, 2020). Despite the advantages of these skills in the correctional worker workspace and the perception that these abilities aid in the performance of job duties, women correctional workers may experience misogyny in the workplace, as feminine qualities are viewed more negatively than macho masculine traits in corrections (Ricciardelli & McKendy, 2020).

The conflict between work and home lives also creates personal health and relational stress for correctional workers, enabling burnout (Johnston et al., 2022a). For both men and women correctional workers, work–family conflict and role conflict present a high-stress effect on workers (Griffin, 2006). Some correctional workers report a lack of understanding from family and friends about their work, which may exacerbate tensions and stresses (Konyk et al., 2021). As previously stated, crossover stress permeates correctional worker families, where family members carry uneven responsibilities for logical, administrative, and family duties (Cox, 2022; Tjin,2022; Young, 2014). Families of correctional workers can experience unpredictability in scheduling due to staff shortages in prisons and overtime requirements, specific to correctional work. For example, prisons must maintain a required level of staffing, leading to mandatory overtime, which can result from burnout and absenteeism in prison staff (Klinoff et al., 2018). Prison incidents such as lockdowns, critical incidents involving prisoners, or safety concerns can influence correctional worker schedules and ability to get off work on time.

Stress also stems from dealing with the public, in how the public understands the profession (Konyk et al., 2021; Ricciardelli et al., 2020), the media representation of the job (Ricciardelli, Stoddart et al., 2024), and the resulting scrutiny (Ricciardelli, Stoddart et al., 2020). Correctional staff are often portrayed negatively in the media (Ricciardelli et al., 2024) and do not have the ability to speak publicly about workplace matters – as public servants, they are exposed to public criticism but unable to clear up falsehoods or address public rumours due to privacy concerns (of prisoners and themselves) and internal policies (Adorjan & Ricciardelli, 2023). Posting on social media from a correctional worker capacity can lead to disciplinary consequences (Adorjan & Ricciardelli, 2023), and disconnection between how the media represents correctional work and correctional worker experiences can cause strain, stress, and anxiety for correctional workers (Ricciardelli, Carleton et al., 2024).

Finally, characteristics of correctional workers can influence stress levels, as they can view prison work differently, and, resultantly, how they handle relationships can vary (Crew & Leibling, 2012; Crew et al., 2015; Ricciardelli, 2016; Ricciardelli & McKendy, 2020). Punitive and rehabilitative mindsets can lead to higher stress levels due to the lack of consequences workers can impose for negative behaviour or the watching residents elect not to complete programming, among other reasons (Cassiano & Ricciardelli, 2023; Cullen et al., 1985; Misis et al., 2013). Behaviour within the correctional workspace is performative, where officers project specific acceptable characteristics and deter scrutinized behaviours deemed as marking weakness (Johnston et al., 2022a; Carbonell & Ricciardelli, 2023). As previously discussed, the social norms and workplace culture of Corrections can lead to multifaceted stress, challenges in workplace acceptance, and the overall well-being of correctional workers.

Assessing Job Stress in Correctional Services

The impetus for our work is not simply the presence of diverse sources and types of stress but also how researchers have identified job-specific stress scales (McLennan, 2005), quantifiable job evaluation tools (i.e., Brief Job Stress Questionnaire (as used in Kachi et al., 2020), as well as lengthy generic questionnaires such as the NIOSH Generic Job Stress Questionnaire, (since discontinued; CDC, 2011) and the NIOSH Quality of Worklife Questionnaire (CDC, 2013), which elude employers attempting to evaluate job stress for employees. While reliable and valid tools, the tools are seemingly inaccessible to companies and employees for stress evaluation and policy considerations. The quantitative nature of the surveys or extensive length (i.e., 224 items with the NIOSH Generic Job Stress Questionnaire, 12 pages for the NIOSH Quality of Worklife Questionnaire) make using these methods cost-prohibitive, time-consuming, and challenging – requiring advanced statistical skillsets to analyse data which is hard to acquire due to survey fatigue and the lengthy questionnaires. Research has only limited considered scales that can be used by employers and organizations – as often scales are academic in construction for analysis requiring advanced knowledge rather than useable by the organizations independently.

Further, many analytic tools are job-specific or lack consideration of mitigation measures in place within organizations. Building on these existing frameworks, we expand on the current literature and supplement it through our research experience in the correctional space; we propose a simplified, accessible job stress analysis tool (JSAT) for employees and employers to unpack job stress and inform job support change – a precursor to more extensive evaluation that is robust but less invasive, time-consuming, and affected by complicated analysis. Including physical, psychosocial (i.e., psychological and social), organizational, and operational considerations, we present a streamlined assessment tool to illuminate areas of change within any workplace. The measured process benefits employees, employers, advocacy groups, mental health practitioners, and unions by encouraging an accessible, holistic evaluation of workplace and job stress, allowing stakeholders at all levels to understand the effects of stress, inform positive change, and support positive work environments.

We can unpack the physical, psychological, and social stresses, and cultural factors, that constitute organizational and operational stresses (Rengamani & Murugan, 2012) to evaluate the presence of job stressors within an occupation, specifically in correctional services, building on the literature of known stressors. Unavoidable operational stress inherent to the content of a job, along with systemic and structural organizational stress, combines to create an overall picture of stress. As aforementioned, operational stressors are more obvious and can lead to injury or cognitive disengagement (Bridger et al., 2010). For example, exposure to environmental stressors in prisons, such as high or low heat, loud noise conditions, chemical hazards, vibration hazards, heavy lifting, or work involving heights or confined spaces, have easily recognizable risks (Bierie, 2012; Turner et al., 2023). More opaque, are the organizational stressors, which constitute a major source of stress for workers (Suresh et al., 2013). These, as a reminder, include working hours, work culture, management and supervisory practices, internal policies and procedures, predictability and agency in the workplace, accessibility to training and supports, and whether the workplace has a safety mindset, all of which play a role in employee organizational stress. Each of these types of stress is utilized to inform the sections of the job stress assessment tool (Tables 7.1 and 7.2).

Measurement Issues in Assessment of Stress

There are a number of measurement challenges that should be considered when conducting research or interpreting research findings. Content validity has been defined as "the extent to which a measure provides a comprehensive and true assessment of the key relevant elements of a specified construct or attribute across a defined range, clearly and equitably for a stated target audience and context" (MacDermid, 2021, p. 1). This definition implies the complexity of ensuring that the measure of stress provides a comprehensive assessment of the nature and severity of occupational stressors across the unique context(s) of PSP and the wide diversity of humans who fill those roles.

As discussed, stress is an elusive concept consisting of potential physical, psychological, and social stressors that may be defined differently across researchers and experienced differently amongst survey respondents. Stress, particularly of a psychological or social nature, tends to be measured solely by self-report. As discussed throughout this edited collection, critical incidents considered sources of high stress are almost universal exposures to PSP, such as correctional workers. Epidemiological studies of toxic exposures like noise or chemicals fall under the realm of stress, as assessed by some self-reports, but are often considered independently as environmental exposures that can be physically measured in the workplace. Given that the stressors PSP are exposed to are multiple and often severe, this means generic measures designed for other occupations may not be capturing important sources of stress and thus lack content validity.

All self-report measures are subject to limitations, including print literacy and health literacy challenges, which create difficulties for some people to provide valid responses to the questions posed. This can particularly affect those with English as a second language (since, in many cases, valid cross-cultural translations are not provided) and those with lower levels of education or a health condition affecting their reading and cognition (Epstein, 2015). This is a potential source of bias since it can be expected that their experiences and health might be different, as literacy affects health (Paasche-Orlow & Wolf, 2007). Measures administered in paper format or by smartphone can selectively be inaccessible to people based on vision or technology access. Technology access may affect who participates in research and health monitoring. As the PSP population become increasingly diverse, considerations tied to cross-cultural validity become increasingly important since not all constructs have the same meaning across different cultures. Hence, content validation of outcome measures specific to the specific PSP population with an equity lens is essential to our confidence in the findings across cited literature. Currently, there is a large gap in the development of stress assessment measures and the associated research literature.

Once content validity is established, other psychometric properties become important. Reliability (consistent measures in a stable state), discriminative validity (ability to detect subgroups), or responsiveness (ability to detect real and important changes) can be foundational for different questions or purposes (MacDermid, 2021). Reliability and validity are specific to the population, measurement purpose, and context (Epstein, 2015). Hence, researchers should consider and report the validity indices specific to their purpose when designing studies to understand PSP health and functioning. As an example, MacDermid and colleagues found that when measured, firefighters doing simulated tasks like hose-drag and stair climb in full equipment exhibited the expected normal distribution (MacDermid et al., 2019). However, when reporting their work limitations (on the same day) using a generic self-report measure that has been validated and used for many occupations, the data distribution was highly skewed, with most firefighters having 'no limitations.' This ceiling effect meant that the self-report data was not valid, and the research team are currently designing a firefighter-specific work limitations measure.

Practical issues can also affect the validity of stress measures in research and practice. With increased attention to PSP health concerns has come increased research. This prevalent recognition has led to suggestions for routine monitoring, such as an annual physical and mental health PSP-specific assessment to mitigate the burden of adverse health outcomes from PSP stress (Niemi & Leone, 2019). While both are welcome additions, they both increase the burden of requests for completion of self-report and physical screening measures. A further burden is added if measures have many items. Having many items favours reliability and comprehensiveness and has traditionally been common, particularly for psychological questionnaires. Respondents may refuse, stop responding, or stop attending to questions when the burden increases. Where response rates are low, the responses may not represent the truth.

Shorter measures have been developed for many traditional measures. Shorter measures may be particularly important where multiple constructs are being evaluated, which is essential given the complexity of sources of stress and potential health impacts for PSP. However, shorter measures may lose robust measurement properties and may not fit all populations. The trade-offs between these different psychometric and practical issues must be considered when designing research studies or health monitoring strategies.

Stress Measurements Should Inform Action

While recognizing the challenges in measuring stress constructs, we have chosen to provide an extensive list of sources of stress to aid employers, unions, and employees in evaluating the collective stress of the workplace and building on the established literature on sources of stress in correctional workplaces (Table 7.1). While not exhaustive, we aim to provide stakeholders with a tool that is clear, understandable, and easy to use (and analyse) to articulate the overall combination of stress in a workplace. Considering physical, psychological, and social stresses which constitute organizational and operational stresses, this list provokes consideration of the many sources of stress a worker could experience. This assessment tool is direct and requires nothing more than the tool itself. It motivates evaluators to assess factors they may not have considered, enabling frank and honest conversations between employee levels. It can be easily shared and gives insight into the many elements of stress. The objective of this stress assessment tool is to articulate the needs of workers and workplaces and inform procedure and policy implications within work environments. For example, a manager may complete the stress assessment tool with an understanding of the physical risks to the job, which are well mitigated in terms of protective equipment; however, a holistic view requires the examination of psychological and social stressors, in addition to physical stressors. Ideally, this can aid in the illumination of gaps, highlight where training is needed, and assist employers in creating resources or processes to reduce overall employee stress within the workplace.

Equally important are the mitigating efforts to combat workplace stress (Table 7.2). Traditionally, things like personal protective equipment (PPE) are used to combat physical threats to safety. Examination of solely physical stress mitigators, however, is remiss of other sources of stress. Healthy workplaces employ psychological and social stress mitigation measures and encourage healthy boundaries. A full consideration of all sides of workplace stress is necessary to ensure a healthy work environment for all employees. While no organization can control nor account for all sources of stress, organizations which thoroughly consider the physical, psychological, and social sources

TABLE 7.1 Job stress analysis tool, Part A

1	There are environmental stresses present, such as working in high or low heat and noise conditions
2	There is exposure to chemical hazards, radiation, or vibration
3	There are proprioceptor hazards affecting balance and stability
4	I am required to lift, push, pull, or carry more than 25 lbs
5	I am to perform shift work or irregular hours that include overnights
6	There is regular interpersonal conflict (overt such as arguments, covert such as gossip)
7	I am required to sit for extended periods of time
8	There is exposure to biological hazards such as bacteria, viruses, mould, animals, or biological (i.e., blood, faeces) substances.
9	There is exposure to electricity, heavy equipment, machinery, ladders or tools
10	I am required to work in confined spaces
11	I work more than 40 hours per week
12	I experience a lack of sleep due to the job
13	I perform repetitive tasks or monotony
14	I experience a lack of control over job duties and related work situations
15	I have a high sense of responsibility
16	I perceive a lack of job rewards or lack of recognition in my job
17	I experience high work demands (i.e., time sensitivity) in tasks
18	I experience high stress
	I experience low control
	I work alone or in isolating conditions
19	I feel excluded in the workplace due to underrepresentation (race, ethnicity, disability, gender)
20	I perceive discrimination based on race, ethnicity, disability, gender, mental health, or family status
21	The workplace culture is challenging (i.e., toxic, difficult interpersonal relationships)
22	I am subject to public or media scrutiny
	I am silenced in responding to public or media scrutiny
23	I experience irregular break times or mealtimes
24	I work forced overtime
25	The workplace experiences chronic staffing shortages
26	I have limited access to nourishment/liquids during work hours
27	I experience unpredictable situations in the course of my duties
28	I experience interpersonal work relationship challenges on the job with coworkers
	I experience interpersonal work relationship challenges with supervisors or managers
29	I perceive risks to safety as a part of doing my job
30	I can leave the workplace, if required, during the regular work shift
31	I perceive the workplace as high-risk
32	I am exposed to violence, physical or nonphysical
33	I am exposed to traumatic situations involving the actual or potential loss of life
34	I receive threats from others in the workplace during the course of my duties
35	I handle mental health crisis as a part of my job duties
36	I am exposed to natural disasters as a part of my job duties
37	I have, in the past, experienced life-threatening illness or injury in this workplace
38	I feel vulnerable outside the workplace because of where I work

of stress and their available mitigating supports will employ healthier and happier individuals. It is important to note that surface-level examinations of stress and desultory mitigations will fall short in remedying workplace stress; employers must consider the real and perceived culture of the workplace and the barriers to well-being to take a pragmatic examination of the organization. In workplaces where stigma towards mental health exists and attitudes towards work–life balance are negative, superficial supports will fall flat and potentially have the opposite effect than desired.

Conclusion

Numerous sources of stress have been identified for correctional staff, and expanding on this, occupational and organizational stress can be assessed through accessible and holistic methods for employees and employers. Valid monitoring and a clear, data-informed, collaboratively co-designed action plan

TABLE 7.2 Job stress analysis tool, Part B

1	Personal Protective Equipment is always available
2	Personal Protective Equipment is always worn as instructed
3	Management safety preventative measures exist
4	Management safety preventative measures are always utilized
5	I am given clear work instructions, job duties, and responsibilities
6	Work duties are predictable and can be planned for in advance
7	Task Hazard Analyses have been undertaken for each workplace hazard
8	I am trained in handling each physical, social, and psychological hazard
9	I have access to resources for health and wellness (EAP, access to exercise possibilities, health and wellness training or workshops)
10	Peer support systems exist
11	Career progression options exist
12	I have the means to bring issues forward without fear of reprisal (ombudsman, anonymous whistle-blowing)
13	I have access to resiliency training
14	I have access to wellness leave without reporting the details of the leave
15	Managers are provided training annually, on management practices and workplace wellness
16	I have ready access to ergonomic assessments
17	I have work equipment tailored to my specific physical needs
18	I can reduce work hours as needed
19	Easy-access conflict mediation is available
20	I experience job stability
21	I have trust in management at all levels
22	I perceive there is a fair performance evaluation
23	Team-based training is available
24	Team members experience high collegiality

are needed to mitigate the impact of stress in PSP roles, given the inherently stressful nature of the roles. As such, building on previous quantitative studies evaluating job stress and identifying workplace variables and needs, it is possible to evaluate employee overall stress levels and workplace stress health, focusing on physical, psychosocial, social, psychological, organizational, and occupational considerations. Through directed tools, information can inform how stakeholders assess the climate of safety climate in the workplace to influence policy and practice adaptations aimed at benefiting employee health, particularly in public safety occupational spaces.

Note

1 While attempting to locate job-stress analysis measures (e.g., cited checklists), one of the authors spent numerous hours negotiating paywall systems and sifting through minute mentions in articles, despite having extensive access through institutional libraries.

References

Adorjan, M., & Ricciardelli, R. (2023). Correctional officers and social media: Policies, challenges, and vulnerabilities. *Social Media + Society, 9*(3), 1–12.

Allen, P., Wadsworth, E., & Smith, A. (2008). Seafarers' fatigue: A review of the recent literature. *International Maritime Health, 59*(1–4), 81–92.

Andrews, K. L., Jamshidi, L., Nisbet, J., Teckchandani, T. A., Price, J. A. B., Ricciardelli, R., Anderson, G. S., & Carleton, R. N. (2022). Mental health disorder symptoms among Canadian coast guard and conservation and protection officers. *International Journal of Environmental Research and Public Health, 19*(23), 15696.

Armstrong, G. S., & Griffin, M. L. (2004). Does the job matter? Comparing correlates of stress among treatment and correctional staff in prisons. *Journal of Criminal Justice, 32*(6), 577–592. doi:http://doi.org/10.1016/j.jcrimjus.2004.08.007

Bannerman, E. D. (1997). *Female Police officers: The relationship between social support, interactional style, and occupational stress and strain*. Vancouver: Simon Frasier University.

Bierie, D. M. (2012). The impact of prison conditions on staff well-being. *International Journal of Offender Therapy and Comparative Criminology, 56*(1), 81–95.

Bridger, R. S., Brasher, K., & Dew, A. (2010). Work demands and need for recovery from work in ageing seafarers. *Ergonomics, 53*(8), 1006–1015.

Casas, J., & Benuto, L. (2022). Work-related traumatic stress spillover in first responder families: A systematic review of the literature. *Psychological Trauma, 14*(2), 209–217.

Castle, T. L., & Martin, J. S. (2006). Occupational hazard: Predictors of stress among jail correctional officers. *American Journal of Criminal Justice, 31*(1), 65–80. https://doi.org/10.1007/BF02885685

Coulling, R., Johnston, M. S., & Ricciardelli, R. (2024). "We must be mentally strong": Exploring barriers to mental health in correctional services. *Frontiers in Psychology, 15*, 1258944–1258944. https://doi.org/10.3389/fpsyg.2024.1258944

Cox, M., Norris, D., Cramm, H., Richmond, R., & Anderson, G. S. (2022). Public safety personnel family resilience: A narrative review. *International Journal of Environmental Research and Public Health, 19*(9), 5224.

Crawley, E. (2004). Emotion and performance: Prison officers and the presentation of self in prisons. *Punishment & Society, 6*(4), 411–427.

Crawley, E., & Crawley, P. (2007). Understanding prison officers: Culture, cohesion and conflict. In *Understanding prison staff* (1st ed., pp. 134–152). Essay, Taylor & Francis.

Crewe, B., & Liebling, A. (2012). Are liberal humanitarian penal values and practices exceptional. In T. Ugelvik & J. Dullum (Eds.), *Penal exceptionalism? Nordic prison policy and practice* (pp. 175–198). Routledge.

Crewe, B., Liebling, A., & Hulley, S. (2015). Staff-prisoner relationships, staff professionalism, and the use of authority in public- and private-sector prisons. *Law & Social Inquiry, 40*(2), 309–344. https://doi.org/10.1111/lsi.12093

Cullen, F. T., Link, B. G., Wolfe, N. T., & Frank, J. (1985). The social dimensions of correctional officer stress. *Justice Quarterly, 2*(4), 505–533.

Dowler, K., & Arai, B. (2008). Stress, gender and policing: The impact of perceived gender discrimination on symptoms of stress. *International Journal of Police Science & Management, 10*(2), 123–135.

Duxbury, L., & Higgins, C. (2001). *Work-life balance in the new millennium: Where are we? Where do we need to go*? Retrieved from https://eric.ed.gov/?id=ED465060

Epstein, J., Santo, R. M., & Guillemin, F. (2015). A review of guidelines for cross-cultural adaptation of questionnaires could not bring out a consensus. *Journal of Clinical Epidemiology, 68*(4), 435–441. https://doi.org/10.1016/j.jclinepi.2014.11.021

Farkas, M., & Manning, P. (1997). The Occupational culture of corrections and police officers. *Journal of Crime & Justice, 20*(2), 51–68. doi.org/10.1080/0735648X.1997.9721581

Finney, C., Stergiopoulos, E., Hensel, J., Bonato, S., & Dewa, C. S. (2013). Organizational stressors associated with job stress and burnout in correctional officers: A systematic review. *BMC Public Health, 13*(1), 82–82. https://doi.org/10.1186/1471-2458-13-82

Flaherty, M. G., & Carceral, K. C. (2022). *The cage of days: Time and temporal experience in prison*. Columbia University Press.

Grant, S., & Langan-Fox, J. (2006). Occupational stress, coping and strain: The combined/interactive effects of the Big Five traits. *Personality and Individual Differences, 41*(4), 719–732.

Griffin, M. L. (2006). Gender and stress: A comparative assessment of sources of stress among correctional officers. *Journal of Contemporary Criminal Justice, 22*(1), 5–25.

Johnston, M. S. & Ricciardelli, R. (2023). Documenting the mental health climate in correctional work and the realities of suicide. *Frontiers, 13*(1026821), 1–18.

Johnston, M. S., Ricciardelli, R., & McKendy, L. (2024). Suffering in silence: Work and mental health experiences among provincial correctional workers in Canada. *Corrections: Policy, Practice and Research, 9*(1), 1–19.

Johnston, M. S., Ricciardelli, R., & McKendy, L. (2022a). Fight or flight? Exploring suicide thoughts, experiences, and behaviours among correctional workers and their interventions of agency. *Sociology of Health & Illness, 44*(9), 1500–1516. https://doi.org/10.1111/1467-9566.13526

Johnston, M. S., Ricciardelli, R., & McKendy, L. (2022b). Improving the mental health of correctional workers: Perspectives from the field. *Criminal Justice and Behavior 49*, 951–970.

Kachi, Y., Inoue, A., Eguchi, H., Kawakami, N., Shimazu, A., & Tsutsumi, A. (2020). Occupational stress and the risk of turnover: A large prospective cohort study of employees in Japan. *BMC Public Health, 20*(1), 174–182. https://doi.org/10.1186/s12889-020-8289-5

Klinoff, V. A., Van Hasselt, V. B., Black, R. A., Masias, E. V., & Couwels, J. (2018). The assessment of resilience and burnout in correctional officers. *Criminal Justice and Behavior, 45*(8), 1213–1233.

Konyk, K., Ricciardelli, R., Taillieu, T., Afifi, T. O., Groll, D., & Nicholas Carleton, R. (2021). Assessing relative stressors and mental disorders among Canadian provincial correctional workers. *International Journal of Environmental Research and Public Health, 18*(19), 10018-. https://doi.org/10.3390/ijerph181910018

Lambert, E. G. (2004). The impact of job characteristics on correctional staff members. *The Prison Journal (Philadelphia, Pa.), 84*(2), 208–227.

Lavender, L., & Todak, N. (2021). Exploring organizational risk factors for health & wellness problems in correctional officers. *Criminal Justice Studies, 34*(4), 361–379.

Leung, R., Cook, M. M., Capra, M. F., & Johnstone, K. R. (2022). The contribution of respiratory and hearing protection use to psychological distress in the workplace: A scoping review. *International Archives of Occupational and Environmental Health, 95*(8), 1647–1659. https://doi.org/10.1007/s00420-022-01863-7

MacDermid, J. C. (2021). ICF linking and cognitive interviewing are complementary methods for optimizing content validity of outcome measures: An integrated methods review. *Frontiers in Rehabilitation Sciences, 2*, 702596–702596. https://doi.org/10.3389/fresc.2021.702596

MacDermid, J. C., Tang, K., Sinden, K. E., & D'Amico, R. (2019). Work functioning among firefighters: A comparison between self-reported limitations and functional task performance. *Journal of Occupational Rehabilitation, 29*(1), 194–204.

McKendy, L., & Ricciardelli, R. (2023). "This job has changed me": Work life conflict, self and social identity in correctional work. *Criminal Justice Review (Atlanta, Ga.), 48*(4), 458–473. https://doi.org/10.1177/07340168221121314

McLennan, M (2005). Nurses views on work enabling factors. *Journal of Nursing Administration, 35*, 311–318

Misis, M., Kim, B., Cheeseman, K., Hogan, N. L., & Lambert, E. G. (2013). The impact of correctional officer perceptions of inmates on job stress. *SAGE Open, 3*(2), 1–13. https://doi.org/10.1177/2158244013489695

Moon, B., & Maxwell, S. R. (2004). The sources and consequences of corrections officers' stress: A South Korean example. *Journal of Criminal Justice, 32*(4), 359–370. https://doi.org/10.1016/j.jcrimjus.2004.04.006

National Institute for Occupational Safety and Health. (2011). *Generic job stress questionnaire*. Centers for Disease Control and Prevention. Retrieved from http://www.cdc.gov/niosh/topics/workorg/tools/nioshjob-stress-questionnaire.html.

National Institute for Occupational Safety and Health. (2013). *Quality of worklife questionnaire*. Centers for Disease Control and Prevention. Retrieved from https://www.cdc.gov/niosh/topics/stress/qwlquest.html

Niemi, L., & Leone, C. (2019). *Extraordinary duties, extraordinary stressors: Assessing the need and potential for innovative approaches to first responder's stress injuries* (pp. 1–63). University of Toronto.

Ogungbamila, B., & Fajemirokun, I. (2016). Job stress and police burnout: Moderating roles of gender and marital status. *IAFOR Journal of Psychology & the Behavioral Sciences, 2*(3), 17–32.

Paasche-Orlow, M. K., & Wolf, M. S. (2007). The causal pathways linking health literacy to health outcomes. *American Journal of Health Behavior, 31*(1), S19–S26.

Paleksić, V. (2020). Professional stressors in prison officers: A cross-sectional study. *Scripta Medica, 51*(3), 166–173. https://doi.org/10.5937/scriptamed51-24550

Pogrebin, M. R., & Poole, E. D. (1997). The sexualized work environment: A look at women jail officers. *The Prison Journal (Philadelphia, Pa.), 77*(1), 41–57.

Regehr, C., Dimitropoulos, G., Bright, E., George, S., & Henderson, J. (2005). Behind the brotherhood: Rewards and challenges for wives of firefighters. *Family Relations, 54*(3), 423–435.

Rengamani, J., & Murugan, M. S. (2012). A study on the factors influencing the seafarers' stress. *AMET International Journal of Management, 4*, 44–51.

Ricciardelli, R. (2016). Canadian prisoners' perceptions of correctional officer orientations to their occupational responsibilities. *Journal of Crime and Justice, 39*(2), 324–343.

Ricciardelli, R. (2019). *Also serving time: Canada's provincial and territorial correctional officers*. University of Toronto Press.

Ricciardelli, R., Carbonell, M., Ferguson, L., & Huey, L. (2023). "It's frustrating … I didn't join to sit behind a desk": Police paperwork as a source of organizational stress. *International Journal of Police Science & Management*, 25(4), 516–528. https://doi-org.qe2a-proxy.mun.ca/10.1177/14613557231188578

Ricciardelli, R., Carleton, R. N., Taillieu, T., Dorniani, S., Johnston, M., Carbonell, M., Coulling, R., Andres, E., & Afifi, T. (2024). Provincial and territorial correctional service workers: A Canadian national and jurisdictional assessment of mental health. *Journal of Criminal Justice, 91*(2024), 1–11. https://doi.org/10.1016/j.jcrimjus.2024.102168

Ricciardelli, R., Czarnuch, S., Carleton, R. N., Gacek, J., & Shewmake, J. (2020). Canadian public safety personnel and occupational stressors: How PSP interpret stressors on duty. *International Journal of Environmental Research and Public Health, 17*(13), 1–16. https://doi.org/10.3390/ijerph17134736

Ricciardelli, R., & McKendy, L. (2020). Gender and prison work: The experience of female provincial correctional officers in Canada. *The Prison Journal, 100*(5), 617–639. https://doi-org.qe2a-proxy.mun.ca/10.1177/0032885520956394

Ricciardelli, R., Stoddart, M., & Austin, H. (2024). News media framing of correctional officers: "Corrections is so Negative, we don't get any Good Recognition." *Crime, Media, Culture, 20*(1), 40–58. https://doi.org/10.1177/17416590231168337

Roy, S., & Avdija, A. (2012). The effect of prison security level on job satisfaction and job burnout among prison staff in the USA: An assessment. *International Journal of Criminal Justice Sciences, 7*(2), 524.

Rutter, D. R., & Fielding, P. J. (1988). Sources of occupational stress: An examination of British prison officers. *Work and Stress, 2*(4), 291–299. https://doi.org/10.1080/02678378808257490

Savicki, V., Cooley, E., & Gjesvold, J. (2003). Harassment as a predictor of job burnout in correctional officers. *Criminal Justice and Behavior*, *30*(5), 602–619.

Siqueira Cassiano, M., & Ricciardelli, R. (2023). Sources of stress among Federal Correctional Officers in Canada. *Criminal Justice and Behavior*, *50*(8), 1229–1251. https://doi.org/10.1177/00938548231174900

Stohr, M. K., Mays, G. L., Beck, A. C., & Kelley, T. (1998). Sexual harassment in women's jails. *Journal of Contemporary Criminal Justice*, *14*(2), 135–155.

Summerlin, Z., Oehme, K., Stern, N., & Valentine, C. (2010). Disparate levels of stress in police and correctional officers: Preliminary evidence from a pilot study on domestic violence. *Journal of Human Behavior in the Social Environment*, *20*(6), 762–777. https://doi.org/10.1080/10911351003749169

Suresh, R., Anantharaman, R., Angusamy, A., & Ganesan, J. (2013). Sources of job stress in police work in a developing country. *International Journal of Business and Management*, *8*(13), 102–110.

Sygit-Kowalkowska, E., Orlak, K., & Stolarski, M. (2023). Work for the Prison Service: Selected health consequences – Investigating the role of personal resources, job demands, work stress, and burnout. *International Journal of Occupational Medicine and Environmental Health*, *36*(6), 744–760. https://doi.org/10.13075/ijomeh.1896.02224

Tjin, A., Traynor, A., Doyle, B., Mulhall, C., Eppich, W., & O'Toole, M. (2022). Turning to "Trusted Others": A narrative review of providing social support to first responders. *International Journal of Environmental Research and Public Health*, *19*(24), 16492.

Turner, J., Ricciardelli, R., & Gacek, J. (2023). The "Pains of Employment"? Connecting air and sound quality to correctional officer experiences of health and wellness in prison space. *The Prison Journal (Philadelphia, Pa.)*, *103*(5), 610–632.

Young, M., Schieman, S., & Milkie, M. (2014). "Spouses' work-to-family conflict, family stressors and mental health outcomes among dual-earner mothers and fathers." *Society and Mental Health*, *4*, 1–20.

PART III

Firefighters

8

THE LINK BETWEEN STRESS AND CARDIAC OUTCOMES IN FIREFIGHTERS

An Example of Critical Analysis of Causation

Sara M. Stretton and Joy C. MacDermid

Introduction

Heart disease (HD) is the leading cause of death and disability worldwide; HD includes any disease that affects the heart or blood vessels, such as cardiovascular disease (CVD), heart failure, and cardiomyopathy. The Canadian Chronic Disease Surveillance System estimates that one in 12 Canadian adults over the age of 20 live with diagnosed HD, and that every hour 14 Canadians with HD die (Public Health Agency of Canada, 2022). In 2019, CVD killed 18.6 million people worldwide, and the incidence and deaths have increased over the last decade by 24.6% and 17.1%, respectively (Institute for Health Metrics and Evaluation, 2020). Even more concerning, previous studies have confirmed that firefighters (FFs) "experience the highest proportionate mortality due to CVD while on duty as compared with other occupational groups and public safety officers" (Soteriades et al., 2011b, p. 207). CVD accounts for 45% of on-duty deaths per year, and there are an estimated 17 nonfatal cardiovascular events for every fatal on-duty HD event among line-of-duty FFs (Soteriades et al., 2011b).

Previous human and animal studies among the general population have shown substantial evidence for a relationship between stress and HD. However, unknown is if FFs experience an incremental risk of adverse cardiac outcomes due to the stressful nature of their job and the high prevalence of occupational stress injuries. For example, a 2020 systematic review concluded that the prevalence of posttraumatic stress disorder (PTSD) among FFs worldwide ranges from 6.4% to 57% (Berger et al., 2012; Naim et al., 2020). A 2017 study among Saudi FFs showed that the prevalence of general anxiety disorder and major depressive disorder was 44.4% and 53.3%, respectively (Alghamdi

DOI: 10.4324/9781003424253-12

et al., 2017). In comparison, in Canada, the lifetime prevalence among the general population are 8% for PTSD, 5% for general anxiety disorder, and 11.3% for major depressive disorder (Wagner et al., 2020). Current literature on occupational stress and HD among FFs is limited but has shown that occupational stress increases risk factors for HD, including sleep, smoking, and becoming overweight and obese (Angleman et al., 2022; Yook, 2019). However, a causal relationship between stress and HD among FFs has not been shown in research.

HD is the leading cause of death and disability among the general population, which makes it difficult to determine if there is an excess burden of illness and, if present, that excess burden is attributable to occupational exposures. Our aim in this chapter is to discuss the literature and the extent to which the literature has supported a causal relationship between occupational stress and HD among FFs. We will use The Bradford Hill Criteria for evaluating the current evidence that supports or refutes this causation hypothesis.

Why Critical Analysis of Causation Matters

Performing a critical analysis of causation is important because finding evidence of a causal mechanism between stress and HD will influence prevention and treatment strategies. For example, suppose a causal mechanism is found between occupational stress and HD, then the treatment plan should address modifiable occupational stressors and how the FF responds to those stressors to reduce future risk of cardiac events (Adameova et al., 2009). Potential prevention strategies like stress management, healthy coping mechanisms, and leveraging peer relationships should be tailored to consider the unique experiences and culture of the fire sector.

While many studies evaluate occupational exposures quantitatively, The Bradford Hill Criteria for causation focuses on the interpretation of these risks using a more defined theoretical hypothesis testing approach. Hill proposed nine "aspects of association" to evaluate whether associations support a causal relationship. These criteria include: (1) the larger the association is between an exposure and disease the more likely the association is to be causal (i.e., strength of relationship); (2) consistency of results among various studies with varying methods, populations, and locations (i.e., consistency); (3) exposures that only cause one disease are more likely to be causal (i.e., specificity); (4) exposure must occur prior to the onset of disease (i.e., temporality), refer to Figure 8.1 for an example; (5) if there is a dose–response relationship observed, the relationship is more likely to be causal (i.e., biological gradient); (6) the causal hypothesis must be based on existing biological or social models (i.e., plausibility); (7) the cause-and-effect mechanism should be consistent

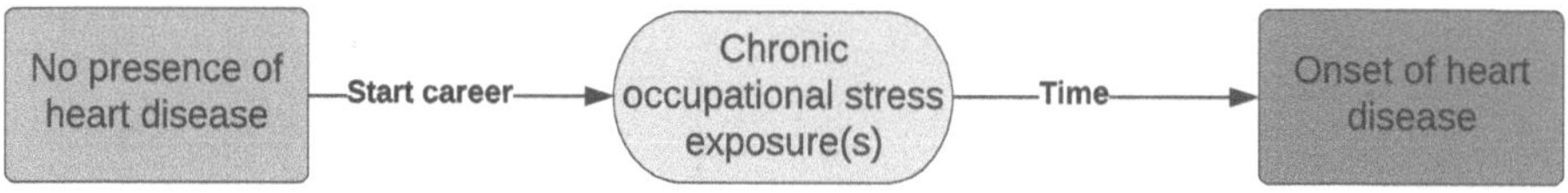

FIGURE 8.1 Temporality example between occupational stress and HD.

with all available knowledge (i.e., coherence); (8) evidence from experimental manipulation may have the strongest support for causality (i.e., experiment); and (9) if there is strong evidence of a causal relationship between an agent and disease, research should be more accepting of weaker evidence between a similar agent and disease (i.e., analogy [Bradford Hill, 1965; Fedak et al., 2015]).

Potential Causal Mechanisms between Stress and HD

The first step in establishing causation is to determine the potential causal mechanism based on existing literature and evidence. In this section, we will discuss the potential causal stress–HD mechanism at the psychological and physiological levels in the general and FF populations.

General

Stress can be described as the physiological response to a stressor, where a stressor is a physical or psychological event that initiates the stress response. The stress response is a cascade of physiological reactions, more commonly known as the fight-or-flight response, which prepares someone to physically protect themselves from a stressful event even if not necessary in the circumstance (McCarty, 2016). For example, Selye's General Adaptation Syndrome (GAS) model describes the body's reactions in response to a stressor and how such reactions may lead to maladaptive outcomes such as HD (Figure 8.2). The GAS model describes three sequential stages that lead to an adaption or maladaptation in response to a stressor: (1) the acute/alarm stage (i.e., the initial response to a stressor), characterized by the fight-or-flight response; (2) the resistance stage (i.e., one's ability to cope with the stressor) – if one can cope, the stress response will end (i.e., acute stress), and if one cannot cope, they will continue to the last stage of the GAS model; and, (3) the recovery or exhaustion stage – if the stressor is removed, they will recover, but if the stressor remains constant (i.e., chronic stress), they will experience mental exhaustion as a result (Kop & Kupper, 2016). Chronic stress and mental exhaustion result in chronic activation of the stress response system, which may lead to maladaptive outcomes such as HD through increased

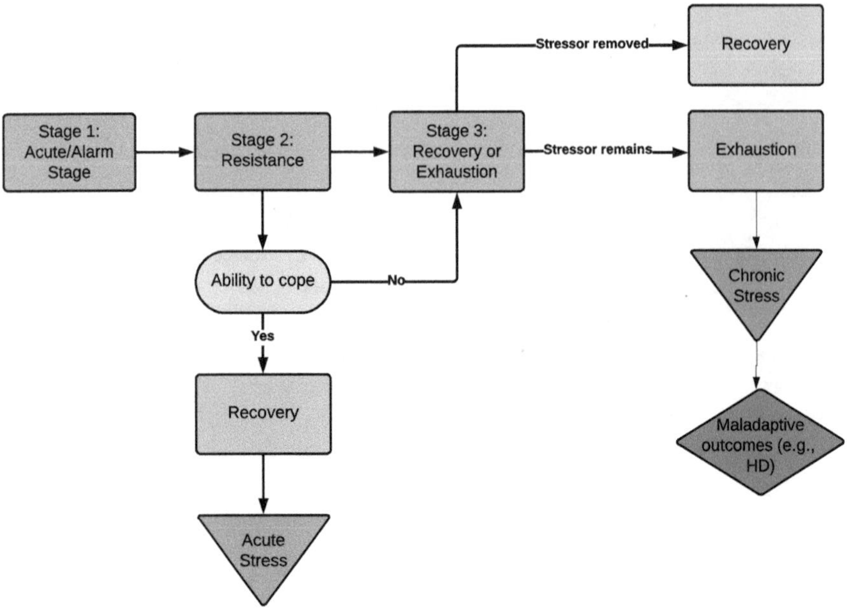

FIGURE 8.2 The GAS model.

cardiovascular strain and cortisol compromising (Hegg-Deloye et al., 2015; Roger, 2016; Igboanugo et al., 2021).

The physiological reactions produced by the stress response (i.e., sympathetic nervous system and hypothalamic–pituitary–adrenal [HPA] axis) include increased heart rate, dilation of blood vessels, increased respiratory rate, and release of catecholamines and glucocorticoids (McCarty, 2016; Adameova et al., 2009). These physiological reactions produced by the stress response system are initially beneficial as they equip someone with the ability to fight or flight; however, they become maladaptive when prolonged and/or frequently occur (Steptoe & Kivimäki, 2013). For example, excess amounts of catecholamines result in cardiac dysfunction, and under stressful conditions, high concentrations of catecholamines have been shown to produce coronary spasms, arrhythmias, cardiac dysfunction, and myocardial cell damage (Adameova et al., 2009). Any stress response has a negative effect on the body; however, chronic stress has been shown to have the most detrimental effects, such as manifestation into subsequent cardiovascular complications such as ischemic HD, myocardial infarction, heart failure, arrhythmias, and sudden death (Adameova et al., 2009). Refer to Figure 8.3 for a detailed explanation of the physiological mechanism of stress manifesting into CVD, as described by Adameova and colleagues (2009).

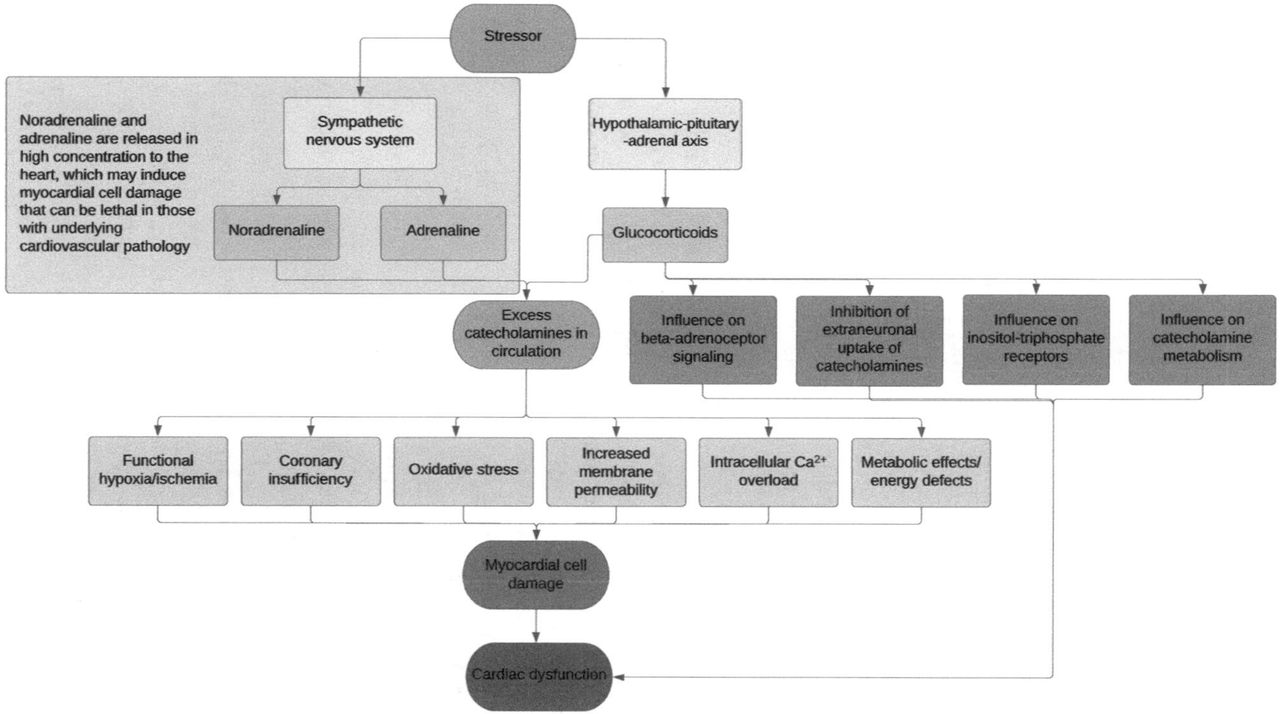

FIGURE 8.3 A summary of the physiological mechanism of stress developing into HD as described by Adameova and colleagues (2009).

Specific to FFs

The mechanism of stress manifesting into HD among FFs differs from the general mechanism regarding the type and frequency of stressors experienced and the physical demands of the job. The mechanism among FFs is rooted in occupational stressors, which is stress experienced as a direct result of work- or workplace-related incidents or environments. FFs experience unique occupational stressors that may make them susceptible to occupational stress injuries and HD, including exposure to workplace critical incidences (CIs), chronic activation of the stress response system, and physical demands during emergency dispatches (Angleman et al., 2022; Soteriades et al., 2011a).

A workplace CI is direct or indirect exposure to a traumatic incident, such as "death, serious injury, or sexual violence" while on the job and can be described as a sudden and overwhelming psychologically traumatic event that "exceeds beyond an individual's normal coping skills" (American Psychiatric Association, 2017; Nazari et al., 2020; Wagner et al., 2020). FFs are often exposed to CIs on the job and are required to respond to and diffuse these situations as part of their job requirements. This exposure to workplace CIs has been widely documented as a high-risk factor for occupational stress injuries among FFs. There are several ways in which exposure to workplace CIs may make an FF more susceptible to HD or on-duty cardiac events: (1) repeated exposure resulting in repeated activation of the stress response system, (2) development of an occupational stress injury (e.g., PTSD, general anxiety disorder) resulting in chronic activation of the stress response system, and (3) CI exposure in someone with an underlying heart condition resulting in an acute cardiac event (e.g., heart attack).

FFs' stress response system is activated each time there is an emergency dispatch; the alarm goes off, and they must immediately spring into action in a potentially life-threatening situation. This repeated activation of the stress response becomes a chronic activation, as their job is to respond to these calls. This chronic activation may then manifest into HD (Figure 8.3). Additionally, the acute transition from rest to peak performance experienced during emergency dispatch may trigger an acute cardiac event in people with an underlying heart condition. For example, data has shown that FFs have different circadian patterns for acute cardiac events compared to the general population (Soteriades et al., 2011b). In FFs, 67%–77% of on-duty acute cardiac deaths occur between noon and midnight, correlating with most emergency alarms and dispatches (Soteriades et al., 2011b). This data highlights stress or strenuous activity as a potential cause for on-duty cardiac deaths, as emergency alarms and dispatches are associated with high stress loads, activation of the stress response system, and strenuous activity. The most strenuous tasks, often associated with emergency dispatch, have been associated with the greatest risk of on-duty cardiac events among FFs (Soteriades et al., 2011b). For example, fire suppression has been cited as the cause of more than 30% of on-duty cardiac events (Soteriades et al., 2011b).

There is a second layer of complexity to the FF-specific stress–HD mechanism, where potential confounding variables must be considered, such as adverse coping mechanisms and sleep disturbances. Several studies have shown evidence that FFs who experience high occupational stress have an increase in HD risk factors such as smoking, poor dietary habits, and sleep disturbances (Angleman et al., 2022; Yook, 2019). Various non-fire-specific studies have also shown that people with stress disorders are more likely to have sleep disturbances and engage in adverse coping mechanisms such as smoking, poor dietary habits, and physical inactivity. Such adverse coping mechanisms are widely known to increase the risk of HD. Therefore, it is unknown if these potential confounding variables are a result of stress or are an external factor, therefore, they must be considered confounders unless proven that they are a result of stress. These potential confounding variables are discussed in detail below and can be observed in the fire-specific theoretical causal mechanism (Figure 8.4).

Confounding

Meaning and Impact of Confounding

Confounding is a type of systematic source of error that threatens the internal validity of a study by influencing the true effect of a relationship (Skelly et al., 2012). Confounding can be described as a "mixing of effects" where there are multiple factors and or interactions between multiple exposure factors that influence the outcome of interest, thereby "distorting" the true relationship between the exposure and outcome, making it difficult to determine a causal relationship (Skelly et al., 2012). There are two general types of confounders, a true confounding factor and a potential confounding factor (PCF). A true confounding factor will predict the outcome of interest in the absence of the exposure (i.e., have an independent relationship), whereas a PCF may or may not predict the outcome; both must be controlled for to avoid a systematic error (Skelly et al., 2012). A confounding factor will be associated with the exposure of interest but is not a proxy or surrogate outcome for the exposure and does not have an intermediate association between the exposure and outcome (Skelly et al., 2012). For example, smoking is a PCF in the stress–HD relationship because smoking is predictive of the outcome (i.e., HD) in the absence of the exposure (i.e., stress), and smoking is also associated with the exposure (i.e., stress) (refer to Figure 8.5). Confounding is a fundamental consideration when determining causality as confounding realities can lead to several errors: under or overestimation of the true relationship, type one error (i.e., false positive), or type two error (i.e., false negative). Therefore, to

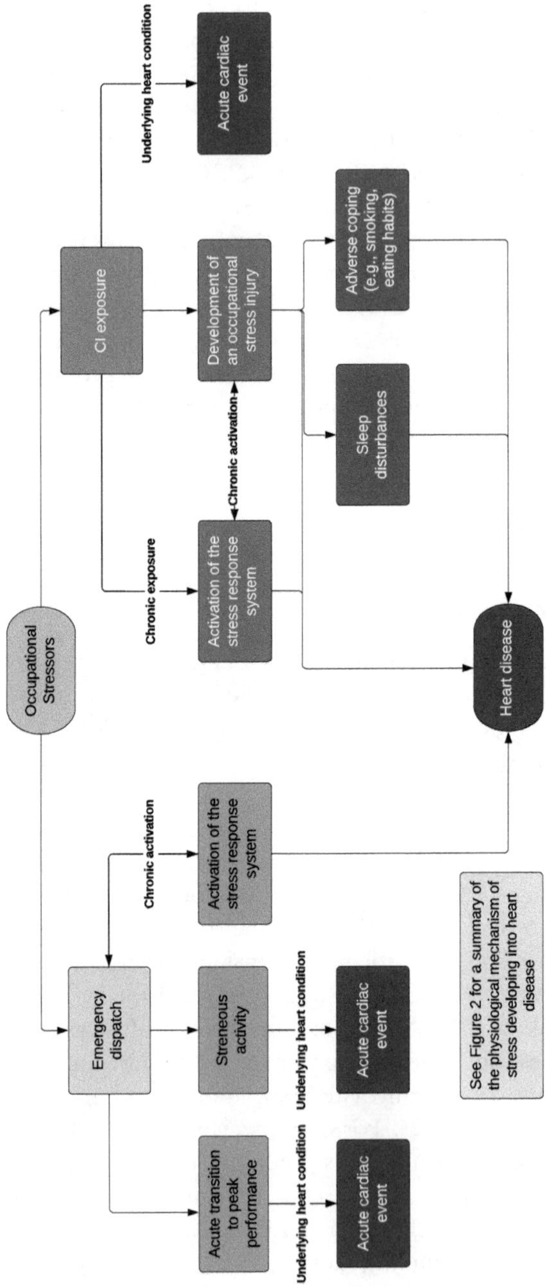

FIGURE 8.4 The theoretical FF stress–HD causal mechanism.

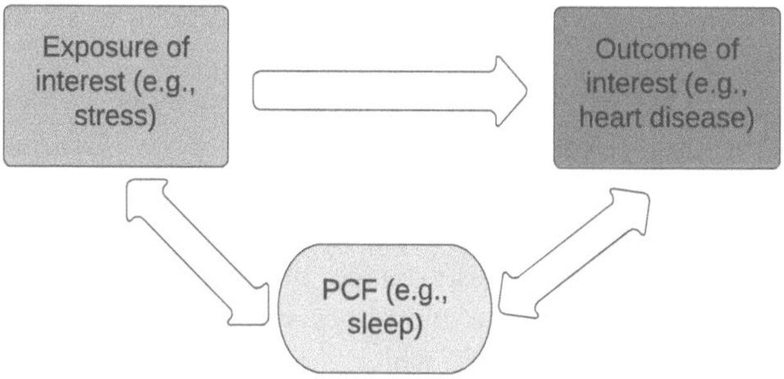

FIGURE 8.5 PCF example.

determine the true causal relationship confounding needs to be considered and controlled for. To control for confounding, all confounding factors (true and potential) must be reported, measured, and mathematically adjusted for in the analysis.

Potential Confounders in the Stress–HD Causal Hypothesis

There are various confounders that must be accounted for and controlled for in the stress–HD causal hypothesis among FFs, including sleep disturbances/shiftwork, diet, being overweight and obese, smoking, physical activity levels, genetics, age, and gas/particulate inhalation. The confounding factors in the stress–HD hypothesis among FFs are where the mechanism gets increasingly difficult to determine causality. Some confounders may or may not be due to workplace stressors, and determining whether these confounders would be present in the absence of these stressors is difficult. Since "confounding" factors in terms of the stress–HD causal hypothesis might be other exposures that are the more appropriate treatment targets, understanding which associations are causal and which are spurious or confounded is necessary. Below are the confounding factors that must be considered in the stress–HD causal hypothesis.

Sleep Disturbances/Shiftwork

FFs are required to provide 24-hour emergency services; this means they must work shift schedules, which has been shown to have detrimental effects on mental and heart health. There is a variation in shift schedules depending on country and location; for example, typically, most career FFs in Canada work rotating 24-hour on and 48-hour off or 48-hour on and 96-hour off shifts (Cramm et al., 2021). Shiftwork may result in an increased risk of HD through various factors, such as circadian misalignment, sleep disruption, and adverse mental health outcomes (Chellappa et al., 2019; Cramm et al., 2021; Soteriades et al., 2011b).

Animal and human studies have shown evidence of how shiftwork increases the risk for CVD through circadian misalignment and sleep disturbances (Chellappa et al., 2019). Circadian misalignment may result in coronary artery disease (CAD), cardiomyopathy, hypertension, stroke, and kidney disease (Chellappa et al., 2019). Sleep disturbances have been associated with atherosclerosis and changes in heart rate, blood pressure, autonomic nervous system functioning, and fluid homeostasis, which result in an increased risk of CVD (Chellappa et al., 2019).

The continuous disruption of the circadian rhythm and sleep disturbances have been shown to stimulate the HPA axis, which may induce activation of the stress response system and result in subsequent adverse heart and mental health outcomes (Cramm et al., 2021). For example, a 2021 study by Cramm and colleagues showed that FFs with insomnia had increased odds ratios and frequencies for "PTSD (OR = 4.98), generalized anxiety disorder (OR = 7.15), panic disorder (OR = 6.88), social phobia (OR = 4.98), and major depressive disorder (OR = 7.91)" (p. 1). Studies have also shown that shift workers may experience social isolation and psychological and psychosocial stress, which may result in stress disorders such as anxiety and mood disorders (Cramm et al., 2021). Lastly, FFs who have experienced CIs or have existing occupational stress injuries have also been shown to have an increased risk for sleep disturbances (Cramm et al., 2021). Therefore, shiftwork is a PCF in the stress–HD relationship because shiftwork is predictive of HD in the absence of stress, and shiftwork is also associated with stress.

Diet

The impact that diet has on HD is widely established in the literature, which shows how poor dietary choices can result in obesity, high blood pressure, and diabetes, all of which are risk factors for HD. Shiftwork has been suggested to adversely affect dietary habits, such as skipping meals, increased food consumption at night, and higher consumption of "unhealthy foods" (e.g., high saturated fats and soft drinks), which may increase one's risk for HD (Souza et al., 2019). Additionally, stress disorders may make people more likely to engage in poor dietary habits and subsequently have an increased risk for HD. For example, a 2018 systematic review and meta-analysis showed that individuals with PTSD were 5% less likely to have healthy diets (OR = 0.95; 95% CI: 0.92, 0.98) (van den Berk-Clark et al., 2018). Thus, diet is a PCF in the stress–HD relationship because diet is predictive of HD in the absence of stress, and diet is also associated with stress.

Being Overweight and Obese

Being overweight and obese is another well-known risk factor for HD. Most literature on the relationship between weight and HD focus on obesity. There is limited literature assessing the difference between being overweight and obese and its effect on HD. Additionally, most studies have grouped being overweight and obese as one factor rather than assessing them separately. The available literature suggests that the severity of being overweight or obese increases the risk of HD, namely, CVDs (Amani-Beni et al., 2023). This suggests that there may be a dose–response relationship among weight and HD. Due to the limited available literature, for the purpose of this chapter, we have assumed that the mechanism and risk factors of being overweight and obese are the same and that people who are obese are at higher risk for such adverse outcomes.

Obesity may cause changes in cardiac hemodynamics, structure, function, and conduction, which may increase the risk of heart failure and other HD risk factors, such as hypertension, sleep apnea, diabetes, and atrial fibrillation (Ebong et al., 2014). Obesity also may cause metabolic changes (e.g., insulin resistance, adipokine release, and inflammation) that can result in endothelial dysfunction and atherogenesis, which can result in CAD, cardiomyopathy, and heart failure (Ebong et al., 2014). Obesity is an independent risk factor for HD; however, stress and related stress disorders, such as PTSD, have been shown to increase the risk for obesity. For example, a 2018 systematic review and meta-analysis showed that individuals with PTSD were 31% more likely to be obese (pooled adjusted $OR = 1.31$; 95% CI:1.25, 1.38) (van den Berk-Clark et al., 2018). Therefore, obesity is a PCF in the stress–HD relationship because obesity is predictive of HD in the absence of stress, and obesity is also associated with stress.

Smoking

Smoking is another well-established independent risk factor for HD. Smoking can increase the risk of atherosclerosis, myocardial infarction, stroke, transient ischemic attacks, and peripheral vascular disease (Fagerström, 2002). Literature has also shown that people with stress disorders, such as PTSD, are more likely to be current smokers. For example, a 2018 systematic review and meta-analysis showed that individuals with PTSD were 22% more likely to be current smokers (pooled adjusted $OR = 1.22$; 95% CI: 1.19, 1.26) (van den Berk-Clark et al., 2018). A recent study on PTSD symptoms and CVD among a sample of US FFs found a medium association between PTSD symptoms and current smoking status ($r = 0.328$, $t = -3.198$, $p < 0.01$) (Angleman et al., 2022). However, another study observed no such correlations between occupational work stress and smoking status among an FF sample in Korea

(Yook, 2019). Smoking is thus a PCF in the stress–HD relationship because smoking is predictive of HD in the absence of stress, and smoking may also be associated with stress.

Physical Activity Levels

Physical activity levels are a well-established factor that may increase or decrease one's risk for HD. Various epidemiological and experimental studies have shown evidence of a causal relationship between low physical activity levels and increased risk of atherosclerosis and HD (Archer & Blair, 2011; Soteriades et al., 2011b). In contrast, regular physical activity has been widely shown to be a cardioprotective factor (Archer & Blair, 2011; Soteriades et al., 2011b). Studies have also shown how stress disorders are linked to physical inactivity. For example, a 2018 systematic review and meta-analysis showed that people with PTSD were 9% less likely to engage in physical activity (pooled adjusted OR = 0.91; 95% CI: 0.88, 0.93) (van den Berk-Clark et al., 2018). Therefore, physical activity is a PCF as it is predictive of HD in the absence of stress and may also be associated with stress.

Genetics

Genetics is an independent risk factor that may predispose people to have an increased risk of developing HD. For example, arrhythmias, congenital HD, cardiomyopathy, and high blood cholesterol may be inherited and can lead to heart attack, stroke, and heart failure (University of Ottawa Heart Institute, n.d.). Thus, genetics can be seen as a true confounder predictive of HD in the absence of stress.

Age

HD typically takes decades to develop and is more common in older adults, which makes increasing age an independent predictor of HD and a true confounder.

Gas/Particulate Inhalation

FFs are exposed to gas and particulate inhalation on the job, which may increase their risk for HD. Exposure to fine particulate matter ($PM_{2.5}$) has been linked to increased blood pressure, thrombosis, insulin resistance, vascular injury, and accelerated atherogenesis (Bhatnagar, 2021). Animal studies also suggest that $PM_{2.5}$ may be associated with oxidative stress, inflammation, and activation of the autonomic nervous system, which may increase the risk for HD (Bhatnagar, 2021). Today gas and particulate exposure among FFs has been significantly reduced by personal protective equipment; however, FFs may not wear their safety equipment for the entire duration of the dispatch call (e.g., after fire suppression) (Soteriades et al., 2011b). Therefore, FFs may be exposed to gas and particulate matter while on the job, which is an independent predictor of HD and, thereby, a true confounder.

Critical Analysis of the Quality of Evidence

After determining the theoretical causal mechanism based on existing literature and evidence, a critical analysis of the quality of evidence may be performed. Determining the quality of evidence will determine how confident we are in the results and conclusions made about causality. The analysis of the quality of evidence must be performed prior to the analysis of causation, as the analysis of quality will influence several areas of Hill's Criteria. To determine the quality of evidence, several important steps must be taken, including consideration of study design, synthesis of evidence, and critical appraisal of evidence. Below we will discuss how to perform each step and the important considerations of each in the stress–HD relationship among FFs.

Importance of Study Design

The study design is one of the strongest considerations when determining causality among a presumed cause and observed effect. The study design relates to several of Hill's aspects of association, consistency, temporality, and experiment, and when designing or evaluating a study, they should be taken into consideration. Consistency should be taken into consideration by designing a study with varying methods, populations, and locations compared to the existing literature to be able to show consistency among the results. Temporality means that associations are more likely to be causal if the exposure occurred prior to the onset of the disease. Temporality is difficult to determine in diseases with long latency, like HD and cancer. For example, in the stress–HD relationship, a longitudinal design would ideally follow FFs during training and follow them for decades and continually assess exposures of interest and confounding variables. Performing such a prospective cohort study is limited by cost, time, and likely large loss of follow-up rates among respondents. Lastly, experiments are the strongest design to show causality. Experimental designs distribute known and unknown confounders evenly across exposure groups and strengthen confidence that the exposures were causal. However, experimental designs are impossible/unethical to perform, as it is inhumane to perform an experiment where participants are subjected to occupational stressors as experienced by FF to assess HD outcomes. Cross-sectional designs are most common among the stress–HD relationship, which fails to show temporality and experiment, providing low certainty on causation.

Synthesis of Evidence

To determine causality among the stress–HD relationship, or any relationship, all available and relevant literature should be identified and synthesized. Evidence synthesis may be performed through a systematic or scoping review, where a systematic approach is used to identify all relevant literature, and all relevant data is collated and synthesized. These results, along with the critical appraisals for each included article, will be the basis of the critical analysis of causation. For the stress–HD relationship, various information should be extracted to perform a critical analysis of quality and causation, including author(s), year of publication, country of publication, type of study, number of participants, participant information/demographics, measurement of stress, measurement of HD, confounding variables accounted for, and results. All extractions should be performed independently among two reviewers to ensure accuracy and non-biased reporting; any disagreements should be resolved by reaching a consensus or consulting a third reviewer.

Critical Appraisal of Evidence

Critically appraising articles when determining causality is another key step. Depending on the study design, there are various critical appraisal tools, such as the Cochrane risk of bias tool for randomized trials (ROB2) and the Quality in Prognosis Studies tool (QUIPS). Performing a critical appraisal will determine the quality of the study by assessing several domains of bias, which will influence how confident we are in the results of the study. For the stress–HD relationship, the critical appraisal tool that can be used is the QUIPS tool. The QUIPS tool assesses six domains of bias: study participation, study attrition, prognostic factor measurement, confounding measurement and account, outcome measurement, and analysis and reporting (Hayden et al., 2013). Each domain of bias is rated as high, moderate, or low. The overall risk of bias is determined based on the individual ratings of each domain with an emphasis on the most important domains (identified a priori) (Hayden et al., 2013). The appraisals should be performed for each included article independently among two reviewers to ensure accuracy and non-biased reporting; any disagreements should be resolved by reaching a consensus or consulting a third reviewer.

Critical Analysis of Causation Using Hills Rules of Causation

After systematically identifying relevant literature, synthesizing data, and critically appraising the literature, a critical analysis of causation can be performed using Hill's nine aspects of association. However, the currently available literature on the stress–HD relationship among FFs is not sufficient to be able to determine causation. The literature has shown that occupational stress increases risk factors for HD, including sleep, smoking, and overweight/obesity (Angleman et al., 2022; Steptoe & Kivimäki, 2013; Yook, 2019). However, this literature is limited by a small number of studies, methodological design (i.e., unable to show temporality), risk of overfit sample sizes (i.e., largely male samples and cohorts from a singular location), and measurement of predictor outcomes (i.e., not measuring HD directly). The remainder of this section will review the nine criteria in terms of their role in establishing causation in the stress–HD relationship among FFs.

Strength of Relationship

The strength of the relationship between stress and HD is an argument for causation; specifically, the larger the association, the more likely it is to be causal (Fedak et al., 2015). One must consider the quality of the evidence when assessing the strength of the relationship, as biases, as described by the QUIPS tool, can influence the results of a study. For example, a study examining the relationship between posttraumatic stress symptoms and CVD risk in FFs found a medium association for triglycerides, current smoking status, and an overall number of CVD risk factors ($r = 0.297, 0.328$, and 0.281, $p < 0.01$) (Angleman et al., 2022). However, this study is at risk for an overfit sample, as they sampled one specific special operations fire unit that regularly engaged in physical activity (CVD protective factor) and had a small homogenous sample. These results must be interpreted in conjunction with the critical appraisal and potential biases present in the study. In this example, the results of this study did not show a large association, but if they did, these results would still not be sufficient for an argument of causation as the sample size has several potential biases.

Consistency

The consistency of the results refers to consistent results among various studies with varying methods, populations, and locations (Fedak et al., 2015). If the included studies have homogenous study methods, populations, and locations, the sample is at risk of being overfit, and the results would not be generalizable to the entire FF population. To determine causation, the methods and samples of studies should vary while still showing consistent results. In the stress–HD relationship, most studies are cross-sectional or cohort studies, which has negative implications for consistency and temporality. Study populations and locations among these studies are often sampled at one location or geographical area, which may put each individual study at risk for overfitting. However, by performing a systematic review and meta-analysis and pooling the results from these studies from various locations and geographical locations, there will no longer be a concern for overfit samples.

Specificity

The criteria specificity suggests that exposures that only cause one disease are more likely to be causal (Fedak et al., 2015). This criterion has been considered "weak" because many diseases have multiple causes and risk factors that may influence the etiology of the disease (Fedak et al., 2015). The failure to meet this criterion should not diminish the results of the remaining criteria in proving causality. In the stress–HD, relationship specificity will never be able to be proven in the general or FF population, as there are numerous confounding variables that may influence the development of HD.

Temporality

The criterion of temporality is essential to determine a causal relationship and states that exposure must occur before the onset of disease (Fedak et al., 2015). In the stress–HD relationship, this means participants must not have HD or predictor outcomes of HD (e.g., high cholesterol, genetic predisposition) prior to stress exposure(s). HD is the leading cause of death and disability worldwide; thus, finding a large enough sample size that does not have HD or predictor outcomes would be difficult among the general and FF populations. Additionally, the study design must be longitudinal, following FFs for decades starting before their career and continually assessing their stress, CI exposure, confounders, and HD predictors and outcomes. A study of this design and nature would be limited by cost, time, and likely large dropout/lost to follow-up rates among participants. Due to these limitations, often cross-sectional or cohort study designs are often chosen, which fail to be able to show temporality.

Biological Gradient

The criteria biological gradient suggests that if there is an observed dose–response relationship, the relationship is more likely to be causal (Fedak et al., 2015). In the stress–HD relationship, we would aim to determine if the incidence of HD increases as stress levels increase. Several measures and scales can be used to predict the level of stress FFs may be experiencing, such as the number/duration of CI exposures, the perceived stress scale, and symptom severity for mental health outcomes (e.g., posttraumatic stress symptom severity). These results can then be compared with HD incidence/outcomes and used to calculate a dose–response curve.

Plausibility

The criteria plausibility states that a causal hypothesis should be based on existing biological or social models (Fedak et al., 2015). In the stress–HD relationship among FFs, existing biological and social models have shown that stress increases the risk for adverse mental health outcomes, and FFs have high occupational stress loads and incidence of adverse mental health outcomes (Berger et al., 2012; Naim et al., 2020), where such adverse mental health outcomes and chronic stress increase the risk for predictor outcomes of HD (Angleman et al., 2022; Steptoe & Kivimäki, 2013; Yook, 2019). Therefore, the plausibility behind the stress–HD relationship among FFs is coherent with the literature and meets this criterion.

Coherence

The criteria coherence is similar to plausibility and states that the cause-and-effect mechanism should be consistent with all available knowledge/evidence of the disease (Fedak et al., 2015). As explained above in the theoretical stress–HD hypothesis, the cause-and-effect mechanism is consistent with all available knowledge and evidence (Adameova et al., 2009; McCarty, 2016; Steptoe & Kivimäki, 2013). Thus, the criterion coherence has been met in the stress–HD relationship.

Experiment

The criterion evidence states that evidence from experimental manipulation may have the strongest support for causality (Fedak et al., 2015). Experimental studies are performed in highly controlled environments where temporality and confounders can be manipulated and controlled to observe the cause-and-effect relationship unbiasedly. To perform such an experiment among participants, they would have to be exposed to highly stressful situations, including traumatic CIs experienced among FFs for an extended period, to determine if they develop HD, which is grossly unethical and thereby impossible to conduct an experiment based on this relationship. Notably, to perform such an experiment among animals is impossible, as certain stress exposures (i.e., CIs) among FFs would be unable to be reproduced in animal studies.

Analogy

The last criterion is an analogy, which states that if there is strong evidence of a causal relationship between an agent and a disease, then research should be more accepting of weaker evidence between a similar agent and disease (Fedak et al., 2015). Studies have been performed among the general population, and animal studies have shown promising evidence for a causal relationship between stress and HD. These studies showed large associations in human and animal studies between chronic stress and risk of coronary HD (~40%–60% increased risk), and various methods, populations, and locations were used among these studies (Steptoe & Kivimäki, 2013; Wirtz & von Känel, 2017). Additionally, these studies suggested that work stress, social isolation, and loneliness play a role in the development of HD (~1.5-fold increase risk) (Steptoe & Kivimäki, 2013). However, controlled longitudinal studies that focus on the role of psychological stress in various cardiovascular outcomes are needed to explore causality further among the general population (Steptoe & Kivimäki, 2013; Wirtz & von Känel, 2017). This evidence for a potential causal relationship among the general population can be applied to the FF population as they have the same risk factors, but they also have additional risk factors to be considered in their causal mechanism.

Summary

In this chapter, we discussed the literature and the extent to which it has supported the causation of the stress–HD relationship among FFs and identified why critical appraisal and critical analysis of causation should be considered in combination when attempting to analyze this potential relationship. Currently, there is not enough literature or evidence to perform a critical appraisal or analysis of causation among FFs. However, using the existing literature, the theoretical mechanism, steps, and considerations to perform an analysis of causation have been discussed. Future studies on the stress–HD relationship among FFs should focus on longitudinal study designs among diverse samples with varying methods and locations and measuring HD directly. When there is a variety of literature available from different populations and locations performed using various methods, a critical analysis of causation may be performed. As discussed, certain aspects of Hills criteria are less relevant in the stress–HD relationship among FFs. We suggest that the criteria that should be focused on when designing studies or performing an analysis of this mechanism are the strength of the relationship, consistency, temporality, and biological gradient. We hope to facilitate and encourage the use of Bradford Hill's Criteria in designing and analyzing the stress–HD relationship among FFs and other similar research areas.

Conflicts of interest: We have no conflicts of interest to disclose. *Acknowledgments:* JCM is funded by the Canadian Institutes for Health Research (FRN: 162539 and 165070). JCM is supported by a Canada Research Chair (Tier 1) in Musculoskeletal Health Outcomes and Knowledge Translation and the Dr. James Roth Research Chair in Musculoskeletal Measurement and Knowledge Translation.

References

Adameova, A., Abdellatif, Y., & Dhalla, N. S. (2009). Role of the excessive amounts of circulating catecholamines and glucocorticoids in stress-induced heart disease. Canadian Journal of Physiology and Pharmacology, 87(7), 493–514. https://doi.org/10.1139/Y09-042

Alghamdi, M., Hunt, N., & Thomas, S. (2017). Prevalence rate of PTSD, depression and anxiety symptoms among Saudi firefighters. Journal of Traumatic Stress Disorders & Treatment, 06(01). https://doi.org/10.4172/2324-8947.1000164

Amani-Beni, R., Darouei, B., Zefreh, H., Sheikhbahaei, E., & Sadeghi, M. (2023). Effect of obesity duration and BMI trajectories on cardiovascular disease: A narrative review. Cardiology and Therapy. https://doi.org/10.1007/s40119-023-00317-6

American Psychiatric Association. (2017). *Diagnostic and statistical manual of mental disorders: DSM-5*. Arlington, VA: American Psychiatric Association.

Angleman, A. J., van Hasselt, V. B., & Schuhmann, B. B. (2022). Relationship between posttraumatic stress symptoms and cardiovascular disease risk in firefighters. Behavior Modification, 46(2), 321–351. https://doi.org/10.1177/0145445521 1061320

Archer, E., & Blair, S. N. (2011). Physical activity and the prevention of cardiovascular disease: From evolution to epidemiology. Progress in Cardiovascular Diseases, 53(6), 387–396. https://doi.org/10.1016/j.pcad.2011.02.006

Berger, W., Coutinho, E. S. F., Figueira, I., Marques-Portella, C., Luz, M. P., Neylan, T. C., Marmar, C. R., & Mendlowicz, M. V. (2012). Rescuers at risk: A systematic review and meta-regression analysis of the worldwide current prevalence and correlates of PTSD in rescue workers. Social Psychiatry and Psychiatric Epidemiology, 47(6). https://doi.org/10.1007/s00127-011-0408-2

Bhatnagar, A. (2021). Annual review of medicine cardiovascular effects of particulate air pollution. https://doi.org/10.1146/annurev-med-042220

Bradford Hill, A. B. (1965). The environment and disease: Association or causation?. Proceedings of the Royal Society of Medicine, 58(5), 295–300.

Chellappa, S. L., Vujovic, N., Williams, J. S., & Scheer, F. A. J. L. (2019). Impact of circadian disruption on cardiovascular function and disease. Trends in Endocrinology and Metabolism, 30(10), 767–779). https://doi.org/10.1016/j.tem.2019.07.008

Cramm, H., Richmond, R., Jamshidi, L., Edgelow, M., Groll, D., Ricciardelli, R., Macdermid, J. C., Keiley, M., & Nicholas Carleton, R. (2021). Mental health of Canadian firefighters: The impact of sleep. International Journal of Environmental Research and Public Health, 18(24). https://doi.org/10.3390/ijerph182413256

Ebong, I. A., Goff, D. C., Rodriguez, C. J., Chen, H., & Bertoni, A. G. (2014). Mechanisms of heart failure in obesity. Obesity Research and Clinical Practice, 8(6), e540–e548). https://doi.org/10.1016/j.orcp.2013.12.005

Fagerström, K. (2002). The epidemiology of smoking health consequences and benefits of cessation. Drugs, 62.

Fedak, K. M., Bernal, A., Capshaw, Z. A., & Gross, S. (2015). Applying the Bradford Hill criteria in the 21st century: How data integration has changed causal inference in molecular epidemiology. Emerging Themes in Epidemiology, 12(1), 14. https://doi.org/10.1186/s12982-015-0037-4

Hayden, J. A., van der Windt, D. A., Cartwright, J. L., Cô, P., & Bombardier, C. (2013). Assessing bias in studies of prognostic factors. www.annals.org

Hegg-Deloye, S., Brassard, P., Prairie, J., Larouche, D., Jauvin, N., Poirier, P., Tremblay, A., & Corbeil, P. (2015). Prevalence of risk factors for cardiovascular disease in paramedics. International Archives of Occupational and Environmental Health, 88(7). https://doi.org/10.1007/s00420-015-1028-z

Igboanugo, S., Bigelow, P. L., & Mielke, J. G. (2021). Health outcomes of psychosocial stress within firefighters: A systematic review of the research landscape. Journal of Occupational Health, 63(1).` https://doi.org/10.1002/1348-9585.12219

Institute for Health Metrics and Evaluation. (2020, October 15). Cardiovascular diseases – Level 2 cause. Healthdata.org. Retrieved August 4, 2022, from www.healthdata.org/results/gbd_summaries/2019/cardiovascular-diseases-level-2-cause

Kop, W. J., & Kupper, H. M. (2016). Fatigue and stress. In G. Fink (Ed.), *Stress: Concepts, cognition, emotion, and behavior; stress: Concepts, cognition, emotion, and behavior* (pp. 345–350, Chapter xiii, 487 Pages) Elsevier Academic Press, San Diego, CA.

McCarty, R. (2016). The alarm phase and the general adaptation syndrome. In G. Fink (Ed.), *Stress: Concepts, cognition, emotion, and behavior; stress: Concepts, cognition, emotion, and behavior* (pp. 69–90). Amsterdam: Elsevier Academic Press.

Naim, M., Salleh, M., Ismail, H., & Yusoff, H. M. (2020). Prevalence and predictors for post-traumatic stress disorder (PTSD) among firefighters: A systematic review. International Journal of Public Health Research, 10.

Nazari, G., MacDermid, J. C., Sinden, K., D'Amico, R., Brazil, A., Carleton, N., & Cramm, H. (2020). Prevalence of exposure to critical incidents in firefighters across Canada. Work, 67(1), 215–222. https://doi.org/10.3233/WOR-203267

Public Health Agency of Canada. (2022). Heart disease in Canada. Retrieved November 16, 2020, from www.canada.ca/en/public-health/services/publications/diseases-conditions/heart-disease-canada.html

Roger, D. (2016). Rumination, stress, and emotion. In G. Fink (Ed.), *Stress: Concepts, cognition, emotion, and behavior* (pp. 261–266). Ontario: Elsevier Academic Press.

Skelly, A., Dettori, J., & Brodt, E. (2012). Assessing bias: The importance of considering confounding. Evidence-Based Spine-Care Journal, 3(01), 9–12. https://doi.org/10.1055/s-0031-1298595

Soteriades, E. S., Smith, D. L., Tsismenakis, A. J., Baur, D. M., & Kales, S. N. (2011a). Cardiovascular disease in US firefighters. Cardiology in Review, 19(4), 202–215. https://doi.org/10.1097/CRD.0b013e318215c105

Soteriades, E. S., Smith, D. L., Tsismenakis, A. J., Baur, D. M., & Kales, S. N. (2011b). Cardiovascular disease in US firefighters: A systematic review. Cardiology in Review, 19(4), 202–215. https://doi.org/10.1097/CRD.0b013e318215c105

Souza, R. V., Sarmento, R. A., Carnevale De Almeida, J., & Canuto, R. (2019). The effect of shift work on eating habits. Scandinavian Journal of Work, 45(1), 7–21. https://doi.org/10.2307/26567055

Steptoe, A., & Kivimäki, M. (2013). Stress and cardiovascular disease: An update on current knowledge. Annual Review of Public Health, 34, 337–354. https://doi.org/10.1146/annurev-publhealth-031912-114452

van den Berk-Clark, C., Secrest, S., Walls, J., Hallberg, E., Lustman, P. J., Schneider, F. D., & Scherrer, J. F. (2018). Supplemental material for association between posttraumatic stress disorder and lack of exercise, poor diet, obesity, and co-occuring smoking: A systematic review and meta-analysis. Health Psychology. https://doi.org/10.1037/hea0000593.supp

Wagner, S. L., White, N., Regehr, C., White, M., Alden, L. E., Buys, N., Carey, M. G., Corneil, W., Fyfe, T., Matthews, L. R., Randall, C., Krutop, E., & Fraess-Phillips, A. (2020). Ambulance personnel: Systematic review of mental health symptoms. Traumatology, 26(4). https://doi.org/10.1037/trm0000251

Wirtz, P. H., & von Känel, R. (2017). Psychological stress, inflammation, and coronary heart disease. Current Cardiology Reports, 19(11). Current Medicine Group LLC 1. https://doi.org/10.1007/s11886-017-0919-x

Yook, Y.-S. (2019). Firefighters' occupational stress and its correlations with cardiorespiratory fitness, arterial stiffness, heart rate variability, and sleep quality. PLOS ONE, 14(12). https://doi.org/10.1371/journal.pone.0226739

9

OVERVIEW OF STRESS AND FIREFIGHTER MENTAL HEALTH

Maria D. H. Koeppel and Sara A. Jahnke

Modern-Day Firefighter: Responders to Everything

Initially organized to respond to neighbourhood fires in early European colonies, modern-day firefighters are responsible for far more than their title suggests, working in more dangerous environments than those faced by their predecessors. To begin with, modern building materials and structure styles result in fires that burn hotter and faster than legacy structures or those built prior to 1940 (Tobin & Shady, 2022). The increased use of synthetic materials, mixed with the decreased use of solid wood, also means structures are prone to collapsing at a faster rate, making an already dangerous environment even more so for firefighters (Williams, 2016). As the actual number of structure fires has trended downwards due to an increased emphasis on building safety and fire prevention (Hall & Evarts, 2022), fire departments have broadened their response scope as a means of job security. In addition to fire suppression, firefighters are now tasked with a slew of emergency services, including rescue operations, hazardous materials management, natural and man-made disaster response, and providing emergency medical care. The wide variety of emergency responses, in conjunction with increasing calls for service, leaves firefighters vulnerable to unprecedented occupational stress and adverse mental health outcomes.

Occupational Stress in the Fire Service

Fire suppression is a physically and mentally taxing component of the job. Personal protective equipment (PPE) can weigh over 50 pounds, while hose lines filled with water charged at high pressures weigh several hundred pounds.

DOI: 10.4324/9781003424253-13

Firefighters are tasked with manoeuvring and controlling hose lines, rescuing patients, pulling ceilings and walls, climbing ladders, and using machinery while under the load of their PPE and in environments reaching well over 1,000 degrees Fahrenheit. The physical strain contributes to significant cardiovascular and thermal strain (Barr et al., 2011; Dorman & Havenith, 2009; Smith et al., 2001), in addition to mental strain. The physicality, in conjunction with the responsibility associated with the job, as well as the dangerous environment in which firefighters operate, creates a unique form of mental stress. This stress includes task management in high-pressure situations, maintaining constant situational awareness for the safety of self and others, and physiological responses to heat, dehydration, and muscle fatigue (Canetti et al., 2022). Fire suppression activities temporarily decrease cognitive abilities, including cognitive capacity and visual and auditory performances (Canetti et al., 2022; Hemmatjo et al., 2020).

Beyond the mental strain of firefighting, the growing responsibilities of responding to natural disasters, man-made tragedies, pandemics and epidemics, and medical calls add an unpredictable level of stress to being on duty. For example, firefighters on duty during natural disasters must navigate an internal struggle between service to the community and service to their families. These events are accompanied by an influx of service calls, splitting the focus of the firefighter between doing their job while attempting to ascertain the safety and whereabouts of their family members. The intentional nature associated with active-shooter incidents or tragedies like 9/11 results in extreme forms of stress as firefighters actively juggle their own life safety while tending to patients. These events uniquely impact the trauma process, as firefighters may project their children's faces onto young victims, while their privacy to cope may be greatly impacted by constant media coverage (DeMarco, 2018). Working during pandemics and epidemics places firefighters at high risk for the contraction of viruses, negatively impacting their home lives as spouses and children take precautions for their health (Wang, 2020).

Nationally, 65% of emergency calls are medical in nature and range from service calls such as lift assists to simple medical calls involving sprains or strains to traumatic events involving death and mutilation (Rindge, 2018). As a result of the growing call volume (NFPA, 2021), in addition to their expanding job description (Bureau, 2018), repeated exposure to trauma is now considered an occupational hazard of the fire service (Jahnke et al., 2016), as over 90% of firefighters are estimated to be exposed to trauma (Meyer et al., 2012). In addition to direct exposure to trauma, firefighters experience "secondary trauma" or "vicarious trauma," as well as "compassion fatigue." The former refers to the negative psychological impact on firefighters who come into contact with trauma through the experiences of others (Fisher & Etches, 2003), while the latter is the negative psychological impact associated with helping others (Clay, 2022). Significant research has been dedicated to understanding the impact these occupational stressors have on the health and wellness of firefighters. An additional growing body of research has found considerable links between occupational stressors such as chronic traumatic exposure to a number of adverse mental health concerns, including symptoms of depression and anxiety, as well as posttraumatic stress disorder (PTSD), and substance use (Haddock et al., 2011; Jahnke et al., 2016; Meyer et al., 2012; Poston et al., 2013; Wagner et al., 2021), outcomes which may be exacerbated by other job characteristics, including intense work hours, and frequent separation from family (Bartlett et al., 2019; Fisher & Etches, 2003; Saijo et al., 2008).

Depression Disorder

Depression disorder is characterized by the experience of negative emotions greatly impacting daily cognitive, emotional, social, and occupational function (Tao et al., 2022). Depression, as a symptom or disorder, leaves an individual feeling sad, hopeless, apathetic, and fatigued and impacts millions of people around the world. Rates of major depressive disorder in the United States have steadily increased over the past decade, hitting almost 20%, with associated costs topping over $325 billion (Greenberg et al., 2021). The recent COVID-19 pandemic pushed rates even higher, with healthcare workers experiencing a substantial increase in the disorder (Ettman et al., 2020; Li et al., 2021). Despite such high prevalence among the general population, pre-pandemic depression symptoms among firefighters were found to be even greater. Up to 27% of sampled career and volunteer firefighters report significant depressive symptoms (Haddock et al., 2011), while more than a quarter of surveyed firefighters responding to a natural disaster were in the range of concern for a depressive disorder (Tak et al., 2007). The prevalence of depressive disorder among international firefighters ranges from 18.2% to 53.3% (Alghamdi et al., 2017; Majani et al., 2022).

The prevalence of major depressive disorder and symptoms of depression among firefighters is no surprise when one considers the job description. In general, exposure to lifetime traumatic experiences is associated with increased depressive symptoms (Tracy et al., 2014). Given the close relationship between being a first responder and being exposed to trauma (Alghamdi et al., 2017; Jahnke et al., 2016; Majani et al., 2022; Meyer et al., 2012), this relationship is exacerbated among firefighters. As a result, frequent job-related trauma exposure is a strong predictor of depression symptoms among firefighters (Alghamdi et al., 2017; Majani et al., 2022). Trauma experienced by firefighters may include a diverse range of experiences, such as providing care to seriously injured victims, arriving on scene to death or dismemberment from intentional violence, working with patients in mangled vehicles, or deaths or injuries of coworkers while working. Additionally, experiencing trauma may occur repeatedly throughout a short period or occur over longer periods with time in between events, making traumatic events impossible to mentally prepare for witnessing it.

Aside from a positive relationship between repeated exposure to trauma, several other occupational factors leave firefighters vulnerable to depressive symptoms. Sleep, which is discussed later, is one such factor. Firefighters with clinical insomnia are six times more likely to experience major depressive disorder than firefighters without insomnia (Cramm et al., 2021). Exposure to natural disasters is another factor, as the condition has been found to be a common problem for populations experiencing natural disasters (Fullerton et al., 2004; Ginexi et al., 2000). Firefighters responding to Hurricane Katrina had a higher risk of depression disorder if they had health challenges (such as respiratory issues) or extended time away from families (Tak et al., 2007). Meanwhile, a systematic review indicated that incident-related factors, including severity and duration of disaster and trauma exposure, are directly related to the manifestation of depression disorder in a cross-national sample of firefighters (Wagner et al., 2021). Finally, low social support, feelings of insecurity, and a perceived lack of control are determinants of depressive symptoms (Regehr et al., 2000; Saijo et al., 2008).

Anxiety Disorders

As one of the most common mental health concerns in North America, anxiety disorders include generalized anxiety disorder, social anxiety disorder, panic disorder, and a host of phobias. In general, experiencing symptoms of anxiety manifests as excessive nervous-related emotional and behavioural responses, including avoidant behaviour (Tao et al., 2022), while physical manifestations include increased heart rate, hyperventilation, sweating, and trembling (National Institutes of Health, 2022). Up to 19% (over 40 million) of adults in the United States have an anxiety disorder, with rates increasing as a result of the recent pandemic (National Alliance on Mental Health, 2017; Terlizzi & Villarroel, 2020).

Despite often being grouped together by research examining mental health, less focus has been placed on anxiety among firefighters. A national sample found that over 10% of firefighters reported an anxiety disorder ever diagnosed by a physician (Poston et al., 2013), while a Canadian study found that up to 19% of sampled firefighters experienced anxiety disorders (Carleton, Afifi, Turner et al., 2018). The prevalence of anxiety jumped to 44% in a small Saudi Arabian firefighter sample (Alghamdi et al., 2017). These prevalences are not surprising given several occupational characteristics placing firefighters at high risk for anxiety. Similar to major depressive disorder, anxiety may result from psychological costs associated with exposure to traumatic events (Alghamdi et al., 2017), a known trait associated with firefighting. Additionally, firefighters with insomnia, a common occurrence in the fire service, were over seven times more likely to screen positive for generalized anxiety disorder (Cramm et al., 2021).

PTSD

Perhaps the most studied mental health concern for firefighters, PTSD is the most common adverse effect associated with repeated traumatic exposure. Defined as a psychiatric disorder resulting from experiencing or witnessing a traumatic event(s), PTSD's history is largely rooted in the combat experiences of veterans (National Center for posttraumatic stress disorder [PTSD], 2022). After returning from war, veterans would experience panic, sleep problems, and emotional volatility. Although the name of these symptoms has evolved from "shell shock" to "combat stress reaction" to "posttraumatic stress disorder," the overall meaning has been the same – reoccurring, long-lasting, and/or extreme reactions to trauma (National Center for PTSD, 2022). As the definition of trauma expanded during the development of the diagnosis to include more than combat experience, research unveiled just how common PTSD is in the general population. On average, the prevalence of PTSD in the United States general population is around 6% (National Center for PTSD, 2021), with women experiencing slightly higher rates than men (National Center for PTSD, 2021).

As stated previously, firefighters are repeatedly exposed to various forms of trauma while on duty. Trauma related to emergency medical calls may include the discovery of a dead body, while trauma related to motor vehicle accidents may include dismemberment, disembowelment, or decapitation. Responses to fires and natural disasters include witnessing the destruction of life and property, potentially while homeowners stand by watching. Additionally, volunteer firefighters are at an increased risk of responding to friends and family, adding an additional layer of complexity to the trauma they experience. Given these reoccurring scenarios, it is unsurprising to find that the prevalence of PTSD in the fire service may reach as high as 37% (Berninger et al., 2010; Bryant & Harvey, 1995; Corneil et al., 1999; Haslam & Mallon, 2003; Heinrichs et al., 2005; North et al., 2002), with a direct correlation between experiencing high levels of cumulative trauma exposure and the increased likelihood of experiencing PTSD (Brewin et al., 2000; Guo et al., 2004; Harvey et al., 2016; Milligan-Saville et al., 2018). International prevalence of PTSD among firefighters includes up to 57% in Saudi Arabia (Alghamdi et al., 2017), 13.5% in Canadian firefighters (Carleton, Afifi, Turner, et al., 2018), and over 18% of Malaysian (Majani et al., 2022) and German firefighters (Wagner et al., 1998) (a notable eight times the German national prevalence rate [Maercker et al., 2008]). Varying prevalences of PTSD among countries may be a result of differing job descriptions, acceptance rates of speaking about mental health, and accessibility to mental health resources (Alghamdi et al., 2017).

Continued research on PTSD in the fire service has unearthed valuable patterns and associations. For example, as a proxy for experiencing high levels of trauma exposure, years of service also have a significant positive association with PTSD among firefighters (Harvey et al., 2016; Kehl et al., 2014; Nydegger et al., 2011; Wagner et al., 1998). Firefighters with insomnia, a relatively common condition in the fire service, were up to five times more likely to be screened for PTSD (Cramm et al., 2021), while the comorbidity of anxiety and depressive disorders and PTSD cannot be understated. Not only are PTSD symptoms significantly and positively associated with anxiety and depressive disorders (Alghamdi et al., 2017), but also firefighters with depressive symptoms are over 14 times more likely to develop PTSD symptoms than firefighters not experiencing depressive symptoms (Majani et al., 2022). Occupational stress, such as intergroup conflict, role ambiguity, and low support from supervisors, was also associated with a higher prevalence of PTSD (Meyer et al., 2012; Saijo et al., 2012), while feelings of insecurity, lack of personal control, and alienation from others were linked to an increased risk of PTSD (Regehr et al., 2000). Finally, a longitudinal study found that personality traits of having a high level of hostility and a low level of self-efficacy before beginning the job were significant predictors of developing PTSD symptoms two years into the job (Heinrichs et al., 2005).

Protective factors associated with decreased PTSD development or symptom severity include a number of personal and social characteristics. The previously mentioned longitudinal study conversely found that individuals with low levels of hostility and high levels of self-efficacy experienced no change in their PTSD symptom scores across the two-year period (Heinrichs et al., 2005). Being married led to a significant decrease in PTSD symptom scores, as marriage was perceived as emotional support at home (Alghamdi et al., 2017). Meanwhile, perceived social support has been found to be significantly and inversely associated with PTSD (Mitani et al., 2006; Regehr et al., 2001; Skeffington et al., 2017), which includes support from friends and family (Regehr et al., 2001). Finally, adaptive coping, which includes active coping, positive reframing, acceptance, humour, and emotional support, resulted in significantly decreased PTSD scores (Skeffington et al., 2017).

Suicidal Ideations

Occupational research has demonstrated that certain groups have different rates and correlates of suicidal behaviours as a result of job-related exposures and hazards (Milner et al., 2013; Stanley et al., 2015). One such occupational group facing an elevated risk is firefighters. Often linked to substance use, sleep disruptions, and mental health issues, suicidal ideation and suicide are growing concerns in the fire service. Firefighters are at an increased risk for death by suicide compared to other occupational groups (Tiesman et al., 2015) and, in general, have higher rates of suicidal thoughts and behaviours compared to the general population (Martin, Tran, et al., 2017; Stanley et al., 2015, 2017b). Some research found firefighters have career estimates of suicidal ideation, plans, and attempts over twice that of the general population (46.8% vs. 13.5%; 19.2% vs. 3.9%; 15.5% vs. 4.6%, respectively [Kessler et al., 1999; Nock et al., 2008; Stanley et al., 2015]), although due to sampling methods, these results may be biased and limited in generalizability. With such high rates, a fire department may be three times more likely in a given year to lose a firefighter to suicide than to a line-of-duty death (National Fallen Firefighters Foundation, 2014).

Theoretical models of suicide risk suggest that exposure to painful and traumatic events may lower one's fear of death while simultaneously increasing one's pain tolerance, creating conditions resulting in suicidal behaviours (Joiner, 2005; Van Orden et al., 2010). Exposure to trauma is only one of several occupational characteristics that leave firefighters vulnerable to suicidal thoughts and behaviours. Others include shift work, issues with sleep, substance use, and additional behavioural and mental health concerns (Joiner, 2005; Kessler et al., 1999). Firefighters who experienced PTSD symptoms faced a higher risk of suicide, a pattern seen in both male and female firefighters (Boffa et al., 2018; Martin, Tran, et al., 2017; Stanley et al., 2017a). Additionally, greater anxiety sensitivity and more symptoms of depression were also associated with an increased suicide risk (Boffa et al., 2018; Martin, Tran, et al., 2017; Stanley et al., 2017a). Sleep disturbances, including insomnia and nightmares, have been linked to an increased risk of suicide ideation and attempts (Bernert et al., 2015; de Barros et al., 2013; Pigeon et al., 2012), while alcohol use is associated with increased suicide risk (Martin, Tran, et al., 2017; Martin, Vujanovic, et al., 2017). Demographics associated with increased risk of suicide thoughts and behaviours among firefighters include being younger, unmarried, non-white, female, and suffering cancer or chronic pain (Stanley et al., 2015). Working in a department responsible for emergency medical services also increases the risk of suicide behaviour (Stanley et al., 2015).

While firefighters experience a number of risks associated with increased suicidal thoughts and behaviours, the occupation also comes with a number of unique potential protective factors, including camaraderie and social support, familial, social support, and a sense of purpose. These factors, included in theoretical models of suicide risk (Joiner, 2005; Van Orden et al., 2010), emphasize the importance of social bonding and connection in protecting against suicide risk. Firehouses are excellent breeding grounds for such connections, as time around the kitchen table with a cup of coffee is a well-known resilience mechanism for the stress of the job (Caruso, 2022; Virgin, 2022). Firefighters often speak of the "brotherhood" or "sisterhood" of the fire service, indicating a tight-knit bond with other firefighters. This social support serves as a protective factor among firefighters (Carpenter et al., 2015; Chu et al., 2016) and may explain why some studies found rates of suicidal ideation and attempts decreased after joining the fire service (Martin, Tran, et al., 2017), while others found years of service to be negatively associated with suicide risk (Chu et al., 2016; Martin, Tran, et al., 2017; Stanley et al., 2015).

Substance Use

Although substance use can be considered its own mental health disorder (NIMH, 2021), substance use in the fire service is largely considered a byproduct or outcome of other mental health concerns, rather than the initial mental health concern. Substance use is a common form of coping with the stress and trauma associated with the fire service (Bacharach et al., 2008; Jitnarin et al., 2016; Pfefferbaum et al., 2002; Skeffington et al., 2017). As a result, it is not surprising to find substance use rates higher for firefighters than those in the general population. To begin with, while cigarette use in the fire service has declined (primarily due to smoke-free department policies) and is lower than the general population (Haddock et al., 2011), the use of smokeless tobacco among male firefighters is considerably higher (18.4% vs. 7.0%) (Jitnarin et al., 2013, 2015). Of note, adjust rates of firefighters who started smokeless tobacco use after joining the fire service were as high as 38.2%, compared to the 0.8% late initiation rate of the general population (Jitnarin et al., 2016).

More problematic, however, is alcohol use among firefighters, especially when compared to the general population. While around 20% of the general population has reported binge drinking in the last 30 days (CDC, 2020), that rate more than doubles to 58% of firefighters reporting binge drinking behaviours (Carey et al., 2011; Haddock et al., 2012, 2017). The binge drinking rate in the fire service is even substantially higher than that of active duty military members, which stands at 33% (Meadows et al., 2018), and that of law enforcement, which also stands at 33% (Ballenger et al., 2011). Additionally, 30% of firefighters met the criteria for alcohol dependence (Paulus et al., 2017), a condition in which the individual craves alcohol and is unable to control their drinking, six times the rate of the general population (Cherpitel, 2002).

The relationship between substance use and mental health in the fire service is clear, consistent, and growing. Firefighters who use tobacco were not only more likely to engage in heavy and binge drinking, a pattern seen in both male and female firefighters (Haddock et al., 2011; Jitnarin et al., 2013, 2015, 2019), but they were also more likely to show signs of depressive symptoms (Jitnarin et al., 2015). Specifically, firefighters who started using smokeless tobacco after joining the fire service had significantly higher depression symptom scores, providing support for the association between substance use and work stress (Jitnarin et al., 2016). Additionally, tobacco users were almost six times more likely to have been diagnosed with an anxiety disorder (Haddock et al., 2011). Depressed firefighters were more likely to engage in hazardous drinking behaviours, including binge drinking (Carey et al., 2011; Paulus et al., 2017), while a positive association between PTSD symptoms and alcohol dependency, including the quantity of alcohol consumed, has also been found (Paulus et al., 2017; Skeffington et al., 2017). Among female firefighters, problematic drinkers were 2.5 times more likely to have been diagnosed with depressive disorder or experience PTSD symptoms (Haddock et al., 2017).

Sleep

Sleep is an often overlooked yet essential foundational piece to general mental health through a number of avenues (Walker, 2018). To begin with, decreased sleep can drastically impact an individual's mood and emotions through its relationship with the amygdala, the part of the brain linked to the fight or flight response (Walker, 2018). A sleep-deprived amygdala leads to a 60% increase in emotional responses compared to a rested brain, responses which may include rage and anger. Uncontrolled reactivity leads to unstable mood swings and emotional decision-making, affecting work and personal relationships as well as personal wellness (Walker, 2018). Additionally, there is a bidirectional relationship between mental health and sleep. A lack of sleep has been found to be a causal trigger of psychiatric episodes associated with bipolar disorder, while improving sleep quality for patients with several psychiatric conditions can improve symptom severity and remission rates. Meanwhile, healthy people can have mental health symptoms induced with sleep disturbance (Walker, 2018).

Sleep in the fire service is a tentatively growing subject with startling findings. The majority of career firefighters are on-duty from 24 to 48 hours at a time, requiring them to sleep at the station. As they are tasked with responding to emergency calls around the clock, this means their sleep is often interrupted by calls for service. These nights of fragmented sleep add up quickly during the course of a career, leading to sleep-related health issues. Meanwhile, volunteer firefighters are on-call daily and respond from their own homes. While sleeping in one's own bed may seem advantageous, a better understanding of the job means these volunteers are never guaranteed a restful night of sleep, unlike their career counterparts who do not respond off-duty.

While it has been widely accepted that firefighters do not experience quality sleep while on duty, quantitative measures capture to what extent that may be true. It is estimated that over 37% of firefighters screen positive for having a sleep disorder (Barger et al., 2015), while over 20% screen positive for insomnia (Cramm et al., 2021). Almost 60% of firefighters report being sleep deprived (Carey et al., 2011), while nearly 70% reported -than-ideal sleep quality (Cramm et al., 2021). These sleep-related issues lead to a number of mental health concerns among firefighters. Compared to their well-rested counterparts, firefighters with insomnia were almost five times more likely to screen for PTSD, six times more likely to experience major depressive disorder, and up to seven times more likely to experience anxiety disorders (Barger et al., 2015; Cramm et al., 2021). Conversely, firefighters who reported suicidal ideation were more than twice as likely to experience sleep disturbances (de Barros et al., 2013). Unhealthy alcohol use and psychological distress measures were also associated with an increased likelihood of sleep disturbances (de Barros et al., 2013), highlighting the bidirectional nature of sleep and mental health. Circling back to sleep's ability to impact mood, sleep disturbances among firefighters have been found to impair emotion regulation, increasing the risk of negative affect and major depressive disorder (Hom et al., 2016).

Women's Health and Wellness

In the United States, the fire service is the public safety field with the smallest percentage of women. While women comprise 11% of the volunteer fire service, less than 5% of career firefighters are women (NFPA, 2020). As a result, women have historically been ignored in health research as their small sample sizes were often omitted from data analysis. Over the past decade, research has begun to rectify that as scientists recognize the role of women in the fire service and examine unique stressors and health outcomes. For example, a small number of studies found that women firefighters had higher levels of PTSD symptoms compared to men (Corneil et al., 1999; Ogińska-Bulik, 2016; Skeffington et al., 2017), a pattern reflective of the general population (Kessler et al., 2005). Additionally, similar to their male counterparts, women engage in high rates of binge drinking, with over 40% reporting binge drinking during the past 30 days, and problematic drinkers were 2.5 times more likely to have been diagnosed with depression or experience PTSD symptoms (Haddock et al., 2017).

Most notable, however, is the emerging research examining the discrimination and harassment experienced by women firefighters and its impact on health and wellness. Almost 70% of women firefighters have experienced differential treatment based on gender (Jahnke et al., 2019). Forty per cent have experienced shunning or social isolation, while 37% have been verbally harassed. The same amount have experienced sexual advances from coworkers, while 5% have been physically or sexually assaulted (Jahnke et al., 2019). When compared to women who experienced little or no harassment, women who experienced high severity of harassment or discrimination are 300% more likely to suffer from depression, 150% more likely to experience PTSD, twice as likely to have driven while intoxicated, and are more likely to report poor health days (Jahnke et al., 2019).

In addition to experiencing high rates of harassment and discrimination, women firefighters are in unique positions to suffer from a number of reproductive health concerns. To begin with, miscarriage rates among women firefighters are over twice as high as the national average (29.1% vs. 13.5%) (Jahnke et al., 2018). Additionally, rates of pre-term birth and rates of infertility among women firefighters are also higher than national averages (Jahnke et al., 2018). These concerns require consideration as research continues to examine mental health among women firefighters. Given the trauma and stress associated with experiencing a miscarriage, future research would benefit greatly from exploring the impact of reproductive health challenges on the mental health outcomes of women firefighters.

Conclusion: What the Future Holds

A growing body of research seems to indicate that the profession of firefighting is detrimental to one's mental health in several ways. Despite that ominous association, over a million firefighters continue to serve their communities during community and individual emergencies. Research on the mental health of firefighters not only uncovered and brought awareness to problematic patterns, it also provided a set of guidelines to address the issue. These guidelines provide opportunities for communities to give back to their firefighters in the form of support, resources, and programme development to improve the well-being of firefighters.

Across the nation, communities, organizations, and departments have responded to the mental health needs of firefighters. From both within the fire service (IAFF, n.d.; NVFC, n.d.) and outside the fire service (Florida A&M University, 2019; Mental Health Education For First Responders, 2022), organizations are focused on breaking stigmas attached to talking about the mental health of firefighters. Trained clinicians are dedicating themselves to learning about the uniqueness of the fire service to better serve their firefighter clients (Gulliver, 2022), and networks of firefighter-friendly providers are being formed (Gulliver, 2022; Jones, 2022). Scientists are empirically assessing the ability of traditional therapies to heal and support firefighters (Alshahrani et al., 2022; IAFF Center of Excellence, 2022; Spell, 2019) while developing and testing innovative interventions (Horses & Heroes, n.d.; Liriano et al., 2019). Fire departments are emphasizing the value of peer support teams and critical incident debriefings, breaking down barriers of isolation and silence to create cultures of support and openness (Conant, 2019; IAFF Staff, 2018; Lanning, 2020; Raney, 2019).

Collectively, these are strong and swift responses to the emerging understanding of the fragility of the human mind in the face of trauma. They highlight the resilience and tenacity of the human spirit, the power of committed groups, and a firefighter's unwavering drive to serve their community. The fire service will never be without trauma and mental health concerns; however, a future full of accessible programmes and support suggests the fire service will be more responsive to the mental health needs of their own, saving lives and improving the quality of service to the community.

References

Alghamdi, M., Hunt, N., & Thomas, S. (2017). Prevalence rate of PTSD, depression and anxiety symptoms among Saudi firefighters. *Journal of Traumatic Stress Disorders & Treatment*, 2017. https://doi.org/10.4172/2324-8947.1000164

Alshahrani, K. M., Johnson, J., Prudenzi, A., & O'Connor, D. B. (2022). The effectiveness of psychological interventions for reducing PTSD and psychological distress in first responders: A systematic review and meta-analysis. *PLOS ONE*, *17*(8), e0272732. https://doi.org/10.1371/journal.pone.0272732

Bacharach, S. B., Bamberger, P. A., & Doveh, E. (2008). Firefighters, critical incidents, and drinking to cope: The adequacy of unit-level performance resources as a source of vulnerability and protection. *Journal of Applied Psychology*, *93*, 155–169. https://doi.org/10.1037/0021-9010.93.1.155

Ballenger, J. F., Best, S. R., Metzler, T. J., Wasserman, D. A., Mohr, D. C., Liberman, A., Delucchi, K., Weiss, D. S., Fagan, J. A., Waldrop, A. E., & Marmar, C. R. (2011). Patterns and predictors of alcohol use in male and female urban police officers. *The American Journal on Addictions*, *20*(1), 21–29. https://doi.org/10.1111/j.1521-0391.2010.00092.x

Barger, L. K., Rajaratnam, S. M. W., Wang, W., O'Brien, C. S., Sullivan, J. P., Qadri, S., Lockley, S. W., Czeisler, C. A., & Harvard Work Hours Health and Safety Group. (2015). Common sleep disorders increase risk of motor vehicle crashes and adverse health outcomes in firefighters. *Journal of Clinical Sleep Medicine: JCSM: Official Publication of the American Academy of Sleep Medicine*, *11*(3), 233–240. https://doi.org/10.5664/jcsm.4534

Barr, D., Reilly, T., & Gregson, W. (2011). The impact of different cooling modalities on the physiological responses in firefighters during strenuous work performed in high environmental temperatures. *European Journal of Applied Physiology*, *111*(6), 959–967. https://doi.org/10.1007/s00421-010-1714-1

Bartlett, B. A., Gallagher, M. W., Tran, J. K., & Vujanovic, A. A. (2019). Military veteran status and post-traumatic stress disorder symptomatology among urban firefighters: The moderating role of emotion regulation difficulties. *Journal of Nervous & Mental Disease*, *207*(4), 224–231. https://doi.org/10.1097/NMD.0000000000000958

Bernert, R. A., Kim, J. S., Iwata, N. G., & Perlis, M. L. (2015). Sleep disturbances as an evidence-based suicide risk factor. *Current Psychiatry Reports*, *17*(3), 554. https://doi.org/10.1007/s11920-015-0554-4

Berninger, A., Webber, M. P., Cohen, H. W., Gustave, J., Lee, R., Niles, J. K., Chiu, S., Zeig-Owens, R., Soo, J., Kelly, K., & Prezant, D. J. (2010). Trends of elevated PTSD risk in firefighters exposed to the world trade center disaster: 2001–2005. *Public Health Reports*, *125*(4), 556–566. https://doi.org/10.1177/00333549101 2500411

Boffa, J. W., Stanley, I. H., Smith, L. J., Mathes, B. M., Tran, J. K., Buser, S. J., Schmidt, N. B., & Vujanovic, A. A. (2018). PTSD symptoms and suicide risk in male firefighters: The mediating role of anxiety sensitivity. *The Journal of Nervous and Mental Disease*, *206*(3), 179–186. https://doi.org/10.1097/NMD.0000000000000779

Brewin, C. R., Andrews, B., & Valentine, J. D. (2000). Meta-analysis of risk factors for post-traumatic stress disorder in trauma-exposed adults. *Journal of Consulting and Clinical Psychology*, *68*(5), 748–766. https://doi.org/10.1037/0022-006X.68.5.748

Bryant, R. A., & Harvey, A. G. (1995). Post-traumatic stress in volunteer firefighters: Predictors of distress. *Journal of Nervous and Mental Disease*, *183*(4), 267–271. https://doi.org/10.1097/00005053-199504000-00014

Bureau, E. M. T. (2018, November 23). Expanding job duties provide challenges for fire departments. *The Quad-City Times*. https://qctimes.com/news/local/government-and-politics/expanding-job-duties-provide-challenges-for-fire-departments/article_55a22539-e581-561a-bfb7-245d55415f72.html

Canetti, E. F. D., Gayton, S., Schram, B., Pope, R., & Orr, R. M. (2022). Psychological, physical, and heat stress indicators prior to and after a 15-minute structural firefighting task. *Biology*, *11*(1), 104. https://doi.org/10.3390/biology11010104

Carey, M. G., Al-Zaiti, S. S., Dean, G. E., Sessanna, L., & Finnell, D. S. (2011). Sleep problems, depression, substance use, social bonding, and quality of life in professional firefighters. *Journal of Occupational and Environmental Medicine / American College of Occupational and Environmental Medicine*, *53*(8), 928–933. https://doi.org/10.1097/JOM.0b013e318225898f

Carleton, R. N., Afifi, T. O., Taillieu, T., Turner, S., Krakauer, R., Anderson, G. S., MacPhee, R. S., Ricciardelli, R., Cramm, H. A., Groll, D., & McCreary, D. R. (2018). Exposures to potentially traumatic events among public safety personnel in Canada. *Canadian Journal of Behavioural Science / Revue Canadienne Des Sciences Du Comportement*, *51*(1), 37. https://doi.org/10.1037/cbs0000115

Carleton, R. N., Afifi, T. O., Turner, S., Taillieu, T., Duranceau, S., LeBouthillier, D. M., Sareen, J., Ricciardelli, R., MacPhee, R. S., Groll, D., Hozempa, K., Brunet, A., Weekes, J. R., Griffiths, C. T., Abrams, K. J., Jones, N. A., Beshai, S., Cramm, H. A., Dobson, K. S., … Asmundson, G. J. G. (2018). Mental Disorder Symptoms among Public Safety Personnel in Canada. *Canadian Journal of Psychiatry. Revue Canadienne De Psychiatrie*, *63*(1), 54–64. https://doi.org/10.1177/0706743717723825

Carpenter, G. S. J., Carpenter, T. P., Kimbrel, N. A., Flynn, E. J., Pennington, M. L., Cammarata, C., Zimering, R. T., Kamholz, B. W., & Gulliver, S. B. (2015). Social support, stress, and suicidal ideation in professional firefighters. *American Journal of Health Behavior*, *39*(2), 191–196. https://doi.org/10.5993/AJHB.39.2.5

Caruso, J. (2022). The firehouse kitchen table: more than a place to eat. *Crisis, Stress, and Human Resilience: An International Journal*, *3*(4), 192–194.

CDC. (2020). BRFSS Prevalence & Trends Data: Alcohol consumption 2011–2020. https://nccd.cdc.gov/BRFSSPrevalence/rdPage.aspx?rdReport=DPH_BRFSS.ExploreByLocation&rdProcessAction=&SaveFileGenerated=1&irbLocationType=States&islLocation=98&islState=&islCounty=&islClass=CLASS01&islTopic=TOPIC07&islYear=2020&hidLocationType=States&hidLocation=98&hidClass=CLASS01&hidTopic=TOPIC07&hidTopicName=Binge+Drinking&hidYear=2020&irbShowFootnotes=Show&rdICL-iclIndicators=_RFBING5&iclIndicators_rdExpandedCollapsedHistory=&iclIndicators=_RFBING5&hidPreviouslySelectedIndicators=&DashboardColumnCount=1&rdShowElementHistory=divClassUpdating%3dHide%2cislClass%3dShow%2cdivTopicUpdating%3dHide%2cislTopic%3dShow%2cdivYearUpdating%3dHide%2cislYear%3dShow%2c&rdScrollX=0&rdScrollY=0&rdRnd=59344

Cherpitel, C. J. (2002). Screening for alcohol problems in the U.S. general population: Comparison of the CAGE, RAPS4, and RAPS4-QF by gender, ethnicity, and service utilization. Rapid Alcohol Problems Screen. *Alcoholism, Clinical and Experimental Research*, *26*(11), 1686–1691. https://doi.org/10.1097/01.ALC.0000036300.26619.78

Chu, C., Buchman-Schmitt, J. M., Hom, M. A., Stanley, I. H., & Joiner, T. E. (2016). A test of the interpersonal theory of suicide in a large sample of current firefighters. *Psychiatry Research*, *240*, 26–33. https://doi.org/10.1016/j.psychres.2016.03.041

Clay, R. (2022, July 11). Are You Experiencing Compassion Fatigue? American Psychological Association. www.apa.org/topics/covid-19/compassion-fatigue

Conant, J. (2019, April 22). Firefighter Peer Support: The Missing Piece of the Mental Health Puzzle. *Lexipol.* www.lexipol.com/resources/blog/firefighter-peer-support-the-missing-piece-of-the-mental-health-puzzle/

Corneil, W., Beaton, R., Murphy, S., Johnson, C., & Pike, K. (1999). Exposure to traumatic incidents and prevalence of post-traumatic stress symptomatology in urban firefighters in two countries. *Journal of Occupational Health Psychology*, *4*(2), 131–141. https://doi.org/10.1037/1076-8998.4.2.131

Cramm, H., Richmond, R., Jamshidi, L., Edgelow, M., Groll, D., Ricciardelli, R., MacDermid, J. C., Keiley, M., & Carleton, R. N. (2021). Mental health of Canadian firefighters: The impact of sleep. *International Journal of Environmental Research and Public Health*, *18*(24), 13256. https://doi.org/10.3390/ijerph182413256

de Barros, V., Martins, L. F., Saitz, R., Bastos, R. R., & Ronzani, T. M. (2013). Mental health conditions, individual and job characteristics and sleep disturbances among firefighters. *Journal of Health Psychology*, *18*(3), 350–358. https://doi.org/10.1177/1359105312443402

DeMarco, H. (2018, July 4). The Other Victims: First Responders To Violent Disasters Often Suffer Alone. NPR. www.npr.org/sections/health-shots/2018/07/04/625784687/the-other-victims-first-responders-to-violent-disasters-often-suffer-alone

Dorman, L. E., & Havenith, G. (2009). The effects of protective clothing on energy consumption during different activities. *European Journal of Applied Physiology*, *105*(3), 463–470. https://doi.org/10.1007/s00421-008-0924-2

Ettman, C. K., Abdalla, S. M., Cohen, G. H., Sampson, L., Vivier, P. M., & Galea, S. (2020). Prevalence of depression symptoms in US adults before and during the COVID-19 pandemic. *JAMA Network Open*, *3*(9), e2019686. https://doi.org/10.1001/jamanetworkopen.2020.19686

Fisher, P., & Etches, B. (2003). *A Comprehensive Approach to Workplace Stress & Trauma in Firefighting: A Review Document Prepared for The International Association of Firefighters 17th Redmond Symposium* (p. 13). International Association of Fire Fighters.

Florida A&M University. (2019). About the 2nd Alarm Project. 2nd Alarm Project. www.2ndalarmproject.org/about

Fullerton, C. S., Ursano, R. J., & Wang, L. (2004). Acute stress disorder, post-traumatic stress disorder, and depression in disaster or rescue workers. *The American Journal of Psychiatry*, *161*(8), 1370–1376. https://doi.org/10.1176/appi.ajp.161.8.1370

Ginexi, E. M., Weihs, K., Simmens, S. J., & Hoyt, D. R. (2000). Natural disaster and depression: A prospective investigation of reactions to the 1993 Midwest floods. *American Journal of Community Psychology*, *28*(4), 495–518. https://doi.org/10.1023/a:1005188515149

Greenberg, P. E., Fournier, A.-A., Sisitsky, T., Simes, M., Berman, R., Koenigsberg, S. H., & Kessler, R. C. (2021). The economic burden of adults with major depressive disorder in the United States (2010 and 2018). *PharmacoEconomics*, *39*(6), 653–665. https://doi.org/10.1007/s40273-021-01019-4

Gulliver, S. (2022). *Warriors Research Institute*. Baylor, Scott, & White Health. www.bswhealth.med/research/Pages/institutes-and-centers/warriors-research-institute.aspx

Guo, Y.-J., Chen, C.-H., Lu, M.-L., Tan, H. K.-L., Lee, H.-W., & Wang, T.-N. (2004). Post-traumatic stress disorder among professional and non-professional rescuers involved in an earthquake in Taiwan. *Psychiatry Research*, *127*(1), 35–41. https://doi.org/10.1016/j.psychres.2004.03.009

Haddock, C. K., Jahnke, S. A., Poston, W. S. C., Jitnarin, N., Kaipust, C. M., Tuley, B., & Hyder, M. L. (2012). Alcohol use among firefighters in the Central United States. *Occupational Medicine*, *62*(8), 661–664. https://doi.org/10.1093/occmed/kqs162

Haddock, C. K., Jitnarin, N., Poston, W. S. C., Tuley, B., & Jahnke, S. A. (2011). Tobacco use among firefighters in the central United States. *American Journal of Industrial Medicine*, *54*(9), 697–706. https://doi.org/10.1002/ajim.20972

Haddock, C. K., Poston, W. S. C., Jahnke, S. A., & Jitnarin, N. (2017). Alcohol use and problem drinking among women firefighters. *Women's Health Issues*, *27*(6), 632–638. https://doi.org/10.1016/j.whi.2017.07.003

Hall, S., & Evarts, B. (2022). *Fire Loss in the United States during 2021* (p. 12). National Fire Protection Association.

Harvey, S. B., Milligan-Saville, J. S., Paterson, H. M., Harkness, E. L., Marsh, A. M., Dobson, M., Kemp, R., & Bryant, R. A. (2016). The mental health of firefighters: An examination of the impact of repeated trauma exposure. *Australian & New Zealand Journal of Psychiatry*, *50*(7), 649–658. https://doi.org/10.1177/0004867415615217

Haslam, C., & Mallon, K. (2003). A preliminary investigation of post-traumatic stress symptoms among firefighters. *Work & Stress*, *17*(3), 277–285. https://doi.org/10.1080/02678370310001625649

Heinrichs, M., Wagner, D., Schoch, W., Soravia, L. M., Hellhammer, D. H., & Ehlert, U. (2005). Predicting posttraumatic stress symptoms from pretraumatic risk factors: A 2-year prospective follow-up study in firefighters. *American Journal of Psychiatry*, *162*(12), 2276–2286. https://doi.org/10.1176/appi.ajp.162.12.2276

Hemmatjo, R., Hajaghazadeh, M., Allahyari, T., Zare, S., & Kazemi, R. (2020). The effects of live-fire drills on visual and auditory cognitive performance among firefighters. *Annals of Global Health*, *86*(1), Article 1. https://doi.org/10.5334/aogh.2626

Hom, M. A., Stanley, I. H., Rogers, M. L., Tzoneva, M., Bernert, R. A., & Joiner, T. E. (2016). The association between sleep disturbances and depression among firefighters: Emotion dysregulation as an explanatory factor. *Journal of Clinical Sleep Medicine: JCSM: Official Publication of the American Academy of Sleep Medicine*, *12*(2), 235–245. https://doi.org/10.5664/jcsm.5492

Horses & Heroes. (n.d.). Our Programs. Horses and Heroes. Retrieved December 11, 2022, from www.horsesandheroes.org

IAFF. (n.d.). IAFF Center of Excellence—Rehab & Treatment for Fire Fighters. IAFF Recovery Center. Retrieved December 11, 2022, from www.iaffrecoverycenter.com/

IAFF Center of Excellence. (2022). *Fire Fighter Treatment for Mental Health*. IAFF Center of Excellence. www.iaffrecoverycenter.com/treatment/mental-health/

IAFF Staff, I. (2018, January 8). Peer Support Fire Fighters, How Peer Support Can Combat Addiction and PTSD. IAFF Recovery Center. www.iaffrecoverycenter.com/blog/peer-support-combat-addiction-ptsd/

Jahnke, S. A., Haddock, C. K., Jitnarin, N., Kaipust, C. M., Hollerbach, B. S., & Poston, W. S. C. (2019). The prevalence and health impacts of frequent work discrimination and harassment among women firefighters in the US Fire Service. *BioMed Research International*, *2019*, e6740207. https://doi.org/10.1155/2019/6740207

Jahnke, S. A., Poston, W. S. C., Haddock, C. K., & Murphy, B. (2016). Firefighting and mental health: Experiences of repeated exposure to trauma. *Work*, *53*(4), 737–744. https://doi.org/10.3233/WOR-162255

Jahnke, S. A., Poston, W. S. C., Jitnarin, N., & Haddock, C. K. (2018). Maternal and child health among female firefighters in the U.S. *Maternal and Child Health Journal*, *22*(6), 922–931. https://doi.org/10.1007/s10995-018-2468-3

Jitnarin, N., Haddock, C. K., Poston, W. S. C., & Jahnke, S. (2013). Smokeless tobacco and dual use among firefighters in the central United States. *Journal of Environmental and Public Health*, *2013*, 675426. https://doi.org/10.1155/2013/675426

Jitnarin, N., Poston, W. S. C., Haddock, C. K., & Jahnke, S. A. (2019). Tobacco Use among Women Firefighters. *Women's Health Issues*, *29*(5), 432–439. https://doi.org/10.1016/j.whi.2019.05.006

Jitnarin, N., Poston, W. S. C., Haddock, C. K., Jahnke, S. A., & Day, R. S. (2015). Tobacco use pattern among a national firefighter cohort. *Nicotine & Tobacco Research*, *17*(1), 66–73. https://doi.org/10.1093/ntr/ntu131

Jitnarin, N., Poston, W. S. C., Haddock, C. K., Jahnke, S. A., Day, R. S., & Severson, H. H. (2016). Prevalence and correlates of late initiation of smokeless tobacco in US firefighters. *Nicotine & Tobacco Research*, ntw321. https://doi.org/10.1093/ntr/ntw321

Joiner, T. E. (2005). *Why People Die by Suicide*. Harvard University Press.

Jones, A. (2022). 42 CARES. Local 42 CARES. www.42cares.org

Kehl, D., Knuth, D., Hulse, L., & Schmidt, S. (2014). Post-traumatic reactions among firefighters after critical incidents: Cross-national data. *Journal of Aggression, Maltreatment & Trauma*, *23*(8), 842–853. https://doi.org/10.1080/10926771.2014.938143

Kessler, R. C., Chiu, W. T., Demler, O., Merikangas, K. R., & Walters, E. E. (2005). Prevalence, severity, and comorbidity of 12-month DSM-IV disorders in the National Comorbidity Survey Replication. *Archives of General Psychiatry*, *62*(6), 617–627. https://doi.org/10.1001/archpsyc.62.6.617

Kessler, R. C., Mickelson, K. D., & Williams, D. R. (1999). The prevalence, distribution, and mental health correlates of perceived discrimination in the United States. *Journal of Health and Social Behavior*, *40*(3), 208–230.

Lanning, M. (2020, April 10). *The Power of Peer Support in the Fire Service*. Fire Engineering. www.fireengineering.com/health-safety/the-power-of-peer-support-in-the-fire-service/

Li, Y., Scherer, N., Felix, L., & Kuper, H. (2021). Prevalence of depression, anxiety and post-traumatic stress disorder in health care workers during the COVID-19 pandemic: A systematic review and meta-analysis. *PLOS ONE*, *16*(3), e0246454. https://doi.org/10.1371/journal.pone.0246454

Liriano, F., Hatten, C., & Schwartz, T. L. (2019). Ketamine as treatment for post-traumatic stress disorder: A review. *Drugs in Context*, *8*, 212305. https://doi.org/10.7573/dic.212305

Maercker, A., Forstmeier, S., Wagner, B., Glaesmer, H., & Brähler, E. (2008). Post-traumatic stress disorder in Germany. Results of a nationwide epidemiological study. *Der Nervenarzt*, *79*(5), 577–586. https://doi.org/10.1007/s00115-008-2467-5

Majani, A. F., Ghazali, S. R., Yong, C. Y., Pauzi, N., Adenan, F., & Manogaran, K. (2022). Job-related psychological trauma, post-traumatic stress disorder (PTSD), and depressive symptoms among Malaysian firefighters. *Asian Journal of Psychiatry*, *76*. https://doi.org/10.1016/j.ajp.2022.103248

Martin, C. E., Tran, J. K., & Buser, S. J. (2017). Correlates of suicidality in firefighter/EMS personnel. *Journal of Affective Disorders*, *208*, 177–183. https://doi.org/10.1016/j.jad.2016.08.078

Martin, C. E., Vujanovic, A. A., Paulus, D. J., Bartlett, B., Gallagher, M. W., & Tran, J. K. (2017). Alcohol use and suicidality in firefighters: Associations with depressive symptoms and post-traumatic stress. *Comprehensive Psychiatry*, *74*, 44–52. https://doi.org/10.1016/j.comppsych.2017.01.002

Meadows, S., Engel, C., Collins, R., Beckman, R., Cefalu, M., Hawes-Dawson, J., Doyle, M., Kress, A., Sontag-Padilla, L., Ramchand, R., & Williams, K. (2018). 2015 Department of Defense Health Related Behaviors Survey (HRBS). RAND Corporation. https://doi.org/10.7249/RR1695

Mental Health Education For First Responders. (2022). On the Job and Off. https://onthejobandoff.com/

Meyer, E. C., Zimering, R., Daly, E., Knight, J., Kamholz, B. W., & Gulliver, S. B. (2012). Predictors of post-traumatic stress disorder and other psychological symptoms in trauma-exposed firefighters. *Psychological Services*, *9*(1), 1–15. https://doi.org/10.1037/a0026414

Milligan-Saville, J., Choi, I., Deady, M., Scott, P., Tan, L., Calvo, R. A., Bryant, R. A., Glozier, N., & Harvey, S. B. (2018). The impact of trauma exposure on the development of PTSD and psychological distress in a volunteer fire service. *Psychiatry Research*, *270*, 1110–1115. https://doi.org/10.1016/j.psychres.2018.06.058

Milner, A., Spittal, M., Pirkis, J., & LaMontagne, A. (2013). Suicide by occupation: Systematic review and meta-analysis. *The British Journal of Psychiatry*, *203*, 409–416.

Mitani, S., Fujita, M., Nakata, K., & Shirakawa, T. (2006). Impact of post-traumatic stress disorder and job-related stress on burnout: A study of fire service workers. *The Journal of Emergency Medicine*, *31*(1), 7–11. https://doi.org/10.1016/j.jemermed.2005.08.008

National Alliance on Mental Health. (2017, December). Anxiety Disorders. National Alliance on Mental Illness. www.nami.org/About-Mental-Illness/Mental-Health-Conditions/Anxiety-Disorders

National Center for PTSD. (2021). How Common is PTSD in Adults? [General Information]. U.S. Department of Veterans Affairs. www.ptsd.va.gov/understand/common/common_adults.asp

National Center for PTSD. (2022, August 30). *What is PTSD?* [General Information]. U.S. Department of Veterans Affairs. www.ptsd.va.gov/understand/what/index.asp

National Fallen Firefighters Foundation. (2014, August 15). The National Fallen Firefighters Foundation Issues a Statement About Suicide Prevention. National Fallen Firefighters Foundation. www.firehero.org/2014/08/15/national-fallen-firefighters-foundation-issues-statement-suicide-prevention/

National Institutes of Health. (2022, April). Anxiety Disorders. National Institute of Mental Health (NIMH). www.nimh.nih.gov/health/topics/anxiety-disorders

NFPA. (2020). While the number of women is increasing, females still make up less than 10 percent of the U.S. fire service. www.nfpa.org/News-and-Research/Publications-and-media/Press-Room/News-releases/2020/Females-still-make-up-less-than-10-percent-of-the-US-fire-service

NFPA. (2021). *Fire department calls* [National Fire Protection Association]. www.nfpa.org/News-and-Research/Data-research-and-tools/Emergency-Responders/Fire-department-calls

NIMH. (2021, March). Substance Use and Co-Occurring Mental Disorders. National Institute of Mental Health. www.nimh.nih.gov/health/topics/substance-use-and-mental-health

Nock, M. K., Borges, G., Bromet, E. J., Cha, C. B., Kessler, R. C., & Lee, S. (2008). Suicide and suicidal behavior. *Epidemiologic Reviews*, *30*(1), 133–154. https://doi.org/10.1093/epirev/mxn002

North, C. S., Tivis, L., McMillen, J. C., Pfefferbaum, B., Cox, J., Spitznagel, E. L., Bunch, K., Schorr, J., & Smith, E. M. (2002). Coping, functioning, and adjustment of rescue workers after the Oklahoma City bombing. *Journal of Traumatic Stress*, *15*(3), 171–175. https://doi.org/10.1023/A:1015286909111

NVFC. (n.d.). Share the Load. National Volunteer Fire Council. Retrieved December 11, 2022, from www.nvfc.org/programs/share-the-load-program/

Nydegger, R., Nydegger, L., & Basile, F. (2011). Post-traumatic stress disorder and coping among career professional firefighters. *American Journal of Health Sciences (AJHS)*, *2*(1), Article 1. https://doi.org/10.19030/ajhs.v2i1.4365

Ogińska-Bulik, N. (2016). Personal resources and negative and positive effects of traumatic events in a group of medical rescuers. *Medycyna Pracy*, *67*(5), 635–644. https://doi.org/10.13075/mp.5893.00409

Paulus, D. J., Vujanovic, A. A., Schuhmann, B. B., Smith, L. J., & Tran, J. (2017). Main and interactive effects of depression and post-traumatic stress in relation to alcohol dependence among urban male firefighters. *Psychiatry Research*, *251*, 69–75. https://doi.org/10.1016/j.psychres.2017.02.011

Pfefferbaum, B., North, C. S., Bunch, K., Wilson, T. G., Tucker, P., & Schorr, J. K. (2002). The impact of the 1995 Oklahoma City bombing on the partners of firefighters. *Journal of Urban Health*, *79*(3), 364–372. https://doi.org/10.1093/jurban/79.3.364

Pigeon, W. R., Pinquart, M., & Conner, K. (2012). Meta-analysis of sleep disturbance and suicidal thoughts and behaviors. *The Journal of Clinical Psychiatry*, *73*(09), e1160–e1167. https://doi.org/10.4088/JCP.11r07586

Poston, W. S., Haddock, C. K., Jahnke, S. A., Jitnarin, N., & Day, R. S. (2013). An examination of the benefits of health promotion programs for the national fire service. *BMC Public Health, 13*(1), 805. https://doi.org/10.1186/1471-2458-13-805

Raney, R. (2019, December 4). *Fire Departments Step Up Their Mental Health Game.* American Psychological Association. www.apa.org/members/content/firefighters-mental-health

Regehr, C., Hemsworth, D., & Hill, J. (2001). Individual predictors of post-traumatic distress: A structural equation model. *The Canadian Journal of Psychiatry, 46*(2), 156–161. https://doi.org/10.1177/070674370104600207

Regehr, C., Hill, J., & Glancy, G. D. (2000). Individual predictors of traumatic reactions in firefighters. *The Journal of Nervous and Mental Disease, 188*(6), 333–339. https://doi.org/10.1097/00005053-200006000-00003

Rindge, B. (2018, February 17). Firefighters respond to more medical emergencies than fires. *AP News.* https://apnews.com/article/15e06ad3778f4ee88b67a1bdb bc97c29

Saijo, Y., Ueno, T., & Hashimoto, Y. (2008). Twenty-four-hour shift work, depressive symptoms, and job dissatisfaction among Japanese firefighters. *American Journal of Industrial Medicine, 51*(5), 380–391. https://doi.org/10.1002/ajim.20571

Saijo, Y., Ueno, T., & Hashimoto, Y. (2012). Post-traumatic stress disorder and job stress among firefighters of urban Japan. *Prehospital and Disaster Medicine, 27*(1), 59–63. https://doi.org/10.1017/S1049023X12000222

Skeffington, P. M., Rees, C. S., & Mazzucchelli, T. (2017). Trauma exposure and post-traumatic stress disorder within fire and emergency services in Western Australia. *Australian Journal of Psychology, 69*(1), 20–28. https://doi.org/10.1111/ajpy.12120

Smith, D. L., Petruzzello, S. J., Chludzinski, M. A., Reed, J. J., & Woods, J. A. (2001). Effect of strenuous live-fire fire fighting drills on hematological, blood chemistry and psychological measures. *Journal of Thermal Biology, 26*(4), 375–379. https://doi.org/10.1016/S0306-4565(01)00047-X

Spell, J. (2019). PTSD treatments for firefighters. FireRescue1. /www.firerescue1.com/health-wellness/articles/ptsd-treatments-for-firefighters-FCqoCFOFO T8luc0F/

Stanley, I. H., Hom, M. A., Hagan, C. R., & Joiner, T. E. (2015). Career prevalence and correlates of suicidal thoughts and behaviors among firefighters. *Journal of Affective Disorders, 187*, 163–171. https://doi.org/10.1016/j.jad.2015.08.007

Stanley, I. H., Hom, M. A., Spencer-Thomas, S., & Joiner, T. E. (2017a). Examining anxiety sensitivity as a mediator of the association between PTSD symptoms and suicide risk among women firefighters. *Journal of Anxiety Disorders, 50*, 94–102. https://doi.org/10.1016/j.janxdis.2017.06.003

Stanley, I. H., Hom, M. A., Spencer-Thomas, S., & Joiner, T. E. (2017b). Suicidal thoughts and behaviors among women firefighters: An examination of associated features and comparison of pre-career and career prevalence rates. *Journal of Affective Disorders, 221*, 107–114. https://doi.org/10.1016/j.jad.2017.06.016

Tak, S., Driscoll, R., Bernard, B., & West, C. (2007). Depressive symptoms among firefighters and related factors after the response to Hurricane Katrina. *Journal of Urban Health: Bulletin of the New York Academy of Medicine, 84*(2), 153–161. https://doi.org/10.1007/s11524-006-9155-1

Tao, Y., Liu, X., Hou, W., Niu, H., Wang, S., Ma, Z., Bi, D., & Zhang, L. (2022). The mediating role of emotion regulation strategies in the relationship between big five personality traits and anxiety and depression among Chinese firefighters. *Frontiers in Public Health*, *10*, 901686. https://doi.org/10.3389/fpubh.2022.901686

Terlizzi, E., & Villarroel, M. (2020, September 21). *Symptoms of Generalized Anxiety Disorder among Adults: United States, 2019*. Centers for Disease Control and Prevention. www.cdc.gov/nchs/products/databriefs/db378.htm

Tiesman, H. M., Konda, S., Hartley, D., Menéndez, C. C., Ridenour, M., & Hendricks, S. (2015). Suicide in U.S. workplaces, 2003–2010: A comparison with non-workplace suicides. *American Journal of Preventive Medicine*, *48*(6), 674–682. https://doi.org/10.1016/j.amepre.2014.12.011

Tobin, C., & Shady, L. (2022, June 1). Reconnaissance of Legacy Buildings—Firefighters and Building Construction. Fire Engineering. www.fireengineering.com/fire-prevention-protection/firefighter-training-reconnaissance-of-legacy-buildings/

Tracy, M., Morgenstern, H., Zivin, K., Aiello, A. E., & Galea, S. (2014). Traumatic event exposure and depression severity over time: Results from a prospective cohort study in an urban area. *Social Psychiatry and Psychiatric Epidemiology*, *49*(11), 1769–1782. https://doi.org/10.1007/s00127-014-0884-2

Van Orden, K. A., Witte, T. K., Cukrowicz, K. C., Braithwaite, S. R., Selby, E. A., & Joiner Jr., T. E. (2010). The interpersonal theory of suicide. *Psychological Review*, *117*, 575–600. https://doi.org/10.1037/a0018697

Virgin, Y. (2022, December 6). Fire stations' kitchen table a place to help with mental stress. *KABB*. https://foxsanantonio.com/news/yami-investigates/fire-stations-kitchen-table-a-place-to-help-with-mental-stress

Wagner, D., Heinrichs, M., & Ehlert, U. (1998). Prevalence of symptoms of post-traumatic stress disorder in German professional firefighters. *American Journal of Psychiatry*, *155*(12), 1727–1732. https://doi.org/10.1176/ajp.155.12.1727

Wagner, S. L., White, N., Buys, N., Carey, M. G., Corneil, W., Fyfe, T., Matthews, L. R., Randall, C., Regehr, C., White, M., Alden, L. E., Krutop, E., Fraess-Phillips, A., & Fleischmann, M. H. (2021). Systematic review of mental health symptoms in firefighters exposed to routine duty-related critical incidents. *Traumatology*, *27*(3), 285–302. https://doi.org/10.1037/trm0000275

Walker, M. (2018). *Why We Sleep: Unlocking the Power of Sleep and Dreams*. Scribner.

Wang, H. L. (2020, April 23). "I Hear The Agony": Coronavirus Crisis Takes Toll On NYC's First Responders. *NPR*. www.npr.org/2020/04/23/842011186/i-hear-the-agony-coronavirus-crisis-takes-toll-on-nyc-s-first-responders

Williams, C. (2016, September 7). Smoked Out: Are Firefighters in More Danger than Ever Before? *EHS Today*. www.ehstoday.com/emergency-management/article/21917746/smoked-out-are-firefighters-in-more-danger-than-ever-before

10

AN INTEGRATIVE REVIEW TO DEVELOP THE UNIFIED NEUROMATRIX ALLOSTATIC LOAD AND RESILIENCY MODEL (UNALARM) AND APPLY IT TO THE HEALTH OF FIREFIGHTERS AND OTHER PUBLIC SAFETY PERSONNEL

Joy C. MacDermid, Temitope Osifeso, and Kathryn E. Sinden

Problem Identification

We used models to explain complex phenomena and test theoretical relationships between different constructs or phenomena that can support or refute those models. Models, while valuable, often focus on a limited perspective or "slice" of a larger reality. In understanding firefighter and other public safety personnel (PSP) health, we need a holistic perspective since PSP are exposed to high social, physical, cognitive, and emotional demands/loads in their work, which occurs in a unique and complex context (Carleton et al., 2018) with many decisions and choices that have to be made under duress and time pressures. Focusing on the psychosocial aspects of occupational exposures is important but neglects important interrelationships between the physical, social, and psychological domains of health.

All PSP are at risk of mental health injuries due to their exposure to critical and chronic occupational stressors incidents (Carleton et al., 2018; MacDermid et al., 2019). Firefighters have biological, social, and psychological exposures that can be associated with mental health injuries (Carey et al., 2011; Carleton et al., 2018; Cramm et al., 2021; Henderson et al., 2016; Jones, 2017; Kim et al., 2018; Stanley et al., 2017), musculoskeletal disorders (Beaton et al., 2002; Carr-Pries et al., 2022; Killip et al., 2023; Kim et al., 2013; Nazari, MacDermid, & Cramm, 2020; Negm et al., 2017; Ramsden et al., 2018), and cancer (Bates, 2007; Daniels et al., 2013; Golden et al., 1995; Guidotti, 2007; LeMasters et al., 2006). These are very different

DOI: 10.4324/9781003424253-14

diseases, but they share common symptoms, like pain (Beaton et al., 2002; Nazari, Macdermid, Sinden, et al., 2020) and sleep disturbances (Billings & Focht, 2016; Cramm et al., 2021; Cabrera et al., 2021). Individual PSP occupational diagnoses have some unique risk factors, symptoms, prognosis, and treatment requirements. However, they may share common pathways between occupational stress injury (OSI) and chronic disease (Cramm et al., 2021; Cabrera et al., 2021). Health can be affected by multiple occupational illnesses that occur concurrently or sequentially. To understand PSP health in a way that considers interactions between different biopsychosocial exposures, different risk pathways, and health trajectories, we required a more holistic model or theory. While we explore a proposed model in the context of all PSP, some examples will relate specifically to firefighters, given that some toxic exposure disease associations are more prevalent in that sector, like toxic chemicals and cancer.

The purpose of this integrative review was to integrate different theories or models. Theories were selected that focus on stress or loading exposures while integrating their unique emphasis to develop a more comprehensive model that considers the cumulative impacts of mental, social, and physical health exposures within a biopsychosocial framework. An integrative review is a literature synthesis intended to integrate different types of knowledge such as theory, mechanistic studies, empirical studies, and qualitative research. The method is ideally suited to our purpose of creating an integrative model that focuses on the life exposures affecting the overall health of firefighters and other PSP.

Therefore, our purposes in the integrative review were:

1 To review the primary tenants of three relevant biopsychosocial models that focus on adaptation to exposures and resulting symptoms: the Neuromatrix Theory of Pain, the Allostatic Load Model, and Selye's General Adaptation Syndrome Theory.
2 To summarize systematic reviews that specifically used the Neuromatrix Theory or the Allostatic Load Model in any population, limiting ourselves to conditions of relevance to firefighters/PSP (all-cause mortality, cancer, MSK, sleep disorders, or mental health outcomes).
3 To propose a Unified Neuromatrix Allostatic Load and Resiliency Model (UNALARM).
4 To discuss exemplar firefighter-specific studies that have assessed mechanisms that support or refute UNALARM.
5 To conduct a meta-analysis of the relationship between psychological stress and musculoskeletal pain in firefighters or other PSP to assess whether this research supports or refutes UNALARM.

Literature Search and Synthesis Strategy by Objective

The following search strategies were used to address the specific purposes above:

1 The primary articles describing the theoretical models by the model developer were identified and summarized.
2 Systematic reviews that summarized evidence on the Allostatic Load Model or Neuromatrix Theory were summarized if the review primarily focused on mental health, cardiovascular, or work disability in any working-age population were identified through PubMed with no date limits.
3 A search was conducted in PubMed, PsycINFO, and CINAHL to identify studies that applied the Allostatic Load Model to firefighter health by searching articles that combined "allostatic or allostatic AND firefighter".
4 A systematic review and meta-analysis were conducted based on a search of three literature databases (PubMed, PsycINFO, and CINAHL) from inception to November 3, 2023. The following search terms were used: TOPIC ("firefighter*" OR "fire fighters" OR "firemen*" OR "fire rescue" or "firefighter" OR "police officers" OR "policemen" OR "public safety personnel" OR EMT OR paramedic* AND stress* or stressor* OR "job stress" OR "occupational stress" OR "work stress" AND pain* or "chronic pain" or "musculoskeletal pain*" OR "acute pain" OR "sub-acute pain").

Study Selection for Systematic Review and Meta-Analysis

All articles identified from the electronic database search were exported to Covidence software (Version 2). After the removal of duplicates, one reviewer (TO) independently screened all titles and abstracts using pre-defined inclusion and exclusion criteria and excluded studies that did not meet the inclusion criteria. Two reviewers (TO and JMD) then retrieved the full texts of the remaining articles and all the full texts alphabetically, by author. The reviewers' discussion of all remaining articles resulted in fitting inclusions/exclusion criteria. Disagreements in each phase were resolved through a consultation meeting.

Eligibility Criteria

Quantitative, qualitative, and mixed method empirical studies that were peer-reviewed, published in English, or that could be translated to English and included PSP (firefighters, police officers, and paramedics) as participants were included. Literature reviews, grey literature, editorials, personal opinions, unpublished literature, conferences, and meeting reports were all excluded.

Data Extraction

One reviewer (TO) extracted the data from the included articles using a self-developed data extraction sheet in Microsoft Excel 365. The reviewers (TO and JMD) later met to resolve any disagreements or inconsistencies. Each reviewer then extracted the following data from their portion of the included articles: (1) name of author(s); (2) year of publication; (3) the country the study was conducted in; (4) research objective; (5) type of PSP population (e.g., firefighters, paramedics/EMT, or police officers); (6) participant characteristics (e.g., mean age of participants, gender/sex, sample size); (7) study design (i.e., qualitative, quantitative, mixed methods); (8) definition of work stress; (11) study themes (if qualitative); (12) tools/outcome measures; (if quantitative or mixed-methods); (15) results; and (16) conclusions.

A narrative synthesis was performed to integrate the findings from the different types of research and was used to develop a conceptual framework. The results of these different sources of evidence were integrated by description, inter-weaving and synthesis into a model and then evaluating current literature to see the extent to which it was consistent with the integrated model.

Integrative Review Findings

Individual Theoretical Frameworks

The Neuromatrix Theory

Ron Melzack was a Canadian psychologist who collaborated with Professor Patrick Wall, a physician and neuroanatomist from the UK. In 1965, they published the Gate Control Theory of pain, a landmark theory in our understanding of pain (Melzack & Wall, 1965). The novel aspect of the Gate Control Theory was that it proposed that descending pathways from the brain modulate activity in the spinal cord dorsal horn interneurons by influencing input from peripheral nerves to affect the pain experience.

Melzack continued to expand and apply his work by explaining that pain is subjective, multidimensional, and processed in several regions of the brain (Katz & Rosenbloom, 2015; Melzack& Wall, 1965; Melzack, 1996; Melzack & Wall, 1994; Odajnyk, 1991). The Neuromatrix Theory (Melzack, 2001) extended hypotheses on how pain signals are processed beyond physical damage or inputs, recognizing that complex interactions between sensory, emotional, and cognitive processes occur in the brain to regulate the pain experience.

The theory proposes the brain contains a "neuromatrix," or a network of neurons that are activated in response to peripheral inputs (Melzack, 2001). In addition to the peripheral neural inputs from the sensory signals, the network is shaped by an individual's experiences, beliefs, and emotions through cognitive processes and emotional inputs from the limbic system. This model considers pain as a psychophysical phenomenon interpreted by the brain. Pain outputs include the pain experience, which has sensory, cognitive, and emotional components, as well as voluntary and involuntary action programmes and stress regulation programmes, which are the active programmes initiated by the brain in response to pain. Melzack proposed that there is cyclical processing and synthesis of inputs into neuromatrix, which has regions or networks that are specialized to process information related to major sensory events (such as injury, temperature change, and stimulation of erogenous tissue) that contribute to a neurosignature. The neurosignature is a continuous outflow from the body-self neuromatrix that creates ever-shifting awareness in the sentient neural hub and initiates action programmes such as the neural networks that produce movement (Melzack, 2001).

The Neuromatrix Theory is useful because of its focus on cognitive integration as determining the pain experience. Melzack (2001) proposed that injury produces neural signals that enter a dynamic nervous system where past experience, culture, and a host of other environmental and personal factors are processed. These brain processes actively participate in the selection, abstraction, and synthesis of information from a flood of sensory input. Reflecting on our focus on OSI and illness in this book, the model is useful as it emphasizes that emotional, cognitive, and sensory experiences act as inputs into the neuromatrix that influence the pain and suffering experienced due to physical illness or OSI. One might expect that physical, social, and psychological loads operate through some shared pathways. A gap in the Neuromatrix Theory is that the model does not explicitly address social inputs into the cognitive neuromatrix, although these can be operationalized through sensory, cognitive, and emotional components. Further, the model does not directly consider time and recalibration, although this is implied since we know the brain is in a constant learning or remodelling mode. This includes adaptive responses to stress (De Kloet et al., 2005; Doewes et al., 2021; Kaul et al., 2021; Lupien et al., 2009; Sandi & Haller, 2015). Melzack (2001) emphasized the link between pain and stress and homeostasis in stating:

> We are so accustomed to considering pain as a purely sensory phenomenon that we have ignored the obvious fact that injury does not merely produce pain; it also disrupts the brain's homeostatic regulation systems, thereby producing "stress" and initiating complex programs to reinstate homeostasis.
>
> *(p. 1380)*

No systematic reviews were found that explicitly evaluated the evidence for this theory, particularly with respect to understanding pain and stress mechanisms.

The Allostatic Load Model

The Allostatic Load Model describes the cumulative wear and tear on the body's systems as a result of ongoing stress (Boulos & Rosenwasser, 2015; Fava et al., 2019; Glei et al., 2007; McEwan, 1998; McEwen, 2006, 2015; Schulkin & Sterling, 2004; Wingfield, 2015). The theory proposes that when the body is exposed to stress, the body activates a physiological response that involves the release of hormones such as cortisol and adrenaline. This "fight or flight" response is beneficial for PSP in the short term as the response helps PSP deal with critical incidents. The model emphasizes the biologic aspects of stress through the neuroendocrine, autonomic nervous, and immune systems which are mediators of adaptation to life challenges, referred to as allostasis, meaning "maintaining stability through change." In the longer term, stress can result in heightened mental or physical resiliency, which can occur through biologic adaptation, improved coping, and neural or cognitive adaptations. However, if stress continues for an extended period or exceeds the capacity to adapt, it can lead to a state of chronic stress and exhaustion with reduced capacity, which can have negative effects on health. Excess allostatic load can arise from (1) frequent or chronic activation of allostatic systems; (2) failure to shut off allostatic activity after exposure to stress; and (3) inadequate response of allostatic systems to meet the nature or size of the allostatic load. Allostatic load refers to the long-term physiological and psychological effects of chronic stress, including changes in the immune system, cardiovascular system, and metabolic function.

Allostatic processes will vary between individuals because there are individual differences in how people respond to potentially stressful situations. After studying critical incidents in firefighters where our initial approach was to study the prevalence of events, we later realized the importance of capturing the meaning of the events to the individual firefighter (MacDermid et al., 2019; Nazari et al., n.d.). McEwan (1998, 2005) describes these individual differences as depending on two principal factors. Firstly, whether the individual perceives and interprets the situation as a threat and the associated nature and extent of the behaviours and physiological responses to a threat. If the situation is not perceived as a threat, then the responses either do not occur or are relatively minor. This partially explains why different PSP vary in their reactions to the same critical incident. The second aspect of individual differences concerns the individual's "fitness," which has physical (physical resiliency or capacity) and mental (mental resiliency) components.

Where threats cannot be prevented, as is the case for PSP, it becomes essential to build physical and mental resiliency to protect PSP against the negative consequences of their occupational exposures.

In terms of similarities, both the Neuromatrix Theory (Melzack, 1999, 2001) and the Allostatic Load Model (Bizik et al., 2013; Christensen et al., 2022; De Kloet et al., 2005; Fava et al., 2019; Lenart-Bugla et al., 2022; McEwen, 2006; Schulkin, 2015) acknowledge the complex interplay between psychological and physiological factors in the perception of symptoms, and the response to stress. Both theories suggest that the brain and body are interconnected, and changes in neural processing or physiological responses affect each other. The Neuromatrix Theory (Melzack, 1999, 2001) emphasizes the sensory receptors and pathways involved in pain, particularly in terms of central processing, but did embrace the concept of stress. The Allostatic Model focuses on the periphery but also includes the impact of repeated stress on brain function, especially the hippocampus, which influences episodic and declarative memory and is especially important for the memory of "context," that is, the time and place where events occur and associated emotional bias. Stress can induce hippocampal dysfunction and memory impairment partially due to the influence of adrenal steroids in the stress response. This explains mechanisms for cognitive fog, emotive responses to reminders of past events, and impaired memory that often occurs with OSI. Repeated stress can cause permanent changes in the brain, including atrophy of dendrites of pyramidal neurons in the hippocampus, through a mechanism involving both glucocorticoids and excitatory amino acid neurotransmitters released during and in the aftermath of stress (Lenart-Bugla et al., 2022). Melzack's views were aligned with the allostatic load model: "The neuromatrix, as a result of homeostasis regulation patterns that have failed, produces the destructive conditions that may give rise to many of the chronic pains that so far have been resistant to treatments" (Melzack, 2001, p. 1381).

Measurement of allostatic load is important to support or refute the theory and for the application of the model in the real world (Beese et al., 2022; Bizik et al., 2013; Yoneda et al., 2023). An initial battery of ten biomarkers has been used to quantify allostatic load and has been used to construct cumulative indicators of stress adaptation (Fava et al., 2019; Logan & Barksdale, 2008; McCaffery et al., 2012; Stewart, 2006). The initial allostatic load battery was composed of four primary mediators (indicating the biochemical changes in the neuroendocrine system that confirm that the stress response was initiated) and six secondary mediators (representing structural remodelling of receptors sites of the cardiovascular, immune, and metabolic systems due to long-term activation of the stress response). The original primary mediators included cortisol, noradrenaline (norepinephrine), adrenaline (epinephrine), and dehydroepiandrosterone (DHEA). These mediators are responsible for triggering the hypothalamic–pituitary–adrenal axis and the sympathetic–adrenal medullary axis cascades of the stress response, or that reflect the outcome of the primary cascades. Secondary mediators measure the symptom manifestations of a prolonged stress response. The original six secondary mediators included systolic blood pressure, diastolic blood pressure, waist-to-hip ratio, high-density lipoprotein, total cholesterol, and glycosylated haemoglobin (McEwan, 2005). These measures have been used to assess the physical aspects of stress and the allostatic systems affected. A systematic review evaluated studies that identified single or repeated stressor exposures, including heart rate variability, among first responders and tactical operators. Lower resting HRV was associated with lower situational awareness and impaired decision-making performance in marksmanship and navigation tasks (Fava et al., 2019; Logan & Barksdale, 2008; McCaffery et al., 2012; Stewart, 2006). This demonstrates the relationship between indicators of allostatic load (i.e., HRV) and job performance. There were insufficient studies to evaluate the utility of HRV to assess allostatic load in repeated stress contexts (Corrigan et al., 2021). With the emergence of wearable sensors with the capability to track biophysical measures linked to allostatic load (i.e., core temperature, cardiac indicators, respiration), there is the possibility to advance our understanding of individual variation in firefighter/PSP responses to physical and mental stress, fitness testing (Nazari et al., 2018, 2019), simulated firefighting (Nazari et al., 2021), and other real-world occupational exposures.

An important aspect of allostasis and allostatic load is the role of anticipation. Although originally introduced in relation to explaining a vascular reflex, anticipation also implies psychological states such as worry and anxiety, as well as cognitive preparation for a coming event. PSP who are more fearful and reactive will have larger reactive physiological responses, whereas those individuals who have proactive planning skills and psychological resiliency will have less reactive responses and more stability in their responses. This provides a biologic mechanism for the effects of cumulative stress and posttraumatic stress disorder (PTSD), and for the recent focus on resiliency training amongst PSP.

The Allostatic Load Model describes what is commonly called the fight–flight–freeze responses. This is needed in the short term, especially for PSP, as the model supports drawing upon emergency reserves to deal with critical events. However, if this response becomes persistent, it can be maladaptive. Maladaptive responses can be *Overactive*, which exposes the person to ongoing stress responses. If the responses are *Inadequate* from any of the allostatic mechanisms, this can lead to pressure on other systems and overall system failure. Maladaptive responses can include a failure to shut off the stress response, where people are unable to activate rest and recovery when tasks or shifts are over. This mechanism can partially explain the link between OSI and musculoskeletal (MSK) pain and how this varies by sex, since chronic muscle tension, abnormal motor control, or altered physiologic responses can contribute to musculoskeletal disorders (Heikkinen et al., 2019; Phyomaung et al., 2014; Vun et al., 2018; Bouffard et al., 2018; Côté, 2012). Inappropriately timed allostatic responses can be maladaptive as they disrupt sleep (Christensen et al., 2022; McEwen, 2006), appetite, and mood. Chronic physiological dysregulation has been linked to a range of health problems, such as heart disease, depression, and diabetes (Bergen-Cico et al., 2015; Friedman & McEwen, 2005; Igboanugo & Mielke, 2023). Understanding these responses and how to facilitate better coping and homeostasis mechanisms can be underlying mechanisms in resiliency, mental health awareness training, and cognitive behavioural therapy. These pathways demonstrate the link between physical input and pathways with pain and stress, which form a basis for physical interventions like diet and exercise that are beneficial for mental health. Conversely, mental health stress enacts allostatic loads that adversely affect physical health, including potential risks for musculoskeletal injuries, cancer, and heart disease. This is confirmed by statistical models that demonstrate the predictive strength of physical and behavioural health measures where PTSD was shown to be strongly associated with depression, anxiety, poor sleep quality, musculoskeletal pain, cortisol, and BMI (Bergen-Cico et al., 2015).

A difference between the two theories is how the Neuromatrix Theory focuses specifically on the perception of pain, while the Allostatic Load Model is more broadly concerned with the effects of chronic loading across multiple stress-regulating systems. The Allostatic load is a whole-body physiologic approach emphasizing that stress affects more than the brain. These systems include the HPA axis; the autonomic nervous system; the metabolic systems–thyroid axis, insulin, glucagon, the gut, and the immune system (McEwen, 2006, 2015; Wingfield, 2015). Thus, while the Neuromatrix Theory suggests pain is primarily a product of the brain, the Allostatic Load Model emphasizes the importance of body-wide physiological responses to stress, including changes in hormone levels and other bodily processes. The Allostatic Load Model explains why the cardiovascular system is susceptible to stress, and this explains potential associations between OSI and heart disease, as reviewed in the chapter in this book by Stretton. The gut is increasingly a focus of interest with respect to mental health both in terms of understanding mechanisms, links across mental and physical health and potential new mental health treatments (Bruce-Keller et al., 2018; Holingue et al., 2020; Järbrink-Sehgal & Andreasson, 2020; Rieder et al., 2017).

Systematic reviews have addressed allostatic load in non-PSP adult populations and the association with all-cause mortality, cancer, musculoskeletal, sleep disorders, or mental health outcomes. These concluded:

1 Based on 11 studies that met eligibility, a meta-analysis of correlation coefficients indicated a small but significant positive association between

neuroticism and allostatic load and small but significant inverse associations between both conscientiousness and openness with allostatic load (Yoneda et al., 2023).

2 A synthesis review of 238 studies published from 1995 to 2020 that focused on how allostatic load has been measured found that the original ten biomarkers (listed above) were most often used. More recently, body mass index and C-reactive protein have additionally been frequently used to measure the allostatic load burden (McEwan, 2005).
3 A total of 13 studies evaluated the association of the allostatic index with brain structure and functioning. All studies confirmed the associations between a higher allostatic index and brain changes, especially: (1) the hippocampus, white matter volume, grey matter volume, and density in older adults; (2) the cortex, fornix, hippocampus, and choroid plexus in patients with schizophrenia spectrum disorders; and (3) whole-brain white matter tracts, cortical grey matter volume, and cortical thickness in overweight subjects (Lenart-Bugla et al., 2022).
4 Sleep disturbance was significantly associated with higher allostatic load based on 17 studies of 26,924 participants included in a meta-analysis (Christensen et al., 2022).
5 High allostatic load was associated with increased risk of all-cause mortality across all 17 individual studies included in a systematic review (hazard ratio = 1.08–2.75) and 6 of 8 studies examining cardiovascular disease mortality (hazard ratio = 1.19–3.06) (Parker et al., 2022).
6 From 7 studies with 902 African Americans, higher chronic stress levels and experiences of racial discrimination were associated with telomere shortening, while lower income and higher chronic stress levels were associated with an increase in allostatic load among people of colour (Murkey et al., 2022).
7 Significant associations were found between allostatic load in 12 studies with variables such as cancer-related stress, positive cancer history, posttraumatic growth, resilience, tumour pathology, and cancer-specific mortality. A mini meta-analysis found that a one-unit increase in allostatic load was associated with a 9% increased risk of cancer-specific mortality (Mathew et al., 2021).
8 A total of 20 studies supported the hypothesis that social connectedness correlates negatively with allostatic load. Several moderators of this relationship were also identified, including gender, social status, and quality of social ties (Sonderlund et al., 2019).
9 Mixed evidence was found across 24 studies with respect to the relationship between psychosocial resources and allostatic load. Most (14/24) studies used a cross-sectional design, and only one investigated whether a psychosocial resource predicted change in allostatic load. Both psychological (8/11) and social (10/16) resources had similar findings (Sonderlund et al., 2019).

Three studies were identified that specifically addressed the application of the Allostatic Load Model in firefighters.

Igboanugo and Mielke (2023) published a comprehensive narrative review that applied the Allostatic Load Model to understand firefighter health. They reviewed the occupational characteristics that may cause psychosocial stress within firefighters, leading to dysregulation across various physiological systems. They provided a summary of how allostatic load can be measured and touched on the framework's utility for studying the cumulative effects of work-related stress on firefighter health. They discussed factors mediating the pathways from stress exposure to health outcomes considering other non-modifiable (age, sex, and ethnicity) and modifiable (psychosocial resources and behavioural habits) factors. These authors (Igboanugo et al., 2022) applied the theory in an empirical study where they found a positive relationship but a nonsignificant association between psychosocial stress and allostatic load, but a small association between age and allostatic load ($B = 0.09$, $p = 0.04$). They noted firefighters reported the mitigating effects of social support. Corrigan (2022) investigate the utility of heart rate variability in measuring allostatic load in firefighters (discussed above).

General Adaptation Syndrome (GAS)

Selye's General Adaptation Syndrome (GAS) model describes a three-stage physiological response to stress: alarm, resistance, and exhaustion (Selye, 1950), which we have adapted in our revised model below to alarm, resist, and change to reflect that change can be positive or negative. In the alarm stage, the body reacts to stress by activating the sympathetic nervous system, leading to an increase in heart rate, blood pressure, and respiration. In the resistance stage, the body attempts to adapt to the stressor and return to homeostasis. In the exhaustion stage, if the stressor persists for an extended period, the body's resources can become depleted, leading to exhaustion and possibly illness. GAS aligns with the principles of the Allostatic Load Model. The Allostatic Load Model and Selye's GAS model are both concerned with how the body responds to stress. However, there are some nuanced differences. While the GAS and Allostatic Load Models focus on the physiological response to stress, the Allostatic Load Model considers the psychological and social factors that contribute to stress. As such, it emphasizes that chronic stress can have different exposures and health outcomes, leading to unique trajectories for different people. The GAS theory has been used to explain cardiovascular disease in this book (Chapter 7).

Social Stress Theories

Although not the focus of this review, social theories have been well explored in other chapters of this book. Social theories acknowledge that people with disadvantaged social status are more likely to be exposed to stressors and to be more vulnerable to stress because they have limited psychosocial coping resources, which is a potential pathway to mental injury or illness. Social stress is often persistent, which may contribute to chronic stress. Social inequalities, such as poverty and discrimination, can lead to poor health outcomes by creating unequal access to resources and opportunities. Social determinants of health, such as housing, employment, and access to healthcare, have a role in shaping health outcomes (Moin et al., 2018; van Ingen & Matheson, 2021; Zygmunt et al., 2020). Social theories are particularly relevant in the context of firefighting, which is a masculine-dominated occupation, and the social context of this work is highly defined by the unique history and culture (Beaton et al., 1997; Johnson et al., 2019; Kaur et al., 2023; Taber et al., 2012). While career firefighters have compensation for their service, there can be economic and social disparities between volunteer and career roles. Social theories of health emphasize the social, and political factors that contribute to health, while the Allostatic Load and Neuromatrix Theory focus more on the individual-level factors that affect health and disease, with social influences as mediators that exist in the background.

The Unified Neuromatrix Allostatic Load and Resiliency Model (UNALARM) Adaptation Model

Figure 10.1 illustrates our integrated model to explain the cumulative impacts of physical, psychological, and social loads. From left to right, the model illustrates how people at one point in time have a health state that supports their current well-being and role functioning. Over time, life events happen, including injuries, trauma, life events, and ageing, that act as inputs/loads into the neuromatrix and allostatic systems. These "alarms" require a response to maintain homeostasis. These exposures include physical, mental, and social inputs into the body-self neuromatrix. The "resist" phases are the combined cognitive, sensory, and affective responses in the brain neuromatrix and the peripheral nervous, immune endocrine, musculoskeletal, and cardiovascular responses that encompass the allostatic stress regulator programmes. These programmes are reflected in symptoms and behavioural action programmes. The optimal outcome of this process is positive homeostasis, which leads to an improved health state where adaptation results in better resilience and enhanced capacity. Conversely, where the system cannot adequately compensate for the allostatic load, this leads to exhaustion, chronic stress, and negative coping strategies that lower health and well-being, with an expected resultant loss of role functioning. Multiple symptoms and diseases could arise from the cumulative and interactive loading and ongoing biopsychosocial processes that are engaged to try and achieve homeostasis and resiliency.

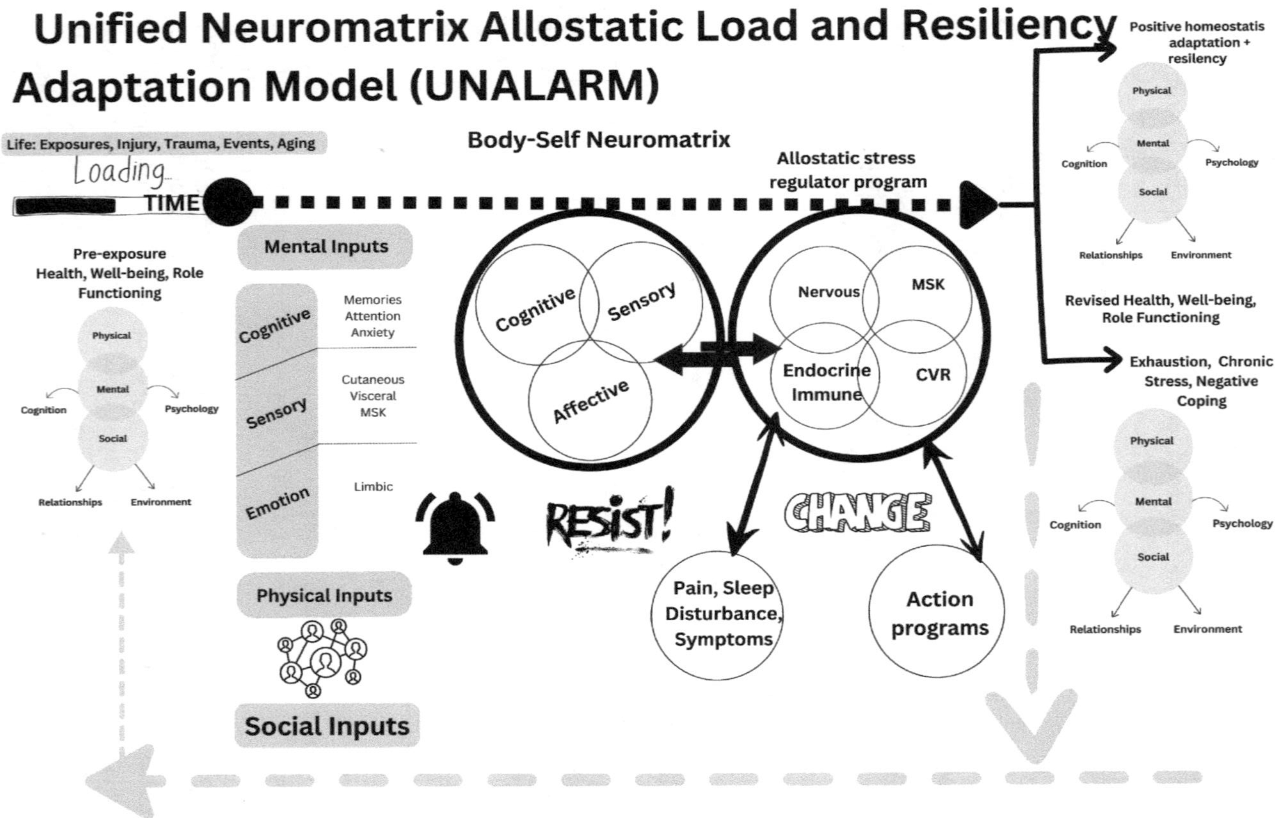

FIGURE 10.1 Unified neuromatrix allostatic load and resiliency adaptation model (UNALARM).

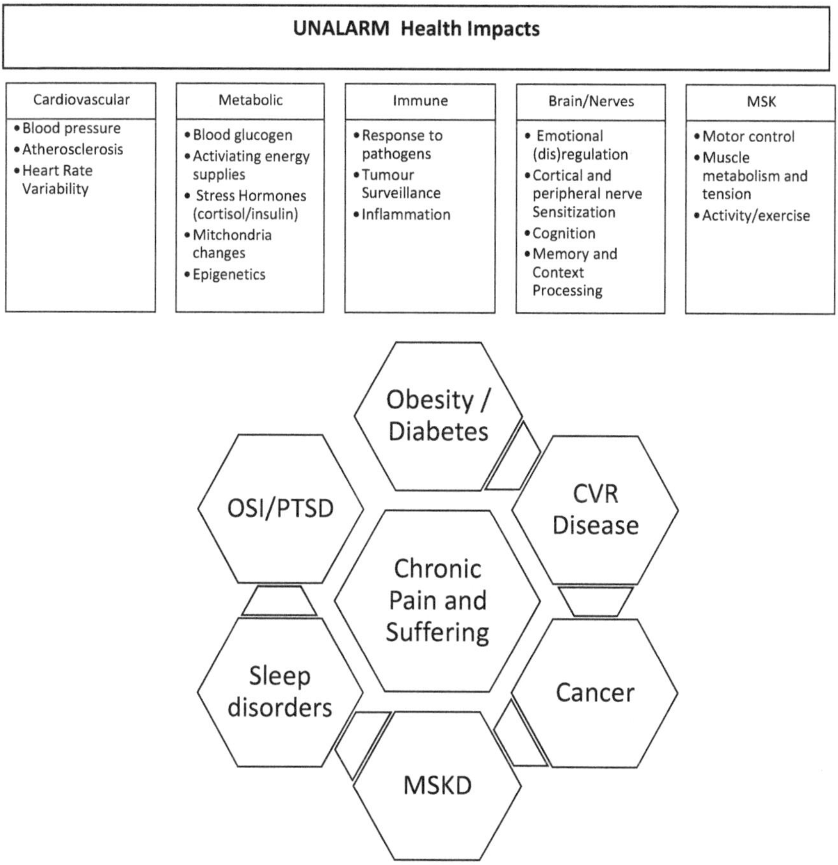

FIGURE 10.2 UNALARM health impacts.

Figure 10.2 illustrates the common health disturbances that occur on firefighters and other PSP. These are consistent with multi-system allostatic loading responses that build resiliency or lead to systemic exhaustion that compromises health.

Testing Hypothesis of the Neuromatrix Allostatic Stress Adaptation Model in Firefighters

UNALARM describes how life exposures and the resulting "homeostatic" reactions affect multiple body systems and can increase the risk for multiple physical and mental health disorders. The model is useful in the case of firefighters, and other PSP, who are at elevated risk of multiple health problems since we tend to view these physical and mental problems as having different risk factors, although they are likely linked. This differs from disease models that expect a direct relationship between an exposure, like an infection, where a specific outcome is expected. As an example of multiple pathways to disease, firefighters are at increased risk of cancer (LeMasters et al., 2006) due to their exposure to toxic chemical exposures on the front line. Our *Neuromatrix Allostatic Load Model* illustrates how, in addition to toxic chemical/air exposures from fire, other stressors can affect the immune system responses that protect firefighters against cancer. Thus, while toxic chemicals can be the primary exposure, stress can be a secondary cause or mediator of the causal pathway.

As a second example, chronic musculoskeletal pain is prevalent among firefighters (Nazari, MacDermid, & Cramm, 2020; Nazari, Macdermid, Sinden, et al., 2020), which is assumed to be primarily due to their highly demanding physical tasks performed under urgent conditions, in awkward postures and emergency circumstances with precarious environmental conditions. However, physical changes in neuromuscular functioning due to cognitive "fog" resulting from OSI could be a contributing factor in musculoskeletal injuries. We know musculoskeletal injuries often occur in training (Carr-Pries et al., 2022; Frost et al., 2015), where there are high physical demands (Kajaks et al., 2023) potentially without the same "meaningfulness" – such that injury risks are affected by lower situational awareness. Similarly, shift work can affect the allostatic load in firefighters. Choi et al. (2016) studied stressors in long firefighting shifts and proposed a theoretical model to explain how these stresses affect elements consistent with allostatic load. Others have shown changes in inflammatory markers in firefighters exposed to computerized firefighting strategies and tactics in decision-making challenges while participating in moderate-intensity exercise (Igbboanugo et al., 2022). A study of firefighters who exercised at 60% VO2max while participating in a computerized Fire Strategies and Tactics Drill and again at the same intensity without the mental challenge found no differences in the amount of work performed between the two conditions, but that cortisol responses were significantly elevated across with the concurrent physical and mental challenges (Webb et al., 2011). Others have shown that both cortisol and inflammatory markers are associated with psychosocial stress in firefighters (Wolkow et al., 2016). The exacerbated responses of stress hormones with mental and physical demands support that allostatic mechanisms may represent common pathways to different diseases and health outcomes. The link between occupational climate and organizational systems and lower heart rate variability in firefighters demonstrates how macro-climate variables can affect individual physiologic allostatic responses (Shin et al., 2016). Occupational stress was also shown to alter the neuromatrix of firefighters, as indicated by associations with large-scale neural networks (Shin et al., 2016). In a study of firefighters, abundant social support was inversely associated with perceived stress that mediated the total allostatic load (Igboanugo et al., 2022). These mechanistic studies support the intersectional effects of physical, mental, and social health consistent with UNALARM.

Systematic Review and Meta-analysis of Pain and Stress Associations in all PSP

Included Studies

Database search results initially identified 171 articles. There were 148 articles remaining after duplicates were removed and 12 after full-text screening was completed (see Figure 10.3). The 12 studies focused on diverse PSP populations, including firefighters, police officers, and paramedics (see Table 10.1). All 12 studies were quantitative studies and the articles included in this review were published between 1992 and 2019, with research conducted in 7 different countries, mainly across North America.

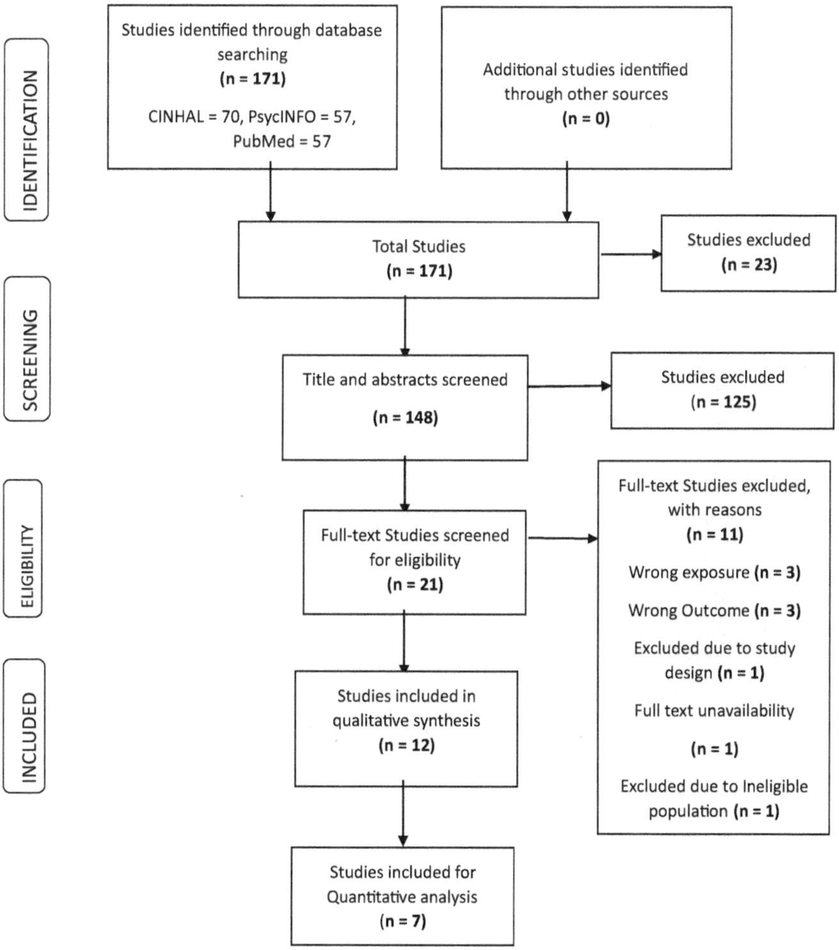

FIGURE 10.3 PRISMA flow chart.

Study Descriptions

The total sample size for all included studies (*n* = 12) was 22,197 participants (range: 90–4665 participants across studies), which comprised various PSP subgroups (see Table 10.1). The age range was from 19 years to greater than 60 years, and the average years of service was from less than 4 years to more than 15 years. Studies that included firefighters as the primary population reported a total of four studies (Damrongsak et al., 2018; Kim et al., 2013, 2017; Soteriades et al., 2019), while studies reported police officers as the primary sample had the highest number of studies with a total of six studies (Avdija, 2014; Douma et al., 2018; Burton et al., 1996; Kirkcaldy & Cooper, 1992; Mohr et al., 2003). Two studies reported a mixed PSP subgroup of firefighters, police officers, paramedics, correctional officers, etc. (Beaton et al., 1996; Carleton et al., 2018) (see Table 10.1). Ten studies implemented a cross-sectional design (Avdija, 2014; Beaton et al., 1996; Carleton et al., 2018; Kim et al., 2013, 2017; Larsen et al., 2019; Mohr et al., 2003; Soteriades et al., 2019), one study used a case-control design (Burton et al., 1996), while the remaining study used a non-experimental correlational design (Avdija, 2014). Sex and gender were primarily self-reported by completing a demographic questionnaire, and there were no reports of gender-diverse people. One study in the review excluded all female firefighters from their study sample because of their small numbers, with only 4.9% female participants compared to the 83.6% male participants in the study (Kim et al., 2013, 2017).

Synthesis of Findings

PSP Subgroups and Occupational Stressors

Firefighters

Six studies reported various musculoskeletal pain experienced by firefighters, which were found to be associated with physical and psychosocial stressors at work (Beaton et al., 1996; Carleton et al., 2018; Damrongsak et al., 2018; Kim et al., 2013, 2017; Soteriades et al., 2019). Two studies reported back pain as the primary location of musculoskeletal pain site linked to stressors at work (Damrongsak et al., 2018; Kim et al., 2017). The remaining four studies reported back and other locations of pain sites, including shoulders, hands, knee, neck, ankle, and foot regions, as the outcome of work-related stressors (Beaton et al., 1996; Carleton et al., 2018; Kim et al., 2013; Soteriades et al., 2019) (see Table 10.1).

Police

Three studies reported the back region as the primary musculoskeletal pain sites among police officers linked to physical and psychosocial stressors at work

TABLE 10.1 Summary of studies examining the relationship between psychosocial stressors and musculoskeletal pain

Author, Year, Country	*PSP Group*	*Years of Service*	*Study Design*	*Sample Size*	*Sex (Male)*	*Age M(SD)*	*MSK Pain Site*	*Assessment Toos/Outcomes*
Avdija 2014, USA (Avdija, 2014)	Police officers	12.8	CSS	1632	87.1%	37(8)	Back pain	Self-reported high blood pressure, work-related back pain and self-reported headaches
Beaton 1996, USA (Beaton et al., 1996)	FFs and Paramedics	NR	CSS	2000 (FFs = 1730; Paramedics = 253)	97%	NR	Neck, back, and shoulder regions	A 16-item measure of subjective pain complaints was derived from the Symptoms of Stress (SOS) inventory, SOS Pain Scale. A 57-item measure of job-related stressors inherent and/or related to employment as a professional firefighter and/or paramedic was developed by the first and second authors.

(*Continued*)

TABLE 10.1 (Continued)

Author, Year, Country	*PSP Group*	*Years of Service*	*Study Design*	*Sample Size*	*Sex (Male)*	*Age M(SD)*	*MSK Pain Site*	*Assessment Toos/Outcomes*
Burton 1996, UK (Burton et al., 1996)	Police officers	RUC: 14.8; GMP: 15.2	Case-Control	1885 (Case-RUC = 1508; control-GMP = 337)	RUC: 92%; GMP: 87%	RUC: 38(8); GMP: 37(7)	LBT – Low back trouble	Psychosocial Aspects of Work (PAW) questionnaire, 12-item General Health Questionnaire (GHQ). Self-administered questionnaires that had been piloted and refined. The requested information covered data relating to the experience of LBT (e.g., first-onset, subsequent temporal patterns, perceived cause) and data relating to the duties and activities performed (including exposure to body armour, extent of use of vehicles, and participation in sports activities)

Carleton 2018, Canada (Carleton et al., 2018)	Public Safety Personnel (PSP)	<4years=19.3%(47);CSS 4–9 years = 30.9% (270); 10–15 years = 40.7% (474);>15years=44.9 (1226)	2025 (participants with any chronic pain)	40.3 %	19–29 – 26.4% (100), 30–39 – 34.2% (483), 40–49 – 41.3% (766), 50–59 – 48.7% (598), >= 60 – 47.3% (78)	All cases of chronic pain	Current chronic pain experiences were assessed with self-report items based on work done by the International Association for the Study of Pain (IASP); Current mental disorder symptoms were assessed with several validated self-report mental disorder screening measures, PTSD (past month) was assessed with the PTSD Check List 5 (PCL-5)

(*Continued*)

TABLE 10.1 (Continued)

Author, Year, Country	*PSP Group*	*Years of Service*	*Study Design*	*Sample Size*	*Sex (Male)*	*Age M(SD)*	*MSK Pain Site*	*Assessment Toos/Outcomes*
Damrongsak 2018, USA (Damrongsak et al., 2018)	Firefighters	12.5	Non-experimental, correlational design	298	100%	39 (9)	Back pain	The Job Stress Survey (JSS), a 30-item self-administered questionnaire designed to assess occupational stress in men and women: Four major domains were assessed, including stress frequency, stress severity, job pressure, and lack of organizational support. Health Risk Appraisal Questionnaire: Personal factors collected via the health risk appraisal questionnaire included age, history of back pain, and report of current back pain

Douma 2018, Canada (Benyamina Douma et al., 2018)	Police officers	12.1	CSS	2208	68.1%	35 (8)	Low back pain (acute, sub-acute and chronic)	French-Canadian version of the Nordic Musculoskeletal Questionnaire (NMQ) – Low Back pain section; Car-patrol police officers were then questioned about their 12 last months' work schedule, mean number of hours worked per week, and mean number of breaks in a 9-hour work shift. The proportion of hours spent wearing body armour, wearing a duty belt, sitting in a patrol car (in motion or stationery), sitting in the patrol car as a driver, or doing desk tasks in a stationary patrol car was assessed, in addition to the use of a patrol car equipped with Mobile Data Terminal (MDT). Perceived stress over the last four weeks was measured by the 4-item Perceived Stress Scale (PSS-4)

(*Continued*)

TABLE 10.1 (Continued)

Author, Year, Country	*PSP Group*	*Years of Service*	*Study Design*	*Sample Size*	*Sex (Male)*	*Age M(SD)*	*MSK Pain Site*	*Assessment Toos/Outcomes*
Kim 2013, South Korea (Lee et al., 2022)	Firefighters	11	CSS	2362 (Work-related Musculoskeletal Disorders)	83.6% Male; 4.9% excluded female firefighter	39 (6) (WMSDs FFs)	Back, neck, foot, and shoulder pain complaints.	The job stress factors were measured by the short form of the Korean Occupational Stress Scale (KOSS-26); Work-related musculoskeletal disorders were measured by the Korean NIOSH Symptom Survey.
Kim 2017, South Korea (Lee et al., 2022)	Firefighters	NR	CSS	4665 (Reported Back pain symptoms)	100%	20–29 = 361 (18.1%); 30–39 = 2153 (21.1%); 40–49 = 1765 (19.1%); 50–59 = 386 (14.1%)	Low back pain	Job stress was measured by the Korean Occupational Stress Scale–Short Form (KOSS-SF); Structured questionnaire for the measurement of MSK symptoms, including frequency, duration and severity.

Kirkcaldy and Cooper 1992, Germany (Kirkcaldy & Cooper, 1992)	Police officers	12	CSS	90	93%	< 26 (3.33 %) years, 26–30 (2.22%), 31–35 (5.56%), 36–40 (14.44%), 41–45 (1 1.1 1%), 46–50 (26.67%), 51–55(20%), 56–60 (13.33%), >60 (2.22%)	Physical ill health	Occupational Stress Indicator was implemented, which measured seven different aspects of occupational stress. These subscales include four independent variable measures: (a) sources of job stress (61 items), (b) type A behaviour patterns (14 items), (c) locus of control (12 items), (d) coping strategies (28 items); and three dependent variable measures: (e) job satisfaction (22 items), and (f) mental (18 items) and (g) physical health (12 items).

(*Continued*)

TABLE 10.1 (Continued)

Author, Year, Country	*PSP Group*	*Years of Service*	*Study Design*	*Sample Size*	*Sex (Male)*	*Age M(SD)*	*MSK Pain Site*	*Assessment Toos/Outcomes*
Larsen 2019, Sweden (Larsen et al., 2019)	Police officers	NR	CSS	3899	74.3%	25–39 (70%)	(a) Upper back or neck; (b) shoul-dersorarms; (c) lower back; and (d) hips, legs, knees, or feet.	The Swedish Work Environment Survey (SWES) aims to describe the physical and psychosocial work environment of the Swedish working population. Additional questions were added to capture demographics, physical exercise and police-specific information. Multi-site musculoskeletal pain was the main outcome variable, with pain at various body sites measured separately and assessed with the question, "During the last three months, have you, after work, experienced pain in [body site] ...?" response alternatives were given on a 5-point scale

Mohr 2005, USA	Police officers	NR	CSS	733		78.6%	37.1 (6.9%)	Pains in the lower back, muscle soreness, numbness/tingling, and heavy feelings in arms or legs.	Somatization Subscale of the Symptom Checklist-90-R (SCL-Som). This scale measures the intensity of self-reported somatic complaints during the previous week, including headache, faintness/dizziness, pains in the heart or chest, pains in the lower back, muscle soreness, numbness/tingling, and heavy feelings in arms or legs. Items related to sleep were removed. Traumatic stress symptoms secondary to critical incidents during police service were evaluated by the Mississippi Scale–Civilian Version (MS-CV), which is a modification of the Mississippi Scale for Combat-Related Posttraumatic Stress Disorder.

(*Continued*)

TABLE 10.1 (Continued)

Author, Year, Country	*PSP Group*	*Years of Service*	*Study Design*	*Sample Size*	*Sex (Male)*	*Age M(SD)*	*MSK Pain Site*	*Assessment Toos/Outcomes*
Soteriades 2019, Cyprus (Soteriades et al., 2019)	Firefighters	NR	CSS	430	88.4%	(21–30 = 76(17%); 31–40 = 170 (29.5%); 41–50 =114 (26.5%) and 51–60 = 70 (16.3%)	Back pain, shoulder pain, knee problems, neck pain, upper extremities, upper back, and ankles.	Copenhagen Psychosocial Questionnaire and Depression, Anxiety and Stress Scale-19 dimensions to measure the level of psychosocial stressors at work; Depression, Anxiety and Stress Scale (DASS). For the purposes of the survey, the short version of the scale (DASS-21) was used, which consists of 21 items and all questions are evaluated on a Likert scale; To assess musculoskeletal problems, the Nordic Musculoskeletal Questionnaire (NMQ) was used. This scale consists of structured, multiple-choice questions, and all answers are in the form of a dichotomous yes/no response assessing musculoskeletal issues.

Note: NR – Not reported; FFs -Firefighters; CSS – Cross-sectional study; MSK-Musculoskeletal.

(Avdija et al., 2014; Burton et al., 1996; Douma et al., 2018). The remaining four studies also reported back pain in combination with other musculoskeletal pain sites such as neck, hips, legs, knees, and feet as associated with work-related stressors among police officers (Carleton et al., 2018; Kirkcaldy & Cooper, 1992; Larsen et al., 2019; Mohr et al., 2005) (see Table 10.1).

Paramedics

There were two studies that reported musculoskeletal pain sites as the outcome of work-related stressors among paramedics (Beaton et al., 1996; Carleton et al., 2018). Both studies were a mixed population of other PSP subgroups, including firefighters and police officers. The first study was a mix of paramedics and firefighters, and the outcome of work-related stressors was linked to multiple locations of pain in the body (Beaton et al., 1996). The remaining study was a mix of many PSP subgroups, including police officers, firefighters, correctional workers, and call dispatchers, and the experience of chronic pain symptoms was the outcome of being exposed to work-related mental stressors such as PTSD, anxiety, and depression (Carleton et al., 2018) (see Table 10.1 and Table 10.5).

Meta-Analysis and Subgroup Analysis

Seven studies were included for the meta-analysis of a combined PSP sample size of 17,221 participants (Avdija et al., 2014; Carleton et al., 2018; Douma et al., 2018; Kim et al., 2013, 2017; Larsen et al., 2019; Soteriades et al., 2019). Using a random effects model, the forest plot of pooled odds ratio (ORs) showed a significant association between job-related stressors and chronic pain among PSP (see Figure 10.3). The overall result for the PSP population, OR = 1.6 (95% CI, 1.4–1.9), showed that PSP are 1.6 more likely to report chronic pain when faced with work-related stressors. Similarly, a subgroup analysis of the PSP subgroups included four studies each for police officers (Avdija et al., 2014; Carleton et al., 2018; Douma et al., 2018; Larsen et al., 2019) and firefighters (Carleton et al., 2018; Kim et al., 2013, 2017; Soteriades et al., 2019). Subgroup analysis for police officers, OR =1.9 (95% CI, 1.3–2.6), showed they were 1.9 times more likely to report chronic pain when experiencing job-related stressors. While our results for firefighters, OR =1.5 (95% CI, 1.2–1.8), showed they were 1.5 times more likely to report chronic pain when experiencing job-related stressors (see Figures 10.4).

Assessment of Heterogeneity

Statistical heterogeneity was quantified using I^2, with values of 25%, 50%, and 75% indicating low, moderate, and high heterogeneity, respectively (Higgins

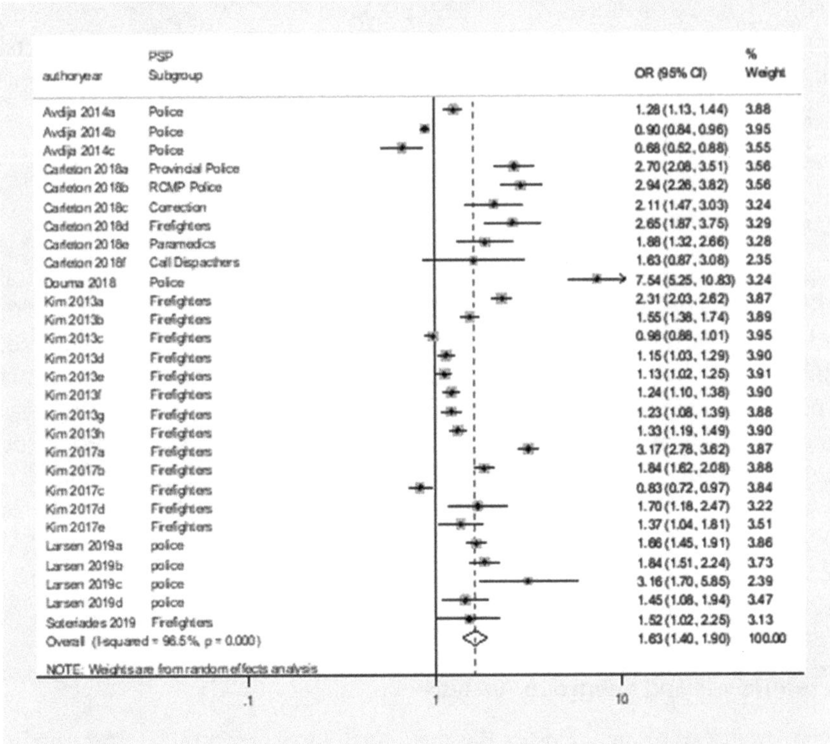

FIGURE 10.4 Forest plots showing the odds ratio between job stress and musculoskeletal pain among public safety personnel.

et al., 2003). Our meta-analysis showed a substantial heterogeneity among studies, statistically (I-squared = 96.5%) and on visual inspection. This might be due to the variability in the PSP population and the various outcome measures utilized in the included studies (see Table 10.1).

Publication Bias

The funnel plot on visual inspection showed asymmetry of all studies at the top and bottom of the plot (see Figures 10.5 and 10.6). Egger's test was used to test the significance of publication bias (Egger & Smith, 1998), and the result showed that there was significant publication bias ($p < 0.05$). This suggests studies linking occupational stress and chronic pain among PSP might be unpublished in literature due to their non-significant or weak findings and hence excluded from this review. Therefore, the results should be interpreted with caution based on this finding.

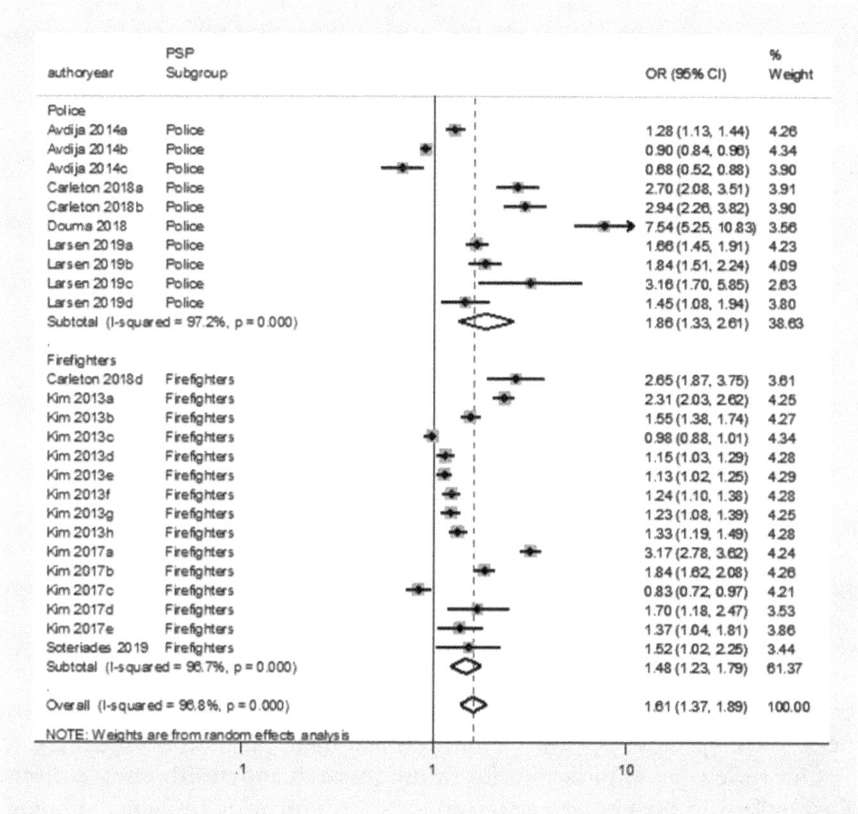

FIGURE 10.5 Forest plots showing the subgroup analysis of the odds ratio between job stress and musculoskeletal pain among police officers and firefighters.

Conclusions and Implications

The UNALARM was developed based on prior theory and current evidence to reflect how people respond to acute and chronic loading from physical, mental, and social factors to enact multi-system coping responses that attempt to maintain homeostasis. Positive adaptation enhances resiliency, whereas insufficient allostatic responses or maladaptive strategies can result in chronic loading with associated symptoms and negative health outcomes. Generic evidence on the individual theories was incomplete but supportive of the pathways proposed in UNALARM. Studies relating allostatic loading to firefighters and studies addressing the relationship between pain and psychological factors in PSP also provided incomplete but generally positive support for the hypotheses within UNALARM. Overall, this suggests that the model was useful in the context of PSP health. Most of the literature we

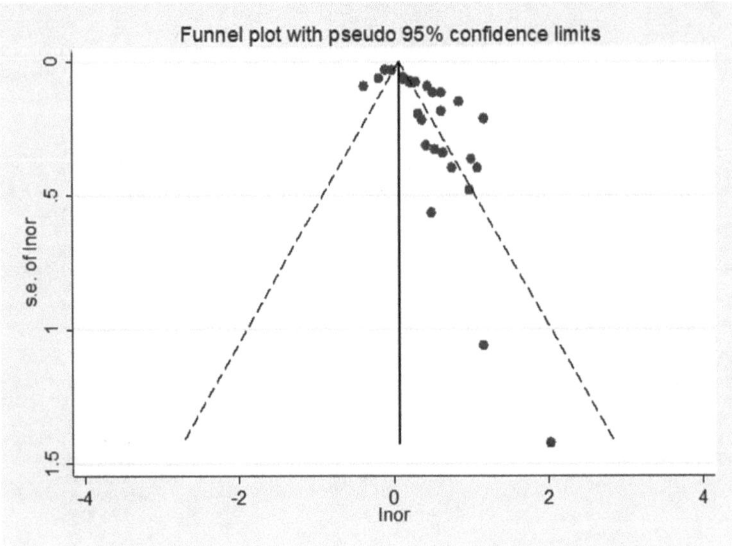

FIGURE 10.6 Funnel plot showing the odds ratio and the standard error of the odds ratio.

reviewed focused on negative outcomes of allostatic loading, but importantly, negative and positive pathways are in constant flux.

Our review has implications for future research and health interventions. First, efforts in the fire service to reduce stigma, provide resiliency training, and address culture are theoretically sound as they are all aimed at reducing psychosocial allostatic loads. Operational training, situational awareness training, and physical preparedness can reduce physical loading. Screening for cardiovascular health and cancer is aimed at early identification of the multiple health outcomes that can arise from allostatic loads and reducing the overall burden of physical disease. Unfortunately, too often, the management of mental and physical health is siloed, which means the interactions between physical, psychological, and social exposures are under-appreciated and, thus, comprehensive health screening is not fully operationalized. Future research that assesses multiple dimensions of allostatic loading and how they relate to specific health outcomes should be considered in comprehensive intervention design and research studies. Experimental studies with comprehensive outcome assessments that test the strength of the proposed pathways would help provide a more comprehensive understanding of the mechanisms and optimal management of PSP health. Nevertheless, the model is not PSP-specific and can serve a variety of purposes.

References

Avdija, A. S. (2014). Stress and law enforcers: testing the relationship between law enforcement work stressors and health-related issues. *Health Psychology and Behavioral Medicine: An Open Access Journal*, *2*(1), 198–210. https://doi.org/10.1080/21642850.2014.886957

Bates, M. N. (2007). Registry-based case – control study of cancer in California firefighters. *American Journal of Industrial Medicine*, *50*, 339–344. https://doi.org/10.1002/ajim.20446

Beaton, R. D., Murphy, S. A., Pike, K. C., & Corneil, W. (1997). Social support and network conflict in firefighters and paramedics. *Western Journal of Nursing Research*, *19*(3), 297–313. https://doi.org/10.1177/019394599701900303

Beaton, R., Murphy, S., & Pike, K. (1996). Work and nonwork stressors, negative affective states, and pain complaints among firefighters and paramedics. *International Journal of Stress Management*, *3*(4), 223–237. https://doi.org/10.1007/BF01857685

Beaton, R., Murphy, S., Salazar, M., & Johnson, L. C. (2002). Neck, back, and shoulder pain complaints in urban firefighters: the benefits of aerobic exercise. *Journal of Musculoskeletal Pain*, *10*(3), 57–67. https://doi.org/10.1300/J094v10n03_04

Beese, S., Postma, J., & Graves, J. M. (2022). Allostatic load measurement: a systematic review of reviews, database inventory, and considerations for neighborhood research. *International Journal of Environmental Research and Public Health*, *19*(24). https://doi.org/10.3390/ijerph192417006

Benyamina Douma, N., Côté, C., & Lacasse, A. (2018). Occupational and ergonomic factors associated with low back pain among car-patrol police officers. *Clinical Journal of Pain*, *34*(10), 960–966. https://doi.org/10.1097/AJP.0000000000000617

Bergen-Cico, D., Lane, S., Thompson, M., Wozny, S., Zajdel, M., Barduhn, M., & Noce, J. (2015). The impact of post-traumatic stress on first responders: analysis of cortisol, anxiety, depression, sleep impairment and pain. *International Paramedic Practice*, *5*(3), 78–87. https://doi.org/10.12968/ippr.2015.5.3.78

Billings, J., & Focht, W. (2016). Firefighter shift schedules affect sleep quality. *Journal of Occupational and Environmental Medicine*. https://doi.org/10.1097/JOM.0000000000000624

Bizik, G., Picard, M., Nijjar, R., Tourjman, V., McEwen, B. S., Lupien, S. J., & Juster, R.-P. (2013). Allostatic load as a tool for monitoring physiological dysregulations and comorbidities in patients with severe mental illnesses. *Harvard Review of Psychiatry*, *21*(6), 296–313. https://doi.org/10.1097/HRP.0000000000000012

Bouffard, J., Yang, C., Begon, M., & Côté, J. (2018). Sex differences in kinematic adaptations to muscle fatigue induced by repetitive upper limb movements. *Biology of Sex Differences*, *9*(1), 17. https://doi.org/10.1186/s13293-018-0175-9

Boulos, Z., & Rosenwasser, A. M. (2015). A chronobiological perspective on allostasis and its application to shift work. In Schulkin, J. (ed.), *Allostasis, homeostasis, and the costs of physiological adaptation*. Cambridge University Press. https://doi.org/10.1017/CBO9781316257081.010

Bruce-Keller, A. J., Salbaum, J. M., & Berthoud, H.-R. (2018). Harnessing gut microbes for mental health: getting from here to there. *Biological Psychiatry*, *83*(3), 214–223. www.embase.com/search/results?subaction=viewrecord&from=export&id=L618728444%0Ahttp://dx.doi.org/10.1016/j.biopsych.2017.08.014

Burton, A. K., Tillotson, K. M., Symonds, T. L., Burke, C., & Mathewson, T. (1996). Occupational risk factors for the first-onset and subsequent course of low back trouble: a study of serving police officers. *Spine*, *21*(22), 2612–2620. https://doi.org/10.1097/00007632-199611150-00011

Carey, M. G., Al-Zaiti, S. S., Dean, G. E., Sessanna, L., & Finnell, D. S. (2011). Sleep problems, depression, substance use, social bonding, and quality of life in professional firefighters. *Journal of Occupational and Environmental Medicine*, *53*(8), 928–933. https://doi.org/10.1097/JOM.0b013e318225898f

Carleton, R. N., Afifi, T. O., Taillieu, T., Turner, S., El-Gabalawy, R., Sareen, J., & Asmundson, G. J. G. (2018). Anxiety-related psychopathology and chronic pain comorbidity among public safety personnel. *Journal of Anxiety Disorders*, *55*, 48–55. https://doi.org/10.1016/j.janxdis.2018.03.006

Carleton, R. N., Afifi, T. O., Taillieu, T., Turner, S., Krakauer, R., Anderson, G. S., MacPhee, R. S., Ricciardelli, R., Cramm, H. A., Groll, D., & McCreary, D. R. (2018). Exposures to potentially traumatic events among public safety personnel in Canada. *Canadian Journal of Behavioural Science*. https://doi.org/10.1037/cbs0000115

Carr-Pries, N. J., Killip, S. C., & MacDermid, J. C. (2022). Scoping review of the occurrence and characteristics of firefighter exercise and training injuries. *International Archives of Occupational and Environmental Health*, *95*(5), 909–925. https://doi.org/10.1007/s00420-022-01847-7

Choi, B. K., Schnall, P., & Dobson, M. (2016). Twenty-four-hour work shifts, increased job demands, and elevated blood pressure in professional firefighters. *International Archives of Occupational and Environmental Health*, *89*(7). https://doi.org/10.1007/s00420-016-1151-5

Christensen, D. S., Zachariae, R., Amidi, A., & Wu, L. M. (2022). Sleep and allostatic load: a systematic review and meta-analysis. *Sleep Medicine Reviews*, *64*, 101650. https://doi.org/10.1016/j.smrv.2022.101650

Corrigan, S. L. (2022). *Soldier performance management: The utility of heart rate variability to evaluate allostatic load* (Doctoral dissertation, Deakin University).

Corrigan, S. L., Roberts, S., Warmington, S., Drain, J., & Main, L. C. (2021). Monitoring stress and allostatic load in first responders and tactical operators using heart rate variability: a systematic review. *BMC Public Health*, *21*(1), 1–16. https://doi.org/10.1186/s12889-021-11595-x

Côté, J. N. (2012). A critical review on physical factors and functional characteristics that may explain a sex/gender difference in work-related neck/shoulder disorders. *Ergonomics*, *55*(2), 173–182. https://doi.org/10.1080/00140139.2011.586061

Cramm, H., Richmond, R., Jamshidi, L., Edgelow, M., Groll, D., Ricciardelli, R., Macdermid, J. C., Keiley, M., & Nicholas Carleton, R. (2021). Mental health of Canadian firefighters: the impact of sleep. *International Journal of Environmental Research and Public Health*, *18*(24). https://doi.org/10.3390/ijerph182413256

Damrongsak, M., Prapanjaroensin, A., & Brown, K. C. (2018). Predictors of back pain in firefighters. *Workplace Health and Safety*, *66*(2), 61–69. https://doi.org/10.1177/2165079917709020

Daniels, R. D., Kubale, T. L., Yiin, J. H., Dahm, M. M., Hales, T. R., Baris, D., Zahm, S. H., Beaumont, J. J., Waters, K. M., & Pinkerton, L. E. (2013). *Mortality and cancer incidence in a pooled cohort of US firefighters from San Francisco, Chicago, and Philadelphia (1950-2009)*. https://doi.org/10.1136/oemed-2013-101662

De Kloet, E. R., Joëls, M., & Holsboer, F. (2005). Stress and the brain: from adaptation to disease. *Nature Reviews Neuroscience*, *6*(6), 463–475. https://doi.org/10.1038/nrn1683

Doewes, R. I., Gangadhar, L., & Subburaj, S. (2021). An overview on stress neurobiology: fundamental concepts and its consequences. *Neuroscience Informatics*, *1*(3), 100011. https://doi.org/10.1016/j.neuri.2021.100011

Egger, M., & Smith, G. D. (1998). Meta-analysis bias in location and selection of studies. *BMJ*, *316*(7124), 61–66.

Fava, G. A., McEwen, B. S., Guidi, J., Gostoli, S., Offidani, E., & Sonino, N. (2019). Clinical characterization of allostatic overload. *Psychoneuroendocrinology*, *108*, 94–101. https://doi.org/10.1016/j.psyneuen.2019.05.028

Friedman, M. J., & McEwen, B. S. (2005). Posttraumatic stress disorder, allostatic load, and medical illness. *Trauma and Health: Physical Health Consequences of Exposure to Extreme Stress*, 157–188. https://doi.org/10.1037/10723-007

Frost, D. M., Beach, T. A. C. C., Crosby, I., & McGill, S. M. (2015). Firefighter injuries are not just a fireground problem. *Work*, *52*(4), 835–842. https://doi.org/10.3233/WOR-152111

Glei, D. A., Goldman, N., Chuang, Y.-L., & Weinstein, M. (2007). Do chronic stressors lead to physiological dysregulation? Testing the theory of allostatic load. *Psychosomatic Medicine*, *69*(8), 769–776. https://doi.org/10.1097/PSY.0b013e318157cba6

Golden, A. L., Markowitz, S. B., & Landrigan, P. J. (1995). The risk of cancer in firefighters. *Occupational Medicine (Philadelphia, Pa.)*, *10*(4), 803–820.

Guidotti, T. L. (2007). Evaluating causality for occupational cancers: the example of firefighters. *Occupational Medicine*, *57*(7), 466–471. https://doi.org/10.1093/occmed/kqm031

Heikkinen, J., Honkanen, R., Williams, L., Leung, J., Rauma, P., Quirk, S., & Koivumaa-Honkanen, H. (2019). Depressive disorders, anxiety disorders and subjective mental health in common musculoskeletal diseases: a review. *Maturitas*, *127*, 18–25. https://doi.org/https://doi.org/10.1016/j.maturitas.2019.05.011

Henderson, S. N., van Hasselt, V. B., LeDuc, T. J., & Couwels, J. (2016). Firefighter suicide: understanding cultural challenges for mental health professionals. *Professional Psychology: Research and Practice*. https://doi.org/10.1037/pro0000072

Higgins, J. P., Thompson, S. G., Deeks, J. J., & Altman, D. G. (2003). Measuring inconsistency in meta-analyses. *BMJ*, *327*(7414), 557–560.

Holingue, C., Budavari, A. C., Rodriguez, K. M., Zisman, C. R., Windheim, G., & Fallin, M. D. (2020). Sex differences in the gut-brain axis: implications for mental health. *Current Psychiatry Reports*, *22*(12). https://doi.org/10.1007/s11920-020-01202-y

Igboanugo, S., Chaurasia, A., Bigelow, P. L., & Mielke, J. G. (2022). Biological embedding of psychosocial stressors within a sample of Canadian firefighters: an exploratory analysis. *Journal of Occupational and Environmental Medicine*, *64*(10), 856–864. https://doi.org/10.1097/JOM.0000000000002590

Igboanugo, S., & Mielke, J. (2023). The allostatic load model: a framework to understand the cumulative multi-system impact of work-related psychosocial stress exposure among firefighters. *Health Psychology and Behavioral Medicine*, *11*(1). https://doi.org/10.1080/21642850.2023.2255026

Järbrink-Sehgal, E., & Andreasson, A. (2020). The gut microbiota and mental health in adults. *Current Opinion in Neurobiology*, *62*, 102–114. https://doi.org/10.1016/j.conb.2020.01.016

Johnson, C. C., Vega, L., Kohalmi, A. L., Roth, J. C., Howell, B. R., & Van Hasselt, V. B. (2019). Enhancing mental health treatment for the firefighter population: understanding fire culture, treatment barriers, practice implications, and research directions. *Professional Psychology: Research and Practice*, *51*(3), 304–311. https://doi.org/10.1037/pro0000266

Jones, S. (2017). Describing the mental health profile of first responders: a systematic review. *Journal of the American Psychiatric Nurses Association*. https://doi.org/10.1177/1078390317695266

Kajaks, T., Ziebart, C., Galea, V., Vrkljan, B., & MacDermid, J. C. (2023). Posture evaluation of firefighters during simulated fire suppression tasks. *Workplace Health & Safety*, *71*(12), 606–616. https://doi.org/10.1177/21650799231214275

Katz, J., & Rosenbloom, B. N. (2015). The golden anniversary of Melzack and Wall's gate control theory of pain: celebrating 50 years of pain research and management. *Pain Research and Management*, *20*(6), 285–286. https://doi.org/10.1155/2015/865487

Kaul, D., Schwab, S. G., Mechawar, N., & Matosin, N. (2021). How stress physically re-shapes the brain: impact on brain cell shapes, numbers and connections in psychiatric disorders. *Neuroscience and Biobehavioral Reviews*, *124*(January), 193–215. https://doi.org/10.1016/j.neubiorev.2021.01.025

Kaur, N., Ricciardelli, R., Fletcher, A., & Carleton, R. N. (2023). 'You are safe. You are not alone:' gender and Social Support Coping (SSC) in public safety personnel. *Journal of Gender Studies*, *32*(4), 343–358. https://doi.org/10.1080/09589236.2021.2011168

Killip, S. C., MacDermid, J. C., Thayalan, N., Lomotan, M., Gewurtz, R. E., & Sinden, K. E. (2023). Exploring Canadian career firefighters' understanding of the return-to-work process after musculoskeletal injuries. *Journal of Occupational Rehabilitation*, 0123456789. https://doi.org/10.1007/s10926-023-10147-x

Kim, J. E., Dager, S. R., Jeong, H. S., Ma, J., Park, S., Kim, J., Choi, Y., Lee, S. L., Kang, I., Ha, E., Cho, H. B., Lee, S., Kim, E. J., Yoon, S., & Lyoo, I. K. (2018). Firefighters, posttraumatic stress disorder, and barriers to treatment: results from a nationwide total population survey. *PLoS ONE*. https://doi.org/10.1371/journal.pone.0190630

Kim, M. G., Kim, K.-S., Ryoo, J.-H., & Yoo, S.-W. (2013). Relationship between occupational stress and work-related musculoskeletal disorders in Korean male firefighters. *Annals of Occupational and Environmental Medicine*, *25*(1), 9. https://doi.org/10.1186/2052-4374-25-9

Kim, M. G., Seo, J. il, Kim, K. S., & Ahn, Y. S. (2017). Nationwide firefighter survey: the prevalence of lower back pain and its related psychological factors among Korean firefighters. *International Journal of Occupational Safety and Ergonomics*, *23*(4), 447–456. https://doi.org/10.1080/10803548.2016.1219149

Kirkcaldy, B. D., & Cooper, C. L. (1992). Managing the stress of change: occupational stress among senior police officers in Berlin. *Stress Medicine*, *8*(4), 219–231. https://doi.org/10.1002/smi.2460080404

Larsen, L. B., Ramstrand, N., & Fransson, E. I. (2019). Psychosocial job demand and control: multi-site musculoskeletal pain in Swedish police. *Scandinavian Journal of Public Health*, *47*(3), 318–325. https://doi.org/10.1177/1403494818801507

Lee, D., Kim, W., Lee, J. E., Lee, J., Kim, Y. T., Lee, S. K., Oh, S. S., Park, K. S., Koh, S. B., Kim, C., & Jung, Y. C. (2022). Changes in intrinsic functional brain connectivity related to occupational stress of firefighters. *Psychiatry Research*, *314*(November 2021), 114688. https://doi.org/10.1016/j.psychres.2022.114688

LeMasters, G. K., Genaidy, A. M., Succop, P., Deddens, J., Sobeih, T., Barriera-Viruet, H., Dunning, K., & Lockey, J. (2006). Cancer risk among firefighters: a review and meta-analysis of 32 studies. *Journal of Occupational and Environmental Medicine*, *48*(11), 1189–1202. https://doi.org/10.1097/01.jom.0000246229.68697.90

Lenart-Bugla, M., Szcześniak, D., Bugla, B., Kowalski, K., Niwa, S., Rymaszewska, J., & Misiak, B. (2022). The association between allostatic load and brain: a systematic review. *Psychoneuroendocrinology*, *145*(February). https://doi.org/10.1016/j.psyneuen.2022.105917

Logan, J. G., & Barksdale, D. J. (2008). Allostasis and allostatic load: expanding the discourse on stress and cardiovascular disease. *Journal of Clinical Nursing*, *17*(7B), 201–208. https://doi.org/10.1111/j.1365-2702.2008.02347.x

Lupien, S. J., McEwen, B. S., Gunnar, M. R., & Heim, C. (2009). Effects of stress throughout the lifespan on the brain, behaviour and cognition. In *Nature Reviews Neuroscience*, *10*(6), 434–445. https://doi.org/10.1038/nrn2639

MacDermid, J. C., Nazari, G., Rashid, C., Sinden, K., Carleton, N., & Cramm, H. (2019). Two-month point prevalence of exposure to critical incidents in firefighters in a single fire service. *Work*, *62*(3). https://doi.org/10.3233/WOR-192882

Mathew, A., Doorenbos, A. Z., Li, H., Jang, M. K., Park, C. G., & Bronas, U. G. (2021). Allostatic load in cancer: a systematic review and mini meta-analysis. *Biological Research for Nursing*, *23*(3), 341–361. https://doi.org/10.1177/1099800420969898

McCaffery, J. M., Marsland, A. L., Strohacker, K., Muldoon, M. F., & Manuck, S. B. (2012). Factor structure underlying components of allostatic load. *PLoS ONE*, *7*(10). https://doi.org/10.1371/journal.pone.0047246

McEwan, B. S. (1998). Stress, adaptation and disease. *Annals New York Academy of Sciences*, *1*(840), 33–44.

McEwan, B. S. (2005). Stressed or stressed out what is the difference? *Journal of Psychiatry & Neuroscience*, *30*(5), 315–318.

McEwen, B. S. (2006). Sleep deprivation as a neurobiologic and physiologic stressor: allostasis and allostatic load. *Metabolism: Clinical and Experimental*, *55*(SUPPL. 2), 23–26. https://doi.org/10.1016/j.metabol.2006.07.008

McEwen, B. S. (2015). Protective and damaging effects of the mediators of stress and adaptation: allostasis and allostatic load. In Schulkin, J. (ed.), *Allostasis, homeostasis, and the costs of physiological adaptation* (pp. 65–98). Cambridge University Press. https://doi.org/10.1017/CBO9781316257081.005

Melzack, D, R., & Wall, P. (1965). Pain mechanisms: a new theory. *Advancement of Science*, *150*, 971–979.

Melzack, R. (1996). Gate control theory. *Pain Forum*, *5*(2), 128–138. https://doi.org/10.1016/s1082-3174(96)80050-x

Melzack, R. (1999). From the gate to the neuromatrix. *Pain*, *Suppl 6*(1), S121–S126. https://doi.org/10.1016/S0304-3959(99)00145-1

Melzack, R. (2001). Pain and the neuromatrix in the brain. *Journal of Dental Education*, *65*(12), 1378–1382.

Melzack, R., & Wall, P. D. (1994). Pain mechanisms: a new theory. *Pain Clinic*, *7*(1), 57–72. https://doi.org/10.1017/cbo9780511759048.009

Mohr, D., Vedantham, K., Neylan, T., Metzler, T. J., Best, S., & Marmar, C. R. (2003). The mediating effects of sleep in the relationship between traumatic stress and health symptoms in urban police officers. *Psychosomatic Medicine*, *65*(3), 485–489. https://doi.org/10.1097/01.PSY.0000041404.96597.38

Moin, J. S., Moineddin, R., & Upshur, R. E. G. (2018). Measuring the association between marginalization and multimorbidity in Ontario, Canada: a cross-sectional study. *Journal of Comorbidity*, 8(1), 2235042X1881493. https://doi.org/10.1177/2235042x18814939

Murkey, J. A., Watkins, B. X., Vieira, D., & Boden-Albala, B. (2022). Disparities in allostatic load, telomere length and chronic stress burden among African American adults: a systematic review. *Psychoneuroendocrinology*, *140*(October 2021), 105730. https://doi.org/10.1016/j.psyneuen.2022.105730

Nazari, G., Lu, S., & MacDermid, J. C. (2021). Quantifying physiological responses during simulated tasks among Canadian firefighters: a systematic review and meta-analysis. *Journal of Military, Veteran and Family Health*, *7*(1), 55–75. https://doi.org/10.3138/JMVFH-2019-0063

Nazari, G., MacDermid, J., & Cramm, H. (2020). Prevalence of musculoskeletal disorders among Canadian firefighters: a systematic review and meta-analysis. *Journal of Military, Veteran and Family Health*. https://doi.org/10.3138/jmvfh-2019-0024

Nazari, G., Macdermid, J. C., Sinden, K., & D'Amico, R. (2020). Prevalence of musculoskeletal symptoms among Canadian firefighters. *Work*, *67*(1). https://doi.org/10.3233/WOR-203264

Nazari, G., MacDermid, J., Sinden, K. E., D'Amico, R., Brazil, A., Carleton, R. N., & Cramm, H. A. (2020). Prevalence of exposure to critical incidents in firefighters across Canada. *Work*, *67*(1): 215–222.

Nazari, G., MacDermid, J. C., Sinden, K. E., & Overend, T. J. (2018). The Relationship between Physical Fitness and Simulated Firefighting Task Performance. *Rehabilitation Research and Practice*. https://doi.org/10.1155/2018/3234176

Nazari, G., MacDermid, J. C., Sinden, K. E., & Overend, T. J. (2019). Comparison of Canadian firefighters and healthy controls based on submaximal fitness testing and strength considering age and gender. *International Journal of Occupational Safety and Ergonomics*, *25*(1). https://doi.org/10.1080/10803548.2017.1372086

Nazari, G., Osifeso, T. A., & MacDermid, J. C. (2020). Distribution of number, location of pain and comorbidities, and determinants of work limitations among firefighters. *Rehabilitation Research and Practice*, 2020. https://doi.org/10.1155/2020/1942513

Negm, A., MacDermid, J., Sinden, K., D'Amico, R., Lomotan, M., & MacIntyre, N. J. (2017). Prevalence and distribution of musculoskeletal disorders in firefighters are influenced by age and length of service. *Journal of Military, Veteran and Family Health*, *3*(2), 33–41. https://doi.org/10.3138/jmvfh.2017-0002

Parker, H. W., Abreu, A. M., Sullivan, M. C., & Vadiveloo, M. K. (2022). Allostatic load and mortality: a systematic review and meta-analysis. *American Journal of Preventive Medicine*, *63*(1), 131–140. https://doi.org/10.1016/j.amepre.2022.02.003

Phyomaung, P. P., Dubowitz, J., Cicuttini, F. M., Fernando, S., Wluka, A. E., Raaijmaakers, P., Wang, Y., & Urquhart, D. M. (2014). Are depression, anxiety and poor mental health risk factors for knee pain? A systematic review. *BMC Musculoskeletal Disorders*. https://doi.org/10.1186/1471-2474-15-10

Ramsden, R., Smith, J., Turcotte, K., Garis, L., Kunz, K., Maxim, P., … , & Pike, I. (2018). *Determinants of injury and death in Canadian firefighters*. British Columbia Injury Research and Prevention Unit..

Rieder, R., Wisniewski, P. J., Alderman, B. L., & Campbell, S. C. (2017). Microbes and mental health: a review. *Brain, Behavior, and Immunity*, *66*, 9–17. https://doi.org/10.1016/j.bbi.2017.01.016

Romero Cabrera, J. L., Sotos-Prieto, M., García Ríos, A., Moffatt, S., Christophi, C. A., Pérez-Martínez, P., & Kales, S. N. (2021). Sleep and association with cardiovascular risk among midwestern US firefighters. *Frontiers in Endocrinology*, *12*. www.frontiersin.org/articles/10.3389/fendo.2021.772848

Sandi, C., & Haller, J. (2015). Stress and the social brain: behavioural effects and neurobiological mechanisms. *Nature Reviews Neuroscience*, *16*(5), 290–304. https://doi.org/10.1038/nrn3918

Schulkin, J. (2015). Adaptive fear, allostasis, and the pathology of anxiety and depression. In *Allostasis, homeostasis, and the costs of physiological adaptation*. Cambridge University Press. https://doi.org/10.1017/CBO9781316257081.009

Schulkin, J., & Sterling, P. (2004). Principles of allostasis: optimal design, predictive regulation, pathophysiology and rational therapeutics. In Schulkin, J. (ed.), *Allostasis, homeostasis, and the costs of adaptation* (pp. 17–64). Cambridge University Press.

Selye, H. (1950). Stress and the general adaptation syndrome. *British Medical Journal*, 4666–4679. https://doi.org/10.1159/000227975

Shin, J. H., Lee, J. Y., Yang, S. H., Lee, M. Y., & Chung, I. S. (2016). Factors related to heart rate variability among firefighters. *Annals of Occupational and Environmental Medicine*, 28(1). https://doi.org/10.1186/s40557-016-0111-6

Sonderlund, A. L., Thilsing, T., & Sondergaard, J. (2019). Should social disconnectedness be included in primary-care screening for cardiometabolicdisease? A systematic review of the relationship between everyday stress, social connectedness, and allostatic load. *PLoS ONE*, *14*(12), e0226717.

Soteriades, E. S., Psalta, L., Leka, S., & Spanoudis, G. (2019). Occupational stress and musculoskeletal symptoms in firefighters. *International Journal of Occupational Medicine and Environmental Health*, *32*(3), 341–352. www.embase.com/search/results?subaction=viewrecord&from=export&id=L627180312%0Ahttp://dx.doi.org/10.13075/ijomeh.1896.01268

Stanley, I. H., Boffa, J. W., Hom, M. A., Kimbrel, N. A., & Joiner, T. E. (2017). Differences in psychiatric symptoms and barriers to mental health care between volunteer and career firefighters. *Psychiatry Research*. https://doi.org/10.1016/j.psychres.2016.11.037

Stewart, J. A. (2006). The detrimental effects of allostasis: allostatic load as a measure of cumulative stress. *Journal of Physiological Anthropology*, *25*(1), 133–145. https://doi.org/10.2114/jpa2.25.133

Taber, N., Scott, T., Scott, C., Myers, K. K., Rothmann, S., Regehr, C., Hill, J., Knott, T., Sault, B., PALMER, C. E., Nydegger, R., Nydegger, L., Basile, F., Miller, L., Milen, D., Lowery, K., Stokes, M. A., Landen, S. M., Wang, C.-C. D. C., … Yafe, E. (2012). Stress and coping strategies among firefighters and recruits. *Journal of Traumatic Stress*, *25*(4), 350–364. https://doi.org/10.1177/1049732313519867

Van Ingen, T., & Matheson, F. I. (2021). The 2011 and 2016 iterations of the Ontario Marginalization Index: updates, consistency and a cross-sectional study of health outcome associations. *Canadian Journal of Public Health*. https://doi.org/10.17269/s41997-021-00552-1

Vun, E., Turner, S., Sareen, J., Mota, N., Afifi, T. O., & El-Gabalawy, R. (2018). Prevalence of comorbid chronic pain and mental health conditions in Canadian Armed Forces active personnel: analysis of a cross-sectional survey. *CMAJ Open*, *6*(4), E528–E536. https://doi.org/10.9778/cmajo.20180093

Walter Odajnyk, V. (1991). Psychological perspectives. *Psychological Perspectives*, *25*(1). https://doi.org/10.1080/00332929108405634

Webb, H. E., Garten, R. S., McMinn, D. R., Beckman, J. L., Kamimori, G. H., & Acevedo, E. O. (2011). Stress hormones and vascular function in firefighters during concurrent challenges. *Biological Psychology*, *87*(1), 152–160. https://doi.org/10.1016/j.biopsycho.2011.02.024

Wingfield, J. C. (2015). Allostatic load and life cycles: implications for neuroendocrine control mechanisms. In Schulkin, J. (ed.), *Allostasis, homeostasis, and the costs of physiological adaptation*. Cambridge University Press. https://doi.org/10.1017/CBO9781316257081.011

Wolkow, A., Aisbett, B., Reynolds, J., Ferguson, S. A., & Main, L. C. (2016). Acute psychophysiological relationships between mood, inflammatory and cortisol changes in response to simulated physical firefighting work and sleep restriction. *Applied Psychophysiology Biofeedback*, *41*(2), 165–180. https://doi.org/10.1007/s10484-015-9329-2

Yoneda, T., Lozinski, T., Turiano, N., Booth, T., Graham, E. K., Mroczek, D., & Muniz Terrera, G. (2023). The Big Five personality traits and allostatic load in middle to older adulthood: a systematic review and meta-analysis. *Neuroscience and Biobehavioral Reviews*, *148*(October 2022), 105145. https://doi.org/10.1016/j.neubiorev.2023.105145

Zygmunt, A., Tanuseputro, P., James, P., Lima, I., Tuna, M., & Kendall, C. E. (2020). Neighbourhood-level marginalization and avoidable mortality in Ontario, Canada: a population-based study. *Canadian Journal of Public Health*, *111*(2), 169–181. https://doi.org/10.17269/s41997-019-00270-9

11

SOCIAL MEDIA AS AN OCCUPATIONAL STRESSOR

The Impact of Social Media on the Mental Health and Occupational Performance of Volunteer Firefighters and Other Public Safety Personnel

Robin Campbell Bromhead and Crystal Dieleman

Introduction

> Content is fire. Social media is gasoline.
>
> *(Baer, 2014)*

Social media has become a dynamic, powerful platform for social interaction, changing how individuals and communities consume and share information, where users can add their own content and continually modify information by sharing photographs, videos, and commentary (Giesbrecht, 2020; Goldsmith, 2015; Waters, 2012). The evolving social media landscape is putting a spotlight on the actions and behaviours of first responders (Tucker et al., 2022). Platforms such as Facebook, Twitter, Instagram, YouTube, Snapchat, and TikTok allow information to be shared and seen in record time. With the societal shift to sourcing news and information through these platforms, social media has created an opportunity for the public to have access to emergency situations and first responders like never before. While this unparalleled public access can allow for greater transparency and understanding of first responders and their agencies, it can also have considerable negative consequences.

First responders are public safety personnel; however, the category of first responders is more limited often referring to police, firefighters, and paramedics. Instead, the broader category of public safety personnel includes, but is not limited to, the occupations of police, paramedics, firefighters (paid and volunteer), public safety communicators (e.g., emergency dispatchers), correctional workers, intelligence officers, and search and rescue personnel (Carleton, et al., 2018). Responding to emergency situations places first responders at an increased risk for mental disorders (e.g., posttraumatic

DOI: 10.4324/9781003424253-15

stress disorder [PTSD]) and mental health challenges such as symptoms of depression, suicidality, anxiety, panic, sleep disturbances, moral injury, and substance use (Jones, 2017; Brazil, 2017; Beshai & Carleton, 2016; Carleton, et al., 2020; Carleton, et al., 2018) – all potential outcomes of occupational stress.

McCreary and Thompson (2006) developed measures for evaluating occupational stress among police which have been applied among other public safety personnel sectors. Similar work was conducted by Duxbury and Higgins (2009), who divide occupational stress into two categories: organizational and operational. Operational stressors are related to the job content and are inherent to the job, thus potentially placing responders' safety at risk and exposing them to suffering, injuries, and death (Acquadro, Zedda, & Varetto, 2018). Organizational stressors are found within the job context, related to organizational tasks or environments, such as leadership and management, training, bureaucratic procedures, and organizational culture. Sources of stress can be from relationships with colleagues and supervisors, and public perception (Acquadro et al., 2018).

Social media can be a double-edged sword for public safety personnel and their organizations (Lev-on & Yavetz, 2020). One edge is the opportunity for responders to send and receive information with the public during ongoing incidents, engage with the public, and promote the mandate of their organizations in a more efficient and effective manner. The other edge is the opportunity for social media users to have immediate access to emergency scenes, to express solidarity with, or rancour towards, those affected by emergency incidents, and to aggressively criticize their actions. Emergency incidents and the actions of public safety personnel draw a great deal of attention on social media, where there are almost no constraints on what can be posted (Waters, 2012; Tucker et al., 2022). Social media not only presents risks for the careers and integrity but can also impact the perceptions of their organization's reputation and effectiveness (Goldsmith, 2015). The diversity of opinions and voices on social media, the social media user perspective, and the narrative on emergency incidents can have lasting impacts. Some studies have found that coverage of emergency incidents is more negative on social media than on traditional media channels such as television and radio (Lev-on & Yavetz, 2020). This is likely due to the nature of reporting by social media users rather than journalists following a professional code of conduct. Furthermore, re-exposure to potentially traumatic events can be triggering and have lasting implications for their mental health and well-being (Dohmen, 2021). Issues related to PTSD and moral injury among public safety personnel have been at the forefront of the research literature in recent years, but there is little to no research on the effect of social media on their mental health.

Social media has changed the media landscape for public safety personnel. Within the realm of social media, they perceive only one side of the story is heard, with their perspective not being included, which leads to strengthening public mistrust and the anti-establishment discourse (Lev-on & Yavetz, 2020).

Public Perceptions

> Social media is the biggest issue that we face. People will hang you in the court of public opinion before all the facts are in.
>
> *(Saunders et al., 2019, p. 46)*

Social media has the potential to be a significant tool for building public trust and representation for public safety agencies but has also been shown to have negative impacts (Lev-on & Yavetz, 2020). Public shaming on social media and issues of cancel culture are common concerns. The fear of cancel culture is real for public safety personnel and their organizations. Cancel culture is a socially constructed practice on social media where users respond to unacceptable behaviour by blocking support for an individual or organization (Haskell, 2021; Velasco, 2020). The act is a form of justice-seeking that places power in the hands of the public, which can be concerning due to the information spreading like wildfire online and having immediate consequences that can destroy lives. Individuals participating in online cancel culture may not necessarily understand the entire context of the situation but still engage in the activity (Haskell, 2021). As a form of public shaming online, the concept of cancelling and cancel culture is a unique phenomenon specific to social media, and the reasoning behind cancelling is always changing (Velasco, 2020).

Being criticized and attacked on social media is a stark reality. Many responders are moving forward with the assumption that everything will be shared, and nothing is hidden on social media, generating stress and anxiety about what might be captured and how the events are portrayed online (Lev-on & Yavetz, 2020). The presence of negative coverage on social media is damaging the image and reputation of public safety organizations due to online criticism and attacks (Lev-on & Yavetz, 2020). For those in positions of authority and trust within the communities they serve, cancel culture and public shaming online have the power to lessen public trust in the personnel and organizations meant to protect and serve them. There is the utmost desire to safeguard image and reputation (Ballam, 2015). To do so, organizations have been quick to respond to issues of social media by creating organizational policies concerned with minimizing responses to negative content (Waters, 2012; Tucker et al., 2022). With social media posts by the public being out of the control of responder organizations, organizations only have the ability to control internal factors through restrictive policies on their own social media accounts and their personnel (Waters, 2012; Tucker et al., 2022).

Having actions and behaviours judged and critiqued by the masses on social media can have a detrimental impact on the individual and/or the organization's reputation and image. Public safety personnel are increasingly inept or unable to respond to those criticisms. They are not equipped with the tools to cope with or manage negative social media attention, especially when organizational rules and policies constrain their actions and behaviours online (Lev-on & Yavetz, 2020). A sense of helplessness ensues due to the public's ability to instantly share anything they desire on social media and the personnels' inability to respond (Lev-on & Yavetz, 2020). There is the perspective from public safety personnel, particularly firefighters, that when inappropriate or bad behaviour from one firefighter spreads on social media, it impacts the image of the fire service as a whole (Ballam, 2015). There have been cases of responders commenting and defending actions online that have led to disciplinary actions and further organizational policy restrictions to reduce their commentary (Waters, 2012; Tucker et al., 2022). The dominant principle in these policies is that public safety personnel are responsible for the content on their personal social media platforms and should be conscious of how it reflects on the organizations and the communities they serve (Tucker et al., 2022).

Social Media and Mental Health

After a potentially traumatic incident, media attention adds significantly to overall stress and can increase depression, anxiety, aggression, social isolation, chronic stress, and decreased overall well-being (McHugh et al., 2018; Regehr et al., 2003; Scott, 2004; Tucker et al., 2022). With social media becoming a prominent fixture in most people's daily lives, its impact on the mental health of different populations has been heavily researched, particularly among adolescents. Ease of access and exposure to traumatic imagery through social media, image-based trauma as a form of vicarious trauma, has also been identified as an emerging concern (Naftulin, 2020; Isen, 2022).

The immediate ability to scroll through multiple social media platforms, and experiencing constant, indirect, and repeated access to imagery and commentary of traumatic events, can cause and reinforce mental health concerns (Isen, 2022). Regardless of the accuracy or truth of social media posts, negative comments can leave lasting impressions (Waters, 2012). Research of media/social media coverage of the Boston Marathon bombing and the 9/11 terrorist attacks has linked PTSD to viewing coverage of traumatic events (Ahern, Galea, Resnick, & Vlahov, 2004; Bernstein, et al., 2007; Busso, McLaughlin, & Sheridan, 2014; Mash, Fullerton, & Ursano, 2018; Otto, et al., 2007; Tucker, Bratina, & Caprio, 2022). Twenty per cent of individuals with no history of trauma were impacted by traumatic incidents viewed on social media (Ramsden, 2017). If the impact of viewing imagery on social media can have this level of impact on those who were not at the traumatic incident, re-exposure to the incident for responders and involved personnel is even more concerning.

Re-exposure to traumatic incidents through videos and photos posted to social media channels from bystanders at emergency incidents, prompting trauma reminders, is a prevalent experience for first responders (Dohmen, 2021). Trauma reminders, also referred to as cues or triggers, are various internal and external cues that prompt sensory experiences, emotions, and bodily reactions that remind the individual of the traumatic event and can evoke intrusive and distressing feelings, thoughts, and/or mental images of the event (Glad et al., 2017; Layne et al., 2006). External cues may include sensory experiences such as sounds, tastes, touches, and smells from the external environment, while internal cues are thoughts, dreams, images, and emotions.

Most research on social media and those serving public safety has focused on the significant issue of police violence (Dawson, 2019; Lev-on & Yavetz, 2020). Due to a considerable number of incidents circulated on social media channels suggesting police abuse of power with devastating effects on individuals and communities, public sentiment towards police and other personnel has deteriorated and eroded public trust (Lev-on & Yavetz, 2020; Dawson, 2019; Saunders, Kotzias, & Ramchand, 2019). The evolution of social media as public communication has provided the public with an avenue to show evidence of major societal issues, such as police brutality, racism, and abuses of power, ensuring that they can no longer be ignored (Giesbrecht, 2020; Isen, 2022; Saunders et al., 2019). At the same time, issues of 'cop-baiting,' when individuals intentionally create confrontational situations for officers and exploit them for personal or political motives, draw attention away from genuine concerns about police conduct and artificially amplify irreparable damage to the integrity and reputation of the police officer and their police agency (Waters, 2012).

Holding police officers and others accountable for their actions is important (Giesbrecht, 2020). The ease and convenience of personal technologies, such as smartphones, where bystanders to emergency incidents and involvement of first responders are more commonly capturing and posting select recordings and commentary to social media. In doing this, social media users choose what they want to show on social media, providing opportunities to share some aspects of events and miss or omit others, often painting a very negative and damaging picture of the occupation as a whole (Naftulin, 2020; Saunders, Kotzias, & Ramchand, 2019). With minimal fact-checking and instantaneous sharing, this generates biased perspectives with a limited understanding of the full context of events and creates an uninformed image of the public safety organization (Lev-on & Yavetz, 2020; Giesbrecht, 2020). The power behind the portrayed narrative, when only pieces of the entire incident are shown, is heavily influencing negative public perceptions, and the stress and pressure felt by police has spread to other responders (Franklin et al., 2019; Tucker, Bratina, & Caprio, 2022).

Growing fear and stress due to increased scrutiny on social media is evident among public safety personnel when aspects of emergency incidents are presented out of context, and the criticism has a negative impact on their mental health (Belasky, 2022; Giesbrecht, 2020; Saunders et al., 2019; Saunders, Kotzias, & Ramchand, 2019). First responders have reported that having bystanders record emergency scenes and share the content online creates a heightened stressful atmosphere at emergency scenes and leads them to continually worry about how their behaviours and actions on emergency scenes will be dissected and interpreted online by those who lack an understanding of the high-risk nature of the work (Giesbrecht, 2020; Saunders et al., 2019). Police officers have reported this increased attention has made them more likely to second-guess themselves and their abilities due to the ongoing worry of being under a microscope with the concern of potential consequential threats of reputational damage or public critique (Saunders, Kotzias, & Ramchand, 2019). There is a collective shame in the negative image that can be portrayed on social media.

Considering all these factors, police and other public safety personnel face high levels of scrutiny, and tough criticisms, online, yet there has been very little research to date on the effect of social media on the populations, beyond police, and their organizations. More research is needed to understand the impact of social media stress on personnel who are at a higher risk of developing mental health disorders and illnesses due to their exposure to traumatic incidents, the high level of online scrutiny and criticism, and the impact of re-exposure to traumatic events through imagery and commentary shared on social media.

Sound the Siren Research Study

The purpose of this study was to understand how the occupational environment impacts the mental health and well-being of volunteer firefighters in rural Nova Scotia. While examining how volunteer firefighters interpret factors within their occupational environment that impact their mental health and well-being, social media emerged as a trying factor.

Methodology

Purposive and convenience sampling was used to engage three rural fire departments and a total of 30 firefighters for this qualitative study (Creswell, 2013). To answer the research questions, a series of three interviews were held with nine frontline volunteer firefighters (five men and four women). Each interview was built upon the previous, with the second interview involving photo-elicitation where research participants selected photographs to share with the researcher that explored three questions: What are the most important aspects of the work you do as a volunteer firefighter? What would you want people to understand about being a volunteer firefighter? And what aspects of volunteer firefighting have an impact on your mental health? All firefighters selected photos, with the majority retrieved from social media. This laid the foundation and reference point to further explore the social media phenomenon during the third interview.

Additionally, 20 officers (18 men and 2 women), which included safety officers, lieutenants, captains, deputy chiefs, and chiefs, were invited to participate in focus groups that explored leadership decision-making and perspectives on mental health and well-being. One officer participated in an individual interview since they were not available for the focus group.

All interviews and focus groups were held in-person and were recorded and transcribed with the participants' consent. Thematic analysis was used for both transcripts and photographs. Initial narrative mapping was used to identify emerging themes and patterns throughout the data collection process. Photographs were analysed during the photo-elicitation interview in collaboration with research participants through a joint-theorizing process (Harper, 2002). Thematic analysis using open coding was used to identify themes and patterns from the transcripts. Thematic discourse analysis was also applied to illuminate social relationships and cultural values through the language used in the transcripts (Souto-Manning, 2014; Czarniawska, 1997). The patterns and themes were linked between the different data sources. Three social media topics emerged as areas of occupational stress for volunteer firefighters: fear of criticism; image and reputation; and moral dilemmas and trauma reminders.

Results

Fear of Criticism

The predominant challenge frontline firefighters face with social media is the negative criticism they receive online. Issues related to "keyboard warriors" who write negative comments on social media posts about firefighters and emergency incidents have a substantial impact. Online criticism from the public was generally related to firefighter performance, such as long response times, firefighting techniques, and on-scene decision-making. This perception and criticism are based on only certain pieces of the entire fire incident shared on social media. Firefighter F states,

> The biggest thing that really pisses me off, like mentally…it's the… First of all, we don't get paid. Second of all [the comments]...well they couldn't

> do this or they couldn't do that. Well, you don't understand. You don't understand the conditions of that fire. You don't understand the conditions of that accident. But sometimes you see people getting bashed over Facebook or social media. Just like shut up... You have no idea what they had to go through to get that done and that gets frustrating.

Most firefighters expressed a complete lack of awareness or understanding of volunteer firefighting resulted in these types of criticisms. Firefighter F illustrates the problem of having only one perspective of the larger story being told through social media. This provides the opportunity for social media users to dissect and critique the firefighter's execution of their roles and tasks. Firefighter F also explained how online comments can be harsh and malicious, with social media users bashing firefighters. The negative emphasis within online comments is frustrating. Firefighter D explains,

> [Social] media is our Achilles heel. [They] like to focus on bad when it comes to the fire service. You could save a family of twelve and only have to put one band-aid on one person, but you trip and fall carrying one person because you're just utterly exhausted and [they] will jump on that and spin it. But [social]media is the Achilles heel of a lot of good that can happen because they always want to focus on the crap.

A difficult reality for firefighters is that the outcome of their efforts is not always positive. Sometimes the house is not saveable, and sometimes the person does not survive. Firefighters continually deal with the negative aspects of their work. Firefighter G explains, "Not all outcomes are all rainbows and unicorns. But you still...you did what you could to [the] best of your ability, and that's all you can ever ask...." To cope with negative outcomes, firefighters focus on how they performed their occupation to the best of their abilities. With increased social media attention, their capabilities are being criticized online. The harsh comments intensify stress for firefighters already dealing with a heightened level of internal pressure experienced by reliving their occupational performance on the fire ground.

Another challenge firefighters experienced is online criticism from fellow firefighters outside their fire department. When peers make negative comments, the comments create frustration, but even worse, mistrust. Fire departments do not work in silos; they depend on neighbouring fire departments to assist them with larger emergency events. Firefighters need to work together and risk their lives together on the fire ground and need to be able to trust each other. When firefighters attack each other online, this can erode trust and influence how firefighters work together on the fire ground.

A natural reaction by firefighters is the desire to defend their actions, but many fire departments have strict social media policies that prohibit them from engaging in certain ways online. Firefighters found that the inability to defend themselves or their fire department left them with feelings of frustration and disempowerment. They feared saying the wrong thing and having that reflect poorly on the fire department, which led to feelings of being silenced and not feeling able to defend their actions. The sentiment takes the control of the narrative completely away from the firefighter and can make firefighters feel unappreciated by the individuals they risk their lives for every day. Firefighter C stated,

> Social media sucks and you read the comments from the keyboard warriors that are like, well it took them forever to do that. And why did they do that? Oh my God, look the house burned down. And it's like you don't know what we're up against. Like it's easy for you to sit back and judge us, but you have no idea what it's like on the other end of the line…we're running into a burning building when everyone else is running out… give us a little appreciation.

The lack of appreciation and judgement can take its toll on firefighters. Reading negative online comments impacts how a firefighter responds to the next emergency. The malicious comments and critiques, while feeling silenced and disempowered, create a level of fear of doing and saying the wrong thing and having it misinterpreted on social media. When responding to future emergencies, this plays in the back of their mind while still having the pressure to perform high-stress, intense firefighting tasks. Firefighter H explains,

> You watch on Facebook, almost instantaneous any fire scene. Because there's so many people just...information is, it's like there. Whether it's typing or pictures or whatever. So you have to be so conscious of who's around, what's around. Don't say this. Don't say that. You have to act accordingly.

If a firefighter is spending their mental efforts on a fire scene looking over their shoulder and trying to be conscious of who is around and what they say, that has the potential to impede their occupational performance. Firefighter G further explains,

> People don't get that when time [is of the] essence and shits gotta happen and that shit had to happen yesterday...Sometimes the actions are ugly to get to there. They're not as pretty as what you see [on] TV because people see it on TV and it's so prim and proper and everything just happens perfect. And that's not the case by any means.

This further emphasizes the linkages between fear of criticism and public image. This perpetuates cancel culture and the desire by the public for firefighters and other first responders to live up to the performance perfection that is portrayed in popular culture. The reality of emergencies is that they are not pretty or perfect, and firefighters are not perfect, they are human.

Image and Reputation

Lack of control and power over content shared on social media is concerning, even upsetting, for firefighters. Volunteer firefighters hold a unique position of trust within their communities, with the traditional image of a firefighter as someone who is there to save the day and help the community. The fire department is seen as a staple within communities, a warm and friendly station that is there when they need help. With the onset of social media, there is unprecedented, constant access to firefighters. Citizens can capture firefighters on emergency scenes or at their fire department and post these images to social media platforms. The control firefighters previously had on their public image and what they want in the public realm is slowly disappearing. As an essential emergency service, the public feels entitled to this access, and firefighters feel helpless in controlling what is shared on social media. Firefighter F explains,

> We have [local social media users], all those local guys that come and take pictures and videos and post them online. And whether we like it or not, it's allowed to happen because they're on public property. As long as they don't get under the fire scene, we don't really have any control over them.

The lack of control over social media user's access to capturing fire scenes on public property is a struggle. Firefighters discussed the approach that social media users take when sharing images online. There are those who want to capture the gruesomeness of the emergency scene. They want to show the house burning down or the horribly damaged car from the motor vehicle accident. This type of content provides shock value and is generally a mechanism for garnering attention, while others want to show the firefighters without the gruesomeness. This type of social media content focuses on the firefighter occupation rather than the traumatic aspects of the emergency. When an individual is taking photos or videos at an emergency scene, the firefighter does not know what they are capturing, and this can be distracting. The loss of control and power over the content and type of imagery being captured and shared online can impede the firefighters' ability to do their job on the fire ground because they are distracted.

Firefighters expressed concerns regarding public perception and reputation on social media. Many firefighters describe their fire department and fellow firefighters as their second family or the brotherhood/sisterhood. There is a sense of pride, belonging, trust, and protection of the fire family and the desire to ensure the reputation of the fire department is protected. Firefighters fear how individual actions can create repercussions for the fire department. Firefighter H explains,

> Maybe I'm being defensive a little bit about it, but I don't want it to look bad on the fire department… one person can bring the appearance down of the whole department. And that's not why I'm here, I'm here to actually help people. If the public thinks that the fire department sits one way, then they may not want you there when you arrive.

The reputation of the fire service directly affects public perception and trust, so firefighters generally take the approach of silence with criticism on social media. As Firefighter H further describes,

> It's very challenging because you want to reply to them, but you can't. Well, you probably could, but it wouldn't look good. Because my opinion reflects on the department. It's just not my opinion. It's how, if I replied, like, oh, they said this. No, it's like I'm saying this, not the department. It's very hard because you want to respond, but you let it go…Deep down you're mad because it's just like why are you even saying that? It's like you don't even know, you weren't there. It's very frustrating.

When firefighters respond to criticism on social media, they are not doing so as anonymous individuals; they represent the fire department and the fire service as a whole. Their actions and behaviours reflect on the fire department and the fire family. Feeling silenced and not able to express opinions creates frustration for firefighters and should be considered an aspect of organizational stress.

Perception and Misinterpretation

One of the struggles many firefighters discussed is how images can be misinterpreted online because they only show a small piece of the entire emergency incident. Common examples were photographs of firefighters responding to a house fire where they are smiling or laughing. To the public, this shows a lack of empathy and compassion. How can a firefighter be happy when someone's home is burning to the ground? That one image with a caption questioning the firefighter's intentions can be damaging to the firefighter and the fire department's reputation. Firefighter D shares,

> I've seen different times [when] different [social media users]…catch those moments in time where someone might be smiling or someone might be laughing. And we [have] gotten flack from social media for it. Why are you

> laughing at such a horrible situation? And I understand people don't realize, they might not understand what was going on in that moment in time.

As evidenced in the words of Firefighter D, to manage the stress of responding to potentially traumatic events, first responders engage in joking culture and dark humour, which allows them to put their emotions aside, compartmentalize, and ultimately distract from what they are experiencing (Thurnell-Read & Parker, 2008). Dark humour tends to make fun of life-threatening or traumatic situations and is considered inappropriate to those outside the first responder culture (Rowe & Regehr, 2010). This is part of the cohesion and camaraderie among those who experience traumatic events together (Willing, 2019; Moran & Roth, 2013; Rowe & Regehr, 2010). This type of coping mechanism is parallel to other common strategies such as depersonalization, dehumanization, and disengagement, which are all ways to detach from personal feelings and emotions of traumatic events first responders deal with on a daily basis (Mastracci, Guy, & Newman, 2012). While these coping mechanisms are used by many firefighters and other first responders to deflect the seriousness of the situation, there is increasingly less space in our society for saying anything that could be perceived as offensive or disrespectful. When images of firefighters are captured and portrayed such that their actions and behaviours are considered inappropriate or inconsiderate to the situation, this leads to a misunderstanding by members of the public. Firefighter F mentions,

> We talked about it last year, it was like maybe we shouldn't have these people on the fire ground taking these pictures and catch that flack. It's getting the general public to understand that we're human and not everything is serious all the time, and while we might be smiling or laughing at that particular time is a way that we can just focus on something that is not so bad.

This negative interpretation can create further mistrust by the public. Firefighter B mentions, "*it's a serious accident. And they have a picture of you laughing. Doesn't look very good on you or the community that you respond or that you're responsible for. So you know the mistrust.*" Firefighters' concerns about issues of mistrust and public resistance are considerable, given what has occurred with police officers. Today's society is less accepting and more critical than ever of public safety organizations for many reasons, foremost due to concerns about the abuse of power that is seen with police (Goldsmith, 2015). Firefighters have a very different role than police in public safety. The public has historically viewed firefighters in a positive light, but there is an underlying fear by firefighters that this perception could change due to social media and have a long-lasting effect on the reputation of the fire service.

Firefighters mentioned how as soon as they are on an emergency scene, the information and pictures are already on social media. The immediate nature of social media leaves little control to the firefighters and fire departments. The need for firefighters to watch what they say and do on the fire scenes is evident, as Firefighter G explains,

> Now we have to be very conscious on what we say on the scenes and how we joke about the situation we're in right now, which we shouldn't probably. Because we're just so used to it. You say, oh comment, house is going good, who brought the hot dogs? And then somebody hears that and we're not saying, making fun of their situation. It's just that we've been down this road so many times. Then somebody sitting there watching us hears that and then they go, that's kind of rude. Person is losing their homes and you're worried about barbecuing hot dogs. So you got to be careful what you say. And we have to be more conscious now because of social media and the cameras. Everybody's got a camera in their pocket.

With widespread access to social media and a camera at one's fingertips, there is little room for mistakes and the stress of this is felt by firefighters.

Moral Dilemma and Trauma Reminders

Firefighters conveyed the moral dilemma they felt by sharing imagery from the fire ground on social media. On one side, they are happy their work as a volunteer firefighter is being shared, but on the other side, they are reminded of the devastation for the victims of those emergencies. Firefighter A stated,

> I have mixed emotions about [social] media. Can't live with it, can't live without it. I like the pictures [that the social media users get] and it's cool to see some of those pictures and they get some really great shots. But I struggle with going back to the victim of that call. I struggle with that part, and I struggle with this internally because we sit here and we're like oh we'd really like to have a fire call today. And we do… that's just who we are. But that's somebody else's worst day. Like, last night we had that call where the guy was pretty injured. And it's like, oh, I'm excited because I got to drive [the fire truck] because I was in town. But then the other part of me [is] dying inside because I'm excited that I get to drive [the fire truck] but I'm driving [the fire truck] to somebody's worst day…that's a great photo, but somebody's [house] just burnt down. So, I struggle with that emotion.

The internal emotional struggle that Firefighter A references is a moral struggle. All volunteer firefighters have a fundamental moral dedication and obligation to serve their communities and help people on their worst days, which can lead to internal moral struggles when viewing fire scene images on social media. On the one hand, it is exciting to showcase the work the firefighter is doing, but on the other hand, the image shows the worst day of someone's life that the firefighter is there to help. Firefighters experience an internal emotional struggle due to the moral dilemma they face seeing images being shared that could be harmful to the people they are trying to help. There is potential for the moral dilemma to lead to issues of moral injury, distress, or harm, a more concerning mental health challenge. When firefighters see an image of a fire scene on social media, there is a flood of memories of their experience at that incident. They remember not just what they saw but also the sounds, smells, and emotions they felt. This sets the foundation for a moral struggle and dilemma by seeing imagery shared for public viewing online without consent from the victim. This act goes against the values and moral beliefs that firefighters feel towards the people they help and provides the leverage for a moral struggle to potentially become a moral injury.

The re-exposure to the fire scene through imagery shared on social media can be trauma reminders for firefighters. When a firefighter sees an image that reminds them of an incident that was traumatic or difficult, it can prompt an unwanted emotional response. That response looks different for each firefighter. Firefighter C states,

> I mean, some days I can talk about that stuff and I'll be okay. And then there's other days where even just looking at the picture, if I sit and, like, think about it too long, I'll pull myself in that funk that no one ever wants to be in.

Viewing certain images on social media returns the firefighter back to the emergency scene, an experience that could be considered similar to a flashback where one vividly remembers and relives the traumatic incident. For Firefighter C, "that funk" is a reminder of their experiences and emotions from that incident. For Firefighter G, they described,

> To this day... I still remember the taste of it, which you actually taste the metallic because that's what's in the iron in the blood. You taste that, that smell...sounds...like when we put [the person] in the body bag. I can still remember all the sounds of fluids and ripping of skin and all that stuff, even though that was... years ago.

For Firefighter G, that trauma reminder induces a response that engages all their senses including smell and sounds. Considering different coping mechanisms used by firefighters to essentially put trauma to the side, such as disengagement, dissociation, and distraction including dark humour, a trauma reminder can have a substantial impact. Given the everyday use of social media, disengagement is not always possible. There may be many photos of fire scenes that will not have any impact on firefighters; however, one bad trauma reminder has the potential to completely derail how the firefighter has been coping with that experience. Photographs elicit an emotional response and remind firefighters of the high-risk and stressful nature of their occupation. The power of imagery being shared freely without restrictions on social media can be harmful and is a strong reminder of incidents firefighters would like to forget.

Social media is now an integral aspect of many firefighters' lives and it is becoming increasingly difficult to avoid going on social media platforms. The reality is firefighters will be continually exposed throughout their careers to trauma reminders and moral dilemmas via social media. Determining ways for firefighters to manage these issues is crucial for the longevity of their mental health and wellness.

Conclusion

Social media is not going anywhere and will continue to evolve as a central aspect of the lives and occupations of public safety personnel. Embracing this reality and identifying strategies to manage social media as an occupational stressor is needed. Social media is a significant source of stress impacting both the occupational performance and mental health of first responders.

The findings from the Sound the Siren study showed social media as an occupational stressor in the following domains: online criticism, image and reputation, trauma reminders, and moral dilemmas. Online criticism related to performance on the fire ground and the harsh comments shared online intensify stress for volunteer firefighters. This leads to a fear of doing and saying the wrong thing, with the potential to impede occupational performance on the fire ground. The lack of control and power over the narratives being shared on social media in relation to actions and behaviours by firefighters during emergency incidents also contributes to occupational stress. The image and reputation of firefighters and the fire department are paramount and impact the public's perspective of the fire service which can lead to misunderstanding, mistrust, or even public resistance. Trauma reminders through imagery shared on social media can prompt an unwanted or unexpected emotional response by firefighters when re-exposed to a potentially traumatic incident. Furthermore, firefighters may experience a moral dilemma or struggle when they see images online that can be harmful to those they are trying to help or protect. The stress of trauma reminders and moral dilemmas can have harmful outcomes for firefighters and potentially results in mental health issues.

More awareness and research into social media as an occupational stressor are required, with attention given to the impact of social media on mental health, particularly concerns of moral dilemma and trauma reminders, and to identify strategies to reduce the occupational stress of social media. Furthermore, there should be more research conducted to understand how social media impacts public perception of first responders and their organizations, and how this influences opinions or attitudes towards them.

References

Acquadro, M., Zedda, M., & Varetto, A. (2018). Organizational and occupational stressors, their consequences and coping strategies: A questionnaire survey among Italian patrol police officers. *International Journal of Environmental Research and Public Health*. https://doi.org/10.3390/ijerph15010166

Ahern, J., Galea, S., Resnick, H., & Vlahov, D. (2004). Television images and probable posttraumatic stress disorder after September 11. *The Journal of Nervous and Mental Disease*, *192*(3), 217–226. Retrieved from https://doi.org/10.1097/01.nmd.0000116465.99830.ca

Baer, J. (2014, April 30). Why content is fire and social media is gasoline [Video]. YouTube. www.youtube.com/watch?v=b4J4NbGhiLc

Ballam, E. (2015, January 30). Managing social media to protect the fire service's image. Retrieved from www.firehouse.com/leadership/news/12039813/firehouse-world-managing-social-media-to-protect-fire-service-image-and-fire-departments

Belasky, J. (2022, November 28). What leaders can do about occupational stress in policing. Retrieved from www.orioncom.com/blog/leaders-occupational-stress-policing

Bernstein, K., Ahern, J., Tracy, M., Boscarino, J., Vlahov, D., & Galea, S. (2007). Television watching and the risk of incident probable posttraumatic stress disorder: A prospective evaluation. *The Journal of Nervous and Mental Disease*, *195*(1), 41–47. Retrieved from https://doi.org/10.1097/01.nmd.0000244784.36745.a5

Beshai, S., & Carleton, R. (2016). *Peer support and crisis-focused psychological intervention programs in Canadian first responders: Blue Paper*. Regina: University of Regina Collaborative Centre for Justice and Safety. Retrieved from www.cipsrt-icrtsp.ca/assets/blue-paper-full-web-final-production-aug-16-2016.pdf

Brazil, A. (2017). Exploring critical incidents and postexposure management in a volunteer fire service. *Journal of Aggression, Maltreatment & Trauma*, *26*(3), 244–257. https://doi.org/10.1080/10926771.2016.1264529

Busso, D., McLaughlin, K., & Sheridan, M. (2014). Media exposure and sympathetic nervous system reactivity predict PTSD symptoms after the Boston marathon bombings. *Depression and Anxiety*, *31*(7), 551–558. Retrieved from https://doi.org/10.1002/da.22282

Carleton, R. N., Afifi, T. O., Turner, S., Taillieu, T., Duranceau, S., LeBouthillier, D. M., . . . Asmundson, G. (2018). Mental disorder symptoms among public safety personnel in Canada. *The Canadian Journal of Psychiatry*, *63*(1), 54–64. https://doi.org/10.1177/0706743717723825

Carleton, R., Afifi, T., Turner, S., Taillieu, T., Vaughan, A., Anderson, G., . . . Hozempa, K. C. (2020). Mental health training, attitudes toward support, and screening positive for mental disorders. *Cognitive Behaviour Therapy*, *49*(1), 55–73. Retrieved from https://doi.org/10.1080/16506073.2019.1575900

Creswell, J. (2013). *Qualitative inquiry and research design: Choosing among five approaches* (3 ed.). Thousand Oaks, CA: Sage Publications Incorporated.

Czarniawska, B. (1997). *Narrating the organization: Dramas of institutional identity.* Chicago, IL: The University of Chicago Press.

Dawson, J. (2019, November). Fighting stress in the law enforcement community. *National Institute of Justice Journal*, 281. Retrieved from https://nij.ojp.gov/topics/articles/fighting-stress-law-enforcement-community

Dohmen, M. (2021, August 13). The aching red: Firefighters often silently suffer from trauma and job-related stress. Retrieved from https://theconversation.com/the-aching-red-firefighters-often-silently-suffer-from-trauma-and-job-related-stress-164994

Duxbury, L., & Higgins, C. (2009). Work-life conflict in Canada in the new millennium. Key findings and conclusions from the 2001 National Work-Life Conflict Study. Ottawa. Retrieved 17 December 2011 from www.hc-sc.gc.ca/ewh-semt/pubs/occup-travail/balancing_six-equilibre_six/index-eng.php

Franklin, A., Perkins, R., Kirby, M., & Richmond, K. (2019). The influence of police related media, victimization, and satisfaction on African American college students' perceptions of police. *Frontiers in Sociology*. https://doi.org/10.3389/fsoc.2019.00065

Giesbrecht, L. (2020, February 28). Social media causing stress for Regina police officers. Retrieved from http://ink.urjschool.ca/social-media-causing-stress-for-regina-police-officers/

Glad, K., Hafstad, G., Jensen, T., & Dyb, G. (2017). A longitudinal study of psychological distress and exposure to trauma. *Psychological Trauma: Theory, Research, Practice, and Policy*, *9*(1), 145–152. Retrieved from http://dx.doi.org/10.1037/tra0000224

Goldsmith, A. (2015). Disgracebook policing: Social media and the rise of police indiscretion. *Policing and Society*, *25*(3), 249–267. Retrieved from https://doi.org/10.1080/10439463.2013

Harper, D. (2002). Talking about pictures: A case for photo-elicitation. *Visual Studies*, *17*(1), 13–26. Retrieved from https://doi.org/10.1080/14725860220137345

Haskell, S. (2021). *Cancel culture: A qualitative analysis of the social media practice of canceling*. Boise State University. Retrieved from https://scholarworks.boisestate.edu/cgi/viewcontent.cgi?article=2984&context=td

Isen, R. (2022). The contribution of social media toward racial trauma and post-traumatic stress disorder in Black Americans: A forensic perspective. *The Journal of Forensic Psychiatry & Psychology*, *33*(5), 692–707. Retrieved from https://doi.org/10.1080/14789949.2022.2105250

Jones, S. (2017). Describing the mental health profile of first responders: A systematic review. *Journal of the American Psychiatric Nurses Association*, *23*(3), 200–214. https://doi.org/10.1177/1078390317695266

Layne, C. M., Warren, J. S., Saltzman, W. R., Fulton, J. B., Steinberg, A., & Pynoos, R. (2006). Contextual influences on posttraumatic adjustment: Retraumatization and the roles of revictimization, posttraumatic adversities and distressing reminders. In L. Stein, H. Spitz, G. Burlingame, & P. Muskin, *Psychological effects of catastrophic disasters: Group approaches to treatment* (pp. 235–287). New York: Haworth Press.

Lev-on, A., & Yavetz, G. (2020, December 19). Police in social media: To protect and share? *First Monday*, *26*(1). Retrieved from https://doi.org/10.5210/fm.v26i1.10459

Mash, H., Fullerton, C., & Ursano, R. (2018). Post-traumatic stress symptoms following sniper attacks: Effects of television viewing and identification with victims. *American Journal of Disaster Medicine*, *13*(1), 29–36. Retrieved from https://doi.org/10.5055/ajdm.2018.0285

Mastracci, S., Guy, M., & Newman, M. (2012). *Emotional labour and crisis response.* New York: M.E. Sharpe.

McCreary, D., & Thompson, M. (2006). Development of two reliable and valid measures of stressors in policing: The operational and organizational police stress questionnaires. *International Journal of Stress Management*, 494–518. https://doi.org/10.1037/1072-5245.13.4.494

McHugh, B. C., Wisniewski, P., Rosson, M. B., & Carroll, J. M. (2018). When social media traumatizes teens. *Internet Research*, *28*(5), 1169–1188. https://doi.org/10.1108/IntR-02-2017-0077

Moran, L., & Roth, G. (2013). Humor in context: Fire service and joking culture. *New Horizons in Adult Education & Human Resource Development*, *25*(3), 14–26. https://doi.org/10.1002/nha3.20028

Naftulin, J. (2020, June 3). Police brutality imagery on social media can cause lasting trauma, especially for black people. Retrieved from www.insider.com/police-brutality-imagery-social-media-trauma-mental-health-2020-6

Otto, M., Henin, A., Hirshfeld-Becker, D., Pollack, M., Biederman, J., & Rosenbaum, J. (2007). Posttraumatic stress disorder symptoms following media exposure to tragic events: Impact of 9/11 on children at risk for anxiety disorders. *Journal of Anxiety Disorders*, *21*(7), 888–902. Retrieved from https://doi.org/10.1016/j.janxdis.2006.10.008

Ramsden, P. (2017). Vicarious trauma, PTSD and social media: Does watching graphic videos cause trauma? *Journal of Depression and Anxiety*, *6*(3), 104172.

Regehr, C., Hill, J., Goldberg, G., & Hughes, J. (2003). Postmortem inquiries and trauma responses in paramedics and firefighters. *Journal of Interpersonal Violence*, *18*(6), 607–622. https://doi.org/10.1177/0886260503251131

Rowe, A., & Regehr, C. (2010). Whatever gets you through the day: An examination of cynical humor among emergency service professionals. *Journal of Loss and Trauma*, *15*(5), 448–464. https://doi.org/10.1080/15325024.2010.507661

Saunders, J., Kotzias, V., & Ramchand, R. (2019). Contemporary police stress: The impact of the evolving socio-political context. *Criminology, Criminal Justice, Law & Society*, *20*(1), 35–52.

Scott, Y. (2004). Stress among rural and small-town patrol officers: A survey of Pennsylvania municipal agencies. *Police Quarterly*, *7*(2), 237–261. https://doi.org/10.1177/1098611103258958

Souto-Manning, M. (2014). Critical narrative analysis: The interplay of critical discourse and narrative analyses. *International Journal of Qualitative Studies in Education*, *27*(2), 159–180. https://doi.org/10.1080/09518398.2012.737046

Thurnell-Read, T., & Parker, A. (2008). Men, masculinities and firefighting: Occupational identity, shop-floor culture and organizational change. *Emotion, Space and Society*, *1*, 127–134. https://doi.org/10.1016/j.emospa.2009.03.001

Tucker, J., Bratina, M., & Caprio, B. (2022). Understanding the effect of news media and social media on first responders. *Crisis, Stress, and Human Resilience: An International Journal*, *3*(4), 106–137. Retrieved from www.crisisjournal.org/article/34152-understanding-the-effect-of-news-media-and-social-media-on-first-responders

Velasco, J. (2020). You are cancelled: Virtual collective consciousness and the emergence of cancel culture as ideological purging. *Rupkatha Journal on Interdisciplinary Studies in Humanities*, *12*(5), 1–7. Retrieved from https://dx.doi.org/10.21659/rupkatha.v12n5.rioc1s21n2

Waters, G. (2012, November 1). Social media and law enforcement. Retrieved from https://leb.fbi.gov/articles/featured-articles/social-media-and-law-enforcement

Willing, L. (2019, November 18). The Internet is forever: Firefighters must be smart on social media. Retrieved from www.firerescue1.com/social-media-for-firefighters/articles/the-internet-is-forever-firefighters-must-be-smart-on-social-media-0cqNAEEvLXhpKipM/

PART IV

Public Safety Personnel

12

HITTING THE MARK

A Survey Process Framework for Informing Evidence-Based Organizational Responses to the Psychological Health Needs of Public Safety Employees

Mary Ann Campbell, Lena Gryshchuk, Laurett Nwaonumah, and R. Michael Young

Introduction

The psychological health of public safety employees (e.g., police, firefighters, public safety communicators, civilian supports) should be of paramount concern to organizational leadership. Across employee sectors, psychologically healthy employees demonstrate higher levels of job satisfaction, organizational commitment, enhanced job performance, fewer concerns with misconduct complaints, reductions in presenteeism (present but unproductive), and reduced employee absences (e.g., Baltes, 2001; Boudrias et al., 2011; Dobson & Schnall, 2009; Weziak-Balowolska et al., 2020). Given their occupational roles, public safety personnel are at greater risk of developing psychological health vulnerabilities (Carleton et al., 2018), the effects of which can be compounded by exposure to negative organizational factors that fail to support or promote psychological health (Edgelow, Scholefield, McPherson, Legassick, & Novecosky, 2022). Thus, given this reality, leadership within public safety organizations should be motivated to engage in management practices intended to support the psychological health of employees, such as those recommended by the Mental Health Commission of Canada in their national standards guidelines for psychologically healthy workplaces (Collins, 2014). We recommend the use of a well-designed psychological health survey to (a) set a baseline for wellness, (b) identify sources of operational, organizational, and personal stress and vulnerabilities negatively impacting employee psychological health, and (c) set benchmarks for future improvement via evidence-informed action planning based on survey findings.

A well-established approach for informing policy, procedures, operations, and impact was developed by Lawrence Sherman for policing contexts and

DOI: 10.4324/9781003424253-17

draws on evidence-based thinking and research practices (Sherman, 2013). The framework articulated in this approach is applicable to any public safety organization given its use of research and evaluation principles and can be useful for understanding factors impacting on the psychological health of employees. This approach is framed around the concepts of Targeting, Testing, and Tracking, otherwise known as the Triple T Framework (Sherman, 2019). Although this concept was developed for the policing context, its underlying principles draw from broader research and evidence-based policy/practices that would benefit all public safety organizations. Foundational to this approach is to gather relevant information to identify and understand the problem (i.e., *targeting*). Once a problem has been identified and understood, solutions to address the problem need to be developed and evaluated to ensure they actually address the problem by measuring outcomes (i.e., testing).

Once a solution has been adopted after testing, it needs to be regularly evaluated over time to ensure that it continues to work as desired without any unintended consequences, and to inform any needed adjustments (i.e., *tracking*). An example of applying this approach to the context of the psychological health of a public safety organization is the identified problem of increased sick time and employee absenteeism. A psychological survey could identify potential factors contributing to this problem, such as occupational burnout due to high workload or stress from employee conflict. Once the contributing factors are identified through targeting, potential solutions to those issues should be implemented and evaluated to determine if they reduce sick time and absenteeism. Over time, successful solutions should be monitored to ensure positive effects are sustained, no negative effects occur, and that needed areas of adjustment are made and then tested. A psychological health survey can provide evidence-based knowledge to inform each step in this process when employee wellness, performance, and conduct issues are an area of concern for an organization.

The Centre for Criminal Justice Studies and Policing Research at the University of New Brunswick in Canada has engaged in psychological health surveys since 2015 with different public safety organizations in Atlantic Canada, including three police services and a fire service that also include public safety/emergency dispatch communicators and other civilian public safety personnel. All partnering organizations have engaged in repeat evaluations, or have one planned, to maintain up-to-date knowledge of the psychological health of their employees and to gauge the impact of implemented strategies intended to address identified needs. One of these surveys was implemented following the death of an employee by suicide, which led organizational leadership to want to understand the psychological health needs of their employees and enact change to minimize the risk of such outcomes for other employees (i.e., targeting to inform testing). Other organizations asked for these surveys to understand the reasons behind a high rate of sick leaves and a perception of general discontent in their organization (i.e., targeting to inform testing), whereas another organization wanted to get employee feedback on their proactive wellness initiatives and to identify any other strengths and gaps for meeting their employee's needs (i.e., testing and tracking).

In the current chapter, we strive to provide a practical survey process framework for (a) what information is relevant to capture in a survey and (b) how to construct and implement a psychological health survey within a public safety organization and offer guidance on how best to use the information learned from such surveys to inform evidence-based planning, based on scientific knowledge, around supporting and promoting the psychological health of employees and, thereby, the organizational system itself. A summary of this process framework is provided in Figure 12.1. This process is based on experience with conducting these types of surveys within public safety organizations, but is also heavily drawn from the research literature on psychological health in the workplace, organizational psychology, as well as survey research practices.

What to Include in a Psychological Wellness Survey

Research (e.g., Wright & Cropanzano, 2000) indicates that employee performance can be influenced by a number of psychological factors. Understanding these factors can help identify the problem (i.e., targeting), as well as guide the implementation of solutions and monitor the effects of these solutions in the short term (i.e., testing) and over time (i.e., tracking). We recommend including content areas that capture the sources of stress impacting employees, the current mental health status of employees, the sources of support and coping resources used by employees, and questions about the helpfulness of existing wellness-focused initiatives as well as the services currently available to employees. Justification for the relevance of these domains to the public safety employee context is outlined in the sections below. Although the sections below will refer to helpful measures of interest to include in a survey, the primary considerations in selecting the most appropriate measures for these domains are (a) how reliable an established measure is in the available research literature where it has been used, (b) how well the measure ties into or represents the construct being measured (i.e., validity), and (c) whether there is any available information about the measure's use within the particular public safety personnel group of interest, such as police officers, when such data exists. If designing new survey questions, rather than adopting a well-validated measure tested by research, one must carefully consider how to best design questions in a way that will not lead to distortion in participant responses (e.g., introducing bias or using confusing questions that generate unhelpful or inaccurate responses; see Jarrett [2021] for a practical guide on survey design and Fowler [2013] for useful information on survey research

What questions is the survey intended to answer?

- identify organizational, operational, or personal stressors hypothesized to be impacting employee psychological health.
- understand the psychological health of employees and impact on work performance and job satisfaction indicators.

What data sources are needed to answer these questions? - Is a survey appropriate?

- are these questions better assessed through other means, such as focus groups, records review, staff interviews - surveys can complement these data sources or stand alone.

Who will construct and manage the survey?

- review availability of internal resource competencies for survey design and implementation.
- consider involvement of an external researcher or evaluation consultant to conduct the work, or at a minimum act as a consultant to review the process and procedures.

What domains need to be captured in the survey to understand the problem and/or the effects of implemented strategies/solutions?

- consider the framing of questions to capture relevant information to address survey goals, using clear, unbiased, unambigous worded items with clear response options, and/or select reliable and valid psychological or occupational measures of the constructs of interest.

What will participants be told about the survey and its use? - Informed consent

- ethical guidelines should be followed for fully informed, non-coerced (voluntary) consent to participate or not as a survey respondent.
- if incentives are used, ensure they are equitable and not so significant they are perceived as coercive.

How will the responses on the survey be protected?

- have a data security plan and protocol that all involved are expected to follow.
- anonymous responding is the best option for maintaining confidential responses, as well as for maximizing survey response rate and honest responding to enhance data quality.

Who interprets the data?

- ensure data is interpreted by parties knowledgable about survey design and the content being assessed, and include objective persons independent from the issues of investigation to minimize biased interpretation and discussion of data.

What process will be used to contextualize the recieved data?

- consider the response rate or and representativeness of the data for the organization or unit being examined, along with other potential limitations to the quality or interpretability of the data coming from the survey.

How will feedback be provided to respondents and relevant parties that making use of this information?

- give thought to how summary feedback will be provided to survey respondents and other relevant stakeholders, while respecting privacy and confidentiality.
- receipt of feedback can enhance uptake in survey completion and adds accountability to using the findings.

How can survey results be used to inform strategic planning ?

- deliberately link the findings to strategic planning and organizational practices to inform these actions in ways that support employee psychological health.

What accountability measures wil be put in place to ensure action from the data?

- prior to knowing the findings, develop a transparent plan for committed action.
- post survey, commit to a plan to enact change based on these results, with continued monitoring.

FIGURE 12.1 A survey framework and process for understanding and monitoring employee and organizational psychological health and workplace impact.

methods, including online mediums of survey delivery). The measures we reference below are ones we have used in our surveys and have found helpful for informing the elements of targeting, testing, and tracking.

Personal, Organizational, and Operational Stressors

Public safety employees are exposed to a variety of stressors shared with the general public (personal stressors like conflict in relationships, financial stress, and parenting), but they also experience stressors unique to their job roles, including operational stressors (i.e., stressors associated with the work itself, such as critical incidents and exposure to violence), and organizational stressors (i.e., stressors related to the work environment, such as interactions with supervisors/colleagues, equipment failure, and workload (Carleton et al., 2020; Edgelow et al., 2022). For example, unpublished data from our most recent survey among Atlantic Canadian public safety organizations (i.e., police, firefighters, public safety communicators, and civilian staff) reflected a high volume of personal life stressors, including health difficulties (60.9%) and dealing with personal and family challenges (57.6%), among others (within the past two years; Campbell et al., 2022). Additionally, these employees commonly dealt with operational stressors such as responding to people in distress (64.6%), dealing with child abuse and neglect (57.4%), and responding to situations in which they were threatened with violence to themselves or their loved ones (52.1%). In addition, more than 70% of employees reported dealing with organizational stressors, such as stressful interactions with co-workers or supervisors, as prominent issues in the workplace. These findings led to recommendations for workplace harassment and anti-bullying interventions for employees, as well as supervisor training on these issues, to effect better supervisory practices and on how to disrupt such behavior among subordinates. Testing and tracking are needed next to determine the benefit of these interventions. Other studies have also reported a higher level of workplace conflict with co-workers and supervisors in public safety organizations, which increases the likelihood of lower job satisfaction and dissatisfaction with one's primary supervisor (e.g., Cash et al., 2019; Rohwer et al., 2022).

Not surprisingly, emerging research has identified organizational stress as a major contributor to various mental health concerns in public safety employees (Marmar et al., 2006; Skogstad et al., 2013). For example, Stanley et al. (2018) assessed 831 firefighters and found that higher levels of organizational stressors were associated with increased suicide risk. Additionally, Chan and Andersen (2020) found that organizational stress and anxiety were positively correlated with depressive symptoms among 109 Canadian police officers. A recent study by Frazer and colleagues (2022) found that Australian female emergency responders (including police officers, firefighters, paramedics, and emergency nurses; $N = 286$) experiencing a lack of workplace respect also reported increased burnout, whereas bullying in the workplace was associated with increased psychological distress and post-traumatic stress disorder/injury (PTSD/I). This finding in particular highlights the importance of a more targeted intervention and prevention approach that should take into consideration unique characteristics of public safety personnel, including gender.

In addition to organizational stressors, a large volume of research has identified a strong association between operational stressors and negative mental health outcomes among public safety employees (Corneil et al., 1999;

Geronazzo-Alman et al., 2017; Jahnke et al., 2016; Motreff et al., 2020). Specifically, Ménard and Arter's (2013) study found that exposure to a higher number of critical incidents, as well as younger police officer age, use of negative coping strategies, and social stressors, were significantly associated with PTSD/I symptoms. Additionally, Ménard and Arter (2013) concluded that critical incidents were positively associated with alcohol use, with this relationship mediated by reliance on the negative strategy of avoidant coping. Thus, exposure to critical incidents matters, as does how an employee copes with such incidents. Personal stressors also have an adverse effect on public safety employees' well-being (Burke & Mikkelsen, 2006; Li et al., 2022; Maguen et al., 2009). For example, Griffin and Sun (2018) concluded that work–family conflict was associated with increased stress and burnout among US police officers. These results were echoed by Lambert and colleagues (2019), who also found an association between work–family conflict and burnout among police officers in India.

Given the volume of stressors that public safety employees experience, and the deleterious effect these stressors can have on their mental health and well-being, it is paramount to look closely at the tools that can be used to appraise the presence, nature, and impact of these stressors within an organization. Our psychological health studies in the public safety context utilize a variety of measures to explore personal, operational, and organizational stressors. Specifically, in line with Sherman's (2013) Triple T framework of evidence-based approaches to understanding potential problems to identify and test solutions, the measurement tools utilized in our own surveys (described below; a short description of measures can also be found in Table 12.1) were chosen on the basis of research supporting the nature of relevant operational, organizational, and personal stressors impacting employees and the mental health and resilience indicators that can stem from these stressors and influence work performance and employee conduct.

At the Centre for Criminal Justice Studies and Policing Research, we created a tool to capture exposure to diverse stressors in our surveys specific to public safety personnel, which we named the Stressful Events Checklist (SEC, available on request). The items on this checklist were developed based on clinical experience and research on known stressors within the public safety work environment and the personal lives of public safety employees. We recently published data from the SEC when used with police officers, finding that officers experienced an average of four different forms of occupational stressors and nearly two additional forms of personal stressors in the two years prior to the survey in which it was used; each of these categories of stress could have included multiple stressful experiences within them and did not significantly vary in types as a function of gender (Nero et al., 2022). The SEC is a self-report checklist of 17stressor types used to capture information from public safety personnel about the occurrence of personal (e.g., "Struggled with

TABLE 12.1 Suggested self-report measures of personal, organizational, and operational stress; mental health symptoms; coping strategies and resilience

Scale Name	*Constructs Measured*	*No. of Items*	*Key Associations*	*Key References*
Personal, Organizational, and Operational Stress				
The Stressful Events Checklist (SEC)	Nature and frequency of operational, personal, and organizational stressor types	17	Indicative of stressor types in various domains of life	Campbell et al. (2022)
Occupational Stress Inventory-Revised (OSI-R)	Domains of occupational adjustment, including occupational stress, psychological stress, and coping resources	140	Associated with difficulties with occupational adjustment	Hicks et al. (2010), Osipow (1998)
The Maslach Burnout Inventory-General Survey (MBI GS)	Level of burnout, including domains of professional efficacy, exhaustion, and cynicism	16	Associated with various domains of job satisfaction and psychological strain	Maslach et al. (1996), Schutte et al. (2009)
The Work Role Over-Load Questionnaire (WROQ)	Sources of work stress specific to law enforcement personnel	17	Predictive of work-related stress	Duxbury et al. (2015)
The Revised Commitment Scale (RCS)	Degree of organizational commitment	17	Associated with job satisfaction and employee retention indicators	Allen and Mayer (1990)
Mental Health and Wellness				
Self-Rated Level 1 Cross-Cutting Symptom Measure (DSM-5 CC)	Screens for symptoms in 13 mental health domains, including depression, anxiety, anger, mania, somatic issues, suicidal ideation, psychosis, sleep problems, memory issues, obsessive–compulsive issues, dissociation, personality dysfunction, and substance use	23	Predictive of potential of mental health difficulties, and need for further mental health evaluation	Doyle et al. (2021), Nero et al. (2022)

(*Continued*)

TABLE 12.1 (Continued)

Scale Name	*Constructs Measured*	*No. of Items*	*Key Associations*	*Key References*
The PTSD Checklist for DSM-5 (PCL-5)	Self-report symptoms of post-traumatic disorder	20	Predictive of probable diagnosis of PTSD	Jetelina et al. (2020), Weathers et al. (2013), Wortmann et al. (2016)
The Alcohol Use Disorder Identification Test (AUDIT)	Severity of problematic alcohol consumption	10	Predictive of potential hazardous alcohol use and alcohol use disorders	Conigrave et al. (1995), Reinert and Allen (2007)
The CAGE Alcohol Misuse Screening Tool (the CAGE)	Concerns about hazardous alcohol use	4	Predictive of excessive alcohol use and disorder	Skogan et al. (2011), Williams (2014)
The Cannabis Use Disorders Identification Test – Revised (CUDIT-R)	Frequency of cannabis use	8	Predictive of problematic cannabis use and cannabis use disorder	Mezquita et al. (2022), Schultz et al. (2019)
Coping Strategies and Resilience				
Cognitive Emotion Regulation Questionnaire (CERQ)	Identify coping styles related to thoughts and emotions	36	Adaptive strategies are associated with mental well-being, whereas maladaptive strategies are linked to poorer mental health	Garnefski et al. (2002), Young et al. (2018)
The Brief Cope	Screens for primary coping styles associated with emotions and behavior	28	Influences the relationship between stress and severity of mental health symptoms	Solberg et al. (2022), Allison et al. (2020)
Connor-Davidson Resilience Scale (CD-RISC)	Measures resilience as a trait/skill	25	Positively influences the experience of reduced stress and trauma	Doyle et al. (2021)
Resilience Scale for Adults (RSA)	Measures resilience as a dynamic process	33	Predicts use of protective factors of mental health such as social support	Machisa et al. (2018), Rossi et al. (2021)

significant financial strain"), operational (e.g., "Responded to an incident in which you had close and prolonged contact with a person who was significantly injured"), and organizational (e.g., "Had a stressful professional relationship with a supervisor") stressor types over the past two years (Yes/No), as well as the frequency of each stressor type over the previous year. In addition, respondents are asked to write out any other stressors they have experienced in their personal or work life not noted on the questionnaire to capture all relevant experiences.

We have found that respondents tend to write detailed narratives of their stressors in these text boxes, providing valuable contextual insight into the experiences impacting their psychological health. As it was highlighted earlier in this chapter, it is of particular importance to tap into the nature and frequency of the variety of stressors experienced by public safety personnel to better understand what it is about them that is associated with mental health issues experienced by employees in response to these stressors. Knowledge about the personal, occupational, and organizational stressors public safety personnel deal with within and outside the work context can help identify relevant targets for intervention and establish a baseline from which to test and track changes and/or improvements over time once these interventions are enacted. Another self-report measure frequently used in our surveys to capture organizational stress is the Occupational Stress Inventory-Revised (OSI-R; Osipow, 1998). The OSI-R comprises the Occupational Role Questionnaire (ORQ), the Personal Strain Questionnaire (PSQ), and the Personal Resources Questionnaire (PRQ). The theoretical model of stress behind the OSI-R assumes that work stressors and coping can have an impact on the perception of work roles (Hicks et al., 2010).

Further, this connection between work-related stress and stressful work roles can create psychological or personal strain which, in turn, can be influenced by an individual's coping resources (Hicks et al., 2010). Therefore, the ORQ (60 items) can be used to measure work-related stress as rooted in stress-inducing work roles; the PSQ (40 items) evaluates the level of psychological strain in such domains as vocational stress, as well as interpersonal, psychological, and physical strain; whereas the PRQ (40 items) assesses various aspects of coping, such as recreation, self-care, social support, and rational/cognitive coping (Osipow, 1998). Taken together, these three subscales can provide a broad picture of both an individual's work-related stress, the impact of this strain, and the methods used to cope with the strain. In contrast to most measures discussed in this chapter, the OSI-R is a copyrighted questionnaire purchased from the test publisher Psychological Assessment Resources (PAR). Purchasers must meet the user qualifications to purchase and use the tool (e.g., purchasers must have a graduate degree in psychology or a field closely related to the intended use of the instruments; must be a licensed healthcare worker or a licensed professional in a field allied to healthcare). This requirement, and its cost, makes the OSI-R a less accessible option for some organizations unless they partner with a professional with the appropriate qualifications and a budget to cover the purchase and use costs. When a researcher is connected to the project, the test publisher may be open to a reduced fee as its use is for research purposes and also allow adaption of the measure to be administered online as part of a larger survey, as we have twice done for our own survey work. We were also successful in just using one of the OSI-R subscales to reduce the number of items to be administered in our survey, as other measures captured some of the same content. Specifically, we used only the ORQ items to measure occupational stress and selected briefer measures to tap into constructs that would have been captured by the other subscales.

Research has identified all sections of the OSI-R as reliable predictors of occupational stress in various employee groups, including police officers (e.g., Cimbura, 1999; Johnstone et al., 2016), and the tool has a public safety employee normative comparison group that allows the user to determine whether levels of reported stress, psychological strain, and coping capacity as measured on the OSI-R are within normal expectations for this professional group versus clinically elevated. Overall, the OSI-R, if used in its entirety, can provide helpful information about the dimensions of occupational adjustment (i.e., occupational stress, psychological strain, and coping resources), which are associated with employees' well-being or a lack thereof, and work performance (Decker & Borgen, 1993). The ORQ scale, utilized on its own, taps specifically into the sources of occupational stress, including role overload (e.g., high workload), role insufficiency (e.g., feeling underutilized), role ambiguity (e.g., uncertain about duties/expectations), role boundary (e.g., competing demands), responsibility (e.g., supervision of others), and physical environment (e.g., exposure to toxins). The information obtained through the ORQ can highlight specific problem areas (e.g., overtime hours, competing responsibilities, unfavorable physical environment) that can be solved by implementing changes at the organizational level. Repeated (i.e., annually or biannually) use of this or similar measures can provide organizations with insight into whether implemented strategies improved/exacerbated/did not have any influence on the level of occupational stress.

Occupational burnout is a product of excessive work stress. The Maslach Burnout Inventory-General Survey (MBI GS; Maslach et al., 1996) is a self-report measure designed to evaluate the degree of occupational burnout that respondents experience. The MBI GS items reflect three dimensions of the experience of burnout: professional efficacy, exhaustion, and cynicism (Maslach et al., 1996; Schutte et al., 2000). The professional efficacy subscale measures one's perceived confidence in their work effectiveness, impact, or value (Schutte et al., 2000). The exhaustion subscale evaluates emotional overextension and work-related exhaustion, whereas the cynicism subscale assesses the presence of indifferent or cynical attitudes about one's work (Schutte et al., 2000; Maslach et al., 1996). According to Schutte and colleagues, high levels of burnout are represented by the combination of low professional efficacy and high emotional exhaustion and cynicism. The MBI GS has adequate validity and reliability with different populations (e.g., Tomás et al., 2016), and, not surprisingly, higher burnout scores have been associated with reduced work performance (Dyrbye et al., 2019). Abbreviated forms of the MBI have been used in a number of studies to measure burnout among civilian and sworn law enforcement employees (Adams & Mastracci, 2019; McCarty & Skogan, 2013).

Assessing occupational burnout provides valuable information for an organization's leaders. For example, a study with EMT professionals found that burnout was associated with an increased risk of using ten or more days of sick time in the past year (Crowe et al., 2018). Such individuals were more likely to have the intention of leaving their role within their organization, significantly impacting workforce levels in that organization (Crowe et al., 2018). Thus, MBI GS provides important insight into the reasons for the employees' satisfactory or poor work performance, giving organizational leaders a chance to create better solutions to improve work conditions that will help to retain public safety personnel. In sum, measures of burnout, such as MBI GS, are useful for all levels of Triple T's (Sherman, 2013) as such measures can identify levels of burnout among employees, and through other measures, determine the cause of the burnout to inform necessary operational or organizational changes needed to reduce occupational burnout. Repeated administrations of burnout measures can then test and track the effectiveness of these changes.

The Work Role Over-Load Questionnaire (WROQ; Duxbury et al., 2015) evaluates sources of work stress specific to law enforcement work contexts; thus, this questionnaire is of limited use for other occupations given its item specificity is for the law enforcement occupational role. The WROQ provides information about the experience of organizational stress related to specific domains of competing work demands, dealing with the court system, working outside the employee's mandate, understaffing, and the experience of non-supportive work culture (Duxbury et al., 2015). The higher the mean score, the more frequently respondents experience stress from a particular stress source. Although this measure has not been widely used yet in the research literature, we frequently utilize the WROQ in our surveys involving law enforcement employees and find the questionnaire helpful. Overall, the WROQ can provide valuable information for police leadership, as this questionnaire identifies sources of work stress that could be contributing to occupational burnout and the associated performance issues that result. Knowing these sources of stress will assist in informing the targeting of operational change and support initiatives intended to alleviate work stress.

The Revised Commitment Scale (RCS; Allen & Mayer, 1990) is another useful self-report measure that can assess respondents' degree of commitment to the organization in which they work. The RCS consists of three subscales: affective commitment (i.e., emotional attachment and involvement in the organization's mission and values), continuance commitment (i.e., commitment tied to what they would lose should they leave the organization, such as loss of benefits or pension impacts, rather than personal investment in the organization itself), and normative commitment (i.e., commitment stemming from a sense of obligation to stay at the organization; Allen & Mayer, 1990). The RCS has been used to measure the level of commitment to the organization among law enforcement employees (McElroy, 1999), and we have successfully used it with our broader public safety employee psychological health surveys. Knowledge of how employees are feeling about their organization and their reasons for staying with that organization are important pieces of information for public safety leadership for retention purposes and for understanding why employees are not stepping up or are unwilling to go above and beyond in their duties. Organizational commitment is an excellent marker of employee morale and level of dedication to serve the mission, goals, and values of the organization. In particular, greater affective commitment to one's organization is the dimension that most positively impacts work performance in general employee groups (Kaplan & Kaplan, 2018; Meyer et al., 1989). Police officers with greater affective commitment to their organization tend to perceive their supervisors are more supportive, report higher levels of work engagement, are more likely to ask for/receive support from colleagues to support their work, and are more willing to do extra work (van Gelderen & Bik, 2016).

Similar findings have been reported among firefighters (Lee & Olshfski, 2002), including findings showing that affective commitment is associated with health and safety compliance and safety participation in their actions on scene among firefighters (Smith, 2020). In our work, organizational commitment has been an informative piece of feedback for senior management. When commitment to the organization is low across the board, it may reflect cultural and systematic issues that require complex solutions to address the multiplicity of effects negatively impacting employee commitment. Specifically, when organizational commitment is low, we have used these findings to advocate for systematic changes in the executive and middle management leadership practices that may be interfering with the emotional investment of employees in the organizations for which they work. The specific practices impacting commitment are captured in the other sections of this chapter.

General measures of job satisfaction also may be useful indicators of stress and overall morale within the workplace. In any given year, a survey could also ask about a specific stressor that may be of potential concern for the organization, such as overtime impact or specific aspects of organizational change that have been implemented, like changes in shift schedules, new policies, and procedures, or critical events potentially impacting a unit or the organization.

Mental Health and Wellness

Given the high exposure to stressful and potentially psychologically traumatic events in the line of duty and work context, existing literature indicates that public safety personnel have a heightened vulnerability to mental health concerns, including but not limited to PTSD/I, major depressive disorder, general and social anxiety disorders, and hazardous substance use (e.g., Carleton, Afifi, Turner, et al., 2018; Kleim & Westphal, 2011; Lewis-Schroeder et al., 2018; Wagner et al., 2021). For example, a study by Jones et al. (2018) with a sample of 220 American firefighters and EMT/paramedics found that 26% of these participants were flagged for PTSD/I symptoms, 31% engaged in hazardous alcohol use and/or experienced alcohol dependence, and 28% reported experiencing moderate to severe anxiety symptoms. Similarly, Carleton, Afifi, Turner, and colleagues (2018) conducted a nationwide study of 5813 public safety personnel in Canada (i.e., public safety communicators, correctional workers, firefighters, municipal/provincial police, paramedics, and Royal Canadian Mounted Police) and found that 23.2% of their sample flagged for PTSD/I concerns, 26.4% for major depressive disorder, and 18.6% for generalized anxiety disorder. Additionally, a large-scale study with a sample of 14,866 Australian police and emergency services employees (Kyron et al., 2022) found that one-third of their sample experienced high psychological distress, 10% were flagged for probable PTSD/I diagnosis, and 60% reported hazardous alcohol use and/or active alcohol use disorders. Data from one of our own published studies (Gryshchuk et al., 2022) using our public safety employee psychological health data from Atlantic Canada (police, firefighters, communication dispatchers) indicated that one-third of the sample exhibited recent symptoms of anxiety and depression, approximately 14% were flagged for suicidal ideation, and slightly more than 40% manifested anger issues. First responders in this same sample were flagged for hazardous alcohol use (22%) and potential PTSD/I diagnosis (23%). Taken together, the results from these studies suggest that public safety personnel within and outside Canada experience a higher rate of mental health and substance use concerns in comparison with the general population (Carleton, Afifi, Turner, et al., 2018; Jones et al., 2018; Kyron et al., 2022). Therefore, it is essential to be able to monitor these concerns among public safety employees at the organizational and individual levels to provide necessary accommodation and intervention, and work toward prevention and early intervention. This approach aligns with the Triple T framework (Sherman, 2013) and helps organizations target the existing vulnerabilities among public safety personnel once identified and then determine the best organizational responses needed that can be subsequently tested and tracked for impact over time on reducing mental health and substance use vulnerabilities of employees.

There are a number of publicly accessible measures that can be used to tap into different domains of mental health functioning. One of the tools we have used in our surveys is the Diagnostic and Statistical Manual – 5th edition (DSM-5) Self-Rated Level 1 Cross-Cutting Symptom Measure (DSM-5 CC; American Psychiatric Association, 2013), a user-friendly and publicly available measure of recent symptoms of mental health. The DSM-5 CC Adult Form is used to screen for recent (past two weeks) mental health concerns in 13 domains, including depression, anxiety, anger, mania, somatic (physical health) issues, suicidal ideation, psychosis, sleep problems, memory issues, obsessive–compulsive issues, dissociation, personality dysfunction, and substance use. The DSM-5 CC has been identified as a reliable tool for measuring psychopathology across various populations, including when using an abbreviated version with police officers (e.g., Bravo et al., 2018; Jiang, 2021). Although the DSM-5 provides valuable information about symptoms of mental illness, it does not confirm whether the severity of these issues is significant enough to warrant a formal diagnosis of mental health disorders. Nevertheless, managers would get a cursory view of potential mental health vulnerabilities in their employees that may be impacting their performance and conduct.

As a common concern among public safety personnel (Carleton, Afifi, Turner, et al., 2018) that can increase the use of sick leave, performance issues, and conduct problems due to the impact of this condition on the executive control functions of the brain (Bisson Desrocher et al., 2021) and risk appraisals influencing the actions of public safety employees (Regehr & LeBlanc, 2017), a measure of PTSD/I should always be included in a psychological health survey. We have often used the PTSD Checklist for DSM-5 (PCL-5; Weathers et al., 2013) as a self-report measure of such symptoms. Respondents are asked to rate the severity of their PTSD/I-related symptoms over the previous month (a version exists the previous week as well). Several studies have explored the psychometric properties of the PCL-5, finding it to be a sound and reliable tool for detecting provisional diagnosis of PTSD/I (Blevins et al., 2015; Ibrahim et al., 2018; Wortmann et al., 2016). We use the civilian, past 30 days version for our surveys to capture more stable symptom reporting. Of note, the PCL-5 is widely used with various groups of public safety employees, including police officers, correctional officers, firefighters, paramedics, and public safety communicators (Carleton, Afifi, Turner, et al., 2018; Easterbrook et al., 2022; McCall et al., 2021).

We also have used a variety of measures to explore hazardous alcohol and drug use in our psychological health surveys, as these issues can be a marker of poor psychological health and also contribute to work performance and conduct concerns. The measures we used are easy to administer, user-friendly, and can be easily accessed via the public domain online. For example, the Alcohol Use Disorder Identification Test (AUDIT; Babor et al., 2001) is a relatively short (ten questions) and user-friendly questionnaire that captures the severity of problematic alcohol consumption. Research supports the AUDIT as a tool that can reliably identify people with alcohol-related issues and predict alcohol-related health and social issues in various populations, including public safety employees (Brunault et al., 2019; Carleton, Afifi, Turner et al., 2018; Conigrave et al., 1995). An even shorter (4 questions) and easy-to-complete measure of hazardous alcohol use among adults is the CAGE Alcohol Misuse Screening Tool (Ewing, 1984). Studies find that the CAGE is a valid efficient screen for alcohol use concerns (Hesse & Thiesen, 2007; Skogen et al., 2011), and has been used to measure hazardous alcohol use among police officers as well as other groups (Fox et al., 2012). Stemming from our own psychological health survey data, Gryshchuk et al. (2022) used the CAGE to identify profiles of first responders based on their exhibited mental health vulnerabilities and alcohol use. Three identified profiles emerged from that study (i.e., Clinical Nonspecific, Anger Specific, and Trauma Impacted) which differed significantly in their alcohol use; the Trauma Impacted profile had the highest rate of hazardous alcohol use (39.1%) in comparison with the other two profiles (Gryshchuk et al., 2022). These results highlight the need to identify the prevalence and severity of hazardous alcohol use in a public safety organization so that its leadership can develop targeted intervention and prevention strategies around alcohol misuse. We have used these findings to advocate for cultural change in public safety organizations that encourage the use of alcohol as a way to socialize and wind down after a long or stressful shift or to cope with trauma and stress (e.g., Haddock et al., 2022).

Drug use among public safety employees has received less attention than alcohol use, but clinical experience and general drug use research give good reason to expect this behavior to negatively impact employee performance and conduct due to intoxication or withdrawn reactions), as well as be associated with poor physical and psychological health of affected employees. Notably, the risk of alcohol and drug use among public safety employees increases when post-traumatic stress symptoms are present (Bonumwezi et al., 2022). To assess drug use in a psychological health survey, there are several quick valid options. The Cannabis Use Disorders Identification Test–Revised (CUDIT-R; Adamson et al., 2010) is an 8-item self-report measure used to measure the frequency of cannabis use over the previous six months. Studies have shown that the CUDIT-R serves as an effective, reliable, and valid tool for cannabis misuse screening (e.g., Mezquita et al., 2022; Schultz et al., 2019). Measures of broader drug use include the Drug Use Identification Test (DUDIT; Berman et al., 2003) and the Drug Abuse Screening Test

(DAST; Skinner, 1982) should there be additional items of relevance to a psychological health survey.

Coping Strategies and Resilience

How employees cope with adverse personal events and stress in the workplace is crucial to mitigating the impact of these factors on their psychological health and work capacities. Coping strategies generally involve thoughts, emotions, and behaviors used to tolerate and manage stressful situations (Folkman & Moskowitz, 2004). The long-term benefits of supportive work environments and adaptive coping strategies are evident in the research on promoting psychological health, including contributing to reduced job stress (Piao & Managi, 2022). Coping strategies can be categorized into being task-oriented (or problem-focused), emotion-oriented, and behavior-oriented (Endler & Parker, 1994; Folkman & Moskowitz, 2004). Task-oriented coping addresses the problem causing distress by engaging in active planning, suppressing competing activities, etc. (Folkman & Moskowitz, 2004). Emotion-oriented coping seeks to reduce the emotions associated with the problem by engaging in positive reframing, acceptance, humor, etc. (Folkman & Moskowitz, 2004; Garnefski & Kraaij, 2006). Finally, behavior-oriented strategies are actions in which an employee engages to reduce the impact of stress. Some actions, like seeking social support, are helpful, whereas other actions, such as turning to substances, are less helpful (Folkman & Moskowitz, 2004).

Choosing an appropriate coping strategy would depend on the type of stressor. For example, if an employee is having financial challenges that contribute to their poor mental health, then seeking financial coaching or budgeting could be appropriate strategies to implement. In contrast, exposure to a chronic stressor outside of the employee's control (e.g., the COVID-19 pandemic or provincial policy changes to an employee's work experience) would require the employee to also engage in emotion-focused strategies. As such, public safety employees should maintain a variety of coping strategies that can be drawn upon as needed. In addition, our own surveys have taught us that quality social support in and outside the organization has positive mental health benefits for public safety personnel (Nero et al., 2022), as have other studies with this population (Prati & Pietrantoni, 2010). Thus, there is value in capturing the perceived quality of social support within and outside the work environment on a psychological health survey. Such information also speaks to the view of the work culture itself as being supportive or not and may contribute to affective commitment to the organization.

In our surveys, we focus on assessing employees' reliance on emotion-oriented coping strategies, given the chronic nature of many of the stressors experienced by public safety employees. For example, police officers and public safety communicators are often exposed to situations that are emotionally charged, and they are expected to regulate and manage their emotional responses in the course of their duties. Using a small sample of European police officers ($n = 31$), Berking et al. (2010) demonstrated that officers were better able to tolerate, accept, and confront emotionally (particularly negative emotions such as distress, fear, and anger) challenging situations after participating in a skill-based training (12 by 45-minute training) relative to a control group that did not receive this training. As such, there is utility in evaluating and enhancing effective emotional regulation skills in this population. To test for emotion-oriented coping strategies in our research, we have used the Cognitive Emotion Regulation Questionnaire (CERQ; Garnefski et al., 2002), a 36-item self-report measure that includes nine subscales assessing a person's cognitive or mental responses to stressful experiences. An 18-item abbreviated version also exists with good psychometric properties (Garnefski & Kraaij, 2006). The CERQ is frequently used to measure coping strategies among law enforcement employees, including police officers, police hostage negotiators, and emergency tactical team officers (e.g., Grubb et al., 2015; Young et al., 2018).

Another distinct but interrelated protective factor against the negative effects of stress is an employee's level of resilience. There is disagreement in the literature regarding the best way to conceptualize resilience, and no clear operational definition currently exists. With no clear definition, it is difficult to compare the concept of resilience across studies and disciplines. What is however emergent from the literature, is that resilience is multidimensional, and tends to be most often conceptualized as a personal resource (trait or skill; e.g., Britt et al., 2016), an outcome, or a process as one interacts with adversity (Bonanno, 2012). Regardless of how it is conceptualized, resilience generally involves the capacity to withstand or recover from significant challenges (Masten, 2001; Van der Hallen et al., 2020). Given the varied conceptualizations of resilience, several measures have been developed to capture the essence of resilience. Most measures focus on resilience as a personal resource, such as the Brief Resilience Scale (BRS – 6 items; Smith et al., 2008) and the Connor-Davidson Resilience Scale (CD-RISC, Connor & Davidson, 2003), whereas the Resilience Scale for Adults (RSA – 33 items; Friborg et al., 2003) measures resilience more as a process that results from tapping into social and protective factors of resilience (e.g., meaningful relationships).

Choosing an appropriate scale for measuring resilience for inclusion in a psychological health survey will depend on the types of questions one seeks to answer. Although no current "gold standard" exists for capturing the multidimensional nature of resilience, the aforementioned questionnaires (i.e., BRS, CD-RISC, RSA) are reliable and valid tools for measuring resilience (Windle et al., 2011). The CD-RISC is a 25-item scale that measures resilience (as a unitary construct) as experienced in the past month. An abbreviated version of CD-RISC with ten items also exists and is a reliable and valid tool for measuring resilience in adult populations, including police officers (e.g., Kuiper et al., 2019; McCanlies et al., 2014). Both versions of the CD-RISC have been utilized in our psychological health surveys. Knowledge generated from our surveys with Atlantic Canadian first responders (Doyle et al., 2021) found that resilience, as measured by the CD-RISC, mediated (influenced) the relationships between various dimensions of occupational stress and the experience of anger. Stronger resilience may reduce anger-related reactions to organizational stress and speaks to the value of resilience-enhancing programs within public safety organizations, especially given the links between anger, organizational stress, and misconduct issues (Bishopp et al., 2019; Fox & Spector, 1999). Selecting employees with high levels of resilience at the hiring stage may offset the risk of developing mental health issues in the line of duty, but that does not mean employees remain unaffected by adverse experiences over their careers.

In addition to evaluating the capacity of employees to engage in adaptive and healthy mental coping strategies, including measures of other coping resources, such as social support quality or use of physical exercise, is helpful when considering the content of a psychological health survey. The OSI-R includes subscales that tap into social support, cognitive resilience coping, and instrumental forms of coping through action (e.g., physical exercise). The Brief COPE measure (28 items) is another public domain measure that provides information about a wide range of healthy (e.g., seeking emotional support, putting things in perspective) and unhealthy (e.g., blaming others, substance use) coping strategies (Carver, 1997; see also Solberg et al., 2022 for a recent review) and has been used with various public safety personnel groups (e.g., firefighters, Nydegger et al., 2011).

Seeking Feedback on Implemented Psychological Health Promotion Initiatives

A public safety organization may have already implemented psychological health and wellness initiatives prior to administering their psychological health survey. In this case, in addition to getting a baseline understanding of the stressors, psychological impacts, and coping resources of the organization, this survey is an opportunity to elicit formal feedback from employees about their use of such initiatives and the perceived value or helpfulness for the employee. This information then can be used to inform decisions about continued investment in said wellness initiatives. Collecting organizational psychological health information over time also provides monitoring data for the impact of strategic employee wellness action plans. In our surveys, we also typically ask employees for their thoughts on potential programs or services that are being considered for implementation to elicit their input in advance, as doing so increases employee engagement post-implementation in keeping with processes that support organizational change (Ford & Ford, 2010; Nadler, 1981). Examples of initiatives we have asked about include the use and helpfulness of critical incident debriefings, formal peer support programs, employee and family support services, capacity to access psychologists, perception of available in-house physical fitness facilities, quality of newsletters sent out by the organization on wellness, and the value of receiving mental health awareness or resilience training for employees and supervisors.

The feedback on available or desired supports and services obtained from these surveys has led to the development of a formal peer support program in one organization that did not have one and the formalization of an informal peer support service in another organization. We also learned that employees were not getting sufficient care from the standard employee and family services program for advanced mental health care needs, and insurance coverage for psychological services was insufficient. Thus, these findings have helped us and employee representatives (e.g., unions and human resources) advocate for changes in the programs intended to support the psychological health of employees within the organization. As an example of these changes, the management and union of one organization contributed to a fund from which employees could seek coverage for psychological services, and another organization's union did something similar for their members. Human Resources in one of our organizations is actively working with their municipality to change the insurance coverage for psychological services for their employee group.

Survey Implementation – Ethical Considerations and Responsibilities of Wellness Survey Implementation

Along with deciding the content of the psychological health survey, consideration must be given to ethical issues around the recruitment of employees to complete the survey, the method of survey delivery, managing and securing data resulting from the survey, how the information obtained from the survey will be interpreted and understood to inform action planning, and what findings will be shared and with whom. Research and professional ethical principles should guide these survey process components, with emphasis on freely given informed consent and respect for privacy and confidentiality (Oldendick, 2012), such as outlined by the Canadian Evaluation Society (2020)'s ethics guidelines and the latest Tri-council Policy Statement for ethical conduct involving human research (Government of Canada, 2022). Moreover, managerial leadership reflecting ethical practices is positively associated with trust and organizational commitment in the workplace (Jha & Singh, 2019), including public safety contexts (Bahadori et al., 2021). Whether using an external consultant or not, it is good practice to engage with organizational leadership, human resource staff, and union or employee group representatives early in the process of survey design to foster a shared, common vision for survey goals that can be later presented to employees as a collaborative effort rather than something to only meet the needs of management. Although requiring more time upfront, we have found this participatory, collaborative process helpful for building a reputation of trust in the survey amongst employees and managers and increasing the likelihood of survey completion. The more people who complete the survey, the more representative it is of the organization, making the findings harder to dismiss or ignore.

Public safety organizations are starting to recognize the value of creating a culture of wellness and ensuring that their focus is on management practices and processes that promote a healthy workforce (Rubim et al., 2020). Some public safety professions have begun a major positive transformational shift in promoting a healthy culture of wellness in their organizations. This includes creating a respectful environment that encourages employees' feedback on issues affecting their work experience (Rubim et al., 2020). Transparency, trust, and having established, functional working relationships among the diverse sectors of an organization are key to successful survey implementation. Each new survey an organization implements hinges on the successful implementation of, and actions stemming from, the previous survey. If a survey is conducted poorly and without sound ethical guidelines (e.g., ensuring privacy and confidentiality of responses) and in the context of poor-quality organizational relationships, then the organization's leadership will likely experience difficulties with employee engagement around survey completion and action planning stemming from the results. We have experienced both sides of this situation. In one organization, we met with individual employee groups, the union executive, managers, and human resources staff to speak about the survey and its relevance. Management also came to these briefings to endorse the survey and their commitment to acting on the findings and committed to the sharing of the findings with all employees whether they participate or not. We experienced a high response rate in this organization for our survey. In contrast, an organization with poor union–management relations and distrust in management leadership led to a lower response rate, as there was active discouragement from some members to complete the survey or question its value for creating change despite our reassurances at briefings. The union of that organization also initiated its own survey on employee morale and organizational leadership close in time to our survey, further lowering our response rate due to survey fatigue. On our part, we should have directly engaged with union leadership from the start to encourage their support for the survey amongst their members.

The best way to promote survey participation, demonstrate transparency, and further build trust in the survey's potential impact is through the use of a competent external/independent partner with expertise in survey research to design, administer, and report the survey findings. We argue this position for several reasons. First, the external/independent partner, especially if affiliated with a university, has the ethical expertise and quality assurance processes required for the administration and management of the survey, including ensuring the anonymity of participants. Second, the consultant can provide an objective, independent expert interpretation of the findings to help organizations understand and see outputs produced by the survey through an evidence-based and unbiased lens (i.e., all data is reported, even if it does not represent the organization in a good light). Finally, using a consultant to administer and manage the data from the survey and interpreting it may increase survey participation. For instance, a recent study found that a sample of 90 active-duty police officers underreported their mental health symptoms on an employer-administered survey relative to when the same survey was administered to them by an independent organization (Marshall et al., 2021). Specifically, only 76.3% of police officers in Marshall and colleagues' study reported the same info on the employer-led survey relative to what they reported on the confidential, independently administered survey by a university partner. The underreporting was most noted for psychologically impacting symptoms of anxiety and post-traumatic stress. Although underreporting was present for symptoms of depression and stress as well, it was not a statistically significant variation from the independently administered survey.

Officers of higher rank tended to endorse symptoms more openly on the employer-led survey than those of lower rank, and officers with more severe mental health challenges were at greater risk of underreporting on the employer-led survey relative to those with lower threshold symptoms. Thus, directly administered employer-led surveys may yield underestimates of stressors and mental health concerns affecting the psychological health of their employees, especially among those of lower rank in their organization and with more significant psychological vulnerabilities. Fortunately, this concern may be mitigated by involving an external/independent partner trusted by the employee group. Having an academic collaborator involved enhances the quality of the data in general, given their expertise in research methodology. Several resources exist that provide helpful insight into practices that support professional–researcher collaborations in the criminal justice sector that can be applied to psychological health surveys in public safety organizations (see Douglas & Braga, 2021; Goode & Lumsden, 2018; Hodgkinson et al., 2023).

As this chapter has highlighted, accurate information is necessary to effectively identify the issues at hand impacting employee psychological health, work performance, and employee conduct – this is the crux of evidence-based decision-making. However, no matter how well-designed a survey is, the data stemming from it can lead to poor decision-making if that survey is not adequately administered, its data security and integrity are not properly maintained, and its findings are not appropriately analyzed and interpreted.

Thus, this next phase of the chapter describes key processes and procedural elements of the recommended survey process framework for administrating a survey, data management, and interpretation and use of the information it generates.

Survey Participant Recruitment

Managers, supervisors, and wellness champion leaders within the organization are assets for maximizing survey response rates, including union engagement and their support for the survey objectives. Specifically, how the survey is discussed and presented to employees is key to engaging them in being interested and willing to share their personal information with the organization through the survey. The involvement of an independent partner can be a helpful component of the informed consent process and participant recruitment. Transparent, honest communication about the survey and its merit from all levels of the organization (i.e., management, union, human resources, trusted wellness supporters within the organization) help to promote its value to employees (i.e., it is viewed as more than a checkbox) and is key to successful participant recruitment. Organizations should view themselves as a team, and the survey is intended to benefit the team. Well-established relationships from the executive level to the frontline level of the organization are the foundation of a team (Willink, 2020). The communication from the organization's leadership needs to be clear and transparent to mitigate any concerns from participants about how the organization will use the survey results. If the organization does not follow through on its original communication and recommendations from the survey's findings, then trust will be broken, thereby impacting team relationships and affecting employee engagement in future surveys.

Surveys can be administered through traditional paper-and-pencil questionnaire packages or online methods such as SurveyMonkey or Qualtrics Inc. In our experience, most public safety personnel prefer online surveys, especially when the platform allows them to complete the survey over a few days, rather than all at once. Should employees be provided permission to participate in the survey during work hours (we recommend this option), an online option allows them to work around unexpected shift duties. Qualtrics Inc. is a secure platform for survey completion that we have used for all our surveys. This platform, however, requires a subscription. Some non-subscription-based online survey platforms may sell respondent data or lack sufficient encryption for data security; as such, we recommend a review of the platform's data security protections prior to use. Google Survey and SurveyMonkey are examples of non-subscription online survey platform options.

From our survey implementation experience, approximately one-third of respondents prefer the paper-and-pencil format. Thus, we typically make both formats available to increase survey participation. In general, online and paper-and-pencil mental health survey administrations tend to produce comparable responses for mental health and personal experience topics (Cronly et al., 2018; Hirsch et al., 2014; Schillewaert & Meulemeester, 2005); however, there are some differences. Some studies have found variations in the characteristics of respondents who choose to complete online versus paper-and-pencil formats (Schillewaert & Meulemeester, 2005). In addition, the psychometric properties of measures may change to some degree when transitioned from a paper-and-pencil medium to an online medium (Van Ballegooiken et al., 2016). Thus, although convenient to administer, online surveys have caveats (Fan & Yan, 2010). Other issues with online survey administration include the problem of low rates of full survey completion, especially for lengthy surveys, and the security risk of internet bots infiltrating the online survey and providing false responses. To mitigate this latter risk, ensuring the survey link is only available to employees rather than the public minimizes intrusions from non-target groups and internet bots. Copyrighted questionnaires will require permission from publishers to modify to include in the online survey, usually at a fee.

If using paper-and-pencil survey versions of the questionnaire package, there is more confidence that responses only come from the target group. However, responses from the paper-pencil format need to be aggregated into an electronic medium to allow for statistical analysis of the data as a whole. As such, the paper-pencil format introduces additional data entry and data management resource demands that need to be considered depending on the organization's size. Paper surveys can be dropped in a sealed box held by a trusted person within the organization and then shared with an external consultant (still sealed) for analysis or given to the staff person responsible for compiling the data. At no time should the consent forms (see below) or identifying information of the employee be stored with the paper survey to protect survey response confidentiality.

Informed Consent Process

For this type of survey, a written consent form should precede the survey. The consent form should clearly state the goals of the survey, the voluntary nature of participation (no consequence for not participating), the confidentiality of the survey and how this will be ensured, what will be expected of them as participants (e.g., topics, survey completion procedures, survey length, and incentives for participation), and whether there are any anticipated risks or benefits they may directly experience from their participation that could influence their decision to participate. Usually, such risks are low in survey research, but some individuals may find answering questions about their personal or work experiences upsetting or triggering given their pre-existing vulnerabilities; thus, it is good practice to include this warning in the consent form and include a list of mental health resources and supports to which any participant can reach out should they feel the need. This list should be for everyone; no one must identify themselves as vulnerable to a third party to get this information. The right to withdraw from the survey and not complete it, or to have their data removed entirely before reporting on the findings also needs to be stated.

Privacy and Confidentiality

The best option is to administer the survey in a way that ensures anonymous participation to both protect employee privacy and maximize the potential for honest reporting (i.e., respondents feel comfortable sharing accurate information about their experiences and perspectives as there is no fear of being judged, embarrassed, or otherwise penalized for their responses). This means that names or other identifying information are not requested in the survey online or in paper format, and if in paper format, no one should be able to view the responses of an individual respondent when they hand in that survey. It should be added to a pile of other anonymous surveys in sealed envelopes separated from their consent forms. If an organization's goal is to track individual employee wellness over time (e.g., longitudinally across repeated surveys), then unique identifiers should be provided to employees for use each time an employee completes the survey. The unique code should exclude their name or employee numbers to ensure their responses are not identifiable and remain anonymous. In addition, procedures need to be arranged to ensure that managers, supervisors, and colleagues do not have access to potentially identifiable responses (where it is possible to track the responses back to a person). Using an independent consultant as the only party with access to the raw survey data helps mitigate this concern, as no employee has access to the database or survey forms, and the organization only receives aggregate (summary) data scrubbed of personal identifying information. Reporting of survey responses should always be de-identified, with any identifying information removed or not reported verbatim.

Once these findings have been compiled and understood, consideration should be given to how the survey findings are shared with employees. Processes of knowledge translation or mobilization should be decided upon when designing the survey and documented when acquiring informed consent. Hence, the employee is aware of how information from the survey will be used and what they will learn from the survey when they decide to (or not to) participate. Being upfront in how one plans to share survey findings reflects transparency, engendering greater trust in the meaningful use of the information employees are being asked to share with the organization. Employees' commitment to transparency is elevated when managers voice openness to the resulting accountability created once findings are known and shared with employees.

Linking Survey Findings to Action Planning

With known survey findings, the next step is to link findings with action items that correspond to identified wellness needs and sources of strain within the organization or to enhance areas of strength to support employee psychological health. Wellness efforts need to be strategically embedded into the everyday culture of organizations to have the desired impact, not just be incorporated in a program or brief training session if outcome longevity is desired. The cultural shift includes countering the view that wellness is only the responsibility of the employee and not of the employer (Blumberg et al., 2022, forward by K.V. Gilmartin). The policing and other public safety environments are ever-changing due to external (societal) and internal (workforce) influences and factors (Cordner, 2019). As this environment is dynamic, successful organizations have built their systems to adapt to the required change (Cordner, 2019). The best way to inform organizations on needed adaptations to their systems, strategies, policies, and programs is through an evidence-informed approach focusing on quality research to answer the question "what works" (Council of Canadian Academies, 2014). The psychological health survey process framework we propose in this chapter is evidence-informed, giving managers the ability to identify organizational vulnerabilities that may be negatively affecting employee behaviors as well as identify realities positively impacting employee behavior (Huey et al., 2017).

Managers can create a healthy work environment by situating the wellness of the organization directly into the vision, mission, values, and leadership principles of the organization (Rubim et al., 2020). These elements should be linked to the organization's strategic plan, which guides efforts to advance the organization by setting clearly defined goals, measurements, and a strategic agenda (More et al., 2012). The findings of an organization's psychological health survey can be used as an index of how the organization is doing with supporting a psychologically healthy work environment, as well as be used to capture key performance indicators for an organization's strategic plan on employee health and wellness (More et al., 2012).

The psychological health action plan process begins with strategic planning to maximize the lessons learned from the survey findings. See Table 12.2 for key strategic steps to be considered when engaging in action planning processes based on survey findings, with an emphasis on employee engagement.

Maintaining and enhancing the psychological health and wellness of public safety employees may involve establishing key programs. In particular, implementing programs that are preventative in nature (i.e., proactive wellness programs that promote and protect psychological health before an employee

TABLE 12.2 Suggested implementation process linking survey findings to action planning

Step	*Purpose*	*Description*
1	Communication and transparency	Before reviewing survey results and action planning, communicate with members of the organization through appropriate channels (e.g., electronic or in-person meetings). Thank employees for providing helpful feedback in the surveys, provide a summary of the survey progress, and eventually summarize results or highlights (e.g., percentage of respondents, breakdown of departments represented in the survey), and share how one hopes to utilize the survey findings. This communication step is crucial as it keeps employees informed and engaged. These steps further build trust and healthy professional relationships.
2	Analysis and interpretation	When analyzing the survey findings in detail, identify the dominant themes that emerge. Classify themes that are strengths and areas for improvement or development. In addition, examine any differences that emerge among various groups (e.g., job role differences or between units if large enough to be non-identifying in what is reported). Taking a team approach here, by including department leaders/representatives who can provide context to understanding the survey findings before they are shared widely, may be helpful. If a previous psychological health survey has been conducted, it would be valuable to compare how the new survey compares to previous surveys.
3	Release survey results	Release survey results to the organization in a way that highlights the strengths while also describing growth areas. Various levels of management and union representatives and wellness champions should be provided with an understanding of the survey findings to ensure they can use the information appropriately and answer questions employees may have about the findings and recommendations.
4	Focus groups	If possible, hold discussions during which the survey results can be discussed to provide any additional context needed for data interpretation and discuss which action items stemming from the survey should be actioned first. These discussions reinforce an organization's commitment to listening to employee feedback and having action items that reflect the feedback. Having members from an organization's wellness committee or other employee leadership groups participate in these discussions can be a useful engagement strategy.

5	Draft action plan	Action items should reflect the emergent themes from survey findings and conversations. Based on the themes that emerged from the survey, having an action plan that spans a few years (3–5 years) can provide an adequate timeline to implement the action items. For example, in our surveys, one of the themes that emerged was difficult interpersonal relationships. As such, an action item tied to this theme was to provide ongoing training on conflict management and training for supervisors on how to have difficult conversations with their employees. Another action item from our surveys led to the creation of a wellness coordinator position to provide a resource to support the development and enacting of these action items. Once action items have been drafted, communicate these action plans to the organization for transparency and accountability purposes.
6	Execute the plan	Actioning a plan requires time and, as such, allows for more time than might be expected to develop appropriate tasks and actions and then implement these identified action items. Collaborate with appropriate department heads and wellness champion leaders to facilitate the actions needed. Having appropriate policies and standard operating procedures might also be helpful to guide behavioral practice around wellness in the organization. Communicate to employees how the action plan will be executed.
7	Evaluate progress	Evaluating the progress of implemented action items is necessary to account for progress. This can be done by polling employees or inviting feedback to inform required changes as needed, or using more elaborative research designs involving external consultants to assess the impact and effectiveness of actioned items. Some of these actioned items might be aimed at creating organizational change, which can be difficult and time-consuming to implement. As such, consider having a dedicated employee(s) be responsible for leading and managing these organizational changes and the initiatives aimed at supporting the psychological health of employees or contracting a knowledgeable party to do so for the organization. Wellness cannot be achieved successfully off the side of someone's desk, someone in the organization should be formally responsible with leadership oversight.

is impacted) while also having programs available when an employee's psychological health has been impacted (i.e., reactive wellness programs) can be helpful in meeting the varied employee needs within the organization. Reactive wellness programs, such as Employee Family Assistance Programs (EFAP), are typically available within public safety organizations and accessed when an employee self-identifies as having an emerging or existing psychological health concern. A recent Canadian study by Milot (2019) found that, when compared to non-EFAP users, EFAP users had significantly better mental health outcomes, including reduced symptoms of depression and anxiety, and EFAP users were better engaged with their work responsibilities. Although EFAP programs provide ample utility within an organization, they do require the employee to take the first step toward help-seeking behavior. In many situations, public safety employees may not recognize that they have a psychological health injury until the injury is quite established. For example, compromised mental health may have a gradual onset, such that the psychologically injured employee is not aware of their condition until they become so overwhelmed due to extreme anxiety and burnout that their work performance and daily functioning are substantially impaired, and they make egregious mistakes or errors in judgment that lead to disciplinary actions, or their health care providers recommend a health leave from work, before their compromised wellness is acknowledged. Psychologically injured or impaired employees may then seek services through their EAFP. The individual, however, has likely moved past the benefits of early or short-term intervention measures provided by most EAFPs at that point. In addition, organizations need to make available additional services to augment the self-initiated counseling services available through EFAP programs, as these are often designed for short-term, mild to moderate psychological issues and can vary in the clinical expertise available within the service provider pool (e.g., limited access to psychologists or professionals who can diagnose mental health conditions and treat complex mental health and substance misuse conditions).

Another popular intervention for public safety personnel intended to prevent psychological stress injuries, or offer early intervention, is the use of Mitchell's Model of Critical Incident Stress Debriefings (CISD) (Mitchell & Everly, 1996) following employees' exposure to a critical incident. Our public safety personnel survey respondents consistently recommend that psychological debriefings become part of their organization's regular operations. However, there are mixed findings about the effectiveness or impact of offering these debriefings to employees (Mitchell et al., 2003), with some experts arguing against CISD's use (American Red Cross Advisory Council on First Aid, Aquatics, Safety and Preparedness, 2010; Skowronski & Kerridge, 2022). These arguments rest on the reality that acute stress reactions are often temporary for most individuals without the aid of such interventions (Bryant, 2004) and indications that the debriefing process may exacerbate post-traumatic injury symptoms (Barboza, 2005; Bledsoe, 2003). Although CISD may benefit broader psychological health functioning (e.g., less alcohol use post-CISD; Tuckey & Scott, 2014), available research generally indicates that there are no meaningful differences in post-traumatic stress injury symptoms (Tuckey & Scott, 2014) and other mental health outcomes for employees who participated in CISD when comparing pre-intervention symptom scores to post-intervention scores (Addis & Stephens, 2008).

There are several proactive wellness programs that may be adopted by public safety organizations to serve preventative and psychological health maintenance goals as part of the everyday life of employees. This work also includes tasks for managers and supervisors to engage in practices that support the psychological health of their supervisees and engender a pro-mental-health organizational culture. Organizations can provide managers and supervisors with the foundation to support practices that promote an organization's psychological health through leadership training and development (Rubim et al., 2020). Transformational leadership focuses on positive leader and follower relationships whereby the leader motivates, inspires, and influences followers to achieve and grow to their fullest potential (More et al., 2012). This leadership style will foster employee engagement, creating employee commitment to the organization and overall employee satisfaction (Rubim et al., 2020). As noted previously, employee engagement and affective commitment to the organization are important elements of employee job satisfaction and likely contribute to, or stem from, the psychological health of the employee and of the organization itself.

Managers also should take care to ask critical questions to determine the efficacy of a considered wellness program and to determine whether a program will be a good fit for the organization to ensure (a) it is actually needed (what data is available to say it is a need in your organization), and (b) if needed, that it will produce the outcomes being claimed for its uptake (test and track it in your organization, but what other studies have been done to support that it works as claimed?). Strong marketing pitches have no informative value when there is little actual data to back up claims of success. A review by Edgelow, Scholefield, McPherson, Mehta, and Ortlieb (2022) on workplace mental health interventions within the context of public safety professions identified stress management and resilience-focused interventions as the most implemented services among public safety employees. These are positive steps toward supporting psychologically healthy workplaces, but these programs are often understudied in terms of their effectiveness with public safety employee groups, especially their long-term benefits over a lengthy public safety career. We also do not yet know how often such initiatives should be provided to maintain their initial benefits. Thus, research is needed to guide the development and testing of wellness programs within public safety organizations to inform their suitability for this setting. Some of this research is emerging, however. For example, Vadvilavičius and colleagues (2023) recently reported on the positive benefits of mindfulness-based interventions for police officers to reduce stress and associated psychological issues (e.g., sleep issues, burnout, PTSD symptoms) in their systematic review of this type of intervention.

Within Canada, Carleton (2021) described a comprehensive initiative to enhance evidence-based supports and services for public safety personnel through the proactive development work of the Canadian Institute for Public Safety Research and Treatment (CIPSRT, www.cipsrt-icrtsp.ca). One of these evidence-informed initiatives is the Before Operational Stress (BOS) program (Stelnicki et al., 2021). The Mental Health Commission of Canada also offers the Working Mind (https://theworkingmind.ca; formally known as Road to Mental Readiness, R2MR). These proactive initiatives aim to reduce mental health stigma and teach employees skills that build resilience to stress and potentially traumatic experiences, though their outcomes are generally modest (Carleton, Korol, Mason, et al., 2018; Stelnicki et al., 2021) and long-term data on sustained benefits is lacking as well as clinical trials and other needed control versus treatment-based evaluations. Resilience and healthy coping skills need to be used as part of one's everyday existence to be maximally beneficial as a prevention strategy, and this may get lost without regular maintenance and reinforcement of their use in the personal and work lives of employees. Another proactive resource that describes practical evidence-informed strategies for enhancing psychological health among public safety employees is the P.O.W.E.R manual by Blumberg and colleagues (2022), which stands for police officer wellness, ethics, and resilience. Although written for police officers, the content within that book is applicable to most public safety personnel. The book provides relevant education on various aspects of psychological health, the role of ethics and values, and content to support resilience. Resources such as these are valuable tools that should be made available to employees for self-directed wellness care, or as content for regular training on wellness and resilience. However, good evidence-based practices require wellness initiatives to be tested (pilot projects are a good start) and then evaluated to ensure that they achieve their intended effects in the specific organization in which they are applied, and do not cause harm. Just because something works in one jurisdiction or employee group, does not necessarily mean it will work in another setting.

Our psychological health surveys clearly demonstrated that a "one-size-fits-all" approach to wellness initiatives would likely not meet the needs of all employees. Specifically, Gryshchuk and colleagues (2022) found three psychologically vulnerable profiles among Atlantic Canadian first responders: a clinical nonspecific group; an anger-specific group; and a trauma-impacted group. Notably, there was no psychologically healthy group in this sample of active-duty employees (representing more than 60% of the organization).

These groups varied in meaningful ways on their psychological needs, organizational stressors, and alcohol use, suggesting value in having access to targeted intervention strategies within organizations for unique issues as well as more global prevention supports. Translating knowledge into action from that study, it is clear that that specific organization is in need of urgent trauma-focused screening and intervention for a portion of their active duty employees (i.e., set up a personalized, confidential screening process for employees with links to mental health care provided for follow-up), while the other two profiles would benefit from general coping and emotional regulation management psycho-education that could be accessed via online training or in-person sessions in groups.

In addition to tailored interventions and resources to meet the diverse needs of employees, it is important to recognize that the psychological health of public safety personnel can be impacted (positively or negatively) by organizational culture, friction between units in an organization, and perceptions of senior leadership (Jacobsson et al., 2020; Orosco & Gaub, 2023; Patterson & King, 2023); thus, deliberate, strategic work to correct or improve these areas also may be required if identified as dominant stressors for employees overall or within a specific unit of the organization. Policies and procedures developed through an organizational justice approach can support positive employee behavior (Rubim et al., 2020). Organizations can further this approach through a performance-based management program focusing on specific objectives, behavioral competencies, and expectations that align with the overall strategic plan, policies, and procedures of the organization that create a psychologically healthy workforce (More et al., 2012).

Conclusion

The psychological health of an organization should be a core point of consideration for any public safety executive management and leadership group within that organization, given the salient ties psychological health has with employee job satisfaction, work performance, employee conduct, and employee absence from work. Working to develop and sustain a psychologically healthy workplace is foundational for a functional organization. As such, public safety leadership must have an evidence-based means of accurately understanding and tracking the psychological health of their employees and their organization as a whole. The Triple T framework (targeting, testing, and tracking; Sherman, 2013) that underlies evidence-based decision-making and practices provides a solid rationale for creating and conducting psychological health surveys within public safety organizations. This chapter provided a review of relevant stressors and psychological factors that can positively or negatively influence the psychological health of an organization and the employees working within it and highlighted the links of these stressors and psychological health factors to workplace behavior and job performance. The link is clear. Enhanced psychological health is associated with positive work performance, conduct, and commitment to one's organization. To guide public safety employee leaders in how to identify the specific stressors and psychological health concerns impacting their employees, we also provided a survey process framework for how to effectively complete a psychological health survey in a public safety employee context. If designed and implemented ethically and in a procedurally fair manner, this survey will provide an evidence base for strategic planning for promoting psychological health in the workplace and the testing and tracking of implemented action items to this end. Such an approach ensures that these initiatives will "hit the mark" and achieve the goals as intended.

To promote transparency and survey participation, our survey process framework recommends the use of an external/independent partner with expertise in survey research to design, administer, and report the survey findings to enhance the quality of the survey, ensure unbiased reporting of results, and maximize trust in the survey by employees less trusting of their organization's leadership. Managers and other employee groups should still have input even if a consultant is used, as relevant context to the organization can identify relevant factors to include in the survey. External/independent partners can provide expert interpretation, provide solutions and strategies for implementation, and conduct/guide appropriate measurements over time to ensure solution/strategy sustainability. This includes tracking and identifying the sources of stress affecting employee wellness, such as personal, organizational, and operational stressors. The use of a psychological health survey also allows for screening of mental health concerns across various domains and measuring hazards contributing to poor coping strategies, such as alcohol and substance use that may relate to work performance, sick use time, and conduct concerns. Evidence-based knowledge of these stressors will help inform strategic planning to improve and sustain the psychological health of employees and work toward embedding wellness initiatives into the everyday culture of organizations. Central here is that employees are the core foundation of the organization and should be a priority above all. Organizations that promote a healthy environment of wellness through evidence-based practices will have created an atmosphere that motivates, inspires, and influences employees in positive ways that improve their work performance, engagement, and commitment to the values and goals of the organization, which ultimately benefits the organizations for which they work. This is a reciprocal relationship that requires contributions from both employers and employees to collaborate on best practices that support the mutual goal of sustaining a psychologically healthy workplace. Effective action on this cause requires evidence-based knowledge.

References

Adams, I., & Mastracci, S. (2019). Police body-worn cameras: Effects on officers' burnout and perceived organizational support. *Police Quarterly*, *22*(1), 5–30. https://doi.org/10.1177/1098611118783987

Adamson, S. J., Kay-Lambkin, F. J., Baker, A. L., Lewin, T. J., Thornton, L., Kelly, B. J., & Sellman, J. D. (2010). An improved brief measure of cannabis misuse: The Cannabis Use Disorders Identification Test – Revised (CUDIT-R). *Drug and Alcohol Dependence*, *110*(1–2), 137–143. https://doi.org/10.1016/j.drugalcdep.2010.02.017

Addis, N., & Stephens, C. (2008). An evaluation of a police debriefing programme: Outcomes for police officers five years after a police shooting. *International Journal of Police Science & Management*, *10*(4), 361–373.

Allen, N. J., & Meyer, J. P. (1990). The measurement and antecedents of affective, continuance and normative commitment to the organization. *Journal of Occupational Psychology*, *63*(1), 1–18. https://doi.org/10.1111/j.2044-8325.1990.tb00506.x

Allison, P., Mnatsakanova, A., McCanlies, E., Fekedulegn, D., Hartley, T. A., Andrew, M. E., & Violanti, J. M. (2020). Police stress and depressive symptoms: Role of coping and hardiness. *Policing: An International Journal*, *43*(2), 247–261.

American Psychiatric Association. (2013). *DSM-5 self-rated level 1 cross-cutting symptom measure—Adult: Online assessment measures.* www.psychiatry.org/practice/dsm/dsm5/online-assessment-measures.

American Red Cross Advisory Council on First Aid, Aquatics, Safety and Preparedness. (2010). *ACFASP scientific review: Critical incident stress debriefing.* www.redcross.org/content/dam/redcross/Health-Safety-Services/scientific-advisory-council/Scientific%20Advisory%20Council%20SCIENTIFIC%20REVIEW%20-%20Critical%20Incident%20Stress%20Debriefing.pdf Retrieved February 16, 2023.

Babor, T. F., Higgins-Biddle, J., Saunders, J. B., & Monteiro, M. (2001). *AUDIT – The alcohol use disorders identification test: Guidelines for use in primary health care.* World Health Organization Department of Mental Health and Substance Use.

Bahadori, M., Ghasemi, M., Hasanpoor, E., Mojtaba Hosseini, S., & Alimohammadzadeh, A. (2021). The influence of ethical leadership on the organizational commitment in fire organizations. *International Journal of Ethics and Systems*, *37*(1), 145–156. https://doi.org/10.1108/IJOES-04-2020-0043

Baltes, B. B. (2001). Psychological climate in the work setting. International Encyclopedia of the Social and Behavioral Sciences. In N. J. Smelser & P. B. Baltes (Eds.), *International encyclopedia of the social and behavioral sciences* (Vol. 18, pp. 12355–12359). Elsevier (Pergamon)

Barboza, K. (2005). Critical incident stress debriefing (CISD): Efficacy in question. *The New School Psychology Bulletin*, *3*(2), 49–70. https://doi.org/10.1037/e741582011-004

Berking, M., Meier, C., & Wupperman, P. (2010). Enhancing emotion-regulation skills in police officers: Results of a pilot controlled study. *Behavior therapy*, *41*(3), 329–339.

Berman, A. H., Bergman, H., Palmstierna, T., & Schlyter, F. (2003). *The drug use disorders identification test manual.* Karolinska Institute, Department of Clinical Neuroscience Section for Alcohol and Drug Dependence Research.

Bishopp, S. A., Piquero, N. L., Worral, J. L., & Piquero, A. R. (2019). Negative affective responses to stress among urban police officers: A general strain theory approach. *Deviant Behavior, 40*(6), 635–654. https://doi.org/10.1080/01639625.2018.1436568

Bisson Desrochers, A., Rouleau, I., Angehm, A., Vasiliadis, H-M., Saumier, D., & Brunet, A. (2021). Trauma on duty: Cognitive functioning of police officers with and without posttraumatic stress disorder. *European Journal of Psychotraumatology, 12*(1): 1959117. https://doi.org/10.1080%2F20008198.2021.1959117

Bledsoe, B. E. (2003). Critical incident stress management (CISM): Benefit or risk for emergency services? *Prehospital Emergency Care, 7*(2). 272–279. https://doi.org/10.1080/10903120390936941

Blevins, C. A., Weathers, F. W., Davis, M. T., Witte, T. K., & Domino, J. L. (2015). The posttraumatic stress disorder checklist for DSM-5 (PCL-5): Development and initial psychometric evaluation. *Journal of Traumatic Stress, 28*(6), 489–498. https://doi.org/10.1002/jts.22059

Blumberg, D. M., Papazoglou, K., & Schlosser, M. D. (2022). *The P.O.W.E.R. manual: A step-by-step guide to improving police officer wellness, ethics, and resilience.* American Psychological Association.

Bonanno, G. A. (2012). Uses and abuses of the resilience construct: Loss, trauma, and health-related adversities. *Social Science and Medicine, 74*(5), 753.

Bonumwezi, J. L., Tramutola, D., Lawrence, J., Kobezak, H. M., & Lowe, S. R. (2022). Posttraumatic stress disorder symptoms, work-related trauma exposure, and substance use in first responders. *Drug and Alcohol Dependence, 237*(Aug), 109439. https://doi.org/10.1016/j.drugalcdep.2022.109439

Boudrias, J-S., Desrumaux, P., Gaudreau, P., Nelson, K., Brunet, L., & Savoie, A. (2011). Modeling the experience of psychological health at work: The role of personal resources, social-organizational resources, and job demands. *International Journal of Stress Management, 18*(4), 372–395. https://psycnet.apa.org/doi/10.1037/a0025353

Bravo, A. J., Villarosa-Hurlocker, M. C., Pearson, M. R., & Protective Strategies Study Team. (2018). College student mental health: An evaluation of the DSM-5 Self-Rated Level 1 Cross-Cutting Symptom Measure. *Psychological Assessment, 30*(10), 1382–1389. https://doi.org/10.1037/pas0000628

Britt, T. W., Shen, W., Sinclair, R. R., Grossman, M. R., & Klieger, D. M. (2016). How much do we really know about employee resilience? *Industrial and Organizational Psychology, 9*(2), 378–404. https://doi.org/10.1017/iop.2015.107

Brunault, P., Lebigre, K., Idbrik, F., Maugé, DEas., Adam, P., El Ayoubi, H., Hingray, C., Barrault, S., Grall-Bronnec, M., Ballon, N., & El-Hage, W. (2019). Posttraumatic stress disorder is a risk factor for multiple addictions in police officers hospitalized for alcohol. *European Addiction Research, 25*(4), 198–206. https://doi.org/10.1159/000499936

Bryant, R. A. (2004). Acute stress disorder: Course, epidemiology, assessment, and treatment. In B. T. Litz (Ed.), *Early intervention for trauma and traumatic loss* (pp. 15–33). Guilford Press.

Burke, R. J., & Mikkelsen, A. (2006). Burnout among Norwegian police officers: Potential antecedents and consequences. *International Journal of Stress Management, 13*(1), 64–83. https://psycnet.apa.org/doi/10.1037/1072-5245.13.1.64

Campbell, M. A., Gryshchuk, L., Smith, E., & Nwaonumah, L. (2022). *Technical report.* Centre for Criminal Justice Studies, University of New Brunswick, Saint John, NB.

Canadian Evaluation Society. (2020). *CES guidance for ethical evaluation practice.* Author. https://evaluationcanada.ca/sites/default/files/CES_Guidance_for_Ethical_Evaluation_approved_09_01_20.pdf

Carleton, R. N. (2021). Collaborating to support the mental health of public safety personnel: The Canadian Institute for Public Safety Research and Treatment. *Canadian Psychology/Psychologie Canadienne, 62*(2), 167–173. https://doi.org/10.1037/cap0000267

Carleton, R. N., Afifi, T. O., Taillieu, T., Turner, S., Mason, J. E., Ricciardelli, R., McCreary, D. R., Vaughan, A. D., Anderson, G. S., Krakauer, R. L., Donnelly, E. A., Camp, R. D., 2nd, Groll, D., Cramm, H. A., MacPhee, R. S., & Griffiths, C. T. (2020). Assessing the relative impact of diverse stressors among public safety personnel. *International Journal of Environmental Research and Public Health, 17*(4), 1234. https://doi.org/10.3390/ijerph17041234

Carleton, R. N., Afifi, T. O., Turner, S., ...Asumnson, G .J. G. (2018). Mental disorder symptoms among public safety personnel in Canada. *The Canadian Journal of Psychiatry, 63*(1), 54–64. https://doi.org/10.1177/0706743717723

Carleton, R. N., Korol, S., Mason. J. E., Hozempa, K., Anderson, G. S., Jones. N. A....Bailey, S. (2018). A longitudinal assessment of the road to mental readiness training among municipal police. *Cognitive Behavior Therapy, 47*(6), 508–528. https://doi.org/10.1080/16506073.2018.1475504

Carver, C. S. (1997). You want to measure coping but your protocol's too long: Consider the brief COPE. *International Journal of Behavioral Medicine, 4*(1), 92–100. https://doi.org/10.1207/s15327558ijbm0401_6

Cash, R. E., White-Mills, K., Crowe, R. P., Rivard, M. K., & Panchal, A. R. (2019). Workplace incivility among nationally certified EMS professionals and associations with workforce-reducing factors and organizational culture. *Prehospital Emergency Care, 23*(3), 346–355. https://doi.org/10.1080/10903127.2018.1502383

Chan, J. F., & Andersen, J. P. (2020). Influence of organizational stress on reported depressive symptoms among police. *Occupational Medicine, 70*(7), 496–502. https://doi.org/10.1093/occmed/kqaa141

Cimbura, J. A. (1999). *An exploration of stress in police officers: A study of the predictive value of pre-employment psychological measures in the development of stress reactions in a sample of Ontario Police officers* [Doctoral dissertation, Ontario Institute for Studies in Education of the University of Toronto]. National Library of Canada Acquisitions and Bibliographic Services. www.collectionscanada.ca/obj/s4/f2/dsk1/tape10/PQDD_0004/NQ41062.pdf

Collins, J. (2014). *Assembling the pieces: An implementation guide to the national standard for psychological health and safety in the workplace.* CSA Group and Mental Health Commission of Canada. https://mentalhealth.apec.org/sites/default/files/Assembling_the_Pieces._An_Implementation_Guide_to_the_National_Standard_for_Psychological_Health_and_Safety_in_the_Workplace.pdf

Conigrave, K. M., Hall, W. D., & Saunders, J. B. (1995). The AUDIT questionnaire: Choosing a cut-off score. *Addiction, 90*(10), 1349–1356. https://doi.org/10.1046/j.1360-0443.1995.901013496.x

Connor, K. M., & Davidson, J. R. (2003). Development of a new resilience scale: The Connor-Davidson resilience scale (CD-RISC). *Depression and Anxiety, 18*(2), 76–82. https://doi.org/10.1002/da.10113

Cordner, G. W. (2019). *Police administration* (10th ed.). Routledge

Corneil, W., Beaton, R., Murphy, S., Johnson, C., & Pike, K. (1999). Exposure to traumatic incidents and prevalence of posttraumatic stress symptomatology in urban firefighters in two countries. *Journal of Occupational Health Psychology*, *4*(2), 131–141.https://doi.org/10.1037//1076-8998.4.2.131

Council of Canadian Academies. (2014). *Policing Canada in the 21st century: New policing for new challenges. Ottawa (ON): The expert panel on the future of Canadian policing models.* Council of Canadian Academies. https://cca-reports.ca/reports/policing-canada-in-the-21st-century-new-policing-for-new-challenges

Cronly, J., Duff, A. J., Riekert, K. A., Perry, A., ...Savage, E. (2018). Online versus paper-based screening for depression and anxiety in adults with cystic fibrosis in Ireland: A cross-sectional exploratory study. *BMJ Open*, *8*, e019305. http://dx.doi.org/10.1136/bmjopen-2017-019305

Crowe, R. P., Bower, J. K., Cash, R. E., Panchal, A. R., Rodriguez, S. A., & Olivo-Marston, S. E. (2018). Association of burnout with workforce-reducing factors among EMS professionals. *Prehospital Emergency Care*, *22*(2), 229–236. https://doi.org/10.1080/10903127.2017.1356411

Decker, P. J., & Borgen, F. H. (1993). Dimensions of work appraisal: Stress, strain, coping, job satisfaction, and negative affectivity. *Journal of Counseling Psychology*, *40*(4), 470–478. https://doi.org/10.1037/0022-0167.40.4.470

Dobson, M., & Schnall, P. L. (2009). From stress to distress: The impact of work on mental health. In P. L. Schnall, M. Dobson., & E. Rosskam (Eds.), *Unhealthy work: Causes, consequences, cures* (pp. 113–132). Baywood Publishing Co.

Douglas, S., & Braga, A. A. (2021). Non-traditional research partnerships to aid in the adoption of evidence-based policing: Innovations in bridging the research-practice. In E. L. Piza & B. C. Welsh (Eds.), *The globalization of evidence-based policing* (pp. 178–190). Routledge. http://dx.doi.org/10.4324/9781003027508-16

Doyle, J. N., Campbell, M. A., Gryshchuk, L. (2021). Occupational stress and anger: Mediating effects of resiliency in first responders. *Journal of Police and Criminal Psychology*, *36*(3), 463–472. https://doi.org/10.1007%2Fs11896-021-09429-y

Duxbury, L., Higgins, C., & Halinski, M. (2015). Identifying the antecedents of work-role overload in police organizations. *Criminal Justice and Behavior*, *42*(4), 361–381. https://doi.org/10.1177/0093854814551017

Dyrbye, L. N., Shanafelt, T. D., Johnson, P. O., Johnson, L. A., Satele, D., & West, C. P. (2019). A cross-sectional study exploring the relationship between burnout, absenteeism, and job performance among American nurses. *BMC Nursing*, *18*, 57–57. https://doi.org/10.1186/s12912-019-0382-7

Easterbrook, B., Brown, A., Millman, H., Van Blyderveen, S., Lanius, R., Heber, A., McKinnon, M., & O'Connor, C. (2022). The mental health experience of treatment-seeking military members and public safety personnel: A qualitative investigation of trauma and non-trauma-related concerns. *Health Promotion and Chronic Disease Prevention in Canada: Research, Policy and Practice*, *42*(6), 252–260. https://doi.org/10.24095/hpcdp.42.6.03

Edgelow, M., Scholefield, E., McPherson, M., Legassick, K., & Novecosky, J. (2022). Organizational factors and their impact on mental health in public safety organizations. *International Journal of Environmental Research and Public Health*, *19*, 13993. https://doi.org/10.3390/ijerph192113993

Edgelow, M., Scholefield, E., McPherson, M., Mehta, S., & Ortieb, A. (2022). A review of workplace mental health interventions and their implementation in public safety organizations. *International Archives of Occupational and Environmental Health, 95*, 645–664. https://doi.org/10.1007/s00420-021-01772-1

Endler, N. S., & Parker, J. D. (1994). Assessment of multidimensional coping: Task, emotion, and avoidance strategies. *Psychological Assessment, 6*(1), 50–60. https://psycnet.apa.org/doi/10.1037/1040-3590.6.1.50

Ewing, J. A. (1984). Detecting alcoholism. The CAGE questionnaire. *JAMA, 252*(14), 1905–1907. https://doi.org/10.1001/jama.252.14.1905

Fan, W., & Yan, Z. (2010). Factors affecting response rates of the web survey: A systematic review. *Computers in Human Behavior, 26*(2), 132–139. https://doi.org/10.1016/j.chb.2009.10.015

Folkman, S., & Moskowitz, J. T. (2004). Coping: Pitfalls and promise. *Annual Review of Psychology, 55*(1), 745–774.

Ford, J. D., & Ford, W. F. (2010). Stop blaming resistance to change and start using it. *Organizational Dynamics, 39*(1), 24–36. https://doi.org/10.1016/J.ORGDYN.2009.10.002

Fowler, Jr., F. (2013). *Survey research methods* (5th ed.). Sage.

Fox, J., Desai, M. M., Britten, K., Lucas, G., Luneau, R., & Rosenthal, M. S. (2012). Mental-health conditions, barriers to care, and productivity loss among officers in an urban police department. *Connecticut Medicine, 76*(9), 525–531.

Fox, S., & Spector, P. E. (1999). A model of work frustration-aggression. *Journal of Organizational Behavior, 20*(6), 915–931. www.jstor.org/stable/3100373

Frazer, H., Hansen, C., Searle, A., Lawrence-Wood, E., & Van Hooff, M. (2022). Exploration of potential indicators of burnout, psychological distress and post-traumatic stress disorder, among Australian female first responders. *Psychiatry Research, 316*, 114771–114771. https://doi.org/10.1016/j.psychres.2022.114771

Friborg, O., Hjemdal, O., Rosenvinge, J. H., & Martinussen, M. (2003). A new rating scale for adult resilience: What are the central protective resources behind healthy adjustment? *International Journal of Methods in Psychiatric Research, 12*(2), 65–76. https://psycnet.apa.org/doi/10.1016/j.paid.2006.04.010

Garnefski, N., & Kraaij, V. (2006). Cognitive emotion regulation questionnaire – Development of a short 18-item version (CERQ-short). *Personality and Individual Differences, 41*(6), 1045–1053.

Garnefski, N., Kraaij, V., & Spinhoven, P. (2002). Negative life events, cognitive emotion regulations and emotional problems. *Personality and Individual Differences, 30*(8), 1311–1327. https://doi.org/10.1016/S0191-8869(00)00113-6

Geronazzo-Alman, L., Eisenberg, R., Shen, S., Duarte, C. S., Musa, G. J., Wicks, J., Fan, B., Doan, T., Guffanti, G., Bresnahan, M., & Hoven, C. W. (2017). Cumulative exposure to work-related traumatic events and current post-traumatic stress disorder in New York city's first responders. *Comprehensive Psychiatry, 74*, 134–143. https://doi.org/10.1016/j.comppsych.2016.12.003

Goode, J., & Lumsden, K. (2018). The McDonaldism of police-academic partnerships: Organizational and cultural barriers encountered in moving from research on police to research with police. *Policing and Society, 28*(1), 75–89. https://doi.org/10.1080/10439463.2016.1147039

Government of Canada (2022). *Tri-Council policy statement: Ethical conduct for research involving humans (TSOS2 2022), The Minister of Health and the Minister of Innovation*, Science and Industry, 2022 Catalogue No: RR4-2/2023E-PDF. https://ethics.gc.ca/eng/policy-politique_tcps2-eptc2_2022.html

Griffin, J. D., & Sun, I. Y. (2018). Do work-family conflict and resiliency mediate police stress and burnout: A study of state police officers. *American Journal of Criminal Justice: The Journal of the Southern Criminal Justice Association*, *43*(2), 354–370. https://doi.org/10.1007/s12103-017-9401-y

Grubb, A., Brown, S., & Hall, P. (2015). Personality traits and coping styles in UK police officers. Do negotiators differ from their non-negotiator colleagues? *Psychology, Crime and Law*, *21*(4), 347–374. https://doi.org/10.1080/1068316X.2014.989165

Gryshchuk, L., Campbell, M. A., Brunelle, C., Doyle, J. N., & Nero, J. W. (2022). Profiles of vulnerability to alcohol use and mental health concerns in first responders. *Journal of Police and Criminal Psychology*, *37*(Sept), 952–961. https://doi.org/10.1007/s11896-022-09546-2

Haddock, C. K., Jitnarin, N., Caetano, R., Jahnke, S. A., Hollerbach, B. S., Kaipust, C. M., & Poston, W. S. C. (2022). Norms about alcohol use among US firefighters. *Safety and Health at Work*, *13*(4), 387–393. https://doi.org/10.1016/j.shaw.2022.08.008

Hesse, M., & Thiesen, H. (2007). The CAGE as a measure of hazardous drinking in the homeless. *The American Journal on Addictions*, *16*(6), 475–478. https://doi.org/10.1080/10550490701641223

Hicks, R. E., Bahr, M., & Fujiwara, D. (2010). The Occupational Stress Inventory-Revised: Confirmatory factor analysis of the original inter-correlation data set and model. *Personality and individual differences*, *48*(3), 351–353.

Hirsch, O., Löltgen, K., & Becker, A. (2014). Comparing health survey data from internet- and paper-based convenience samples of lesbian women in Germany. *Sex Health, Sep 4*. https://doi.org/10.1071/sh14041

Hodgkinson, T., Schaefer, L., Harte, N., Pearson, N., Lonergan, N., & Barber, C. (2023). And you know, we're on each other's team: Lessons from an in-depth analysis of researcher-practitioner partnerships in criminal justice research. *International Journal of Comparative and Applied Criminal Justice* [online first]. https://doi.org/10.1080/01924036.2023.2202868

Huey, L., Blaskovits, B., Bennell, C., Jawaid, Kaylal, H., & Walker, T. (2017). To what extent do Canadian police professionals believe that their agencies are "Targeting, Testing, and Tracking" new policing strategies and programs? *Police Practice and Research*, *18*(6), 544–555. https://doi.org/10.1080/15614263.2017.1363968

Ibrahim, H., Ertl, V., Catani, C., Ismail, A. A., & Neuner, F. (2018). The validity of posttraumatic stress disorder checklist for DSM-5 (PCL-5) as screening instrument with Kurdish and Arab displaced populations living in the Kurdistan region of Iraq. *BMC Psychiatry*, *18*(1), 259–259. https://doi.org/10.1186/s12888-018-1839-z

Jacobsson, A., Backteman Erlanson, S., Brulin, C., & Egan Sjolander, A. (2020). Promoting and hindering health and well-being in firefighter discourse. *SAGE Open*, *10*(4). https://doi.org/10.1177/2158244020979170

Jahnke, S. A., Poston, W. S. C., Haddock, C. K., & Murphy, B. (2016). Firefighting and mental health: Experiences of repeated exposure to trauma. *Work*, *53*(4), 737–744. https://doi.org/10.3233/WOR-162255

Jarrett, C. (2021). *Surveys that work: A practical guide for designing and running better surveys*. Rosenfeld Media.

Jetelina, K. K., Molsberry, R. J., Gonzalez, J. R., Beauchamp, A. M., & Hall, T. (2020). Prevalence of mental illness and mental health care use among police officers. *JAMA Network Open*, *3*(10), e2019658. https://doi.org/10.1001/jamanetworkopen.2020.19658

Jha, J. K., & Singh, M. (2019). Exploring the mechanisms of influence of ethical leadership on employee relations. *IIMB Management Review*, *31*(4), 385–395. https://doi.org/10.1016/j.iimb.2019.07.010

Jiang, Q. (2021). Stress response of police officers during Covid-19: A moderated mediation model. *Journal of Investigative Psychology and Offender Profiling*, *18*(2), 116–128. https://doi.org/10.1002/jip.1569

Johnstone, B., Kaiser, A., Injeyan, M. C., Sappleton, K., Chitayat, D., Stephens, D., & Shuman, C. (2016). The relationship between burnout and occupational stress in genetic counselors. *Journal of Genetic Counseling*, *25*(4), 731–741. https://doi.org/10.1007/s10897-016-9968-3

Jones, S., Nagel, C., McSweeney, J., & Curran, G. (2018). Prevalence and correlates of psychiatric symptoms among first responders in a Southern State. *Archives of Psychiatric Nursing*, *32*(6), 828–835. https://doi.org/10.1016/j.apnu.2018.06.007

Kaplan, M., & Kaplan, A. (2018). The relationship between organizational commitment and work performance: A case of industrial enterprises. *Journal of Economic and Social Development*, *5*(1), 46–50. www.jesd-online.com/dokumenti/upload/separated/Vol_5_No_1_Paper5.pdf

Kleim, B., & Westphal, M. (2011). Mental health in first responders: A review and recommendation for prevention and intervention strategies. *Traumatology*, *17*(4), 17–24. https://doi.org/10.1177/1534765611429079

Kuiper, H., van Leeuwen, C. C., Stolwijk-Swüste, J. M., & Post, M. W. (2019). Measuring resilience with the Connor–Davidson Resilience Scale (CD-RISC): Which version to choose? *Spinal Cord*, *57*(5), 360–366. https://doi.org/10.1038/s41393-019-0240-1

Kyron, M. J., Rikkers, W., Bartlett, J., Renehan, E., Hafekost, K., Baigent, M., Cunneen, R., & Lawrence, D. (2022). Mental health and wellbeing of Australian police and emergency services employees. *Archives of Environmental & Occupational Health*, *77*(4), 282–292. https://doi.org/10.1080/19338244.2021.1893631

Lambert, E. G., Qureshi, H., Keena, L. D., Frank, J., & Hogan, N. L. (2019). Exploring the link between work-family conflict and job burnout among Indian police officers. *The Police Journal: Theory, Practice and Principles*, *92*(1), 35–55. https://doi.org/10.1177/0032258X18761285

Lee, S., & Olshfski, D. (2002). Employee commitment and firefighters: It's my job. *Public Administration Review*, *62*(Sept), 108–114. https://doi.org/10.1111/1540-6210.62.s1.19

Lewis-Schroeder, N. F., Kieran, K., Murphy, B. L., Wolff, J. D., Robinson, M. A., & Kaufman, M. L. (2018). Conceptualization, assessment, and treatment of traumatic stress in first responders: A review of critical issues. *Harvard Review of Psychiatry*, *26*(4), 216–227. https://doi.org/10.1097/HRP.0000000000000176

Li, J. C., Cheung, C., Sun, I. Y., Cheung, Y. K., & Zhu, S. (2022). Work–Family conflicts, stress, and turnover intention among Hong Kong police officers amid the

COVID-19 pandemic. *Police Quarterly, 25*, 281–309. https://doi.org/10.1177/10986111211034777

Machisa, M. T., Christofides, N., & Jewkes, R. (2018). Social support factors associated with psychological resilience among women survivors of intimate partner violence in Gauteng, South Africa. *Global Health Action, 11*(sup3), 1491114.

Maguen, S., Metzler, T. J., McCaslin, S. E., Inslicht, S. S., Henn-Haase, C., Neylan, T. C., & Marmar, C. R. (2009). Routine work environment stress and PTSD symptoms in police officers. *The Journal of Nervous and Mental Disease, 197*(10), 754–760. https://doi.org/10.1097/NMD.0b013e3181b975f8

Marmar, C. R., McCaslin, S. E., Metzler, T. J., Best, S. E., Weiss, D. S., Fagan, J., Liberman, A., Pole, N., Otte, C., Yehuda, R., Mohr, D., & Neylan, T. (2006). Predictors of posttraumatic stress in police and other first responders. *Annals of the New York Academy of Sciences, 1071*(1), 1–18. https://doi.org/10.1196/annals.1364.001

Marshall, R., Milligan-Saville, J., Petrie, K., Bryant, R. A., Mitchelle, P. B., & Harvey, S. B. (2021). Mental health screening amongst police officers: Factors associated with under-reporting of symptoms. *BMC Psychiatry, 21*, 135. https://doi.org/10.1186/s12888-021-03125-1

Maslach, C., Jackson, S. E., & Leiter, M. P. (1996). *Maslach Burnout Inventory.* Consulting Psychologists Press.

Masten, A. S. (2001). Ordinary magic: Resilience processes in development. *American Psychologist, 56*(3), 227.

McCall, H. C., Landry, C. A., Ogunade, A., Carleton, R. N., & Hadjistavropoulos, H. D. (2021). Why do public safety personnel seek tailored internet-delivered cognitive behavioural therapy? An observational study of treatment-seekers. *International Journal of Environmental Research and Public Health, 18*(22), 11972. https://doi.org/10.3390/ijerph182211972

McCanlies, E. C., Mnatsakanova, A., Andrew, M. E., Burchfiel, C. M., & Violanti, J. M. (2014). Positive psychological factors are associated with lower PTSD symptoms among police officers: Post Hurricane Katrina. *Stress and Health, 31*(2), 405–415. https://doi.org/10.1002/smi.2615

McCarty, W. P., & Skogan, W. G. (2013). Job-related burnout among civilian and sworn police personnel. *Police Quarterly, 16*(1), 66–84. https://doi.org/10.1177/1098611112457357

McElroy, J. C., Morrow, P. C., & Wardlow, T. R. (1999). A career stage analysis of police officer work commitment. *Journal of Criminal Justice, 27*(6), 507–516. https://doi.org/10.1016/S0047-2352(99)00021-5

Ménard, K. S., & Arter, M. L. (2013). Police officer alcohol use and trauma symptoms: Associations with critical incidents, coping, and social stressors. *International Journal of Stress Management, 20*(1), 37–56. https://doi.org/10.1037/a0031434

Meyer, J. P., Paunonen, S. V., Gellatly, I. R., Goffin, R. D., & Jackson, D. N. (1989). Organizational commitment and job performance: It's the nature of the commitment that counts. *Journal of Applied Psychology, 74*(1), 152–156.

Mezquita, L., Bravo, A. J., Pilatti, A., Ortet, G., Ibáñez, M. I., & Cross-Cultural Addictions Study Team. (2022). Quantifying cannabis problems among college students from English and Spanish speaking countries: Cross-cultural validation of the Cannabis Use Disorders Identification Test-Revised (CUDIT-R).

Addictive Behaviors, 127, 107209–107209. https://doi.org/10.1016/j.addbeh.2021.107209
Milot, M. (2019). The impact of a Canadian external Employee Assistance Program on mental health and workplace functioning: Findings from a prospective quasi-experimental study. *Journal of Workplace Behavioral Health, 34*(3), 167–191.
Mitchell, A. M., Sakraida, T. J., & Kameg, K. (2003). Critical incident stress debriefing: Implications for best practice. *Disaster Management & Response, 1*(2), 45–51. https://doi.org/10.1016/S1540-2487(03)00008-7
Mitchell, J. T., & Everly, G. S. (1996). *Critical incident stress debriefing (CISD): An operations manual for the prevention of traumatic stress among emergency services and disaster workers* (2nd ed.). Chevron Publishing.
More, H., Vito, G., & Walsh, W. (2012). *Organizational behaviour in law enforcement* (3rd ed.). Prentice Hall.
Motreff, Y., Baubet, T., Pirard, P., Rabet, G., Petitclerc, M., Stene, L. E., Vuillermoz, C., Chauvin, P., & Vandentorren, S. (2020). Factors associated with PTSD and partial PTSD among first responders following the Paris terror attacks in November 2015. *Journal of Psychiatric Research, 121*, 143–150. https://doi.org/10.1016/j.jpsychires.2019.11.018
Nadler, D. A. (1981). Managing organizational change: An integrative perspective. *The Journal of Applied Behavioral Sciences, 17*(2), 191–211. https://doi.org/10.1177/002188638101700205
Nero, J., Campbell, M. A., Doyle, J. N., & Meagher, J. (2022). The link between social support and psychological vulnerability among Canadian police officers. *Journal of Police and Criminal Psychology, 37*(June), 377–391. https://doi.org/10.1007/s11896-022-09505-x
Nydegger, R., Nydegger, L., & Basile, F. (2011). Post-traumatic stress disorder and coping among career firefighters. *American Journal of Health Sciences, 2*(1), 11–19. https://doi.org/10.19030/ajhs.v2i1.4365
Oldendick, R. W. (2012). Survey research ethics. In L. Gideon (Ed.), *Handbook for survey methodology for the social sciences* (pp. 23–35). Springer. https://doi.org/10.1007/978-1-4614-3876-2_3
Orosco, C., & Gaub, J. E. (2023). "I am doing my part, you are doing your part": The sworn-civilian divide in policing dispatching. *Policing; An International Journal, 46*(1), 164–178. https://doi.org/10.1108/PIJPSM-07-2022-0090
Osipow, S. H., & Psychological Assessment Resources, Inc. (1998). *Occupational stress inventory, revised edition (OSI-R)*. Psychological Assessment Resources.
Patterson, S., & King, W. R. (2023). Culture and well-being among sworn officers: An empirical examination. *Policing: An International Journal, 46*(1), 179–193. https://doi.org/10.1108/PIJPSM-06-2022-0078
Piao, X., & Managi, S. (2022). Long-term improvement of psychological well-being in the workplace: What and how. *Social Science & Medicine, 298*(114851), https://doi.org/10.1016/j.socscimed.2022.114851
Prati, G., & Pietrantoni, L. (2010). The relation of perceived and received social support to mental health among first responders: A meta-analytic review. *Journal of Community Psychology, 38*(3), 403–417. https://doi.org/10.1002/jcop.20371
Regehr, C., & LeBlanc, V. R. (2017). PTSD, acute stress, performance and decision-making in emergency service workers. *The Journal of the American Academy of Psychiatry and Law, 45*(2), 184–192. PMID: 28619858

Reinert, D. F., & Allen, J. P. (2007). The alcohol use disorders identification test: An update of research findings. *Alcoholism: Clinical and Experimental Research, 31*(2), 185–199. https://doi.org/10.1111/j.1530-0277.2006.00295.x

Rohwer, E., Velasco Garrido, M., Herold, R., Preisser, A. M., Terschüren, C., Harth, V., & Mache, S. (2022). Police officers' work-life balance, job satisfaction and quality of life: Longitudinal effects after changing the shift schedule. *BMJ Open, 12*(9). https://doi.org/10.1136/bmjopen-2022-063302

Rossi, R., Socci, V., Jannini, T. B., Collazzoni, A., Pacitti, F., Di Lorenzo, G., & Rossi, A. (2021). Validation of a brief version of the resilience scale for adults on an Italian non-clinical sample. *Rivista di Psichiatria, 56*(6), 308–313.

Rubim, F., Rubim, L., & Thornton, A. (2020). Creating a culture of wellness. In K. Papazoglou & D. Blumberg (Eds.), *Power. Police officer wellness, ethics, and resilience* (pp. 171–187). Academic Press.

Schillewaert, N., & Meulemeester, P. (2005). Comparing response distributions of offline and online data collection methods. *International Journal of Market Research, 47*(2), 163–178. https://doi.org/10.1177/147078530504700203

Schultz, N. R., Bassett, D. T., Messina, B. G., & Correia, C. J. (2019). Evaluation of the psychometric properties of the Cannabis Use Disorders Identification Test – Revised among college students. *Addictive Behaviors, 95*, 11–15. https://doi.org/10.1016/j.addbeh.2019.02.016

Schutte, N., Toppinen, S., Kalimo, R., & Schaufeli, W. (2000). The factorial validity of the Maslach Burnout Inventory-General Survey (MBI-GS) across occupational groups and nations. *Journal of Occupational and Organizational Psychology, 73*(1), 53–66. https://doi.org/10.1348/096317900166877

Schutte, N. S., Malouff, J. M., & Bhullar, N. (2009). The assessing emotions scale. In J. D. A. Parker, D. H. Saklofske, & C. Stough (Eds.), *Assessing emotional intelligence: Theory, research, and applications* (pp. 119–134). Springer US.

Sherman, L. W. (2013). The rise of evidence-based policing: Targeting, testing, tracking. *Crime & Justice, 42*(1), 377–451. https://doi.org/10.1086/670819

Sherman, L. W. (2019). Targeting, testing, and tracking: The Cambridge Assignment Management system of evidence based police assignment. In R. J. Mitchell & L. Huey (Eds.), *Evidence based policing: An introduction* (15–27). Policy Press.

Skinner, H. A. (1982). The drug abuse screening test. *Addictive Behavior, 7*(4), 363–371. https://doi.org/10.1016/0306-4603(82)90005-3

Skogen, J. C., Overland, S., Knudsen, A. K., & Mykletun, A. (2011). Concurrent validity of the CAGE questionnaire. The Nord-Trøndelag Health Study. *Addictive Behaviors, 36*(4), 302–307. https://doi.org/10.1016/j.addbeh.2010.11.010

Skogstad, M., Skorstad, M., Lie, A., Conradi, H. S., Heir, T., & Weisæth, L. (2013). Work-related post-traumatic stress disorder. *Occupational Medicine (Oxford, England), 63*(3), 175–182. https://doi.org/10.1093/occmed/kqt003

Skowronski, G., & Kerridge, I. (2022). Critical incident stress debriefing. *Bioethical Inquiry, 19*, 533. https://doi.org/10.1007/s11673-022-10204-9

Smith, B. W., Dalen, J., Wiggins, K., Tooley, E., Christopher, P., & Bernard, J. (2008). The brief resilience scale: Assessing the ability to bounce back. *International Journal of Behavioral Medicine, 15*, 194–200. https://doi.org/10.1080/10705500802222972

Smith, T. (2020). Examination of safety climate, affective organizational commitment, and safety behavior outcomes among fire service personnel. *Disaster Medicine and Public Health Preparedness, 14*(5), 559–562. https://doi.org/10.1017/dmp.2019.117

Solberg, M. A., Gridley, M. K., & Peters, R. M. (2022). The factor structure of the Brief Cope: A systematic review. *Western Journal of Nursing Research, 44*(6), 612–637. https://doi.org/10.1177/01939459211012044

Stanley, I. H., Boffa, J. W., Smith, L. J., Tran, J. K., Schmidt, N. B., Joiner, T. E., & Vujanovic, A. A. (2018). Occupational stress and suicidality among firefighters: Examining the buffering role of distress tolerance. *Psychiatry Research, 266*, 90–96. https://doi.org/10.1016/j.psychres.2018.05.058

Stelnicki, A. M., Jamshidi, L., Fletcher, A. J., & Carleton, R. N. (2021). Evaluation of before operational stress: A program to support mental health and proactive psychological protection in public safety personnel. *Frontiers in Psychology, 12*, 511755. https://doi.org/10.3389/fpsyg.2021.511755

Tuckey, M. R., & Scott, J. E. (2014). Group critical incident stress debriefing with emergency services personnel: a randomized controlled trial. *Anxiety, Stress & Coping, 27*(1), 38–54.

Tomás, J. M., de Los Santos, S., Alonso-Andres, A., & Fernández, I. (2016). Validation of the Maslach Burnout Inventory-General Survey on a representative sample of Dominican teachers: Normative data. *The Spanish Journal of Psychology, 19*(E83), 1–9. https://doi.org/10.1017/sjp.2016.91

Vadvilavičius, T., Varnagirytė, E., Jarašiūnaitė-Fedosejeva, & Gustainienė, L. (2023). The effectiveness of mindfulness-based interventions for police officers' stress reduction: A systematic review. *Journal of Police and Criminal Psychology, 38*(March), 223–239. https://doi.org/10.1007/s11896-022-09570-2

van Ballegooijen, W., Riper, H., Cuijpers, P., van Oppen, P., & Smit, J. (2016). Validation of online psychometric instruments for common mental health disorders: A systematic review. *BMC Psychiatry, 16*(45). https://doi.org/10.1186/s12888-016-0735-7

van der Hallen, R., Jongerling, J., & Godor, B. P. (2020). Coping and resilience in adults: A cross-sectional network analysis. *Anxiety, Stress, & Coping, 33*(5), 479–496. https://doi.org/10.1080/10615806.2020.1772969

van Gelderen, B. R., & Bik, L. W. (2016). Affective commitment, work engagement, and service performance among police officers. *Policing: An International Journal, 39*(1), 206–221. http://dx.doi.org/10.1108/PIJPSM-10-2015-0123

Wagner, S. L., White, N., Buys, N., Carey, M. G., Corneil, W., Fyfe, T., Matthews, L. R., Randall, C., Regehr, C., White, M., Alden, L. E., Krutop, E., Fraess-Phillips, A., & Fleischmann, M. H. (2021). Systematic review of mental health symptoms in firefighters exposed to routine duty-related critical incidents. *Traumatology, 27*(3), 285–302.20201130. https://doi.org/10.1037/trm0000275

Weathers, F. W., Litz, B. T., Keane, T. M., Palmieri, P. A., Marx, B. P., & Schnurr, P. P. (2013). *The PTSD checklist for DSM-5 (PCL-5)*. National Center for PTSD.

Weziak-Bialowolska, D., Bialowolski, P., Leon, C., Koosed, T., & McNeely, E. (2020). Psychological climate for caring and work outcomes: A virtuous cycle. *International Journal of Environmental Research and Public Health, 17*, 7035. https://doi.org/10.3390/ijerph17197035

Williams, N. (2014). The CAGE questionnaire. *Occupational Medicine, 64*(6), 473–474. https://doi.org/10.1093/occmed/kqu058

Willink, J. (2020). *Leadership strategy and tactics*. St. Martin's Publishing Group.

Windle, G., Bennett, K. M., & Noyes, J. (2011). A methodological review of resilience measurement scales. *Health and Quality of Life Outcomes*, *9*(1), 1–18. https://doi.org/10.1186/1477-7525-9-8

Wortmann, J. H., Jordan, A. H., Weathers, F. W., Resick, P. A., Dondanville, K. A., Hall-Clark, B., Foa, E. B., Young-McCaughan, S., Yarvis, J. S., Hembree, E. A., Mintz, J., Peterson, A. L., & Litz, B. T. (2016). Psychometric analysis of the PTSD checklist-5 (PCL-5) among treatment-seeking military service members. *Psychological Assessment*, *28*(11), 1392–1403. https://doi.org/10.1037/pas0000260

Wright, T. A., & Cropanzano, R. (2000). Psychological well-being and job satisfaction as predictors of job performance. *Journal of Occupational Health Psychology*, *5*(1), 84–94.

Young, A. T., Hennington, C., & Eggleston, D. (2018). US SWAT operator experience, personality, cognitive-emotion regulation and decision-making style. *Policing: An International Journal*, *41*(2), 247–261. https://doi.org/10.1108/PIJPSM-10-2016-0156

13

THE IMPACT OF ORGANIZATIONAL CULTURE ON THE MENTAL WELL-BEING OF PUBLIC SAFETY COMMUNICATORS

Nadine Leduc, Stephen Czarnuch, and Rosemary Ricciardelli

Introduction

The term "first responder" typically invokes images of firefighters, paramedics, and police officers, but not necessarily those of public safety communicators (communicators, e.g., 9-1-1, police, fire, and ambulance call-takers and dispatchers) who field the calls for help from the public and other agencies. As public safety personnel (PSP), communicators (referring here to dispatch, call-takers, and trainers) are the first link in the emergency response chain. Despite regular exposure to duty-related psychological trauma and potentially psychologically traumatic events (PPTE), communicators are one of the most understudied groups of PSP (Baseman et al., 2018; Carleton et al., 2018; Carleton et al., 2019; Golding et al., 2017, 2017; Lilly & Allen, 2015; Oliphant, 2016; Steinkopf et al., 2018).

The limited research on public safety communicators has revealed that the prevalence of posttraumatic stress disorder (PTSD) can be higher among communicators than among other PSP (Lilly & Allen, 2015; Pierce & Lilly, 2012; Ramey et al., 2017; Steinkopf et al., 2018). In addition, Carleton et al. (2018) found that Canadian communicators reported a similar or higher prevalence of mental health disorders compared to other PSP, including major depressive disorder, generalized anxiety disorder, social anxiety disorder, panic disorder, alcohol use disorder, and mood disorders. Many factors have been linked to mental health and well-being in PSP, captured by the two themes of (1) Organizational/operational factors (e.g., work environment), and (2) Interactions with others (e.g., management, members of the community, and peers) (Golding et al., 2017).

DOI: 10.4324/9781003424253-18

Carleton et al. (2018), in the largest study of Canadian PSP inclusive of communicators to date, identified the need for further research into the impacts of organizational factors on PSP well-being. In this chapter, we extend the work of Carleton et al. (2018) by exploring how organizational culture influences the ability of employees in emergency communications centres, also called public safety answering points (PSAPs), to perform their occupational duties. We collected data from communicators working in primary and secondary PSAPs. Primary PSAPs receive 9-1-1 calls and either dispatch emergency responders or transfer the call to another agency at a secondary PSAP for dispatch (Canadian Radio-television and Telecommunications Commission, 2020).

Literature Review

Mental Health in the Workplace

The CSA Group (2022), which develops standards designed to enhance public safety and health, maintains that psychologically healthy environments foster employee engagement, increase productivity, are more innovative, and are better positioned to recruit and retain talent. The CSA Group (2022) further contends that psychologically unhealthy workplaces enhance the risks of conflict, high turnover, disability, absenteeism, and poor morale. In 2015, an estimated 500,000 Canadians missed work for mental health reasons weekly, and approximately 30% of all short- and long-term disability claims in Canada can be attributed to mental health challenges (Mental Health Commission of Canada, 2015).

The Centre for Addiction and Mental Health (2020) claims that prevailing stigma in the workplace may inhibit workers from sharing their mental health challenges, thus creating a barrier to receiving support. The inability to disclose is profoundly impactful, as expressed by workers who maintain that dealing with the stigma is oftentimes worse than the disorder itself (Szeto et al., 2019). Workers fear the negative consequences of disclosing mental health challenges, that is, to be perceived as "unreliable, unproductive, and untrustworthy" (Pietrus, 2013, p. 5). Employees who do disclose may be discriminated against, potentially resulting in unemployment, underemployment, or alienation in the workplace (Szeto et al., 2019).

Communicator Mental Health

In the most comprehensive review of communicator mental health to date, Golding et al. (2017) examined the psychological health of emergency communicators working in police, fire, and ambulance communications centres in Europe, Australia, and the United States. Seven qualitative studies (from n = 9 to n = 27) and nine quantitative studies (n = 8 to n = 358) revealed two dominant themes influencing psychological well-being: organizational/operational factors and interactions with others. According to Golding et al. (2017), for communicators, organizational and operational factors are related to the work environment (e.g., feeling undervalued by one's organization, increased exposure to traumatic and abusive calls, and minimal control over individual workload). Communicators expressed regularly feeling invisible and not recognized within their organization and tended to feel unappreciated and treated dismissively or with disrespect (Baseman et al., 2018; Coxon et al., 2016; Golding et al., 2017; Smith et al., 2019; Soria, 2020; Steinkopf et al., 2018). Communicators further reported feeling excluded from awards ceremonies or critical incident debriefs, despite similar or worse negative outcomes to those of "traditional" first responders (i.e., police, firefighters, and paramedics) (Adams et al., 2015; Lilly & Allen, 2015; Pierce & Lilly, 2012; Ramey et al., 2017; Steinkopf et al., 2018). Further studies have identified additional organizational stressors experienced by communicators, including a lack of effective training, rigid policies, outdated mental health culture, poor relationships with colleagues and responders, and poor leadership (Coxon et al., 2016; Ramey et al., 2017; Smith et al., 2019; Steinkopf et al., 2018).

Communicators describe being regularly scrutinized for adherence to protocols (Koopmans et al., 2017), receiving feedback only when mistakes are made (Adams et al., 2015; Deselms, 2016) – despite reporting receiving inadequate training, or no training at all (Adams et al., 2015; Coxon et al., 2016; Golding et al., 2017; Smith et al., 2019; Steinkopf et al., 2018). Inadequate training can increase a communicator's anxiety and stress levels, resulting in feelings of insecurity (Bång et al., 2002; Coxon et al., 2016).

Golding et al. (2017) found that interactions with others influenced communicator's psychological well-being, such as management (e.g., through a lack of support, empathy, or understanding), members of the community they serve (e.g., feeling a communicator's role is invisible and emotionally demanding), and peers, friends, and family (e.g., seeking informal support for job-related issues). Communicators claim inappropriate behaviours from responders, allied agencies, and PSAP colleagues are frequently unaddressed (Golding et al., 2017). Poor supervision, coupled with the perceived lack of support by superiors, contributes to job-related stress, which is amplified by a dearth of positive feedback (Adams et al., 2015; Golding et al., 2017; McCarty & Skogan, 2013; Ramey et al., 2017; Soria, 2020). Golding et al. (2017) posit that the scarcity of organizational support from the upper echelons can, in part, be attributed to managers being too removed from the role, the lack of recognition of communicators' needs, or a lack of appreciation of their hard work, excessive workloads, paucity of breaks, frequent overtime, downstaffing, and generally poor treatment from responders.

Unquestionably, achieving a supportive culture is essential, particularly as several PSP, including communicators, report experiences with toxic workplace cultures and bullying, harassment, and conflict among colleagues, responders, and supervisors (Adams et al., 2015; Baseman et al., 2018; Ramey et al., 2017; Smith et al., 2019). Perhaps most poignant for communicators is the discourse surrounding inadequate briefings after calls, inappropriate training for mental health calls, the demands of high-pressure environments without meaningful downtime, and little recognition of routine exposure to duty-related secondary trauma (Golding et al., 2017; Ramey et al., 2017; Smith et al., 2019). Communicators, who are exposed to secondary trauma as a function of their work, are shown to have higher rates of PTSD than police officers (Patel et al., 2018; Pierce & Lilly, 2012; Ramey et al., 2017), firefighters, and the general population (Lilly & Allen, 2015). Given that PTSD can impair judgement, in an environment where seconds count, poor decisions can cause risks to public health and safety (Lilly & Allen, 2015; Pierce & Lilly, 2012).

Despite the negative aspects of emergency communications, an overwhelming number of communicators report enjoying performing an altruistic role (Golding et al., 2017) and taking pride in their work (Coxon et al., 2016). It is a common sentiment among communicators to view their work as meaningful and significant, finding purpose in their efforts to give back to their communities (Davis, 2023).

Theoretical Framework

Organizational culture and its impacts on the productivity, commitment, and well-being of its members are well-documented (Schein, 2004), yet they are not well-understood in the context of communicators. Schein (2004) defines organizational culture as "a set of structures, routines, rules, and norms that guide and constrain behavior" and is formed through member interactions and shared experiences, as well as is shaped by the behaviours of its leaders (p. 1). Schein (2004) divides organizational culture into three levels, or degrees, to which outsiders observe cultural phenomena: (1) *artefacts*, referring to tangible, identifiable elements seen by the public (e.g., uniforms); (2) *espoused beliefs and values*, describing the behavioural norms, the rules of behaviour, or how a member represents the organization (what ought to be versus what is); and (3) *basic underlying assumptions*, which are unseen by the public but are salient, unconscious behaviours or tacit assumptions that are taken for granted by members and are difficult to articulate. MacQueen (2020) applies a more sociological lens to define organizational culture and describes it as "a symbol rich system by which people in an organization construct and apply meaning about their work lives" (p. 51). In essence, how issues are discussed in the workplace communicates meaning and sets the climate.

This chapter is guided by the framing of organizational culture as having a direct impact on its members, both explicitly and implicitly, or tacitly. Explicit culture is expressed in customs and traditions (e.g., swearing-in ceremonies), rituals (e.g., annual fundraiser), celebrations (e.g., promotions), values (e.g., mission statement), structures (e.g., how the organization is organized, including physical space), and processes (e.g., policies) (Schein, 2004). Implicit or tacit culture, according to Schein (2004), is expressed in group norms and guides behaviour (e.g., they evolve in groups working together); they are the "phenomena that are below the surface" (p. 8), unwritten "rules of the game" (p. 13), and "the way we do things around here" (p. 13). The implicit or tacit culture encapsulates the underlying, implied assumptions and beliefs held within the organization, which are impactful despite being invisible and primarily unconscious (Schein, 2004). Schein (2004) contends that culture exists throughout an organization, invariably creating subcultures with different shared experiences, languages, skill sets, and interpretations of events and policies. Schein (2004) further asserts that conflicting cultural assumptions can occur among subgroups, frequently leading to conflicts, as evidenced in numerous organizations in this study.

According to Schein (2004), subcultures can arise within organizations for several reasons, including functional/occupational differentiation, geographic differentiation, and differentiation by hierarchal level. Functional/Occupational differentiation arises as organizations recruit members to fulfil specific functions, resulting in the creation of units that share cultural assumptions rooted in their education, duties, and responsibilities. Consequently, fundamental differences in roles culminate in divergent occupational identities, often resulting in conflicting priorities and challenges with cultural integration. Geographical differentiation serves to form subcultures based on physical location. Geographic separation can threaten the useful exchange of information among subcultures if managers adopt assumptions held by their subunit. Although assumptions about other subgroups are typically incorrect, they become embedded into the unit culture as the group evolves, potentially fracturing their connection to other units and even the organization. Finally, subcultures manifest through differentiation at the hierarchical level. In addition to unit subcultures, additional subcultures are formed at these hierarchal levels, typically based on rank or status. Commonly, higher-ranking members operate in isolation and have limited interactions with lower-ranking members. Such isolation can also result in assumptions being made about what the lower levels need.

Once subcultural interpretations, practices, and narratives are established, they are passed along to new employees, ensuring the culture's survival through new shared experiences of the group. Schein (2004) argues that within this context, culture is a mechanism of social control by which members are manipulated into "perceiving, thinking and feeling in certain ways"

(p. 20). The command-and-control model typically adopted by emergency service organizations specifically contributes to division among subgroups by assuming that conflict is inherent and expected (Schein, 2004). In the case of communicators, the clash in subcultures can result in conflict and further divide already fractured working relationships, resulting in countercultures. The physical separation, differing tasks and responsibilities, as well as varying products delivered by each unit – despite being members of the same organization – intensifies the division between the subcultures.

Method

The current project is in partnership with the Association of Public-Safety Communications Officials (APCO) Canada.[1] Our overall objectives were to examine self-reported communicator mental health and the impact of organizational culture on communicator well-being and to characterize workplace stressors and treatment-seeking behaviours in communications centres through a cross-sectional survey.

Survey

The survey was intended to capture a snapshot of the mental health screenings and organizational culture of a statistically representative sample of Canadian communicators. The research question analysed here asked participants to "describe the organizational culture in your communications centre."

The cross-sectional survey was a self-administered online questionnaire in which potential respondents followed an anonymous Qualtrics link to access it. In creating the survey, we followed established guidelines for web surveys (e.g., informed consent and confidentiality) (Ashbaugh et al., 2010). Upon initiating the questionnaire, participants were guided to an informed consent page, where we provided a comprehensive explanation of the study's purpose, outlined the potential risks and benefits of participation, and offered relevant resources, including an online directory for locating Canadian therapists[2] and crisis resources for suicide prevention.[3] In addition, we presented an overview of the processes, an estimated survey completion timeline, a detailed confidentiality agreement, instructions on study withdrawal, contact information, and directions on accessing the study results. Upon providing electronic consent, participants were issued a unique computer-generated random identifier. The participants were required to record their own identifier, thus enabling them to access the questionnaire repeatedly. This feature was implemented to address the demanding schedules of communicators, encourage their participation, and facilitate the completion of the questionnaire over several sessions.

Prior to launch, the questionnaire items (see Table 13.1) were piloted with members of the Atlantic Canada Public Safety Research and Innovation

TABLE 13.1 Organizational culture questionnaire questions

Item	*Item phrasing*
1	Please describe the organizational culture in your communications centre.
2	How does the organizational culture impact your ability to do your job?
3	What are three things you like about the organizational culture in your communications centre?
4	What are three things you dislike about the organizational culture in your communications centre?

Lab (n = 16), the APCO Canada executive board members (n = 5), and the APCO Canada mental health sub-committee (n = 7) to ensure the collection of accurate and appropriate data. Following this, the survey was made available for participation in both French and English from 4 November 2020 to 30 April 2021. It included 19 sections and 179 questions; depending on specific responses to screening questions, participants could skip entire sections. While most scales included both closed and open-ended questions, several were measured using Likert scales or offered multi-option responses. The section related to organizational culture was the only one to solicit only open-ended responses.

Similar to the work of Carleton et al. (2018), demographic information was collected (see Table 13.2), including workplace details (e.g., place of work, workplace staffing questions, and employer questions), sex, gender, education, ethnicity, religion, language, marital status, income, and children. No personally identifiable information (e.g., name and phone number) was collected to protect the anonymity and confidentiality of participants.

In total, 696 survey responses were received (27 in French and 669 in English), distributed among police, fire, and paramedic services across Canada. Of these responses, 329 (47.2%) participants answered, "Describe the organizational culture in your communications centre," representing the final sample. The questionnaire generally took 30–90 minutes to complete.

Participants

Most participants were women (74.1%), 20.1% were men, less than 1% self-identified as transgender, other, or "rather not say," while 4.6% did not reply. See Table 13.3 for additional participant demographic and occupational characteristics.

Recruitment

Participation was initially solicited through recruitment emails sent by APCO Canada to their membership, directing interested persons to

TABLE 13.2 Demographic questions

Item	*Item phrasing*
1	What province do you work in?
2	What communications centre do you work for?
3	What geographic area does your public safety communications centre cover?
4	What services do you call take and/or dispatch for (check all that apply)?
5	How many communicators work in your centre (total)?
6	Please select the primary role that best describe your current position.
7	How long have you been in your primary role?
8	Please select any additional role(s) that best describes your current position:
9	What is your salary?
10	Who is your employer?
11	Why did you choose a job in public safety communications?
12	If you have ever qualified as another category of First Responder, Public Safety Personnel, or Military, please indicate the organization (check all that apply).
13	Please indicate your current employment status.
14	What year were you born?
15	At what age did you begin working in public safety communications?
16	Please indicate your biological sex.
17	Please indicate your gender.
18	Please indicate your sexual orientation.
19	Please indicate the highest level of education you have completed.
20	By your own definition, what is your ethnicity?
21	What language did you first learn at home in your childhood?
22	Please indicate your current marital status.
23	Please indicate your total household income.
24	Do you have any children (biological, adopted, step)?
25	Please indicate how many children you have.
26	Please describe your children. – Sex.
27	Please describe your children. – Lives at home.
28	Please describe your children. – Age.

the online questionnaire, and encouraging participants to share the questionnaire link with colleagues within their agency or allied agencies. To be included in the study, participants were required to be employed as fire, police, or ambulance service emergency communicators, or be employed as emergency call-takers for OnStar. Additional recruitment strategies included emails to PSAPs and communications oversight organizations and unions (e.g., NL911; Government of Nova Scotia's Emergency Management Office; E-Comm 911, CUPE 104), social media, and communications newsletters, and snowball sampling (i.e., participants informing other potential participants).

TABLE 13.3 Participant demographics and occupational characteristics

Gender	Female	244	74.1%
	Male	66	20.1%
	Other	3	1.0%
	No response	15	4.5%
Sexuality	Heterosexual	262	79.6%
	Gay	19	5.7%
	Bisexual	15	4.5%
	Rather not say	14	4.3%
	Other	3	1.0%
	No response	16	4.9%
Education	College diploma	105	31.9%
	Partially completed college	72	21.9%
	University degree	70	21.4%
	High school diploma	38	11.6%
	Post-graduate education	14	4.2%
	Other	2	0.7%
Occupation	Dispatchers	115	35.0%
	Call-takers	69	21.1%
	Other	66	20.1%
	Supervisors	42	12.9%
	No response	11	3.4%
	Trainers	11	3.3%
	Managers	6	1.7%
	Quality assurance	4	1.3%
	Directors	3	0.9%
	Technical	0	0.1%
Time in field	>10 years	112	34.1%
	1–9 years	190	57.9%
	<1 year	26	8.0%
Work schedule	Full-time	258	78.3%
	Part-time	24	7.2%
	Casual	8	2.4%
	Disability	8	2.3%
	Leave/Students/Volunteers	3	1.0%
	No response	15	4.5%
	Other	11	3.4%
Employer	Municipality	150	45.7%
	Province/territory	54	16.5%
	Federal	46	13.9%
	Private/commercial	27	8.3%
	Health authority/region	18	5.5%
	No response	14	4.2%
	Other	19	5.9%

Analysis

To conduct a content analysis, the raw online survey data from Qualtrics were exported into an Excel file and then imported into NVivo. NVivo software aided in identifying and tracking emergent themes, as well as coding, as themes were broken into parent, child, and grandchild nodes. An emergent theme was constituted when multiple respondents voiced similar experiences, interpretations, and needs. For example, chronic downstaffing, increased responsibilities, and favouritism were child nodes in the parent node referencing morale and staffing. Once the themes were identified (e.g., management and supervision, division and exclusion, and gender), they informed the theoretical approach. We employed constructivist semi-grounded theory to analyse the themes (see Ricciardelli, 2011; Ricciardelli et al., 2010). Constructivist grounded theory provides a structured analytic framework that allows for flexibility and the emergence of unexpected themes (Charmaz, 2006). To ensure inter-rater reliability, the research team thoroughly reviewed all codes assigned to respondents, engaging in discussions to resolve discrepancies and reach a consensus on the coding. Agreement was reached on the taxonomies of codes for both the parent and child nodes. We did not correct participants' grammar or spelling errors.

Results

A thematic analysis revealed six parent themes: management and supervision, perceptions of organization, morale and staffing, division and exclusion, colleagues, and gender. Similar to Golding et al. (2017), our findings included references to organizational/operational and interactions with others. Furthermore, several participants described their workplace culture as toxic, with inadequate support from both supervisors and organizations. Additionally, the dialogue surrounding discomfort in disclosing mental health struggles to superiors is consistent with previous assessments of PSP experiences (see Oliphant, 2016).

Conversely, positive feedback related to supportive colleagues, management, and organizations emerged. References to satisfactory mental health supports and positive feelings about being part of a team and helping the public were common.

Perceptions of Organization

When asked about their organizational culture, communicators (n = 132, 40.1%) provided equally favourable perceptions (n = 66) and negative descriptors in their responses (n = 66). The former, which we refer to as positive responses (e.g., helpful, encouraging), pointed to a supportive environment and, thus, a positive organizational culture.

Positive Perceptions

A majority of our participants (n = 66, 20.1%) indicated working within organizations that have deliberately made changes to promote the training and skills development of their members and have allocated resources to realize the priorities outlined in strategic planning towards a healthier workplace. While strategic priorities differ by group, successful organizations prioritize efforts to establish a connection between their objectives, such as improved employee retention, and their vision and mission statements. In this regard, Participant 19 wrote, "In the last 6 or 7 years the culture has changed to focus on development, training, hiring practices for additional staff." Participant 44 wrote, "Luckily we have a strong Manager who engages in forward-thinking, staff support, and transparency."

Participants were keenly aware of the support they received from colleagues and management. Participant 36 noted that their organization "values inclusivity and supporting each-other." Inclusivity and support are fundamental to ensure public safety communicators are able to navigate responding to oftentimes distressing calls while administering self-care. Similarly, Participant 88 stated, "Our communications centre is very team orientated and positive. Everyone is willing to help each other out – especially open to helping new hires like me feel comfortable and confident in my new role." The magnitude of providing misinformation to callers can be dire. Thus, to develop their skills, new hires must be encouraged to ask questions and be granted the leeway to make mistakes. Furthermore, Participant 113 stated, "Our Communications Supervisor/Manager does a good job of telling us, every chance she gets, about how dedicated, valued, talented and 'fabulous' we are. She constantly reiterates how we are a team and must always try to work together." Team cohesion thus appears necessary to maintain stable daily operations in a fluid environment.

Lastly, organizations with a culture that aligns with their espoused values put their objectives into action by supporting management practices and processes that reflect principles commonly rooted in corporate value statements. For instance, Participant 324 described their communications centre as "... one of teamwork and professionalism, accountability."

Negative Perceptions

Respondents (n = 66, 20.1%) who characterized the culture in their workplaces as negative described what can be considered unhealthy work environments (e.g., low morale, constant stressors, negativity, high turnover, bullying). Participant 260 defined their communications centre as "chaotic and unorganized, especially during this pandemic." Communications centres were similarly depicted as "hectic and loud" (Participant 149) and "dysfunctional and ineffective" (Participant 138). Participant 145 recalled feeling "belittled" by management, and Participant 198 said their colleagues "are afraid to follow chain of command."

Communicators operating in detrimental environments expressed a lack of safety in voicing their concerns or asking questions, thus feeling unsupported and compromised in their well-being. These less favourable work environments were described as offering "no support and quick to punish" (Participant 214). Others explained that, in their workplace, they were to "do as your [sic] told and do not ask questions, no voice" (Participant 172). Others explained that, at their work, "people are treated more as means to an end, instead of considering individuals" (Participant 254), and "unappreciated" (Participant 234).

Newer employees described enduring more hardships in comparison to those with occupational tenure or who feel accepted within their workspace. Participant 266 remarked that the personnel in their centre are "bullies to younger staff." Participant 255 noted, "We eat our young and piss on our sick." Even seasoned communicators expressed finding it difficult to concentrate in damaging environments and felt their work performance was negatively impacted by increased stress levels. The cyclical effect of a negative atmosphere is that it can contribute to an increased workload when employees are absent, thereby sustaining the harmful effects of a detrimental work environment.

The prevailing theme among the 66 negative responses was the perception of a toxic work environment. Respondents who reported working in toxic atmospheres (n = 26, 7.9%) defined them as "backstabbing, poisonous, harsh" (Participant 144) and "cliquey and juvenile" (Participant 130).

Management and Supervision

Overall, the category of management and supervision yielded the most responses (n = 189, 57.4%), further represented within eight subthemes: supportive leadership, leadership disconnect from the front-line reality, lack of recognition by leadership, unsupportive organizations, ambiguous leadership, deficient inter-organizational communication, injurious leadership, and management's support of mental health. Of the eight subthemes, only one uncovered exclusively positive remarks concerning the leadership in their organization. Leadership positions within emergency services organizations are generally occupied by uniformed members, predominantly men,[4] who have been promoted through their rank structures. Conversely, communicators are largely civilian, or non-uniformed, members, exposing them to different experiences.

Supportive Leadership

Differing occupational identities were not barriers for organizations with supportive leaders, as they genuinely appreciate the hard work and dedication of the communications staff and endeavour to recognize their contributions. Participant 36 stated, "Management always want [sic] Staff support and recognition to be at the forefront." Respondents working in respectful environments, who felt supported personally as well as professionally, shared positive sentiments regarding senior leaders. While respondents shared positive comments (n = 24, 7.3%) about the senior leadership in their organizations, most spoke specifically about their supervisors. Participant 114 relayed that their "supervisor does a good job of trying to boost morale," and Participant 278 shared that their "supervisors are very active and aware and supportive. Management does not care about employee's well-being." Similarly, Participant 133 stated that "the supervisor does everything in her power to mitigate and make the director understand." Schein (2004) posits that front-line supervisors, or the operator subculture, are more attuned to human nature, whereas the executive subculture has a greater focus on economic sustainability. Participant 307 supported Schein's assertion that executives have different priorities, claiming the workers in their centre must "follow the rules even if they do not make sense, look good in Stats for the Province."

Leadership Disconnects from the Front-Line Reality

Participants strongly felt the leaders in their organizations failed to adequately understand the communicators' roles (n = 32, 9.7%) and made managerial decisions based on incorrect assumptions. Participants contended that managers have "no clue what we do" (Participant 13); therefore, they make unreasonable and illogical decisions, constrained by their limited perception of alternatives. Not surprisingly, decisions are commonly "shortsighted and misguided because they don't understand" (Participant 94). Moreover, Participant 82 shared that operational pressures commonly compel managers to "sign off people who are not ready, and/or not the right job for them," increasing the workload of other members. Communicators who endeavoured to address central issues with management felt disregarded, describing their experiences as futile or "screaming into the wind" (Participant 368).

Respondents (n = 33, 10%) suggested that because the leaders in their organizations had only a tangential understanding of their daily lives, management was rendered ineffective. Negative judgements of organizations developed as respondents described managers as unable, or unwilling, to resolve chronic issues. Long-standing staffing issues, in addition to the insufficient allocation of resources required to support communicators, were constant sources of irritation and suggestive of disorganized organizations. The absence of solution-based actions needed to address systemic issues was attributed to "weak supervision and little leadership" (Participant 318). Ineffective leaders, or those who operate with blinders on and routinely avoid dealing with problems, were depicted as having a "don't rock the boat" attitude (Participant 196).

Lack of Recognition by Leadership

Notions of inequality intensified as leaders were viewed to fail to produce meaningful changes to ameliorate conditions for communicators, leaving communicators with the perception that they are less valued than uniformed PSP (n = 7, 2.1%). Notwithstanding the modest number of comments, participants expressed frustration that their contributions were deemed less significant than those of other PSP, such that communicators were left to "feel less than and subservient" to uniformed responders (Participant 268). Likewise, commitment and loyalty to an organization seemed to diminish when members discerned that they were not important enough or were "considered last by organization" (Participant 151).

Unsupportive Organizations

Communicators' beliefs that their mores and values differ from, or are counter to, those of the dominant group, strengthen collective perceptions of unsupportive organizations (n = 17, 5.2%). Management's inadequate support was in part attributed to their indifference towards communicators' daily struggles or career goals. Communicators shared commentaries, such as "Managers don't have your back" (Participant 182), it "does not feel like management is on our side" (Participant 14), and, when given the opportunity, management will "throw us under the bus" (Participant 318). Respondents, as evidenced in the participants' words, characterized their managers and supervisors as quick to discipline, culminating in a paucity of positive feedback. Communicators also inferred that their organizations are equally deficient, as they do not allocate sufficient resources necessary for an arduous job. Participant 33 supported this claim and stated, "there is not a lot of talk about peer support within our centre – CISM [Critical Incident Stress Management] is often thought of for medics and fire immediately but not often offered to comms."

Ambiguous Leadership

In addition to feeling unsupported, communicators acknowledged feeling confused about unclear chains of command but also with inconsistent management decisions resulting from the poorly delineated authority structures (n = 20, 6.1%). An example of a statement came from a call-taker with an ambulance service, who wrote: "Way too many people have roles in higher positions, confusing who is in charge of what and who to go to with which issue" (Participant 13). Seemingly, organizations with top-heavy bureaucracies, when coupled with a high turnover of leaders, can result in miscommunications. Exacerbating matters, supervisors appeared to interpret and subsequently implement, policies differently on their platoons or shifts, creating further confusion: "Nothing is the same across platoons. They try to stay organized but they don't do a good job of communicating with staff and being consistent" (Participant 203).

Deficient Inter-Organizational Communication

Participant 273 characterized the management in their centre as "terrible," with a "lack of communication and people skills." Managers who operate with a "do as I say, not as I do mentality" (Participant 267) were regarded as unsympathetic and disengaged. Due to their physical separation from operations, in addition to most not having worked as communicators, leaders may be unacquainted with the intricacies of communications centres, rendering them "out of touch with the needs of the membership" (Participant 267).

Injurious Leadership

Communicators chronicled working in emotionally abusive environments tolerant of bullying, thereby "contributing to the fear based submissive culture" (Participant 366). Thus, we identified injurious leaders as subtheme number seven (n = 12, 3.6%). The presence of social control was apparent as participants demonstrated reluctance in reporting issues or asking questions, instead choosing to "just bottle up, stay upset and wont deal with the issue" (Participant 198). Participants working in centres with predominantly male leaders experienced gender bias, as described by Participant 305, who states, "People have gotten away with rampant sexual harassment because they are higher up." This suggests that a gap still exists between professed organizational values and actual behaviour norms. Later in this chapter, we explore gendered experiences of workplace cultures.

Management's Support for Mental Health

To this end, the final, and arguably most significant subtheme in the Management and Supervision section pertains to the insufficient recognition of communicator mental health issues (n = 19, 5.8%). "I do find there to still be a stigma (which I have witnessed) against colleagues that suffer from chronic/semi-chronic mental health, specifically relating to time off work" (Participant 44). Leaders were commonly portrayed as uncaring and unsupportive of communicators with operational stress injuries. Communicators disclosed that stigma surrounding mental health issues, be it structural or perceived, is still deeply rooted in the emergency services culture and that more robust PTSD training is needed. For instance, a call-taker for emergency services wrote: "I feel there has been some progress made in regards to seeking help for mental health issues however there is room for improvement so that people feel more comfortable talking about it" (Participant 408).

Conversely, a handful of respondents felt their organization had excellent peer support teams, with one participant reporting that their organization had implemented policies to remove the stigma of calling in sick. Claims that organizations are supportive of mental health initiatives were also interpreted as disingenuous by some participants, who described toxic environments that perpetuate malicious discourse about colleagues with mental health needs. To exemplify, Participant 223 believed that executives are simply paying "lip service" to mental health needs, and Participant 386 wrote that they are "Running down people who need to take time off." When language of this nature is collectively adopted and passed on to new members, it creates an atmosphere that is not conducive to mental health safety (Schein, 2004).

Morale and Staffing

Communicators shared personal sentiments regarding morale and inadequate staffing resources in their centres (n = 54, 16.4%). Five subthemes were identified: favouritism; understaffing; increased levels of responsibilities; diminished morale; and ways forward, the latter being the only positive theme.

Favouritism

Favouritism, the most prevalent theme (n = 21, 6.4%), identified three distinct beneficiaries of preferential treatment: uniformed responders, full-time employees, and chosen communicators. Schein (2004) contends that command-and-control models of operation inherently divide subcultures, creating animosity and conflict among groups, particularly if one appears less supported or valued. Accordingly, communicators expressed resentment that their roles were minimized, and their contributions deemed too insignificant to warrant the same recognition and appreciation bestowed upon responders.

The second subtheme, favouritism related to employment status, was expressed by Participant 106 as "You're in or out. Being part time, you're out." It is reasonable to anticipate a decline in motivation and performance from communicators coping with the stressors of precarious employment while managing the possibility of termination. While only 7% of respondents identified as part-time employees, fiscally constrained centres may be more apt to rely on their part-time cadre to fill operational gaps. Furthermore, not all centres employ part-time members, reducing the ratio of organizations contributing to this inequality in tenure.

Preferential treatment from management arose as the third, and final, subtheme. Statements show that team cohesion eroded when communicators challenged the integrity of decisions or questioned purported equal access to opportunities. Tensions increased when communicators believed that rewards and promotions were based on favouritism, not performance. Participant 305 shared their impression of discrimination in the workplace, stating, "nothing is fair because you are targeted based on how much you are liked." Similarly, Participant 145 expressed working in a "poisoned work environment brought on by management giving jobs to friends," naturally "putting staff against each other." Discord among colleagues was reported as disrupting the harmony needed for the coordination and management of resources, potentially affecting operations, and placing the health and safety of the responders, as well as the public, at risk.

Understaffing

The second dominant subtheme identified was understaffing (n = 16, 4.9%), or compelling communicators to function with fewer resources than required to do the job effectively. Staffing issues were overwhelmingly characterized as chronic, with little confidence that satisfactory solutions would be realized. Communicators shared that habitually inadequate staffing levels directly impacted their stress levels and impeded their ability to decompress. They recounted routinely being unable to leave their stations despite the incessant demands of a high-pressure environment and consistent exposure to PPTE. Participants were powerless to take measures, even nominal ones, to attend to their mental health, as they were regularly unable "to organize breaks and time to debrief after calls as almost always short-staffed" (Participant 46). Unequal access to basic resources supports the perception that communicators are less important to the organization than uniformed responders, who are commonly offered mental health support.

Participant 13 summarized the culture in their centre as "no vacation, extreme short staffing." Similarly, Participant 273 described routinely working as "short staffed, expectation to make up for staffing with less people." Organizations that are reluctant, or unable, to maintain adequate staffing levels and do not provide sufficient mental health supports inevitably create circumstances which contribute to the burnout of their members. Even members loyal to the organization seem incapable of sustaining the never-ending pressure, as described by Participant 109, who asserts they are trying to "feel positive, but hard to when we are extremely short staffed and running consistently without lunches."

Increased Levels of Responsibilities

An equally taxing issue, struggling with increasing responsibilities, also surfaced as a third dominant theme (n = 14, 4.3%). Communicators relayed feeling overburdened by operational pressures and steadily increasing workloads. While communicators expressed exasperation with colleagues who appeared not to pull their weight, most relayed that they pulled together to get the job done when needed; however, inequitable distribution of work occurred when communicators routinely did "the bare minimum… leaving others to put in the 'extra' effort to make up for it" (Participant 398). Any imbalance may be attributed to ineffective supervision, but as underscored earlier, favouritism may also play a role in tolerating substandard performance by some.

While frequent changes in operational practices might be unavoidable, it is conceivable that fewer changes could be required if front-line personnel were consulted, as they are uniquely positioned to recommend efficient solutions. A supervisor in an ambulance communications centre explains that: "There is an imbalance between what gets pushed downline, and what the downline can actually handle. It is death by 1000 cuts, and the cuts keep coming" (Participant 78).

Diminished Morale

Ineffective leaders also have a negative impact on employee morale, either directly, "decisions are made without input even after asking for it and that only leads to negative impact on personnel" (Participant 115), or indirectly "their [sic] is quite a noticeable divide between the communication staff and the administrative team, with often times little communication occurring between the two" (Participant 143). For reasons elucidated thus far, survey respondents who referenced morale (n = 16, 4.9%) largely expressed struggling with low morale, with only two expressing positive feelings. Members shared feeling anxious about going to work, as expressed by Participant 347, who said, "There is a lot of negativity and bullying from all levels. I used to be happy to come to work and now I dread it." Indeed, when "staff are at wit's end," it is difficult to remain optimistic about future directions when "local management has been trained to keep their heads in the sand and not speak up" (Participant 78). Participant 119 illustrates how the literature translates to lived experience when their leadership exclaims, "Do what we say! We don't care what you think! Just get the work done and do it right!"

Ways Forward

Though respondents overwhelmingly expressed dissatisfaction, two provided encouraging comments (n = 2, 0.6%) that indicate positive ways forward.

Nonetheless, these findings must be interpreted with caution due to the limited number of participants expressing these sentiments. Participant 310 characterized the morale in their centre as "decent," suggesting a balance between the negative elements of the job, and the beneficial support provided by colleagues or the organization, or both. With respect to support, the salience of efforts taken to eliminate the stigma or mark of sick leave cannot be understated. Another example of positive ways forward came from a participant whose organization forbids "discussing someone's mental health or off duty sick time while in the workplace"; accordingly, they have not "heard anyone speak badly about another co-worker in a long time" (Participant 272).

Division and Exclusion

Physical division (n = 14, 4.3%) and perceptions of exclusion (n = 21, 6.4%) are inextricably linked and equally impact communicators' impressions about the value of their role in their organizations. Though it is customary for communications centres to be physically separated from the administration, uniformed responders, and other organizational branches, even when in the same building, the impacts of isolation cannot be dismissed. Over time, organizational subunits develop occupational identities, complicating inter-group relations (Schein, 2004). Participant 25 exemplifies the impact of opposing identities, sharing that "general patrol members and communication centre staff are separated and often resent each other and blame the other for service wide issues." In command-and-control organizations, where vertical communication is expected, lateral communication is often restricted (Schein, 2004).

The remoteness of communications centres breeds unfamiliarity, as expressed by Participant 147, who says, "The greater organization doesn't really understand what impacts occur to the staff, let alone what they really do." Participant 356 indicated that "outside our building people tend to forget we exist."

Feelings of exclusion were also linked to policy and procedural decisions made by management, directly impacting communicators' routine tasks, time on tasks, and workload. Specific to policy and programming, Participant 318 maintains that no one from their unit is represented in planning discussions; therefore, "communications is not considered at all in any program or policy planning, but always gets stuck with all the administrative burden and responsibility." Participant 218, who similarly expressed dissatisfaction with the lack of inclusion and communication, states, "We are given policy changes or direction without being asked for our input or at least being given the reason behind the change so that we can better explain it to the members on our shift." Recognizing workload can have an emotional impact, communicators cannot be expected to sustain fast-paced performance levels and remain committed to their organization if they feel unappreciated, overlooked, or forgotten. "It feels like we are an after thought" (Participant 390). Overwhelmingly, communicators revealed feeling repeatedly let down by their leadership, despite explicitly expressing the need for meaningful changes aimed at creating supportive and inclusive cultures.

Colleagues

Relationships with colleagues (n = 34, 10.3%), referring here to portraying colleagues as either positive (n = 9, 2.7%) or negative (n = 25, 7.6%). For example, Participant 124 wrote, "We all get along, get together outside of work." Similarly, Participant 24 indicated they work with "tons of supportive folks who became fast friends outside of work." References to implicit, familial feelings reveal that cohesion regularly appears to emerge naturally from the bonds created between colleagues. Although communicator work groups are not devoid of interpersonal conflict, as relayed by Participant 135, who states, "we're constantly short staffed and there are some people who have negative attitudes, however we all can come together...," their teamwork can create conditions favourable to ensuring continuity of operations.

Respondents working in unhealthy environments shared experiences of being overlooked, undervalued, disrespected, overworked, and belittled in their workplaces. Operational pressures, commonly experienced by emergency services personnel, appeared to routinely add strain to already tenuous relationships, resulting in the mistreatment of subordinates and colleagues alike. Several participants shared sentiments of inferiority; "more senior people get away with breaking rules, unfairly getting their way, telling people what to do" (Participant 380), or "the people with more seniority tend to be more 'dominant' and voice their opinions causing tension with both supervisors and other shift members" (Participant 143). Participant 383 described the culture in their communications centre as "nasty – they eat their young. You are not qualified until you've been there for a couple years and proven yourself to the older staff."

Communicators not only grapple with relationships and communications among other subunits, but they commonly have divisive inter-team relationships, which can be exacerbated when conditions are less than favourable. Supporting this, Participant 198 said, "There are many people who don't or will not 'step up to the plate' when we get busy. Always issues with the same people," suggesting a lack of accountability is a major vexation. When communicators work with "cancerous employees that create more problems than they are worth" (Participant 9), morale can become negatively impacted.

Gendered Experience of Culture

Though gender was not a predominant topic (n = 7, 2.1%), primarily because the research question concerned organizational culture, not diversity, the responses were revealing. While most references were negative, one respondent believed the mix of genders offered a broader perspective, contributing positively to the dynamics of the workplace. Yet, Participant 157 affirms that although gender issues are abating, biases still exist, as "many women are mistaken on the phone as 'just secretaries' and the men who answer those same phones are thought to be 'well trained policemen'." Communicators characterized their organizations as "male dominated" (Participant 412) and "sexist," where there is "far more career growth for male employees" (Participant 161).

Androcentric ideologies, which contribute to gender inequality, can also influence the health and safety of its members and, within this context, their mental health.

> These are all men who have their own complex histories and are often 'old school' and jaded and tend to be more of a 'brush it off' type than a supportive type of manager. It means that many people have to fight to have their workplace mental injuries after traumatic events treated appropriately.
>
> *(Participant 72)*

Unbalanced gendered representation in leadership positions produces culture conflicts with subgroups and creates de facto barriers, as explained by Participant 141, "there is a 'Boys Group' that has recently developed, and the females (70% of staff are female) don't have a means to be heard anymore." Tacit norms and accepted patterns of behaviour seem to influence culture and reflect deeper assumptions and values of the organization, often preventing members of subgroups from speaking up.

Discussion

The current study results build on prior quantitative findings of the prevalence of mental health issues to provide a clearer understanding of the experiences of communicators and provide new insight into the relationship between organizational culture and communicator well-being. Routine exposure to potentially psychologically traumatic events, in addition to the pressures of performing in high-stress situations, can compromise a communicator's capacity to make rapid decisions and function at the high pace required, particularly in chronically down-staffed centres. Still, participants reported that although organizations formally endorse mental health initiatives, supports are commonly absent. Similarly, respondents maintained that stigma surrounding disclosing mental health struggles prevails, shaping cultures that limit and exclude rather than encourage and include. These conclusions reinforce Schein's (2004) position that when the espoused beliefs and values of an organization conflict with the basic underlying assumptions of its members, tacit group norms guide behaviour. Schein further contends that the implicit understanding of "the way we do things around here" is more impactful to its members than the organization's publicly endorsed value statements (Schein, 2004, p. 13). Thus, stigma surrounding the disclosure of mental health struggles prevails in part because negative discourse remains rooted in the tacit culture, most notably in unsupportive organizations. Leaders who rely on outdated mental health belief patterns undermine the health and safety of the organization and contribute to toxic workplaces, corroborating Oliphant's (2016) findings that emergency services remain rife with a suck-it-up culture.

Six predominant themes outlined elements which positively or negatively impacted communicators' well-being: perceptions of organization, management and supervision, morale and staffing, division and exclusion, colleagues, and gendered experience of culture. Positive perceptions were most commonly attributed to organizations taking action to promote employee wellness, agreeing with the importance of transparency about "the way we do things around here" (Schein, 2004, p. 13). Negative perceptions, conversely, were associated with unhealthy work environments (e.g., constant stressors, negativity, and bullying), supporting previous findings that suggest that heightened degrees of stress contribute to burnout, resulting in missed steps and poor decisions, putting the health and safety of the public at risk (Lilly & Allen, 2015; Pierce & Lilly, 2012), and providing more context to previous findings that suggest communicators are subjected to negative treatment from a variety of sources, such as the public, uniformed responders, and supervisors (Golding et al., 2017).

A similar sentiment emerged within discussions around management and supervision, where respondents expressed a lack of recognition by leadership relative to other first responders, corroborating previous findings where communicators felt that supports were systematically offered to uniformed responders, reinforcing the contention that minimal recognition is given to communicators, or the secondary duty-related trauma they are consistently exposed to (Golding et al., 2017; Ramey et al., 2017; Smith et al., 2019). Again, within the theme of management and supervision emerged the idea that inaccurate suppositions made by the leadership subculture about the communications subculture suggest management are either unaware of, or indifferent to, the dynamic and complex minutia of communicators' daily tasks, agreeing with previous findings indicating that leaders may reason, based on incorrect assumptions, that their centres operate optimally, as communicators reliably stay on task, despite excessive workloads, a scarcity of breaks, frequent overtime, and perpetual downstaffing (Golding et al., 2017).

Schein (2004) further contends that although subcultural differences by hierarchy can be appropriate and utilitarian, they can also be used as mechanisms of social control, deterring subordinates from communicating candidly – a sentiment that was clearly expressed by our participants. For example, discussions around male dominance and sexist environments support Schein's (2004) assertion that members will seek to preserve, or even enhance, the prevailing culture as it benefits them. Conditions of understaffing clearly are an operational issue in communication centres, but interestingly, so did sentiments of a need to still complete the job effectively, agreeing with Schein's (2004) concept of operators (i.e., communicators), who regularly exceed their capacity to perform effectively, contributing to the incorrect assumption that "all is well in comms" despite chronic understaffed conditions. Discussions around diminished morale additionally supported extant findings (e.g., Golding et al., 2017; McCarty & Skogan, 2013; Smith et al., 2019; Soria, 2020), in that respondents were sceptical that solutions to key issues impacting their well-being would be found, particularly with respect to communicators feeling unheard, dismissed, and disrespected (Baseman et al., 2018; Coxon et al., 2016; Golding et al., 2017; Smith et al., 2019; Soria, 2020; Steinkopf et al., 2018). Interestingly, while unhealthy work environments contributed to negative affect, participants in this study also depicted their workplace colleagues as toxic, creating conditions that were rife with bullying, harassment, and conflict, agreeing with findings extant in the literature (Adams et al., 2015; Baseman et al., 2018; Ramey et al., 2017; Smith et al., 2019), including the direct and negative impact on psychological well-being (Golding et al., 2017).

Notably, participants communicated strong desires to be recognized as valued members of their organizations, to be included in mental health solutions, to be provided sufficient human resources to adequately perform tasks, to be granted meaningful time away from task while on shift, to be treated with dignity and respect, to have their stress and trauma validated, and to access career opportunities based on skill and not gender. Unfortunately, despite proclamations to address long-standing issues, organizations regularly fall short of gaining traction as they commonly fail to allocate sufficient resources, or are unfamiliar with the unique needs of communicators, or both. These findings corroborate the contentions of Carleton et al. (2018), who assert that the needs of each PSP group should be identified, and that evidence-based treatment options should be developed to support occupation-specific needs.

Limitations

Our reliance on respondents to provide us with contact information for partnering PSAPs was only moderately helpful; therefore, contacting communicators nationwide proved challenging. Efforts were made to reach communications chiefs, managers, and supervisors by phone and email, with limited success. When successful, members regularly advised that they were not in a position of authority to approve the dissemination of the survey, stating they required approval from the "chain of command." Notably, it was challenging to reach people at any level of the chain of command within fire services nationally, though it was beyond the scope of this study to investigate why participation from this sector was less than the rest. Overall, attempts were made to reach fire services via phone and emails to communicators, communications managers and chiefs, service chiefs, provincial fire marshals, fire service unions, fire service women's social media groups, and through social media, all with limited success. Although the precise number of communicators employed in Canada is uncertain, our sample is the largest of any Canadian research and includes participants from all territories, provinces, official languages, and all roles defined in our study.

The reliability of these data may be impacted by the positioning of the organizational culture questions near the end of the survey, with this study's question at 165 out of 179. A further limitation remains that the data were a result of responses to open-ended survey items, not interviews; therefore, we lacked the opportunity to ask follow-up questions or probe for additional information. Additionally, our reliance on participant self-report as our primary data source introduces the possibility of potential issues in our data, including bias. Finally, this population, and other PSP, tend to underreport health issues due to factors such as stigma, suggesting that our sample may not represent the full extent of experiences.

Recommendations

Future research should investigate barriers to accessing communicators and identify measures to facilitate access, markedly within fire services. Emergency services, principally fire services, should be encouraged to share mental health research opportunities with their members, permitting the members to determine if they want to participate. Organizations should: (a) offer training for management, including leadership, equity, diversity and inclusivity, and mental health training; (b) conduct regular screening for mental health needs, like annual evidence-based psychological assessments; and (c) offer interpersonal relationship training to assist with collegiality and professionalism in interactions.

Conclusion

Though stress, exposure to potentially psychological trauma, and high-pressure decision-making are concomitants of the occupation, supportive cultures can mitigate the proliferation of impacts. The dearth of debriefs after stressful or traumatic calls, an inability to take breaks or have meaningful time away from the centre, and the stigma associated with disclosing mental health challenges contribute to behaviour norms, which create barriers to care-seeking. To contribute positively to the well-being of its members, organizations require empathetic and effective leaders, strong mental health supports, and adequate resourcing.

Notes

1 Our research was approved by the Newfoundland and Labrador Human Research Ethics Board (File #20210168).
2 Canadian Psychological Association. Finding the Psychologist for You. www.cpa.ca/public/findingapsychologist/. Last accessed 20 August 2024.
3 Canadian Association for Suicide Prevention. (2024) Resources. http://suicidprevention.ca/thinking-about-suicide/find-a-crisis-centre/. Last accessed 19 August 2024.
4 We were unable to locate official data sources identifying the number of women occupying executive leadership positions in Canadian police, fire, or paramedic services. We reached out to national association leaders and were provided with estimates identifying only a handful of women. Thus, we will use the term "predominantly" to identify male leadership.

References

Adams, K., Shakespeare-Finch, J., & Armstrong, D. (2015). An interpretative phenomenological analysis of stress and well-being in emergency medical dispatchers. *Journal of Loss and Trauma*, *20*(5), Article 5. https://doi.org/10.1080/15325024.2014.949141

Ashbaugh, A. R., Herbert, C. F., Butler, L. D., & Brunet, A. (2010). Internet use in the aftermath of trauma. *A New Frontier: Trauma Research on the Internet*, *72*, 99–120. https://doi.org/10.3233/978-1-60750-626-3-99

Bång, A., Ortgren, P.-O., Herlitz, J., & Währborg, P. (2002). Dispatcher-assisted telephone CPR: A qualitative study exploring how dispatchers perceive their experiences. *Resuscitation*, *53*(2), Article 2. https://doi.org/10.1016/S0300-9572(01)00508-1

Baseman, J., Revere, D., Painter, I., Stangenes, S., Lilly, M., Beaton, R., Calhoun, R., & Meischke, H. (2018). Impact of new technologies on stress, attrition and well-being in emergency call centers: The NextGeneration 9–1-1 study protocol. *BMC Public Health*, *18*(1), Article 1. https://doi.org/10.1186/s12889-018-5510-x

Canadian Radio-television and Telecommunications Commission. (2020). 9-1-1 Services. Canadian Radio-Television and Telecommunications Commission. https://crtc.gc.ca/eng/phone/911/can.htm

Carleton, R. N., Afifi, T. O., Taillieu, T., Turner, S., Krakauer, R., Anderson, G. S., MacPhee, R. S., Ricciardelli, R., Cramm, H. A., Groll, D., & McCreary, D. R. (2019). Exposures to potentially traumatic events among public safety personnel in Canada. *Canadian Journal of Behavioural Science / Revue Canadienne Des Sciences Du Comportement*, *51*(1), Article 1. https://doi.org/10.1037/cbs0000115

Carleton, R. N., Afifi, T. O., Turner, S., Taillieu, T., Duranceau, S., LeBouthillier, D. M., Sareen, J., Ricciardelli, R., MacPhee, R. S., Groll, D., Hozempa, K., Brunet, A., Weekes, J. R., Griffiths, C. T., Abrams, K. J., Jones, N. A., Beshai, S., Cramm, H. A., Dobson, K. S., … Asmundson, G. J. G. (2018). Mental disorder symptoms among public safety personnel in Canada. *The Canadian Journal of Psychiatry*, *63*(1), Article 1. https://doi.org/10.1177/0706743717723825

Centre for Addictions and Mental Health. (2020). Workplace Mental Health—A Review and Recommendations. www.camh.ca/-/media/files/workplace-mental-health/workplacementalhealth-a-review-and-recommendations-pdf.pdf

Charmaz, K. (2006). *Constructing Grounded Theory: A Practical Guide Through Qualitative Analysis.* Sage Publications.

Coxon, A., Cropley, M., Schofield, P., Start, K., Horsfield, C., & Quinn, T. (2016). 'You're never making just one decision': Exploring the lived experiences of ambulance Emergency Operations Centre personnel. *Emergency Medicine Journal*, *33*(9), 645–651. https://doi.org/10.1136/emermed-2015-204841

CSA Group. (2022). Psychological health and safety in the workplace—Prevention, promotion, and guidance to staged implementation (CAN/CSA-Z1003-13/BNQ 9700-803/2013). www.csagroup.org/article/can csa-z1003-13-bnq-9700-803-2013-r2018/

Davis, A. C. (2023). The Flourishing of 911 Communications Workers (Publication No 30313427) [Doctoral dissertation, Capella University]. ProQuest Dissertations Publishing.

Deselms, J. L. (2016). 911,What's My Emergency? Emotional Labor, Work-Related Rumination, and Strain Outcomes in Emergency Medical Dispatchers (Paper No. 632) [Doctoral dissertation, Minnesota State University]. All Theses, Dissertations, and Other Capstone Projects.

Golding, S. E., Horsfield, C., Davies, A., Egan, B., Jones, M., Raleigh, M., Schofield, P., Squires, A., Start, K., Quinn, T., & Cropley, M. (2017). Exploring the psychological health of emergency dispatch centre operatives: A systematic review and narrative synthesis. *PeerJ*, *5*, e3735. https://doi.org/10.7717/peerj.3735

Koopmans, E., Wagner, S. L., Schmidt, G., & Harder, H. (2017). Emergency response services suicide: A crisis in Canada? *Journal of Loss and Trauma*, *22*(7), Article 7. https://doi.org/10.1080/15325024.2017.1360589

Lilly, M. M., & Allen, C. E. (2015). Psychological inflexibility and psychopathology in 9-1-1 telecommunicators: Psychopathology in telecommunicators. *Journal of Traumatic Stress*, *28*(3), Article 3. https://doi.org/10.1002/jts.22004

MacQueen, J. (2020). *The Flow of Organizational Culture: New Thinking and Theory for Better Understanding and Process.* Springer International Publishing. https://doi.org/10.1007/978-3-030-25685-2

McCarty, W. P., & Skogan, W. G. (2013). Job-related burnout among civilian and sworn police personnel. *Police Quarterly*, *16*(1), 66–84. https://doi.org/10.1177/1098611112457357

Mental Health Commission of Canada. (2015). *Case Study Research Project: Early Findings Interim Report.* https://mentalhealthcommission.ca/resource/case-study-research-project-early-findings-interim-report-2/

Oliphant, R. (Chair) (2016). Healthy Minds, Safe Communities: Supporting our Public Safety Officers through a National Strategy for Operational Stress Injuries. Parliament of Canada. Standing Committee on Public Safety and National Security.

www.ourcommons.ca/Content/Committee/421/SECU/Reports/RP8457704/securp05/securp05-e.pdf

Patel, V., Saxena, S., Lund, C., Thornicroft, G., Baingana, F., Bolton, P., Chisholm, D., Collins, P. Y., Cooper, J. L., Eaton, J., Herrman, H., Herzallah, M. M., Huang, Y., Jordans, M. J. D., Kleinman, A., Medina-Mora, M. E., Morgan, E., Niaz, U., Omigbodun, O., … UnÜtzer, Jü. (2018). The Lancet Commission on global mental health and sustainable development. *The Lancet*, *392*(10157), 1553–1598. https://doi.org/10.1016/S0140-6736(18)31612-X

Pierce, H., & Lilly, M. M. (2012). Duty-related trauma exposure in 911 telecommunicators: Considering the risk for posttraumatic stress. *Journal of Traumatic Stress*, *25*(2), Article 2. https://doi.org/10.1002/jts.21687

Pietrus, M. (2013). *Opening Minds Interim Report*. Mental Health Commission of Canada. https://mentalhealthcommission.ca/resource/opening-minds-interim-report/

Ramey, S. L., Perkhounkova, Y., Hein, M., Chung, S. J., & Anderson, A. A. (2017). Evaluation of stress experienced by emergency telecommunications personnel employed in a large metropolitan police department. *Workplace Health & Safety*, *65*(7), Article 7. https://doi.org/10.1177/2165079916667736

Ricciardelli, R. (2011). Masculinity, consumerism, and appearance: A look at men's hair: Masculinity, consumerism, and appearance. *Canadian Review of Sociology/Revue Canadienne de Sociologie*, *48*(2), 181–201. https://doi.org/10.1111/j.1755-618X.2011.01261.x

Ricciardelli, R., Clow, K. A., & White, P. (2010). Investigating hegemonic masculinity: Portrayals of masculinity in men's lifestyle magazines. *Sex Roles*, *63*(1–2), 64–78. https://doi.org/10.1007/s11199-010-9764-8

Schein, E. H. (2004). *Organizational Culture and Leadership* (3rd ed.). Jossey-Bass.

Smith, E. C., Holmes, L., & Burkle, F. M. (2019). Exploring the physical and mental health challenges associated with emergency service call-taking and dispatching: A review of the literature. *Prehospital and Disaster Medicine*, *34*(6), Article 6. https://doi.org/10.1017/S1049023X19004990

Soria, J. R. (2020). Emergency dispatcher vulnerabilities. *Office of Suicide and Violence Prevention*, Winter 2020, 14–16. www.nova.edu/suicideprevention/newsletter.html

Steinkopf, B., Reddin, R. A., Black, R. A., Van Hasselt, V. B., & Couwels, J. (2018). Assessment of stress and resiliency in emergency dispatchers. *Journal of Police and Criminal Psychology*, *33*(4), Article 4. https://doi.org/10.1007/s11896-018-9255-3

Szeto, A., Dobson, K. S., Luong, D., Krupa, T., & Kirsh, B. (2019). Workplace antistigma programs at the Mental Health Commission of Canada: Part 1. Processes and projects. *Canadian Journal of Psychiatry*, *64*(1_suppl), 5S–12S. https://doi.org/10.1177/0706743719842557

14

FAMILY FIRST

The Potential Value of Training Family Members to Provide Psychological First Aid (PFA) to Their First Responders

Michelle O'Toole, Alan M. Batt, Walter Eppich, and Brett Williams

Introduction

Public safety personnel (PSP), including police, firefighters, public safety communicators, and paramedics, regularly encounter critical incidents in the line of duty. As examples, firefighters may struggle emotionally with failed rescue attempts in burning buildings, paramedics may visualize their own children while responding to unresponsive paediatric patients, and public safety communicators must calm anxious callers before directing them to perform CPR on their loved ones (Lawrence et al., 2018; Krakauer et al., 2020). Due to this regular psychologically traumatic exposure, PSP experience increased symptoms of acute or posttraumatic stress, when compared to the general population (Jones et al., 2020; Krakauer et al., 2020). Taking care of others in distress often leads to vicarious or secondary traumatization (May et al., 2023), with PSP described as 'hidden victims' (Regehr et al., 2005), expected to simply continue with the job, sometimes without the time to process the adverse experiences. Secondary traumatic stress occurs as emotional distress after witnessing trauma experienced by others, e.g., a patient, the likelihood of which is influenced by both psychosocial and occupational factors (Renkiewicz & Hubble, 2022).

These critical incidents are not the only stressors contributing to decreased mental well-being in PSP. Non-public facing issues (often referred to as organizational or workplace stressors), such as role ambiguity, interpersonal relationships, poor leadership, health hazards, and perceived lack of support, also impact PSP's ability to optimally serve their communities (Acquadro Maran et al., 2022). Uncertainty surrounding shift end times, lack of protected break times, increasing workload, and reduced opportunities for

DOI: 10.4324/9781003424253-19

continuing professional development are just some examples of common workplace stressors that also cause stress reactions in PSP. Whilst public safety organizations have a duty of care to generally provide support programmes to their staff, family members and friends often appear to fall outside of this remit into an unfortunate 'grey zone.' While some organizations recognize the need to inform family members about the role their loved one is embarking on, emerging education programmes are still in their infancy and are not yet standard practice across all PSP professions. Family and friends of PSP report their willingness and determination to help support their loved ones in dealing with these stressors (Tjin et al., 2022), and we see value in both recognizing and supporting their efforts to maintain PSP well-being. However, PSP worry for the well-being of their family members and demonstrate an innate desire to protect them from vicarious traumatization through secondary exposure (Hill et al., 2023; MacDermid et al., 2021). Therefore, careful consideration is needed to ensure appropriate psychoeducation and support services are available and accessible for those supporting the supporters.

In the current chapter, we outline the role of social support as a proactive, early intervention technique for PSP experiencing normal stress reactions following organizational or operational stressors. We will explore the role of social support both within and outside emergency service organizations, to increase awareness of the usefulness and readiness of family members and friends of PSP as willing and able supporters.

Social Support

Public safety organizations frequently apply social support techniques to assist employees following potentially traumatic events. Rather than focusing on preventing or treating posttraumatic stress disorder (PTSD), early crisis intervention programmes instead help by boosting group cohesion, decreasing absenteeism, and counter-productive stress reactions, as well as enhancing productivity at work (Regel et al., 2012; Price et al., 2022). According to the National Institute for Health and Care Excellence (2018), best practices following psychologically traumatic events include offering practical social support and guidance to those affected. Social support is the emotional or practical help a person receives from their social groups, such as family, friends, and co-workers, during times of crisis and distress (Kshtriya et al., 2020). Social networks organically encourage help-seeking and foster a sense of community. House (1981) details social support as interpersonal transactions leading to feeling cared for through the assistance provided by others and describes four types of support:

1 **Emotional** support offers trust, empathy, love, and care for the help-seeker.
2 **Instrumental** support includes tangible, financial, or practical help.

3 **Appraisal** support provides affirmation, reflection, and interpretation for the purposes of self evaluation.
4 **Informational** support offers knowledge, helping the person to gain clarity and understanding about the situation.

Social support reduces posttraumatic stress, increases positive mental well-being in the general population, and protects first responders' mental health (Pietrantoni & Prati, 2008; Lowery & Cassidy, 2022). A lack of social support increases the likelihood of PTSD; by contrast, receiving social support predicts well-being and posttraumatic growth (Charuvastra et al., 2008). Thus, social support is a multidimensional construct influenced by the culture and context of both its providers and recipients. A recent study illustrated how those from Western cultures are more likely to prefer explicit support, whereas those from Asian cultures benefit more from implicit support (Jobson et al., 2023). Explicit support refers to openly discussing problems and seeking advice, while implicit support is described as reassurance in the company of others, without disclosing the problem. Reasons for the varying values and preferences stem from how different cultures perceive the self, e.g., many Western cultures view the self as individualistic and independent, while many Asian cultures are collectivist, focused on interconnectedness with others (Jobson et al., 2023).

PSP are often characterized as having unique and complex cultures and subcultures, while being wary of outsiders (Young et al., 2014). Crisis intervention as a form of social support aligns with a cultural outlook that focuses on homogenous groups, e.g., firefighters working with firefighters and police working with police. Crisis intervention theory dates to the early 1900s, with Erich Lindemann and Gerald Caplan receiving recognition for the theory's development in the 1940s and 1960s, respectively (Roberts, 2005; Black & Flynn, 2021). Lindemann witnessed acute grief in the survivors and relatives of the 493 people who perished in the 1942 nightclub fire at Cocoanut Grove in Boston. Caplan continued contributing to the body of knowledge in the field of crisis intervention by arguing that "*homeostasis is disrupted when the individual is unable to see a way out of the predicament*," i.e., when their coping mechanisms fail (Roberts, 2005, pp.16–17). Rapoport elaborated on the application of the concept of homeostasis by highlighting the necessity of early intervention or 'rapid access' for those in crisis. The original three principles of crisis intervention, **proximity, immediacy, and expectancy (PIE)**, articulated by Salmon in the early 1900s and expanded by Artiss in the 1960s (Solomon & Benbenishty, 1986), are outlined in Table 14.1. A 20-year longitudinal study demonstrated that veterans who received crisis intervention in the form of PIE fared better in post-military life than those who did not receive PIE (Solomon, 2005).

Typically, crisis intervention support is provided by organizations, with an emphasis on peer-led support (usually internal) and/or professional

TABLE 14.1 Original principles of crisis intervention applied to PSP context

Crisis intervention principle	*Historical military application*	*PSP context (Mitchell, 2006)*
Proximity	Treatment for 'shellshock' was provided near the frontline to enable soldiers to stay close to comrades and commanders.	Techniques such as RITS[a] are provided near the incident location to allow for rest, information, and transition back to work following a brief break.
Immediacy	Treatment was provided as soon as possible after symptoms occurred to enable a speedy return to battle.	Individual and group interventions occur as soon as possible following an incident to encourage reflection on the incident, normalizing reactions through psychoeducation and group cohesion.
Expectancy	Most soldiers were expected to return to battle as soon as their symptoms began to dissipate. Those who did not recover quickly were removed for further treatment.	Most first responders recover from most incidents, most of the time. Following appropriate crisis intervention, only a small number require referral to MHPs[b].

[a] **RITS**: Rest Information Transition Services is an informational group process designed for first response/disaster relief teams to share updates, rehydrate, and provide a safe space after initial exposure to a major incident.

[b] **MHPs**: Mental health professionals: person recognized and registered to conduct professional mental health therapy, e.g., counsellors, psychotherapists, psychologists, psychiatrists, and social workers.

support, namely external assistance (Price et al., 2022). Within the external model, various mental health professionals (MHPs) such as psychotherapists, counsellors, and occupational health psychologists provide care and support to those who identify the need to seek professional help, often through Employee Assistance Programs (EAPs). Stigma often prevents first responders from requesting professional help; men in professions such as firefighting and paramedicine, scholars have found, have been conditioned to not cry in case crying is perceived as a sign of weakness, resultantly they hide their true feelings (Seaton et al., 2019; Jakubowski & Sitko-Dominik, 2021). To tackle stigma and to normalize the stress responses experienced following these potentially distressing incidents, most emergency service organizations now train their own peer support staff to recognize the signs and symptoms of stress, to listen effectively to a colleague, and how to identify if a person needs further support (Price et al., 2022). There are various models of peer support used internationally (e.g., Critical Incident Stress Management (CISM)).

This multi-component suite of both group and individual psychological first aid (PFA) interventions mitigates the after-effects of critical incidents by facilitating early access to crisis intervention (Mitchell, 2006).

Psychological first aid (PFA) is defined by the World Health Organization (WHO) as "a humane, supportive response to a fellow human being who is suffering and may require support" (van Ommeren et al., 2011, p.5) and includes simple interventions such as listening, providing information, comfort, and practical support to address fundamental needs (van Ommeren et al., 2011). According to the National Institute of Mental Health, PFA is the most favoured early intervention technique utilized during or immediately after a crisis (Shultz & Forbes, 2013). Social support was traditionally provided by co-workers or administrators in emergency service professions, but the practice of PFA is not limited to peers or even MHPs (van Ommeren et al., 2011).

Barriers to Seeking Support

Despite the availability of various types of social support in the workplace, they are not reliably accessible, and barriers inhibit their widespread uptake among PSP. Some barriers include a lack of mental health literacy or even an inability to recognize the need for help; stigma or shame; doubts about the confidentiality of the service provided and the potential for negative implications at work; and the fear of being a burden—both financially and socially (Jones et al., 2020). A recent Australian study found the risk factors for reduced help-seeking include being male, having severe psychological distress, having low social support, and being a member of the police service, an additional overarching theme of wanting to manage problems by themselves or with family members/friends (Rikkers et al., 2022). Thus, a 'one-size-fits-all' approach often taken by work-based support systems is not universally effective.

The WHO acknowledges that sex and gender play a crucial role in health care, specifically how males frequently put off seeking medical attention and even refuse to cooperate with the therapy advised (World Health Organisation, 2017). Men are more vulnerable to suicide, with greater rates among those in the armed forces and first responder vocations (Oliffe et al., 2021). Mental health is a significant concern for businesses and society at large, but ways to promote mental health that are gender-sensitive need to be improved in fields where males predominate (McCreary, 2019; Seaton et al., 2019). PSP claim issues such as 'can't show weakness,' 'needing cultural change,' and 'family burden' (Jones et al., 2020, p.48) are some of the hurdles they must jump before seeking help (MacDermid et al., 2021). Masculinities discourage asking for help, encourage unhealthy coping strategies, and change how people see the social support offered (Jones et al., 2020). Continuous demonstrations of toughness, independence, and stoicism are linked to emerging mental health problems such as PTSD (Jakubowski & Sitko-Dominik, 2021) and considerably higher levels of symptoms of anxiety and depression (Seaton et al., 2019). This finding may be influenced by the stereotyped culture of frontline professionals, which views asking for help and even caring, as a quality culturally interpreted as feminine (Kyed, 2020; Jakubowski & Sitko-Dominik, 2021).

Opportunities to Reduce Barriers

Changing workplace culture is the ultimate long-term solution to decreasing stigma and the perception of help-seeking as a character weakness (Henderson et al., 2016). Although this will inevitably take time to both enforce and take effect, there are practical strategies that can be implemented in the short to medium term to improve access to support for all PSP. Fundamentally, all staff levels in emergency service organizations require training on how to recognize the signs and symptoms of stress in themselves and colleagues. Further, alleviating concerns surrounding the impact of stress reactions on career progression will help relieve a burden on those seeking help. Managers must be trained on how to handle mental health disclosures effectively and sensitively in the workplace, and they must strive to provide support pathways that maintain confidentiality (Rikkers et al., 2022) and encourage disclosure without recourse (Henderson et al., 2016). While peer-led trauma support usually stems from in-house personnel, external MHPs must be socialized to the unique culture typical among PSP. This unique culture includes technical terminologies used to describe common practices and dark humour as a coping strategy (Dangermond et al., 2022). Some authors have even suggested that MHPs wishing to work with PSP should be mandated to ride-along for a couple of shifts, to gain insight into life on duty, thus further understanding the culture (Gulliver, 2019; Demoulin et al., 2022).

So, while we patiently try to change workplace culture, how might we address some of these concerns outside the workplace? These acute stress reactions experienced at work do not simply disappear when PSP finish a shift. Despite their best efforts to protect their partners, families, and friends, these reactions creep into home life (Hill et al., 2023), with PSP often unconsciously struggling to leave their emotional backpacks at work. The impact inevitably spills over into the home, causing reduced tolerance, irritability, suboptimal communication, and even increased risk for divorce (MacDermid et al., 2021). Considering the principles of crisis intervention outlined earlier (PIE) in conjunction with House's four categories of social support, we propose an additional, most accessible provider for PFA support: family and friends or 'trusted others' of public safety personnel (Tjin et al., 2022; O'Toole et al., 2022). These normal reactions to abnormal events usually dissipate with time, and trusted others are close-by and readily available in the aftermath, already providing emotional and practical support. If trusted others were better prepared to provide this support, could this help both groups in the wake of trauma? The next section highlights what we currently know about family members provision of support to their PSP.

Two Sides to the Coin

Secondary traumatic stress or vicarious traumatization is a risk inherent with hearing about traumatic events experienced by another (Hill et al., 2023). Firefighters described being 'guarded' about sharing work details, knowing that they need to communicate, and yet, at the same time, wanting to protect their loved ones from the impact of their work (MacDermid et al., 2021). Partners and spouses of PSP have previously described negative reactions such as nausea, anxiety, fear, and sleep disturbances, indirectly experienced due to their partners' profession (Beks, 2016; Friese, 2020; Hill et al., 2020; Casas & Benuto, 2022). Fortunately, in addition to outlining the potentially negative effects of psychological trauma and shift work, family members also characterized their pride in their loved one's work, which often involved the PSP putting themselves at risk to serve their communities for public safety (Landers et al., 2020). Some challenges related to the lack of recognition family members receive for the assistance they provide to their PSPs, as well as the need for proper information and education to continue this often-hidden role (Cox et al., 2022; Tjin et al., 2022). In times of adversity, mutual support is a protective factor in relationships (Jobson et al., 2023); thus, in this light, PSP also need to reciprocate by supporting their families, mitigating the risk of secondary and/or vicarious traumatization for those providing the support.

In the existing literature, many family members recounted how they provide emotional, practical, or instrumental, and appraisal support to their PSP loved ones. Fostering a safe space (Ewles, 2019) and "being there when he needs to talk to someone" (Landers et al., 2020, p.314) were recurring examples of providing emotional support, delicately balanced with giving him time and 'walking on eggshells' (Beks, 2016, p.651). Practical strategies of support included taking on additional household responsibilities, changing the family schedule (Landers et al., 2020; Casas & Benuto, 2022), and "...just feeling like a single parent all the time" (Friese, 2020, pp.413–414), particularly whilst attending children's sporting events or family get-togethers. Spouses reported learning the signs to watch out for to ensure they monitor their first responders' mood before providing verbal reassurance and reminders of previously established helpful coping strategies (Hill et al., 2020; Tjin et al., 2022). Using humour (Bochantin, 2017) and collective language, for example, 'we need' instead of 'I need' (Beks, 2016), seemed to take the edge off the problem, preventing support from coming across as confrontational.

Often, family members and/or spouses prioritized their PSPs' emotional needs over their own by concealing their fears about safety and providing emotional support despite their own deteriorating emotional condition.

> Sometimes I need support, and I feel like that comes, kind of, second place to…'cus the nature of his work is more acute and more intense, and so, I feel like that's a priority over my needs sometimes.
>
> *(Ewles, 2019, p.149)*

This behaviour proved unsustainable and overwhelming for some, with communication issues, substance use, and exhaustion, all cited as barriers to providing support (MacDermid et al., 2021; Tjin et al., 2022). Trusted others also desired recognition, reassurance, and praise for the vital role they play, albeit informal and understated at times. Some found solace in peer support, with other spouses of PSPs, describing "deepening bonds with other law enforcement wives…personal and emotional relief from talking with them" (Landers et al., 2020, p.314). Clearly, there must be a balance in providing and requiring support, and the relationship must be equitable in that one party's needs must not outweigh the others.

Future Directions

Gulliver et al. (2019) state that 67 per cent of firefighters indicated they would seek assistance from informal supporting persons in their lives, suggesting friends and family members of PSP need timely access to educational seminars and training to become adept at noticing signs of distress in a loved one. Hence, organizations must implement psychoeducation regarding clinical indicators and support pathways through in-person seminars, brochures, and web-based approaches (Lizardi & Stanley, 2010; Lawrence et al., 2018). Additionally, programmes that encourage increasing degrees of family involvement in the earliest phases of treatment have shown improvement in patient engagement and motivation (Lizardi & Stanley, 2010; Johnson et al., 2020). Due to the similar cultural complexities of firefighting with other emergency services (i.e., the 'us versus them' culture), we assume that trusted others of all PSP will benefit from this type of training.

To fully support their personnel, PSP organizations must build strong working relationships with local mental health agencies and consider teaming up with researchers, mental health specialists, post-secondary education institutions, and/or stakeholders to design, implement, and deliver effective training solutions proactively rather than reactively. Inviting key stakeholders to co-design these training sessions will also bring authenticity and ensure real-world problems are being addressed. Including family members and PSP as key stakeholders will help them feel empowered to share their lived experiences, highlighting the 'two sides to the coin' (MacDermid et al., 2021, p.5) and promoting learning for those following in their footsteps. Finally, peer support for these key supporters should also be considered, either in person, virtually, or via technology-enabled platforms, to ensure their ability to provide continuing support to their first responders.

Conclusion

In summary, we recognize social support as a mitigator of acute stress in PSP, and various support mechanisms and pathways already exist to provide comfort in times of distress. Family members and friends of PSP continue to provide essential assistance to their loved ones, in the form of emotional, practical, appraisal, and informational support. Due to the delicate balance of providing such support and the simultaneous risk of secondary or vicarious traumatization, we see the need for more formal preparation, such as co-created educational interventions, to ensure family members and friends feel better prepared to continue providing this key support. Models such as CISM reference the need to involve families (Mitchell, 2006) and yet organizations implementing these procedures consistently fail to acknowledge their usefulness and their needs. While researchers and key community stakeholders begin to formalize these approaches as additional complementary pathways to psychological first aid outside of the workplace, tailored peer support for these supporters must also be considered.

Peer support for family members and friends of PSP has not yet received enough attention (Hill et al., 2023), and further work is needed to identify the outcomes of providing social support for these trusted others right across their loved ones' career trajectory, from recruit to retiree.

Partnerships with community-based organizations, mental health agencies, and digital platform providers will provide opportunities for connection for these supporters. Future research is vital to ensure the sustainability of this approach to enhance the well-being of PSP families and friends and perhaps public safety organizations should begin viewing family members of PSP as allies, and members of the team. To ensure its success, future research must be purposeful, pragmatic, and participatory in nature to further identify and address the real-world challenges facing our PSP families, so that they may continue to effectively serve the public, while also prioritizing their own self-care.

References

Acquadro Maran, D., Magnavita, N., & Garbarino, S. (2022). Identifying organizational stressors that could be a source of discomfort in police officers: A thematic review.

International Journal of Environmental Research and Public Health, 19(6), 3720. https://doi.org/10.3390/ijerph19063720

Beks, T. (2016). Walking on eggshells: The lived experience of partners of veterans with PTSD. *The Qualitative Report.* https://doi.org/10.46743/2160-3715/2016.2269

Black, L. L., & Flynn, S. V. (2021). *Crisis, trauma, and disaster: A clinician's guide.* Thousand Oaks, CA: Sage.

Bochantin, J. E. (2017). "Ambulance thieves, clowns, and naked grandfathers." *Management Communication Quarterly, 31*(2), 278–296. https://doi.org/10.1177/0893318916687650

Casas, J. B., & Benuto, L. T. (2022). Work-related traumatic stress spillover in first responder families: A systematic review of the literature. *Psychological Trauma: Theory, Research, Practice, and Policy, 14*(2), 209–217. https://doi.org/10.1037/tra0001086

Charuvastra, A., & Cloitre, M. (2008). Social bonds and posttraumatic stress disorder. *Annual Review of Psychology, 59*(1), 301–328. https://doi.org/10.1146/annurev.psych.58.110405.085650

Cox, M., Norris, D., Cramm, H., Richmond, R., & Anderson, G. S. (2022). Public safety personnel family resilience: A narrative review. *International Journal of Environmental Research and Public Health, 19*(9), 5224. https://doi.org/10.3390/ijerph19095224

Dangermond, K., Weewer, R., Duyndam, J., & Machielse, A. (2022). "If it stops, then I'll start worrying." Humor as part of the fire service culture, specifically as part of coping with critical incidents. *HUMOR, 35*(1), 31–50. https://doi.org/10.1515/humor-2021-0106

DeMoulin, D., Jacobs, S., Nam, Y.-S., Harding, A. B., Moskowitz, A. F., Shi, Y., & Kim, H. (2022). Mental health among firefighters. *Journal of Occupational and Environmental Medicine, 64*(11). https://doi.org/10.1097/jom.0000000000002680

Ewles, G. (2019). Enhancing organizational support for Emergency First Responders and their families: Examining the role of personal support networks after the experience of work-related trauma (thesis).

Friese, K. M. (2020). Cuffed together: A study on how law enforcement work impacts the officer's spouse. *International Journal of Police Science and Management, 22*(4), 407–418. https://doi.org/10.1177/1461355720962527

Gulliver, S. B., Pennington, M. L., Torres, V. A., Steffen, L. E., Mardikar, A., Leto, F., Ostiguy, W., Zimering, R. T., & Kimbrel, N. A. (2019). Behavioral health programs in fire service: Surveying access and preferences. *Psychological Services, 16*(2), 340–345.

Henderson, S. N., Van Hasselt, V. B., LeDuc, T. J., & Couwels, J. (2016). Firefighter suicide: Understanding cultural challenges for mental health professionals. *Professional Psychology: Research and Practice, 47*(3), 224–230. https://doi.org/10.1037/pro0000072

Hill, M. A., Paterson, J. L., & Rebar, A. L. (2023). Secondary traumatic stress in partners of paramedics: A scoping review. Australasian Emergency Care, online ahead of print. https://doi.org/10.1016/j.auec.2023.06.002i

Hill, R., Sundin, E., & Winder, B. (2020). Work–family enrichment of firefighters: "Satellite family members", risk, trauma and family functioning.

International Journal of Emergency Services, *9*(3), 395–407. https://doi.org/10.1108/ijes-08-2019-0046

House, J. S. (1981). *Work stress and social support*. Boston: Addison-Wesley.

Jakubowski, T. D., & Sitko-Dominik, M. M. (2021). The impact of the traditional male role norms on the posttraumatic stress disorder among Polish male firefighters. *PLOS ONE*, *16*(10), e0259025. https://doi.org/10.1371/journal.pone.0259025

Jobson, L., Matharu, T. K., Kulendran, S., Sivakumar, V. D., Lee, Q. Y., Li, H., & Haque, S. (2023). Exploring the associations between social support and symptoms of posttraumatic stress disorder among Malaysian and Australian trauma survivors. *European Journal of Psychotraumatology*, *14*(1), 2192962. https://doi.org/10.1080/20008066.2023.2192962

Johnson, C. C., Vega, L., Kohalmi, A. L., Roth, J. C., Howell, B. R., & Van Hasselt, V. B. (2020). Enhancing mental health treatment for the firefighter population. *Professional Psychology: Research and Practice*, *51*(3), 304–311. https://doi.org/10.1037/pro0000266

Jones, S., Agud, K., & McSweeney, J. (2020). Barriers and facilitators to seeking mental health care among first responders: "removing the darkness." *Journal of the American Psychiatric Nurses Association*, *26*(1), 43–54. https://doi.org/10.1177/1078390319871997

Krakauer, R. L., Stelnicki, A. M., & Carleton, R. N. (2020). Examining mental health knowledge, stigma, and service use intentions among public safety personnel. *Frontiers in Psychology*, *11*, 949. https://doi.org/10.3389/fpsyg.2020.00949

Kshtriya, S., Kobezak, H., Popok, P., Lawrence, J., & Lowe, S. (2020). Social support as a mediator of occupational stressors and mental health outcomes in first responders. *Journal of Community Psychology*, *48*, 2252–2263. https://doi.org/10.1002/jcop.22403

Kyed, M. (2020). Doing care work on the fly – exploring the unnoticed socio-emotional skills of male ambulance staff. *Sociology of Health & Illness*, *42*(3), 433–448. https://doi.org/10.1111/1467-9566.13014

Landers, A. L., Dimitropoulos, G., Mendenhall, T. J., Kennedy, A., & Zemanek, L. (2020). Backing the blue: Trauma in law enforcement spouses and couples. *Family Relations*, *69*, 308–319. https://doi.org/10.1111/fare.12393

Lawrence, D., Kyron, M., Rikkers, W., Bartlett, J., Hafekost, K., Goodsell, B., & Cunneen, R. (2018). Answering the call: National Survey of the Mental Health and Well-being of Police and Emergency Services. Detailed Report. Graduate School of Education, The University of Western Australia. www.beyondblue.org.au/docs/default-source/resources/bl1902-pes-detailed-report.pdf

Lizardi, D., & Stanley, B. (2010). Treatment engagement: A neglected aspect in the psychiatric care of suicidal patients. *Psychiatric Services* (Washington, DC), *61*(12), 1183–1191. https://doi.org/10.1176/ps.2010.61.12.1183

Lowery, A., & Cassidy, T. (2022). Health and well-being of first responders: The role of psychological capital, self-compassion, social support, relationship satisfaction, and physical activity. *Journal of Workplace Behavioral Health*. https://doi.org/10.1080/15555240.2021.1990776

MacDermid, J. C., Lomotan, M., & Hu, M. A. (2021) Canadian career firefighters' mental health impacts and priorities. *International Journal of Environmental Research and Public Health*, *18*, 12666. https://doi.org/10.3390/ijerph182312666

May, K., Van Hooff, M., Doherty, M., & Iannos, M. (2023) Experiences and perceptions of family members of emergency first responders with post-traumatic stress disorder: A qualitative systematic review. *JBI Evidence Synthesis*, *21*(4), 629–668. https://doi.org/10.11124/JBIES-21-00433

McCreary, D. R. (2019). Veteran and first responder mental ill health and suicide prevention: A scoping review of prevention and early intervention programs used in Canada, Australia, New Zealand, Ireland, and the United Kingdom. British Columbia, Canada: Donald McCreary Scientific Consulting. https://uk.movember.com/uploads/files/2020/VFR%20Grants/Movember%20Executive%20Summary%20-%20Veterans%20and%20First%20Responder%20Scoping%20Review.pdf

Mitchell J. (2006). *Critical Incident Stress Management (CISM): Group crisis intervention*. 4th ed. Ellicott City, MD: Chevron.

National Institute for Health and Care Excellence Guideline 116. (2018) Post-traumatic Stress Disorder. Available: www.nice.org.uk/guidance/ng116

Oliffe, J. L., Han, C. S., Drummond, M., Sta. Maria, E., Bottorff, J. L., & Creighton, G. (2015). Men, masculinities, and murder-suicide. *American Journal of Men's Health*, *9*(6), 473–485.

O'Toole, M., Mulhall, C., & Eppich, W. (2022). Breaking down barriers to help-seeking: Preparing first responders' families for psychological first aid. *European Journal of Psychotraumatology*, *13*(1), 2065430. https://doi.org/10.1080/20008198.2022.2065430

Pietrantoni, L., & Prati, G. (2008). Resilience among first responders. *African Health Sciences*, *8*(Suppl 1), S14–S20. https://doi.org/10.4314/AHS.V8I3.7086

Price, J. A. B., Ogunade, A. O., Fletcher, A. J., Ricciardelli, R., Anderson, G. S., Cramm, H., & Carleton, R. N. (2022). Peer support for public safety personnel in Canada: Towards a typology. *International Journal of Environmental Research and Public Health*, *19*(9), 5013. https://doi.org/10.3390/ijerph19095013

Regehr, C., Dimitropoulos, G., Bright, E., George, S., & Henderson, J. (2005). Behind the brotherhood: Rewards and challenges for wives of firefighters. *Family Relations*, *54*, 423–435. https://doi.org/10.1111/j.1741-3729.2005.00328.x

Regel, S., & Dyregrov, A. (2012). Commonalities and new directions in post trauma support interventions: From pathology to the promotion of post-traumatic growth. In Hughes R., Kinder A., & Cooper C. (Eds.), *International handbook of workplace Trauma support* (pp. 48–67). West Sussex: Wiley-Blackwell.

Renkiewicz, G. K., & Hubble, M. W. (2022). Secondary traumatic stress in emergency services systems (STRESS) project: Quantifying and predicting compassion fatigue in emergency medical services personnel. *Prehospital Emergency Care*, *26*(5), 652–663. https://doi.org/10.1080/10903127.2021.1943578

Rikkers, W., & Lawrence, D. (2022). Barriers to seeking help for an emotional or mental health condition among Australian emergency services workers. *Australasian Journal of Disaster and Trauma Studies*, *26*(1), 23–40.

Roberts, A. (2005). *Crisis intervention handbook*. Oxford: Oxford University Press.

Seaton, C. L., Bottorff, J. L., Oliffe, J. L., Medhurst, K., & DeLeenheer, D. (2019). Mental health promotion in male-dominated workplaces: Perspectives of male employees and workplace representatives. *Psychology of Men & Masculinities*, *20*(4), 541–552. http://doi.org/10.1037/men0000182

Shultz, J. M., & Forbes, D. (2013). Psychological first aid. *Disaster Health*, *2*(1), 3–12. https://doi.org/10.4161/dish.26006

Solomon, Z., & Benbenishty, R. (1986). The role of proximity, immediacy, and expectancy in frontline treatment of combat stress reaction among Israelis in the Lebanon War. *American Journal of Psychiatry*, *143*, 613–617. https://doi.org/10.1176/ajp.143.5.613

Solomon, Z., Shklar, R., & Mikulincer, M. (2005). Frontline treatment of combat stress reaction: A 20-year longitudinal evaluation study. *The American Journal of Psychiatry*, *162*(12), 2309–2314. https://doi.org/10.1176/appi.ajp.162.12.2309

Tjin, A., Traynor, A., Doyle, B., Mulhall, C., Eppich, W., & O'Toole, M. (2022). Turning to 'Trusted Others': A narrative review of providing social support to first responders. *International Journal of Environmental Research and Public Health*, *19*(24), 16492. https://doi.org/10.3390/ijerph192416492

van Ommeren, M., Snider, L., & Schafer, A. (2011). (WHO, War Trauma foundation, World Vision International) Psychological First Aid: Guide for Field Workers. Geneva: WHO. www.who.int/publications/i/item/9789241548205

World Health Organisation. (2017). Gender mainstreaming for managers: A practical approach. World Health Organization (Online). https://apps.who.int/iris/handle/10665/44516

Young, P. M., Partington, S., Wetherell, M. A., St Clair Gibson, A., & Partington, E. (2014). Stressors and coping strategies of UK firefighters during on-duty incidents. *Stress and Health*, *30*(5), 366–376. https://doi.org/10.1002/smi.2616

15

EXPLORING THE EFFECTS OF PSP CAREERS ON FAMILIES

Linna Tam-Seto, Heidi Cramm, Rosemary Ricciardelli, and R. Nicholas Carleton

Introduction

Public safety personnel (PSP) include border services, communications officials (e.g., 911 operators, dispatchers), correctional officers, firefighters, police officers, and paramedics. In Canada and internationally, PSP are exposed to occupational stressors that include operational factors such as potentially psychologically traumatic events (PPTE) (Canadian Institute for Public Safety Research and Treatment, 2019) that involve harm, injury, or death as an inherent function of their occupations (Carleton et al., 2019). Associated with exposure to work-related PPTE are experiences of operational stress injuries, compromised well-being, and chronic physical ailments (Carleton et al., 2017, Carleton, Afifi, et al., 2018, Carleton, Duranceau, et al., 2018). Occupational stressors associated with organizational factors, such as job responsibilities and lifestyle changes for PSP, also appear to impact all aspects of PSP lives, including physical, psychological, and social well-being (Carleton et al., 2020; Carleton, Duranceau, et al., 2018; Regehr et al., 2005; Ricciardelli et al., 2018).

There is increasing acknowledgment and understanding of how occupational stress associated with PSP work impacts employees. There is also a growing body of research on the mental health changes associated with this kind of work, with a focus on operational stressors such as frequent PPTE exposures. PSP work involves irregular and demanding occupational responsibilities through organizational factors like shift work, sleep disruption, and job-related stress, all of which negatively impact the lives of PSP and their families (Anderson & Lo, 2011; Fair, 2011; Lammers-van der Holst & Kerkhof, 2014; Wolkow et al., 2015). Less information is available on how the operational and organizational stressors of PSP work impact the family system. The available

DOI: 10.4324/9781003424253-20

research on how PSP work impacts families focuses on specific effects for children or spouses, rather than the family as a system (Anderson & Lo, 2011; Black, 2010; Boulin Johnson et al., 2005; Duarte et al., 2006; Zavala, 2010). Without dedicated research to understand the complex and dynamic patterns of family interactions, there will continue to be important gaps in knowledge necessary to inform any potential programs or supports for PSP and their families. In addition, the current body of work exploring the experiences of PSP family members has reflected international experiences (Kunst et al., 2017; Smith et al., 2018; Thompson et al., 2001); international results must be considered through Canada's own unique social, cultural, and institutional contexts. Canadian-specific research allows for a more nuanced exploration and understanding of the experience of Canadian PSP families.

Conceptualizing families as systems was first introduced by Bowen (1978) and presents individual family members' actions as influencing the family as a whole and vice versa. Bowen's theory includes eight interconnecting factors: (1) differentiation of self; (2) triangular relationships; (3) nuclear family emotional system; (4) family projection process; (5) emotional cut-off; (6) multi-generational transmission process; (7) sibling position; and (8) societal regression (Haefner, 2014). The interactive factors contribute to "inevitable chronic emotional anxiety present in family relationships" (Haefner, 2014, p. 835) and create a complicated dynamic balance between togetherness ("emotional fusion") (Haefner, 2014, p. 835) and individuality ("differentiation of self") (Haefner, 2014, p. 835). Chronic anxiety has been argued by Haefner (2014) to be the root of family dysfunction. The family systems approach facilitates examining a range of family experiences, including experiences interacting with PPTE exposures (MacKay, 2012), intimate partner relationships (Priest, 2015), separation (Palombi, 2016), and specific mental health disorders (Haefner, 2014; Miller et al., 2004). The impact of diverse experiences specific to PSP family systems has not been explored. In addition, PSP family systems in the context of mental health changes that compound lifestyle stressors have also not been explored.

The current work was designed to increase our collective understanding of how occupational stress in Canadian PSP, because of operational and organizational demands, impacts families as a system. Specifically, we explored how PSP perceive the interactions between their vocational requirements, the potential mental health implications, and their families. We present the family-related challenges from the perspectives and experiences of PSP from diverse professions as a means to begin understanding the family as a system. The PSP participants are individuals who have identified as living with increased occupational stress and report on several important foundational issues that can increase awareness, support and catalyze future research, and potentiate additional family-focused resources for PSP.

Approach

The current work reports on a segment of a web-based, self-report survey in both English and French that explored the experiences of mental disorder symptoms in Canadian PSPs. The larger survey consisted of the following self-report screening measures: the post-traumatic stress disorder (PTSD) Check List 5 (PCL-5) (Weathers et al., 2013); the 9-item Patient Health Questionnaire (PHQ-9) (Kroenke et al., 2001); the Panic Disorder Symptoms Severity scale, Self-Report (PDSS-SR) (Shear et al., 1997); the 7-item GAD scale (GAD-7) (Spitzer et al., 2006); the Social Interaction Phobia scale (SIPS) (Carleton et al., 2009); and the Alcohol Use Disorders Identification Test (AUDIT) (Saunders et al., 1993). The survey was open for participation by PSP across Canada from September 1, 2016, to January 31, 2017. Using broadly accepted guidelines for conducting online surveys (Ashbaugh et al., 2010), the survey consisted of well-established scales used to screen for mental disorder symptom levels (see Carleton, Duranceau, et al., 2018, for additional survey details), as well as open-ended questions for additional participant information related to their perceptions and experiences. Participant recruitment took multiple forms, including emails and advertisements administered by employers, unions, professional associations, and researchers. The federal Minister of Public Safety and Emergency Preparedness also provided a public service announcement to describe the study and encourage participation. The University of Regina Institutional Research Ethics Board (file No. 2016-107). provided ethical clearance for the data collection.

A total of n=8520 surveys were completed and 828 participants voluntarily provided comments in response to the following open-ended question: "If you have any additional information you would like to provide or additional feedback, please feel free to do so below." Information for the current chapter is restricted to the PSP participants who shared their thoughts about the effects of their mental health difficulties on their families. The average written response was 129 words in length. Participants self-identified as males (77%) and females (33%) working as police officers (Royal Canadian Mounted Police [RCMP] and municipal police; 27%), paramedics (33%), firefighters (8%), and correctional workers (8%). As with all qualitative data, the thematic results may not generalize beyond the current participants.

A semi-structured grounded approach was used to analyze emergent themes (Charmaz, 2006; Glaser & Strauss, 1967; Ricciardelli et al., 2010). The grounded approach taken in the analysis of the data is best suited for the exploratory nature of the open-ended questions included in the survey. Data were first transferred from the online survey tool to Microsoft Excel and then imported into NVivo Pro, a qualitative data software tool, such that each participant's data constituted a unique case. Salient emergent themes were identified and analyzed using an inductive approach whereby themes and patterns are derived from the data itself rather than being predetermined by the researchers (Charmaz, 2006). Data was transferred into Microsoft Excel spreadsheets (Microsoft Corporation, 2018) and then moved into NVivo Pro (Lumiero, 2017), a qualitative data software program, to verify that each participant was individually coded with their own attributes (e.g., unique demographic information). Two researchers grouped responses into thematic categories representing emerging trends in the data (i.e., parent nodes). The parent nodes were then broken down and recoded into subthemes (i.e., broken down into child nodes and recoded into subthemes with axial coding) (Saldana, 2015; Strauss & Corbin, 1990). Coding continued until each subtheme was representative of all respective emergent themes in the data, and the data in each theme and subtheme were reliably coded.

The quoted comments in the current chapter were made by participants and are included with only minor edits to support flow, comprehension, and anonymity. Participants consented to the inclusion of all quotes presented (i.e., they answered "For any part of the research, including quoting what I wrote" to the item "Please let us know how we can use any additional information and feedback that you have provided in the open text fields"). Due to the anonymous nature of the survey, member checking for triangulation was impossible.

Results

We present derived themes about how Canadian PSP understand the compounding impact of their occupational stressors. Central themes included (1) the effects of organizational occupational stressors on PSP families, and; (2) the effects of operational occupational stressors on PSP families.

Effects of organizational occupational stressors on PSP families

Participants reported feeling torn between the demands of their family and their job. The organizational demands, such as shift work and irregular work hours experienced by many PSP families, were often burdensome and increasingly more stressful in the presence of or contributed to mental health difficulties. Unique to some PSP occupations, such as policing and correctional services, officers may have to relocate regularly depending on their occupational deployment. For example, RCMP officers may relocate every four years, if not more often, to different provinces, territories, or detachments in diverse jurisdictions, particularly when striving toward promotion and career advancement. To demonstrate how relocation can impact families, a member of the RCMP expressed increased stressors related to relocation, comparing his situation with that of municipal police officers. Not only was relocating challenging for his spouse and children, with potential financial and social consequences, but the officer perceived a lack of support from his employer for his family situation. The additional layer of psychological stress can complicate efforts to balance work and family. The perceived lack of support from their organization may be associated with the officer's current situation and emotional state; nevertheless, the result is that PSP perceived their work environment as adding tension between their family needs and their occupational obligations, negatively impacting their overall mental health.

Participants reported challenges fulfilling their familial roles, most often the role of a parent or spouse, given organizational stressors. PSP reported experiencing increased stress when having to sacrifice their family roles to meet the occupational and logistical demands of their jobs, with negative implications for their relationships. For example, a male RCMP officer described missing family events (e.g., birthday parties) and coming home from work too exhausted to talk to his children. Similarly, another RCMP officer shared:

> The amount of times I have come home to my daughter's embrace only to be ripped from her again and cause her the anguish of her father heading out the door to deal with "bad guys" is unbearable.

The words of both RCMP officers highlighted the impact of their work on their families as well as their mental well-being, particularly the organizational requirement to abruptly leave their families for unexpected work "events." In the former excerpt, the exhaustion from the job, described as, "You come home so tired [the children] try to talk to you and you fall asleep in the chair you are sitting in," is evidenced alongside the "missed," often irreplaceable, experiences. The same participant reported emotional turmoil inflicted on his daughter because of the organizational requirements of the job, which implies that he believed that his daughter felt he prioritized "bad guys" over her, leading to feeling of guilt. Most participants reported increased stress while trying to manage their dual roles, the resulting role conflicts, and the impact on their children. A female correctional officer with nine years of experience explained:

> Being a single parent who works full-time very likely affects my children's adjustment although I could not respond that it was a direct negative response linked only to my employment but is rather a culmination of many complex factors.

Factors beyond work may indeed contribute to children's "adjustment," but PSP work experiences appeared to exacerbate challenging home environments or situations when viewing the family as a system. The exacerbation likely results from all members of a PSP family sharing individual and group experiences that impact family well-being.

Effects of operational occupational stressors on PSP families

Evidencing the extent to which families function as a system (Haefner, 2014), all participants described how operational occupational stressors impacted the well-being of their family. Organizational stressors (e.g., shift work), compounded with personal struggles of managing operational occupational stressors such as major depressive disorder and PTSD, seemed to unintentionally cascade into the family system. A paramedic described his family's experience with his work operational stress injury:

> I had an [operational stress injury]. It was five months of pure hell for myself and my family. My anger was intense. I screamed and swore at my family in the middle of the night. My wife would hurry the kids into their rooms when I was enraged just so they wouldn't see it. It took the joy out of the birth of my son.

As evidenced in the paramedic's words, and echoed by others, PSP came to recognize the impact their organizational occupational stressors had on their family and themselves. Symptoms of compromised mental health, as described by participants, included anger, lack of patience, the inability to cope with daily tasks, frustration, and even depressed mood, which shaped the lived experiences of children, spouses, and other family members (Duarte et al., 2006; Ussery & Waters, 2006). For many, the suffering that PSP experience appears to be compounded and exacerbated by feelings of guilt or remorse they endured because of what they "did" to their families. As a result of their mental health symptoms, there were feelings that the balance and flow of family life were affected. For example, an RCMP officer reported:

> Mental illness not only affects the first responder, but moreover, [a]ffects the family. My family suffers much more than I do because of my chosen profession. Agencies need to do so much more to assist the families of their dedicated employees in order to maintain the employee's mental well-being...family and children's groups need to have the same importance to employers as the employee support groups. As the saying goes, "Happy wife, happy life."

Others reiterated the word of the RCMP officer, revealing the complex interconnectedness within family dynamics, where each person influences the other's well-being. PSP may also experience guilt associated with actually or potentially impacting the mental health of their family members. The bidirectional nature of family systems is illustrated in the comments that describe the struggle between role conflict and operational stressors and how the stressors impact the family and, therein, shape PSP experiences as family members.

Some PSP described experiencing the breakdown of their spousal relationship in relation to their operational occupational stressors. Living for protracted periods of time with PPTE can disrupt relationships, particularly when PSP tried to keep those issues to themselves. As a result, the protective efforts of PSP appeared to incidentally push loved ones away. One provincial police officer described the outcome of his efforts and shared, "I suffered alone for ten years before I asked for help… I was very angry, depressed, drank, and threw my marriage away because she was too important to me to hurt." Challenges within spousal relationships were also echoed by some participants who reported having observed such strains among their co-workers:

> A lot of first responders have or are currently going through a relationship breakdown. I believe that needs to be looked into at a deeper level.

As the participant highlights, PSP participants believed the rates of marital and spousal breakdown are higher among paramedics and perhaps among all PSP; however, not all participants reported relationship turmoil. Participants recognized that the nature of their profession posed a strain on their relationships, particularly during challenging periods of intersection between work and personal life (e.g., work events taking precedence over home in select cases). A municipal police officer reported:

> For the last 15–20 years, I have experienced difficulties with a lot of issues including anger, irrational thoughts and behaviours and lack of sleep. This nearly cost me my marriage and boys.

The police officer's words were repeated by others when describing challenges surrounding PSP's occupational stressors, including shift work and persistent exposure to PPTE, which may contribute to marital dissolution by preventing PSP from fulfilling parental and spousal roles, such as being physically present at milestone events or being emotionally present.

Discussion

In the current work, we identified some of the effects that occupational stress can have on PSP families based on the PSP perspectives, contributing to a body of research largely void of the Canadian experience. The work was derived from voluntarily provided text to an open-ended question intended to solicit any additional information participants were wanting to share, in which some PSP shared responses directly connected to families. The current results highlight the interconnectedness of PSP families and how stressors experienced by PSP reflexively influence the health and well-being of individual family members, the family as a unit, and the PSP.

PSP organizational stressors contributed to role conflict between the participants' families and work. The organizational stressors were particularly difficult to navigate and perceived to cause harm to other family members (e.g., children and spouses), reflexively compromising the mental health of the PSP family member. Participants also described substantial impacts from operational stressors, such as PPTE exposures and subsequent changes to their mental health. The mental health impacts seemed to compound existing role conflicts and exacerbate stress on the family as a whole and their interrelationships. The current results are limited given the small number of participants; however, each participant chose to comment on and highlight their families' experiences without being prompted, underscoring the perceived importance for those participants. The unprompted provision of such information both underscores the importance of and provides direction for future research. Future studies should be dedicated to looking to understand the effects of organizational and operational stressors on individual family members and the family as a collective.

The emergent theme of occupational stressors may be further understood through the lens of Greenhaus and Beutell's (1985) work–family conflict model. The work–family conflict described by participants in their study can be seen as a potential source of anxiety that ultimately contributes to family dysfunction from the perspective of Bowen's theory of family systems (Bowen, 1978). In their model, Greenhaus and Beutell (1985) suggest that conflict exists between work and family roles under certain conditions; specifically, when (1) time required to fulfill one's role causes difficulty in fulfilling the demands of another; (2) strain from taking one role may challenge one's ability to meet the requirements of another; and (3) specific behaviors of one role make it difficult to fulfill the requirements of the other. Applying the Greenhaus and Beutell model is supported by extant literature (1985) and helps to contextualize PSP experiences with their families as identified in the current study. The current results evidenced that PSPs struggle to maintain the balance of family responsibilities and the demands of the job on their own time. The Greenhaus and Beutell model has been used to understand experiences of work–family conflict across different kinds of emergency service workers, including probation officers (Westaby et al., 2016) and volunteer firefighters (Cowlishaw et al., 2010a, 2010b). Also supporting the current study were results from the Sharp et al. (2022) systematic review, which identified evidence to support work–family conflict for PSP family members. The systematic review was designed to explore what is known about the mental health and well-being outcomes and experiences of PSP families. The review evidenced operational stressors as inherent to PSP careers and disruptive to the time and emotional energy PSP have for their families, which negatively impacts familial relationships (Sharp et al., 2022). The review results echo several participant statements in the current study regarding the challenges of trying to balance the requirements of the job and their family roles, underscoring the layered and complex nature of occupational stressors specific to public safety careers and their effects on families.

Each factor contributing to conflict and stress was evident in the sample, but the time required to fulfill one role while being at the detriment of the other was very salient. PSP wrote about missing out on family events and not being able to fulfill their family roles (e.g., being present at family events) and responsibilities because of organizational demands (e.g., working overtime), which was reported as directly impacting their mental health status. In turn, the deterioration of PSP mental health as a result of PPTE and how PSP interact with their families (i.e., being emotionally present) seemed to directly contribute to the existing tension of "not having enough time" when balancing home and work life. Viewing the family as a system, the current results describe a reality of insufficient time to balance PSP and family roles, which negatively impacts the family as a whole.

Other organizational stressors, such as working shifts and being called back to work, or held back at work, can also amplify marital tensions as expressed by participants. The current chapter begins to expand our understanding of marital stress partially due to role conflict; specifically, how role conflict comes about due to the cumulative impact of their mental health difficulties and their job roles. Existing research supports the reality of marital tensions among PSP; however, explicit discussion of the role of changing mental health status is not made clear. Hackett and Violante (2003) reported anecdotal evidence that divorce rates are higher among police officers than in the general public; however, the impact of changing mental health status on divorce rates is unknown in either of these populations. There is also evidence of gender-based differences in the ways in which mental health issues are experienced among PSP; for example, female firefighters screened positive for PTSD more often than their male counterparts in the national cross-sectional study (Carleton et al., 2017). US population results have also concluded that the prevalence of divorce among male firefighters was comparable to the general population, but the divorce rate among female firefighters was three times greater than their civilian counterparts Haddock et al. (2016). The current study sample size precludes specific comments on gender differences associated with marital discord, but the data suggests the need for more exploratory work. Further research into gender dimensions of work–family conflict and the contributing factors is warranted, especially in relation to work-related mental health issues based on existing research. Researchers agree that role conflict exists between family and PSP roles and that there are corresponding tensions between work and home life for individuals working as PSP (Roth & Moore, 2009; Westaby et al., 2016), including from the perspective of spouses (Porter & Henriksen,

2015). The current chapter has begun identifying how PSP's work (e.g., organizational stressors, operational stressors) contributes to marital strain leading to divorce; however, the results also underscore that much more work is needed to better understand how PSP stressors interact within families.

The bidirectionality within family systems experiencing mental health changes as a direct result of occupational stressors has been identified in military families (Cramm et al., 2019; Schwartz et al., 2021) and will likely be similar among PSP families. PSP families are systems; accordingly, PSP members are impacted by changes in their family members and vice versa, as evidenced by the current chapter. Regarding the impact on PSP children, another paper based on the current chapter survey data is based on responses from PSP parents about their 4- to 17-year-old children. The child study by Stelnicki and colleagues (2022) found that almost 40% of PSP parents surveyed reported that they observed mental health and well-being difficulties in their children, attributing their children's difficulties to the challenges that accompany PSP careers. Difficulties included experiences of sadness, worries, and fears, disobedience or anger, attention, and friendships (Stelnicki et al., 2022). The results of Stelnicki and colleagues (2022) also evidence the bidirectionality inherent in family systems. PSP occupational stressors interactively impact the mental health and well-being of PSP parents and their children. The current results further evidence the impact of PSP careers on children as a result of both organizational stressors (i.e., work schedule) and operational stressors (i.e., decline in health due to PPTE). The current results provide necessary foundational work to further examine how specific PSP occupational stressors reflexively impact PSP parents and their children.

Greenhaus and Beutell's (1985) model also posited that behaviors required by one role may create challenging conditions for fulfilling the requirements of another role, and therein serve as an additional source of role conflict. Behaviors that are desirable for PSP in their professional life may have a "spillover effect" (Dong et al., 2019; Miller, 2007) when at home, as suggested by some participants in the current study. Being overprotective, suspicious, and hyper-vigilant toward their own family members, as seen in a study of police officers (Miller, 2007), seemed to contribute to feelings of guilt in some study participants while increasing the strain in their family relationships. PSP may start to close themselves off from family members as a way to "protect" their family from the realities of their work and/or the realities of their changing mental health, as evidenced in the words of the participants and supported by existing literature (Cowlishaw et al., 2008; Miller, 2007; Regehr, 2005; Regehr et al., 2005; Thompson et al., 2001). A study with firefighters evidenced withdrawal, social isolation, and avoidance of activities and places as negatively impacting their families (Gagliano, 2009). The current chapter identified family detachment as a strategy used to cope with stressors and illustrated the dynamic impacts detachment can have on individual family members (e.g., children, spouse) as well as the family as a whole. Future researchers should further investigate the patterns of family detachment as a response to operational occupational stressors. It has been identified that PSP who exhibit behaviors such as high attachment avoidance also demonstrate a preference for self-reliance rather than being dependent on others (Halpern et al., 2012; Landon & Wang, 2010). The current results help to explain some of the behaviors that result from PSP trying to manage the interaction of multiple roles (e.g., PSP and family members). Understanding attachment can inform the development of PSP-specific coping strategies that better support their families and minimize the impact of occupational stressors.

There has been increasing recognition that PSP families are a population at increased risk for mental health difficulties, given the careers of their loved ones. For example, PSP families were recognized as a population unduly affected by the pandemic in the Government of Canada's investment of $50 million in 2021 to support projects that address PTSD and psychological trauma (PSPNET, 2022). That investment resulted in the development of PSPNET Families, an online well-being hub created to support the unique needs and challenges of families of PSP (PSPNET, 2022). Evidenced-informed strategies are available to support families (e.g., "extending your support system"; "household tasks"; "communicating with children") as well as couples (e.g., "gratitude and positive reframing"; "goal setting together"; "supporting work to home transitions") based on the understanding that occupational stressors do impact families and partners. The current results can inform more PSP family support programs such as PSPNET Families by bringing to the forefront the interconnectedness of families and by emphasizing that a family systems approach is needed to adequately support the complexities of PSP family life.

Limitations

The current work provides crucial foundational elements for further developing our understanding of how families of Canadian PSP may be impacted by occupational stressors experienced by their PSP family members; however, there are several limitations that provide directions for future research. First, the current sample size is small (n = 13), and the associated results may not generalize beyond the current participants. Future work should engage larger samples that broadly showcase the diversity of PSP professions. Second, the question from which the findings were derived was broad and did not specifically seek out information about PSP and their families; as such, the results do not necessarily reflect the interpretations of the entire study population. Future researchers should consider studies focused specifically on PSP families. Third, the use of a self-report survey prohibited interactive discussions and follow-up questions; as such, there was no opportunity to pursue several potentially important avenues of knowing how Canadian PSP understand the effects of their profession on the well-being of their families. Future researchers should consider using interactive interviews for primary data collection related to PSP family research.

Conclusion

The current chapter explored how Canadian PSP living with increased occupational stressors because of operational and organizational demands perceive effects on the well-being of their families. The results evidenced that PSP experience augmented conflict between their role as family members, typically as a spouse or parent, and their roles by the presence of or development of operational occupational stressors. We highlighted how occupational stressors in PSP careers can compromise the well-being of PSP families, which reflexively negatively impacts PSP. Despite the limitations, the current results provide important initial support for future research with PSP and their families within the Canadian context.

References

Anderson, A. S., & Lo, C. C. (2011, Apr). Intimate partner violence within law enforcement families. *Journal of Interpersonal Violence, 26*(6), 1176–1193. https://doi.org/10.1177/0886260510368156

Ashbaugh, A. R., Herbert, C. F., Butler, L. D., & Brunet, A. (2010). A new frontier: Trauma research on the internet. In A. Brunet, A. R. Ashbaugh, & C. F. Herbert (Eds.), *Internet use in the aftermath of trauma* (pp. 99–120). ISO Press BV.

Black, A. (2010). The treatment of psychological problems experienced by the children of police officers in Northern Ireland. *Child Care in Practice, 10*(2), 99–106. https://doi.org/10.1080/13575270410001693330

Boulin Johnson, L., Todd, M., & Subramanian, G. (2005). Violence in police families: Work-family spillover. *Journal of Family Violence, 20*(1), 3–10. https://doi.org/DOI: 10.1007/s10896-005-1504-4

Bowen, M. (1978). *Family therapy in clinical practice.* Jason Aronson.

Canadian Institute for Public Safety Research and Treatment. (2019). *Glossary of terms: A shared understanding of the common terms used to describe psychological trauma* (Version 2.0). Author.

Carleton, R. N., Afifi, T. O., Taillieu, T., Turner, S., Mason, J. E., Ricciardelli, R., McCreary, D. R., Vaughan, A., Anderson, G. S., Krakauer, R., Donnelly, E. A., Camp, R. D. I., Groll, D., Cramm, H. A., MacPhee, R. S., & Griffiths, C. T. (2020). Assessing the Relative Impact of Diverse Stressors Among Public Safety Personnel. *International Journal of Environmental Research and Public Health, 17.* https://doi.org/10.3390/ijerph17041234

Carleton, R. N., Afifi, T. O., Turner, S., Taillieu, T., Duranceau, S., LeBouthillier, D. M., Sareen, J., Ricciardelli, R., MacPhee, R. S., Groll, D., Hozempa, K., Brunet, A., Weekes, J. R., Griffiths, C. T., Abrams, K. J., Jones, N. A., Beshai, S., Cramm, H. A., Dobson, K. S., Hatcher, S., Keane, T. M., Stewart, S. H., & Asmundson, G. J. G. (2017, Jan 01). Mental Disorder Symptoms among Public Safety Personnel in

Canada. *Can J Psychiatry,* 706743717723825. https://doi.org/10.1177/0706743717723825

Carleton, R. N., Afifi, T. O., Turner, S., Taillieu, T., LeBouthillier, D. M., Duranceau, S., Sareen, J., Ricciardelli, R., MacPhee, R. S., Groll, D., Hozempa, K., Brunet, A., Weekes, J. R., Griffiths, C. T., Abrams, K. J., Jones, N. A., Beshai, S., Cramm, H. A., Dobson, K. S., Hatcher, S., Keane, T. M., Stewart, S. H., & Asmundson, G. J. G. (2018). Suicidal ideation, plans, and attempts among public safety personnel in Canada. *Canadian Psychology/Psychologie canadienne, 59*(3), 220–231. https://doi.org/10.1037/cap0000136

Carleton, R. N., Afifi, T. O., Turner, S., Taillieu, T., Vaughan, A. D., Anderson, G. S., Ricciardelli, R., MacPhee, R. S., Cramm, H. A., Czarnuch, S., Hozempa, K., & Camp, R. D. (2019, Feb 22). Mental health training, attitudes toward support, and screening positive for mental disorders. *Cognitive Behaviour Therapy,* 1–19. https://doi.org/10.1080/16506073.2019.1575900

Carleton, R. N., Collimore, K. C., Asmundson, G. J., McCabe, R. E., Rowa, K., & Antony, M. M. (2009). Refining and validating the Social Interaction Anxiety Scale and the Social Phobia Scale. *Depression and Anxiety, 26*(2), E71–81. https://doi.org/10.1002/da.20480

Carleton, R. N., Duranceau, S., McMillan, K. A., & Asmundson, G. J. G. (2018). Trauma, pain, and psychological distress. *Journal of Psychophysiology, 32*(2), 75–84. https://doi.org/10.1027/0269-8803/a000184

Charmaz, K. (2006). *Constructing grounded theory.* Sage Publications Ltd.

Cowlishaw, S., Evans, L., & McLennan, J. (2008). Families of rural volunteer firefighters. *Rural Society, 18*(1), 17–25.

Cowlishaw, S., Evans, L., & McLennan, J. (2010a). Balance between volunteer work and family roles: Testing a theoretical model of work-family conflict in the volunteer emergency services. *Australian Journal of Psychology, 62*(3), 169–178. https://doi.org/10.1080/00049530903510765

Cowlishaw, S., Evans, L., & McLennan, J. (2010b). Work–family conflict and crossover in volunteer emergency service workers. *Work & Stress, 24*(4), 342–358. https://doi.org/10.1080/02678373.2010.532947

Cramm, H., Norris, D., Schwartz, K. D., Tam-Seto, L., Williams, A., & Mahar, A. L. (2019). Impact of Canadian armed forces veterans' mental health problems on the family during the military to civilian transition. *Military Behavioral Health.* https://doi.org/10.1080/21635781.2019.1644260

Dong, J., Stephenson, E., King, D., & Delongis, A. (2019, Mar 6–9, 2019). *You're stressed, I'm stressed: Spillover and crossover effect of work stress among paramedics and their spouses.* American Psychosomatic Society: Body to Mind, Vancouver, BC.

Duarte, C. S., Hoven, C. W., Wu, P., Bin, F., Cotel, S., Mandell, D. J., Nagasawa, M., Balaban, V., Wernikoff, L., & Markenson, D. (2006, Apr). Posttraumatic stress in children with first responders in their families. *Journal of Traumatic Stress, 19*(2), 301–306. https://doi.org/10.1002/jts.20120

Fair, D. J. (2011). First responder family distraction syndrome. *Annals of Psychotherapy & Integrative Health,* 3(Summer), 84–85.

Gagliano, A. (2009). What every firefighter's spouse should know. *Fire Engineering, 162*(12), 89–92.

Glaser, B. G., & Strauss, A. L. (1967). *The discovery of grounded theory: Strategies for qualitative research.* Aldine.

Greenhaus, J. H., & Beutell, N. J. (1985). Sources of conflict between work and family roles. *Academy of Management Journal, 10*(1), 76–88.
Hackett, D., & Violante, J. (2003). *Police suicide: Tactics for prevention.* Charles C. Thomas.
Haddock, C. K., Jahnke, S. A., Poston, W. S. C., Jitnarin, N., & Day, R. S. (2016). Marriage and divorce among firefighters in the United States. *Journal of Family Issues, 37*(16), 2294–2308. https://doi.org/10.1177/0192513x15583070
Haefner, J. (2014, Nov). An application of Bowen family systems theory. *Issues in Mental Health Nursing, 35*(11), 835–841. https://doi.org/10.3109/01612840.2014.921257
Halpern, J., Maunder, R. G., Schwartz, B., & Gurevich, M. (2012, Feb). Attachment insecurity, responses to critical incident distress, and current emotional symptoms in ambulance workers. *Stress Health, 28*(1), 51–60. https://doi.org/10.1002/smi.1401
Kroenke, K., Spitzer, R. L., & Williams, J. B. (2001). The PHA-9: Validity of a brief depression severity measure. *Journal of General Internal Medicine, 16*, 606–613.
Kunst, M. J. J., Saan, M. C., Bollen, L. J. A., & Kuijpers, K. F. (2017). Secondary traumatic stress and secondary posttraumatic growth in a sample of Dutch police family liaison officers. *Stress and Health: Journal of the International Society for the Investigation of Stress.* https://doi.org/http://dx.doi.org/10.1002/smi.2741
Lammers-van der Holst, H. M., & Kerkhof, G. A. (2014). Shift work tolerance and the importance of sleep quality: a study of police officers. *Biological Rhythm Research, 46*(2), 257–264. https://doi.org/10.1080/09291016.2014.985002
Landen, S. M., & Wang, C.-C. D. C. (2010). Adult attachment, work cohesion, coping, and psychological well-being of firefighters. *Counselling Psychology Quarterly, 23*(2), 143–162. https://doi.org/10.1080/09515071003776028
Lumivero. (2017). NVivo (Version 12) www.lumivero.com
MacKay, L. (2012). Trauma and Bowen family systems theory: Working with adults who were abused as children. *Australian and New Zealand Journal of Family Therapy, 33*(03), 232–241. https://doi.org/10.1017/aft.2012.28
Microsoft Corporation. (2018). Microsoft Excel. Retrieved from https://office.microsoft.com.excel
Miller, L. (2007). Police families: Stresses, syndromes, and solutions. *The American Journal of Family Therapy, 35*, 21–40. https://doi.org/DOI: 10.1080/01926180600698541
Miller, R. B., Anderson, S., & Kaela, D. K. (2004). Is Bowen's theory valid? A review of basic research. *Journal of Marital & Family Therapy, 30*, 453–466.
Palombi, M. (2016). Separations: A personal account of Bowen family systems theory. *Australian and New Zealand Journal of Family Therapy, 37*(3), 327–339. https://doi.org/10.1002/anzf.1170
Porter, K. L., & Henriksen, R. C. (2015). The phenomenological experience of first responder spouses. *The Family Journal, 24*(1), 44–51. https://doi.org/10.1177/1066480715615651
Priest, J. B. (2015, Jul). A Bowen family systems model of generalized anxiety disorder and romantic relationship distress. *Journal of Marital and Family Therapy, 41*(3), 340–353. https://doi.org/10.1111/jmft.12063
PSPNET (2022). Families and Couples Resources. www.pspnet.ca/en/for-families-of-psp/families-and-couples-resources

Regehr, C. (2005). Bringing the trauma home: Spouses of paramedics. *Journal of Loss and Trauma, 10*, 97–114.
Regehr, C., Dimitropoulos, G., Bright, E., George, S., & Henderson, J. (2005). Behind the brotherhood: Rewards and challenges for wives of firefighters. *Family Relations, 54*(3), 423–435.
Ricciardelli, R., Carleton, R. N., Mooney, T., & Cramm, H. (2018). "Playing the system": Structural factors potentiating mental health stigma, challenging awareness, and creating barriers to care for Canadian public safety personnel. *Health* https://doi.org/10.1177/1363459318800167
Ricciardelli, R., Clow, K. A., & White, P. (2010). Masculinity portrayals in men's lifestyle magazines. *Sex Roles: A Journal of Research, 63*(1), 64–78. https://doi.org/10.1007/s11199-010-9764-8
Roth, S. G., & Moore, C. D. (2009, Oct–Dec). Work-family fit: The impact of emergency medical services work on the family system. *Prehospital Emergency Care, 13*(4), 462–468. https://doi.org/10.1080/10903120903144791
Saldana, J. (2015). *The coding manual for qualitative research* (3rd ed.). Sage.
Saunders, T. J., Aasland, O. G., Babor, T. F., de la Fuente, J. R., & Grant, M. (1993). Development of the Alcohol Use Disorders Identification Test (AUDIT): WHO collaborative project on early detection of persons with harmful alcohol consumption II. *Addiction, 88*(6), 791–804. https://doi.org/10.1111/j.1360-0443.1993.tb02093.x
Schwartz, K. D., Norris, D., Cramm, H., Tam-Seto, L., & Mahar, A. (2021). Family members of Veterans with mental health programs: Seeking, finding, and accessing informal and formal supports during military-to-civilian transition. *Journal of Military, Veteran and Family Health, 7*(1). https://doi.org/10.3138/jmvfh-2019-0023
Sharp, M-L., Solomon, N., Harrison, V., Gribble, R., Cramm, H., Pike, G., & Fear, N. T. (2022). The mental health and wellbeing of spouses, partners and children of emergency responders: A systematic review. *PLOS One, 17*(6), e0269659. https://doi.org/10.1371/journal.prone.0269659
Shear, M., Brown, T. A., Barlow, D. H., Money, R., Sholomskas, D. E., Woods, S. W., Gorman, J. M., & Papp, L. A. (1997). Multicenter collaborative panic disorder severity scale. *American Journal of Psychiatry, 154*(1), 1571–1575. https://doi.org/10.1176/ajp.154.11.1571
Smith, T. D., Hughes, K., DeJoy, D. M., & Dyal, M.-A. (2018). Assessment of relationships between work stress, work-family conflict, burnout and firefighter safety behavior outcomes. *Safety Science, 103*, 287–292. https://doi.org/10.1016/j.ssci.2017.12.005
Spitzer, R. L., Kroenke, K., Williams, J. B., & Lowe, B. (2006). A brief measure for assessing generalized anxiety disorder: The GAD-7. *Archives of Internal Medicine, 166*(10), 1092–1097. https://doi.org/10.1001/archinte.166.10.1092
Stelnicki, A. M., Jamshidi, L., Taillieu, T. L., Carleton, R. N. & Afifi, T. O. (2022). Mental health and well-being among children of public safety personnel in Canada. *International Journal of Environmental Research and Public Health, 19*(21). https://doi.org/10.3390/ijerph192114030
Strauss, A., & Corbin, J. (1990). *Basics of qualitative research: Grounded theory procedures and techniques.* Sage.

Thompson, B., Kirk-Brown, A., & Brown, D. (2001). Women police: The impact of work stress on family members. In P. A. Hancock & P. A. Desmond (Eds.), *Stress, workload, and fatigue* (pp. 200–210). Lawrence Erlbaum.

Ussery, W. J., & Waters, J. A. (2006). COP-2-COP Hotlines: Programs to address the needs of first responders and their families. *Brief Treatment and Crisis Intervention, 6*(1), 66–78. https://doi.org/10.1093/brief-treatment/mhj004

Weathers, F. W., Litz, B. T., Keane, T. M., Palmieri, P. A., Marx, B. P., & Schnurr, P. P. (2013). The PTSD Checklist for DSM-5 (PCL-5). U.S. Department of Veterans Affairs. www.ptsd.va.gov/professional/assessment/adult-sr/ptsd-checklist.asp

Westaby, C., Phillips, J., & Fowler, A. (2016). Spillover and work–family conflict in probation practice: Managing the boundary between work and home life. *European Journal of Probation, 8*(3), 113–127. https://doi.org/10.1177/2066220316680370

Wolkow, A., Ferguson, S., Aisbett, B., & Main, L. (2015). Effects of work-related sleep restriction on acute physiological and psychological stress responses and their interactions: A review among emergency service personnel. *International Journal of Occupational Medicine and Environmental Health, 28*(2), 183–208. https://doi.org/10.13075/ijomeh.1896.00227

Zavala, E. (2010). Testing the link between child maltreatment and family violence among police officers. *Crime & Delinquency, 59*(3), 468–483. https://doi.org/10.1177/0011128710389584

CONCLUSION

Knowledge and Ways Forward

Joy Macdermid and Rosemary Ricciardelli

Introduction

Our objective in the current edited collection was to gain insight into how occupational stress injuries present across diverse public safety sectors. We are limited by not being fully inclusive of all public safety sectors, but we do include both many sectors and the collateral consequences of public safety work on families. We do so across 15 chapters, each representing a sector; however, we do recognize an overrepresentation of policing across chapters, although other sectors include correctional workers, firefighters, detachment services assistants, and public safety communicators.

Summary of Findings

In this edited collection, the contributors explored the underlying risks and experiences of operational and organizational stress injuries—occupational stress injuries—arising from a variety of critical incidents and chronic stresses that are inherent in public safety work. While exposure to operational and occupational stress may be considered the norm for PSP, we highlight in this book how there are both shared and unique exposures across different public safety personnel individuals, subgroups, and contexts. These are mediated by gender and position within the organization. This diversity in experience is necessary to understand and contribute to a variety of positive and negative experiences, as well as mental, social, and physical health impacts, each evolving over the course of individual PSP careers (see Chapter 9).

Words like 'stress' and 'risk' have common and scientific meanings, which can sometimes confuse discussions across different disciplines, organizations,

DOI: 10.4324/9781003424253-21

and audiences. Some differentiate trauma, critical incidents/operational stress, other operational stress, and organizational stress (see Chapter 3). Moral injury, where PSP see or enact behaviours that counter their values and moral beliefs can further increase stress for PSP. Some operational exposures are unavoidable and highly traumatic. For example, colleague death in the line of duty, or by suicide, and calls where children are harmed are universally traumatic for PSP (see Chapters 3 and 4). Along with the common PSP experiences, there are sector-specific critical incident exposures, such as for police or correctional officers who may be required to take a life (see, for example, Chapter 3) and firefighters who may have to watch victims burn or have toxic exposures due to fire. The contributors identified many organizational stressors, all of which were discussed in relation to the nature of public safety work, including male-dominated occupational expectations and culture, shiftwork, historical traditions, and hierarchical administrative processes. Many of these stressors are common across different sectors, those we cover, and many beyond the scope of the current collection (i.e., intelligence officers and border services).

Many PSP share a commitment to helping individuals and communities to be safe and healthy and a willingness to put their own health and safety at risk to achieve this goal. The strongly held value is inherent to what attracts people to public safety work and is fundamental for mission success. However, like many PSP-factors, there are two sides to the coin. While mission commitment is important to protect communities, this commitment can also contribute to stigma around mental health problems, a lack of self-care, and ignoring situational risks. The commitment can also heighten the impact of moral injury as people who put their lives on the line will naturally feel betrayed when let down by their organizations or communities.

Operational stress and job demand contribute to critical incidents and are layered on top of ongoing chronic stressors and societal norms. Paramedics and firefighters are often seen as saviours to the public. Correctional officers may perform front line rescues that are hidden from society and are undervalued due to societal attitudes that consider prisoners as not being as valuable to rescue. Some PSP, such as communication officers, do not respond in person to critical incidents, and expressed that their occupational stress was perceived as less valuable, which contributes to their feeling undervalued in their roles. PSP who work more out of the public's line of sight may not experience the public or organizational appreciation to offset their occupational stress, whereas those who perform primarily rescue roles may have more positive affirmations. For police changes in societal attitudes about their role and behaviours can lead to more conflict with the public. Recent trends include a larger manifestation of negative attitudes, opposing organizations, and negative press. Negative societal affirmations might be particularly prevalent and harmful to police, where 70 per cent of officers report this has affected their motivation and most felt that the 'war on cops' lacked legitimacy (see Chapter 3). However, with the increasing presence of social media, all PSP and their families are subject to second-guessing, negative commentary, and a looming presence of risk and trauma (see Chapter 11). This was highlighted in the contributors' chapters, which specifically focused on the impact of social media, as well as recurrent themes across sector-specific chapters that described organizational, operational, and societal stressors affecting PSP. Incorrect public perception of PSP work was also reflected in Chapter 2, where the authors describe how unrealistic portrayals of police work in television drama shows can contribute to stress.

The effect of social systems and culture was a recurrent theme across multiple chapters. PSP are subject to highly unique cultures intended to build camaraderie, social support, pride, and dedication to their mission of public safety. The other side of the coin, however, is how PSP often push themselves beyond their capacity to achieve their mission to avoid letting down their teams and society. Negative attitudes have been associated with a highly masculine culture, a workforce where sexism adversely affects women, and stoicism that adversely affects men and women. PSP can be reluctant to report weakness or seek help in an environment where stoicism and stigma are prevalent. While this affects all types of illness behaviour and reporting, impacts are most predominant in mental health, where stigma has been most profound and long-standing.

The unique nature of PSP culture is layered on societal systems, norms, and power structures. Sexism, racism, and other forms of discrimination influence the stress experienced by PSP internal to their organizations, but also in their public interactions. Lack of access to healthcare services is a common problem where PSP are unable to access clinical services with practitioners who understand their unique needs, while a lack of access to primary care and rehabilitation services is common to many healthcare systems. Thus, PSP are required to provide emergency health care to victims experiencing trauma, mental health crisis, or addictions (see Chapter 3). Conversely, they are often unable to receive care for themselves when they need care. Access to care is highly variant across different sectors or communities and is influenced by who pays for the services and who decides which services are to be made available. For example, governments may be responsible for funding PSP services, while union and management may be involved in negotiation or selection of programs and services. The consequence is substantial differences in coverage for medical and rehabilitation services, particularly when comparing rural and urban services. An example here emerges when comparing career and volunteer services—most notably in firefighting, but also in some other rescue services. Volunteer PSP have less access to training, prevention, healthcare services, and disability management. Further, their employment status and personal or family supports may be compromised by injury in their volunteer role. A recurrent theme across many of the contributors' chapters, also evidenced in sectors, was how these internal and external cultures and healthcare system factors affect their well-being and ability to recover from occupational stress injury.

Recruitment and retention failures exacerbate burnout, presenteeism, and absenteeism which leads to understaffing—another predominant theme across the sectors (see Chapters 3 and 6). The trend has exacerbated since the pandemic as the rates of illness-related absenteeism substantially increased. The importance of understaffing may be underestimated since understaffing is a common concern across many occupations. However, in a large survey of police, an unexpected and exceptional finding emerged, where police rated staff shortages as more stressful than a colleague being killed in the line of duty. This reflects how acute operational stress from critical incidents and chronic occupational stress must both be considered important in research, programs, and policies. In addition to staff shortages, inconsistent policies and treatment (favouritism) were common stressors across PSP including police (see Chapter 3), and communicators (see Chapter 13) . A large quantitative study (see Chapter 6) in the United Kingdom confirmed the qualitative findings, revealing associations between burnout and both operational and organization stress factors.

While it is common in Western Society to treat physical and mental health as separate, our hope is for this collection to highlight how such bias is counterproductive. The predominance of fatigue as a stressor (see Chapter 3) exemplifies how fatigue is a symptom with both mental and physical components and that arises from different health conditions. Physical and psychological health conditions are prevalent in PSP, despite starting their career with an extra healthy worker effect and engaging in ongoing training and health programs aimed at maintaining their health. Thus, in Chapter 10, the contributors bring together physical, mental, and social health, illustrating how the combined allostatic load affects the homeostasis and adaption mechanisms in the brain and periphery that contribute to resilience or chronic stress; while the contributors in Chapter 8 examine some of these components of allostatic load due to occupational stress in more detail related to cardiovascular disease in firefighters, using a critical causation analysis and literature synthesis.

Although the needs of PSP are vast, progress has been made. Increased recognition of the high prevalence of occupational stress injury in PSP has motivated increased funding of research targeting, specifically, the PSP population. Scientists and knowledge mobilization centres specifically focused on PSP have translated research into arguably better programs and policies. Increasing the capacity for applied research focused on the prevention, treatment, and rehabilitation of physical and mental health conditions arising due to PSP service is critical. Examples of progress include better training of PSP prior to active duty, screening programs, preventative wellness initiatives, peer support programs, critical incident debriefing, resiliency training, psychological first aid and health care benefits that include support for physical and mental rehabilitation, PSP-specific professional services and treatment programs, and increased training for PSP competency amongst healthcare professionals (see Chapter 14).

Targeted funding has been important to quickly build capacity and impact in the PSP space. However, a downside to targeted funding is that there is a real possibility, or at minimum a perception, that lower quality research is funded outside of more open competitions. The PSP sector needs and deserves the highest quality research. PSP stakeholders often contend that that research needs to be practical and deliver interventions immediately due to the great need for help in the sector. As a result, there has been a proliferation of studies without control groups or even a comparison group, many of which are underpowered, have low response rates, and/or unstandardized outcome measures. Regression to the mean applies to PSP interventional studies since PSP who enter programs are likely to do so at times of high mental stress, and many could improve at a follow-up assessment—with or without intervention. Clinicians and researchers might interpret a change in scores or symptoms to indicate a program is working when in fact it is due to regression to the mean, or natural recovery. Controlling for this time effect is necessary to provide valid conclusions ("the truth") to PSP stakeholders. Many of the quantitative studies reviewed in this book lacked rigorous control and did not adequately acknowledge reasons for low confidence in the findings. It is unfortunate if low quality research occurs in the PSP sector, particularly at a time when the standards for health research in most other sectors are increasing. Despite the high needs of the PSP sector for prevention and treatment programs to mitigate the high burden of occupational stress injury, or perhaps because of those high needs, it remains exceptionally important that the best interventions be identified. To do so requires rigorous studies that compare different interventions and consider treatment outcomes and cost-effectiveness are needed. The lost opportunities by implementation of programs before they are fully evaluated with rigorous research means programs can have unintended adverse outcomes that are not adequately mitigated, or the system uses up its resources on ineffective programs when research might have identified a better option.

Qualitative studies too are incredibly important to understand PSP experience, how programs work, unintended consequences, how different subgroups might respond, needs, and the workings of complex phenomena. Qualitative research is not meant to be generalizable, although in select cases it can be (i.e., large enough sample, rigorous questioning). Therefore, alone this type of research cannot fully inform decisions about which policies, interventions, or programs are best. Perhaps due to the real challenges in conducting real-world controlled quantitative research with PSP, we have fewer studies of this nature. The lack of high quality quantitative and mixed methods studies is a gap and challenge for the future. However, qualitative research has greatly advanced theoretical frameworks and our understanding of the context and challenges faced by PSP. For example, much of our understanding of PSP culture comes from qualitative research which captures the complexity and meaning of the PSP experience. In Chapter 13, the authors explored correctional officer culture including artefact, espoused beliefs, and values and tacit assumptions that are explicit or implied in affecting this PSP subgroup. In Chapter 15, the authors explored the organizational and operational stressors that affect PSP families.

A reoccurring challenge is the measurement challenges arising in PSP mental health research and ongoing health monitoring. Many psychological constructs are inherently subjective and often overlap with other constructs. Further self-report scales measuring these constructs can have limited content validity or diagnostic accuracy. Attempts to standard diagnostic categories (or mental health disorders) have been important but still rely on human interpretation rather than objective findings that might occur for many physical diseases. Misclassification can delay appropriate treatment and can thwart efforts to understand mental health problems. Measurement tools capturing necessary constructs are essential building blocks to advance mental health research, and many gaps in measurement properties plague commonly used tools. A practical problem in measurement is the burden associated with self-report. Given the complexity of the challenges PSP face and the complexity of human health, there is a tension between burden and comprehensive assessment. The increased attention to PSP research has increased the frequency of research requests. As a result, low response can be a problem in PSP research, which limits the timeliness and validity of PSP research. Similarly routine PSP screening programs can be costly and complicated given multiple domains of health are affected, and the range of potential diseases/disorders that can arise from occupational exposures. In Chapter 12, the authors highlight a process framework that was used to guide these challenges.

Unfortunately, PSP research is sometimes seen as a niche area, which can make attracting trainees difficult. This is reinforced if academic departmental structures at universities do not see this type of research as valuable for their mission or broadly generalizable. This is unfortunate because PSP research can teach us a lot about the effects of trauma since we know PSP enter the workforce healthy and changes in health associated with trauma are more likely to be causal. However, there are dangers in having a small number of academics who do PSP research. First, there is the obvious limitation in the amount of research that can be published by a small number of researchers. However, beyond that, the research is likely to be biased as it will contain a small number of perspectives and methodologies. Third, high-quality, generalizable studies often require larger samples and multi-site/institutional involvement, which can be challenging where the pool of researchers is small. Also challenging are the processes for fostering innovation and excellence where a small number of researchers are widely distributed and do not have sufficient opportunities for collaboration. Trainees and even established researchers may be reluctant to enter a field where there is the perception of a small number of researchers as having cornered the market on research grants and success. PSP sectors will face these challenges and will need to form collaborative and equitable networks to achieve the goal of a rich, diverse, and fully supported research infrastructure that addresses the unique and important concerns of PSP. Organizations and events that bring together the PSP community should include sector champions, frontline personnel, decision-makers and researchers to focus on knowledge sharing, advancing methods, sharing resources, planning strategies to increase impact, and influencing policy.

The organization of the book and the content reflect common threads and unique elements to different PSP occupations. Progress has been made in PSP coming together in ways necessary to advance research and leverage knowledge across different fields. For example, adaptation of programs from one sector to another can greatly accelerate the speed of innovation and its impact. A challenge in these collaborations is ensuring the unique and common threads are adequately addressed such that all PSP sectors benefit from the collaborations. The practice can be invaluable for some smaller PSP sectors lacking capacity and profile. Similarly, there are some areas of PSP work where the sectors have clear occupational scope boundaries, and others that are overlapping. For example, emergency health care is a primary focus for paramedics but has increasingly become a primary role for many firefighters. The health care demands of both groups have been worsened by insufficient capacity in the healthcare system which often increases the burden and inefficiency of paramedic work. For firefighters, insufficient capacity to meet increasing health care demands may contribute to occupational stress as some firefighters may not feel adequately prepared for increasing healthcare roles. For paramedics, insufficient capacity may result in increased stress due to role conflict or job dissatisfaction. Differences in culture and conflicted occupational roles can contribute to occupational stress and may limit diffusion of innovation across sectors. Despite challenges collaboration across PSP sectors and between PSP and military research teams continues to build and strength capacity. This collaboration is a positive trend that may contribute to advancing science and more rapid translation of research into practice.

A reoccurring theme across many of the chapters was the need to consider sex/gender and other intersectional factors that contribute to the marginalization of certain PSP and a source of stress within society at large (see Chapter 13). In Chapter 5, the authors speak to the complex societal issues affecting women on probation and the emotional labour required of women probation staff in a way that illustrates how societal issues are visited on PSP. Qualitative studies have helped define the nature and extent of marginalization. However, quantitative studies have been slow to introduce appropriate sex gender-based analysis to provide quantitative estimates of risk, intervention effectiveness, and outcomes based on sex/gender or other intersectional factors. This remains a gap area. There certainly has been progress in recruitment to have PSP sectors to be more inclusive so they better reflect the communities they serve, although some would argue that the progress is too slow. For example, amongst firefighters, women remain less than 5 per cent of the workforce in many jurisdictions. Other PSP sectors, like police, have made more rapid changes in creating a more gender diverse workforce but have been plagued by cases where sexual harassment and other forms of discrimination have existed within the workforce. It seems that that increased gender representation occurred in a sector that was not adequality prepared to deal with the cultural shifts needed to provide an inclusive work environment. An inclusive workforce is essential for recruitment and retention of PSP, and their ability to deliver effective protection to their communities.

An important aspect of PSP research is the active involvement of the target audience as lay researchers or partners in research undertaken. Partner engagement should include priority setting, conduct of the research, and implementation. PSP need to have key roles in the entire research process to ensure it reflects their unique knowledge, needs, and priorities, and valued outcomes, while ensuring the feasibility of the proposed research, and potential for scaling up research outputs. A unique aspect of these collaborations in the PSP sector is how PSP are often used to directing others and are task-oriented. These can be beneficial attitudes given engagement and partnership between PSP stakeholders and researchers, that will continue to enrich the field. The context in PSP engagement dynamic is quite different than in health care, where patients are used to deferring to clinicians. Since PSP are used to being directive with the public they could bring this approach into their relationships with researchers. Thus, the power dynamics are quite different in research collaboration in the PSP sector as compared to health care. As partnerships evolve, the PSP sector may address this contextual issue to ensure mutual trust, respect, collaboration, and execution during research to capture the full potential for quality and impact. This will also be important to attract future scientists to the field as the challenge of creating high-quality science with a practical application is essential for impact but is not easily achieved.

Ways Forward

In this edited collection, we show the need for rigorous, theoretically informed research with capacity to shape better prevention and management of PSP health. Collaboration is essential to ensure the right research questions are addressed, and they are answered with rigorous research methods that mitigate potential sources of misinterpretation or error. The issues are complex, the research can be challenging, and managing the translational process to ensure the research makes a difference requires persistent and multi-pronged efforts across multiple highly variable contexts. This book highlights excellent work, yet much that remains to be done. Better research methods, support for inclusive teams, training of all team members and use of implementation science that is tailored to the PSP sectors should help build on the foundations outlined in this book.

INDEX

Note: Page numbers in **bold** and *italics* refer to tables and figures, respectively. Endnotes are indicated by the page number followed by "n" and the note number e.g., 111n5 refers to note 5 on page 111.

FSC
www.fsc.org
MIX
Papier | Fördert
gute Waldnutzung
FSC® C083411

Kolibri 360 GmbH
Ferdinand-Jühlke-Straße 7
99095 Erfurt, Deutschland
produktsicherheit@kolibri360.de